PRAYING TO PORTRAITS

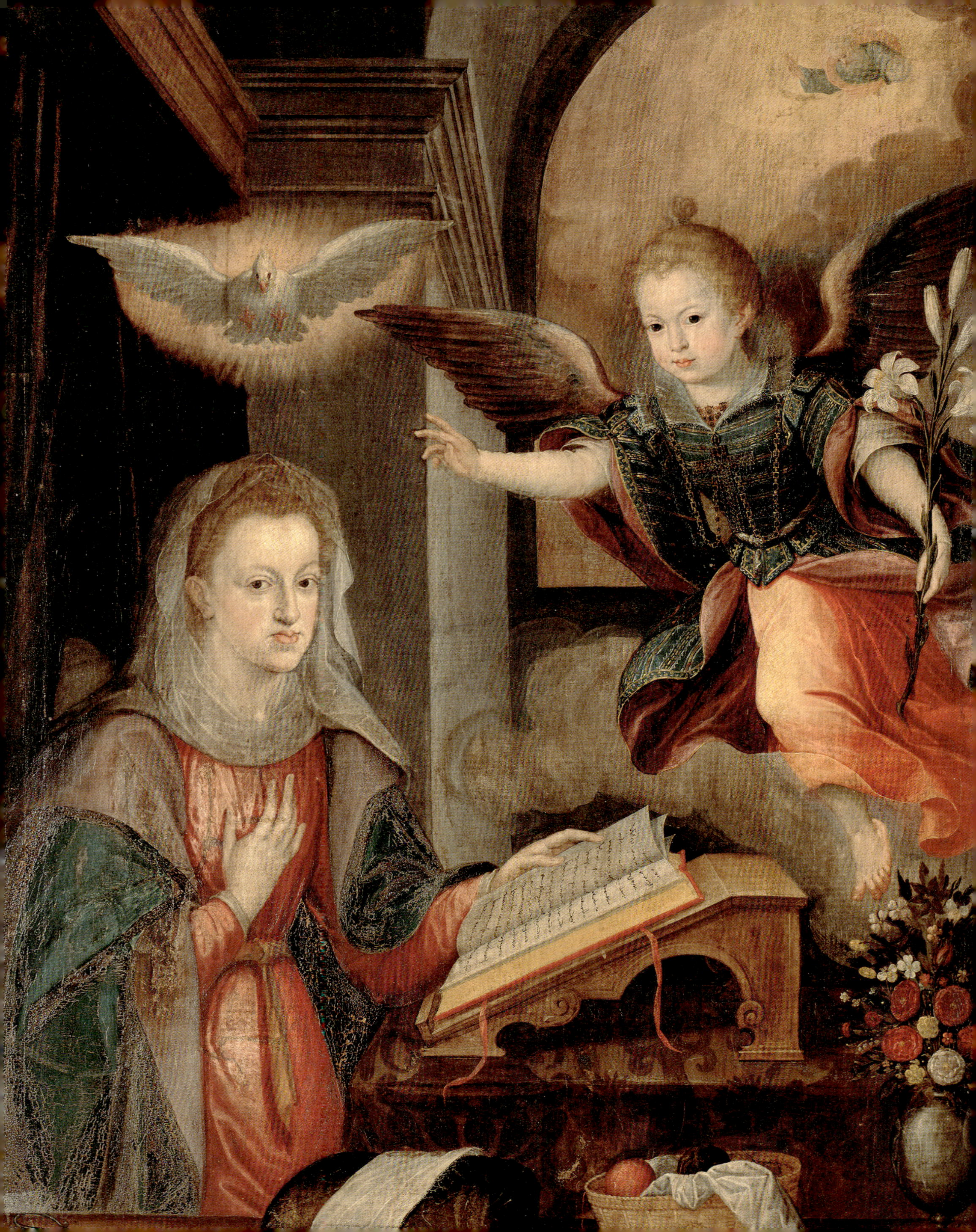

ADAM JASIENSKI

Praying to Portraits

Audience, Identity, and the Inquisition in the Early Modern Hispanic World

The Pennsylvania State University Press | University Park, Pennsylvania

Publication of this book has been supported by a Lila Wallace—Reader's Digest Publications Subsidy at Villa I Tatti, The Harvard University Center for Italian Renaissance Studies, and by a generous grant from SMU Meadows School of the Arts.

Frontispiece: Juan Pantoja de la Cruz, *Annunciation with Portrait of Margarita de Austria as the Virgin Mary*, ca. 1605 (figure 14).

Library of Congress Cataloging-in-Publication Data

Names: Jasienski, Adam, 1985– author.
Title: Praying to portraits : audience, identity, and the Inquisition in the early modern Hispanic world / Adam Jasienski.
Description: University Park, Pennsylvania : The Pennsylvania State University Press, [2023] | Includes bibliographical references and index.
Summary: "Explores sacred portraits in early modern Spain and Latin America and their use in mediating an individual's relationship to the divine, emphasizing the role of the spectator in the production of meaning"—Provided by publisher.
Identifiers: LCCN 2022037341 | ISBN 9780271093444 (cloth)
Subjects: LCSH: Portrait painting, Spanish—16th century. | Portrait painting, Spanish—17th century. | Portrait painting, Latin American—16th century. | Portrait painting, Latin American—17th century. | Christian art and symbolism—Spain—16th century. | Christian art and symbolism—Spain—17th century. | Christian art and symbolism—Latin America—16th century. | Christian art and symbolism—Latin America—17th century.
Classification: LCC ND1322.2 .J37 2023 | DDC 757.0946/09031—dc23/eng/20220922
LC record available at https://lccn.loc.gov/2022037341

Printed in Lithuania by BALTO Print
Published by The Pennsylvania State University Press, University Park, PA 16802–1003

The Pennsylvania State University Press is a member of the Association of University Presses.

It is the policy of The Pennsylvania State University Press to use acid-free paper. Publications on uncoated stock satisfy the minimum requirements of American National Standard for Information Sciences—Permanence of Paper for Printed Library Material, ANSI Z39.48–1992.

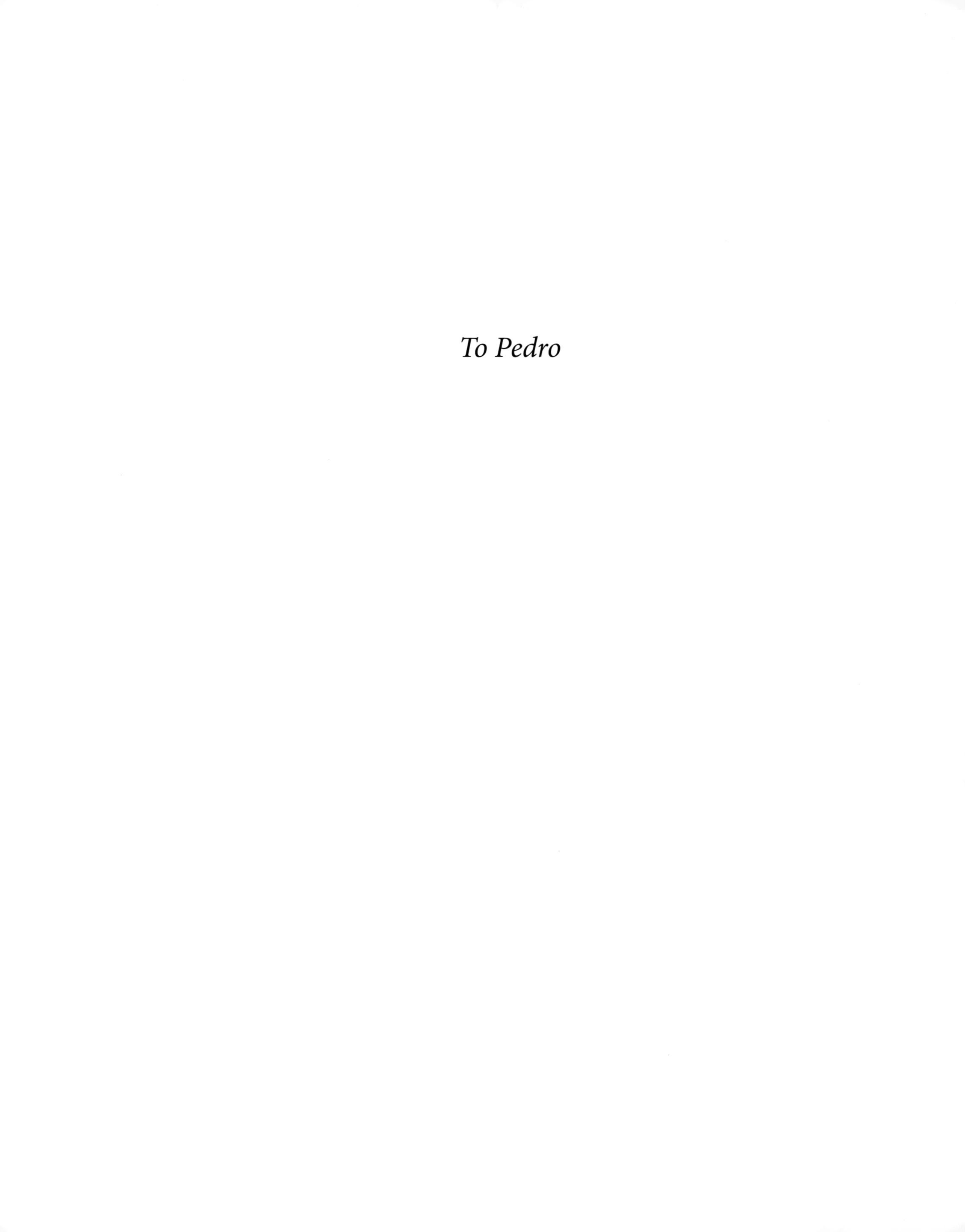

To Pedro

CONTENTS

ILLUSTRATIONS

ACKNOWLEDGMENTS

When I think of this project's decade-long gestation, the parallel that comes to mind is that of the long life of a painting. The many hands that stretched, primed, retouched, varnished, rolled, crated, carried, unpacked, framed, cleaned, conserved, repainted, retouched, revarnished, and hung the canvas are sometimes apparent but, just as often, those social accretions are invisible. Nonetheless, each of those hands has a part in its story. That the hands that helped this book along were well-meaning and generous, motivated by friendship and goodwill, fills me with boundless gratitude.

As a high school student in Poland, I had the good luck of being placed in the Spanish class of Professor Renata Sokólska-Pyzik, who, for six hours a week during four years, fostered my fascination with Spain and the Spanish language. The seed for this book was planted during those early encounters, and it was tended by the mentorship of other teachers along the way, chief among whom is Tom Cummins. I am thankful to him and Kyle Huffman, whose warm, open home was a special place during my years of graduate study. From among my teachers at Harvard University, I would like to especially thank Joseph Connors, Susan Dackerman, Frank Fehrenbach, Ewa Lajer-Burcharth, Mary Malcolm Gaylord, Gülru Necipoğlu, Katharine (Katy) Park, Alina Payne, Felipe Pereda, Suzanne Preston-Blier, Jennifer Roberts, David Roxburgh, Hugo van der Velden, and Henri Zerner. Special gratitude is also due to Deanna Dalrymple. I was lucky to belong to a cohort of generous and brilliant fellow graduate students, which included Francesca Borgo (who looks at pictures more astutely than anyone I know), and Ronah Sadan, Dan Zolli, and Sam Johnson (who read drafts or helped think through difficult sections of the project). In particular, my daily—even hourly—conversations with Aaron Wile helped to refine big arguments and minor points across nearly every page of this book.

I benefitted from a number of fellowships and institutional affiliations and formed part of communities that challenged this project and helped it to develop in crucial ways. At Villa I Tatti, The Harvard University Center for Italian Renaissance Studies, I wish to thank Alina Payne, Lino Pertile, Anna Bensted, Lukas Klič, and all the staff and fellows, particularly Philippa Jackson (who guided me on my first visit to the Archivio Segreto Vaticano) and Nadja Aksamija. Additionally, Villa I Tatti supported the publication of this book through a generous Lila Acheson Wallace–Reader's Digest publications subsidy.

I am also grateful to the staff and fellows of the John Carter Brown Library, where I held the Barbara S. Mosbacher fellowship, including César Manrique Figueroa, Neil Safier, Miguel Martínez, Elvira Vilches, Surekha Davies, Ana Hontanilla, Benjamin D. Reed, Valeria López Fadul, and Amara Solari. In particular, Laura Bass has remained an invaluable interlocutor from my time in Providence. During my years of graduate study, my work was supported by the Jens Aubrey Westengard Fund, the Arthur Kingsley Porter fellowship, the Richard and Susan Smith Foundation fellowship, the Tinker and John Womack grants, the Casa de Velázquez: École des Hautes Études Hispaniques et Ibériques in

Madrid, and the David Rockefeller Center for Latin American Studies in Cambridge.

At the Center for Advanced Study in the Visual Arts (CASVA) at the National Gallery of Art, where I held a Samuel H. Kress Fellowship, I am particularly grateful to Elizabeth Cropper, Peter Lukehart, and Therese O'Malley. Among the fellows, I wish to thank Paul Jaskot, Lihong Liu, Alexa Sand, Thomas Crow, Oscar E. Vázquez, Sarah Blake McHam, Rob Nelson, Vladimir Kulić, and Stephen Houston. Mary Roberts has read innumerable drafts and shared many a chinwag. The friendship that developed among the predoctoral fellows—Miri Kim, Nikolas Drosos, Hannah Friedman, David Pullins, Rachel Saunders, and Kate Cowcher—was a worthwhile recompense for the long days of writing. I am also grateful to Gregory P. J. Most and the staff of the Art Research Library.

Since 2016, I have been fortunate to form part of a supportive department at Southern Methodist University (SMU), which includes Randall Griffin, Anna Lovatt, Abbey Stockstill, Roberto Conduru, Elizabeth Eager, Elyan Hill, and Stephanie Langin-Hooper, all of whom have helped me think in new ways about the issues I explore in the pages of this book. Particular thanks go to Amy Freund and Adam Herring for their friendship and mentorship. At SMU I am also grateful to Kenneth Andrien, Alicia Zuese, Amanda Dotseth, Anne Lenhart, Tippi Polo, and to the late Mark Roglán. My thanks are also due to Samuel Holland, the dean of the Meadows School of the Arts, for generously supporting this project. At SMU my research was also funded by the Sam Taylor Fellowship, University Research Council Grants, and Faculty Development Grants. A grant from the SMU Meadows School of the Arts supported the publication of this book.

In 2018, I served as the inaugural fellow at the Zurbarán Centre for Spanish and Latin American Art at Durham University. I wrote this book's first chapter during that rainy autumn, while sitting in the Senior Common Room of Saint Mary's College, which hosted me warmly during my time in Durham. I am especially indebted to Stefano Cracolici, Edward Payne, Simon Hackett, the late Helen Hackett, Catherine Paine, and Michael Daly.

I presented research that contributed to the book's final form at numerous venues and I am grateful to all of the organizers of and participants in those events, including at the Coloquios investigadores of the Universidad Autónoma de Madrid (especially Juan Luis González García, José Riello, Fernando Marías, María Cruz de Carlos Varona, and Sergio Ramiro Ramírez); Wesleyan Renaissance Seminar (Nadja Aksamija and Michael Armstrong Roche), Villa I Tatti (Maria Berbara, Carmen Fernández Salvador, and Patricia Zalamea Fajardo), the Maius Workshop (Costanza Beltrami), CASVA (Therese O'Malley), the Clark Art Institute (Mary Roberts and Robert Wellington), the University of St. Andrews (Francesca Borgo and Kate Cowcher), and at the annual meetings of the Renaissance Society of America (Katrina B. Olds, Christopher Nygren, Ryan McDermott, Kelley Helmstutler Di Dio, and Almudena Vidorreta Torres), the College Art Association (Cristina Cruz González), and the Sixteenth Century Conference (Linda K. Williams). Portions of chapters 2 and 3 appeared as "Converting Portraits: Repainting as Art Making in the Early Modern Hispanic World," published in the March 2020 issue of *Art Bulletin*, and I am indebted to the editors, anonymous reviewers, and staff of that journal, especially Nick Geller and Lory Frankel.

I also wish to thank the staffs of numerous research institutions, including in A Coruña: the Museo de Belas Artes da Coruña; in Barcelona: the Arxiu Mas in the Institut Amatller d'Art Hispànic (especially Núria Peiris Pujolar and Núria Armengol); in Bogotá: the Museo de la Universidad del Rosario (in particular Ingrid Frederick Obregón, Eliécer Mauricio Tovar Gutiérrez, and Juan Diego Cortés Rodríguez); in Cambridge: Andover-Harvard Theological Library, Houghton Library (especially Susan Halpert and William Stoneman), and the Fine Arts Library; in Madrid: the Museo Lázaro Galdiano (especially Carlos Sánchez Díez), Patrimonio Nacional, the Archivo General de Palacio, the Museo de Historia de Madrid (especially Esther Sanz Murillo), the Archivo de Villa—Ayuntamiento de Madrid, the Archivo Histórico Diocesano de Madrid, the Archivo Histórico de Protocolos, the Biblioteca Nacional de España, the Real Hermandad del Refugio y Piedad, the Archivo Histórico Nacional, and the Palacio Liria (especially Álvaro Romero Sánchez Arjona); in New Haven: the Beinecke Rare Book & Manuscript Library; in New York: the Hispanic Society of America (especially John O'Neill); in Rome: the Archivio Segreto Vaticano, Biblioteca Apostolica Vaticana, and Monsignore Michał Jagosz at the Archivio della Basilica Papale di Santa Maria Maggiore; in San Lorenzo de El Escorial: the Real Biblioteca del Monasterio de El Escorial; in Seville: the Archivo de la Catedral de Sevilla; and in Toledo: the Archivo Histórico Nacional Sección Nobleza and the Biblioteca Capitular.

I am fortunate to have colleagues and friends who were willing to share their thoughts on numerous drafts or to debate the finer points of thorny translations. In particular, José Riello, César Manrique Figueroa, Morgan Ng, Wendy Sepponen, Rebecca Quinn Teresi, Juan Luis González García, and Robert Wellington have been constant sources of scholarly discussion, support, and inspiration. I am also very grateful to Borja Franco Llopis, Jack Balderrama Morley, María Lumbreras, Tatiana Seijas, Aaron Hyman, Andrew Hui, Mark Castro, Luisa Elena Alcalá, Álvaro Pascual Chenel, Byron Hamann, Clara Bargellini, Javier Portús Pérez, and Peter Cherry. Stephen Perkinson generously traveled to Dallas to participate in a transformative book manuscript workshop. Additionally, I wish to thank a number of people for their friendship, support, and interest in this project at its various stages, including Tanya Tiffany, Michael Schreffler, Alejandro Suárez León Plancarte, Kyrah Malika Daniels, Escardiel González Estevez, Allison Caplan, Denva Jackson, Francisco Montes González, Emily C. Floyd, José Luis Colomer, Fernando Marías, Darío Velandia Onofre, Jesús Escobar, Akemi Herráez Vossbrink, Ricardo Fernández Gracia, Annette Schultze, Hilda Pérez, Caitlin Henningsen, Seth Hindin, Cécile Vincent-Cassy, Carmen Fernández Salvador, Elena Calvillo, Piers Baker-Bates, Daniel Giannoni Succar, Francisco Moreno, Stephan Wolohojian, Pablo Pérez d'Ors, Ana García Sanz, Ybeth Arias Cuba, Mercedes Llorente, Vanessa de Cruz Medina, María Cruz de Carlos Varona, Brendan McMahon, Santiago López-Rios Moreno, Dieter (Bobby) Kuehl, David Alan Brown, Kate Holohan, Susan Verdi Webster, Goretti González, Ana Pulido Rull, Benito Navarrete Prieto, Richard Kagan, Dana Leibsohn, Kris Lane, Alexandra Letvin, Layla Bermeo, Victoria Addona, José María Quesada Valera, and Niria Leyva-Gutiérrez.

At Penn State University Press, I am deeply indebted to Eleanor (Ellie) Goodman for seeing the value of this project. She is present in these pages not only as an editor but as a scholar whose work on seventeenth-century royal spaces has informed my own. I am also grateful to Maddie Caso, Annika Fisher, Brian Beer, and to the two anonymous reviewers, whose feedback was essential in strengthening the book's main arguments.

I am so fortunate that my parents, Michał Jasieński and Grażyna Jasieńska, supported my interests and pursuits without falter, challenged ideas, applauded successes, encouraged after failures, and followed me during trips throughout Europe as I went inside any open churches. It was their crossing of an iron curtain and an ocean, when they left Poland for the United States, that set off the chain of events that culminated in my academic path and this book. They are present in every part of this project. I am also grateful to my mother-in-law, Balbina Hérmida Jorge Fleites, who spent much of 2020 with us as I finished work on the manuscript, and to Lupka and Benek, who ensured that I took walks after long days of editing. Finally, most importantly, I thank Pedro José Fernández, whose contributions to this project and to my life would be impossible to summarize in anything less than an entire new volume. They are the reason that this book is dedicated to him.

ABBREVIATIONS

AGI	Archivo General de Indias, Seville
AGN	Archivo General de la Nación, Mexico City
AHN	Archivo Histórico Nacional, Madrid
RAH	Real Academia de la Historia, Madrid
RBME	Real Biblioteca del Monasterio de El Escorial

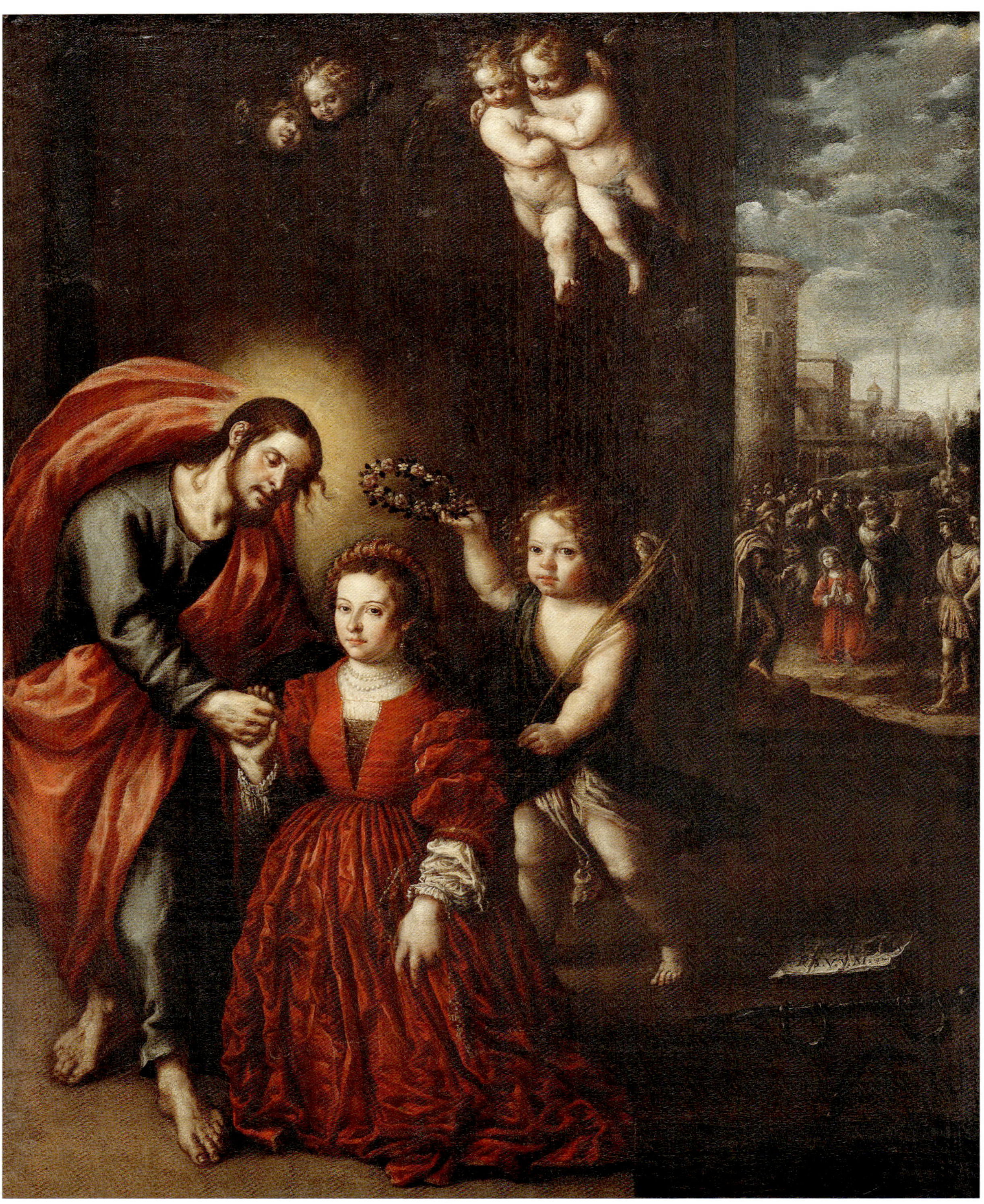

INTRODUCTION

Portraits and Sacred Images in Early Modernity

Ambiguous Images

The woman in red is a saint (fig. 1). This much seems clear. She kneels next to Christ, who grasps her hand, while an angel raises a floral wreath over her head. On the ground lies a piece of paper inscribed with the words "Saint Barbara, virgin and martyr." In the scene beyond them, another woman, also dressed in red, submits to decapitation by a bearded executioner. The women's parallel poses and dress, along with the ambiguous position of the *cartellino*—set in darkened middle ground between the two scenes—imply that both women are Saint Barbara. Barbara's martyrdom in the background is narrative, derived from hagiographic texts: the future saint's own father ordered—and performed—her beheading.[1] In the foreground, the representation of Barbara is iconic, an event that occurs outside of narrative time. Here, directly before the viewer, Saint Barbara, now rendered whole in posthumous sanctity, kneels alongside Christ.[2] Since the woman is a saint, this painting appears to be an image for devotion and prayer, its iconography and composition deriving from a long tradition of Christian art.

At the same time, a number of clues in the painting suggest that the depiction may actually be a portrait, perhaps of the person who commissioned the painting. The woman who kneels in the foreground is represented according to the conventions of period portraiture: her facial features are particularized, and, whereas Christ's face is painterly, with eyes downcast, hers is highly finished and confronts the viewer with a direct gaze. Tellingly, the angel also looks out from the picture: he, too, is a portrait, likely of the sitter's young son. This painting, then, is not only a religious painting but also a portrait, bringing together in one canvas

FIG. 1 Attributed to Mosén Domingo Saura, *Portrait of a Woman as Saint Barbara*, ca. 1650. Oil on canvas, 43.125 × 34.75 in. (109.5 × 88.5 cm). Museo Lázaro Galdiano, Madrid. Photo: Pablo Linés © Museo Lázaro Galdiano, Madrid.

two categories of early modern image making that have long been understood as not only distinct but binarily opposed to each other.

The contemporary individuals inhabit the historic religious scene with seeming ease, but the painting's competing registers—present-day and profane as opposed to ancient and sacred—force the image to exist in a permanent state of tension. The Council of Trent (1545–63) had decreed that "the honor which is shown unto [devotional images] is referred to the prototypes which they represent."[3] In this conception a religious image was a tool—helpful with a task but not an end unto itself—that served to redirect a pious viewer's thoughts to the depicted holy figure. The saintly "prototype" of a religious picture could receive prayer and serve as an intercessor on behalf of the suppliant. On the other hand, portraits of living or once-living sitters could not perform in the same way; their referents, while perhaps imagined by their viewers to be sympathetic listeners, were eschatologically ineffective. In the case of an image with a doubled referent, such as the portrait of a woman in the guise of Saint Barbara, to whom was this honor referred? For early modern ecclesiastics, the question was not merely rhetorical. Prayers could be misdirected and go unheeded, while living individuals might receive veneration worthy only of saints, challenging the Catholic Church's primacy in administering religious cults. The troubling duality of a portrait-icon put souls at stake.

In the painting with Saint Barbara, the artist (perhaps the Valencian painter Mosén Domingo Saura) responded to a request common across early modern Spain and its American and European viceroyalties: to create a religious image that included a likeness of the work's patron.[4] Even within those straightforward parameters, however, artworks that fulfilled the directive could differ radically. Some entirely collapsed the distance between the nonsacred sitters and the sacred scene, thus bringing the two spheres together. Other artworks pointedly accentuated the distance separating the heavens from the world of the profane. For example, a late seventeenth-century central Mexican portrait offers a closely observed, naturalistic depiction of two sitters, Bartolomé Andrés and Agustín Pérez (fig. 2). This painting was almost certainly one of a pair of double donor portraits set on either side of a holy image. The physical and ontological distance between the now-lost sacred scene at the center and the profane ones that framed it was such that the three canvases became separated at some point in their afterlives, with the portrait coming to function as an independent artwork.[5]

The painting of the woman as Saint Barbara is explicit in its sacred iconography. It is therefore plausible that some of its viewers may have treated the work as an object of religious contemplation. However, much the same was true of the Mexican donor portrait, even though there is no explicit religious element in the image aside from the donors' hands grasped in prayer. It, too, could have been understood to be a sacred image, becoming the focus of prayer and veneration. This book's central argument is that the early modern portrait—*any* early modern portrait—could become a sacred image. However latent, the potential was there, both provocative and irrefutable. The possible slippage from one register to the other—from sacred to profane, or from worldly to sacred—could occur in a number of ways, many of which were entirely legitimate from the point of view of the ecclesiastical establishment. The iconography of Saint Ignatius of Loyola, for example, was centered

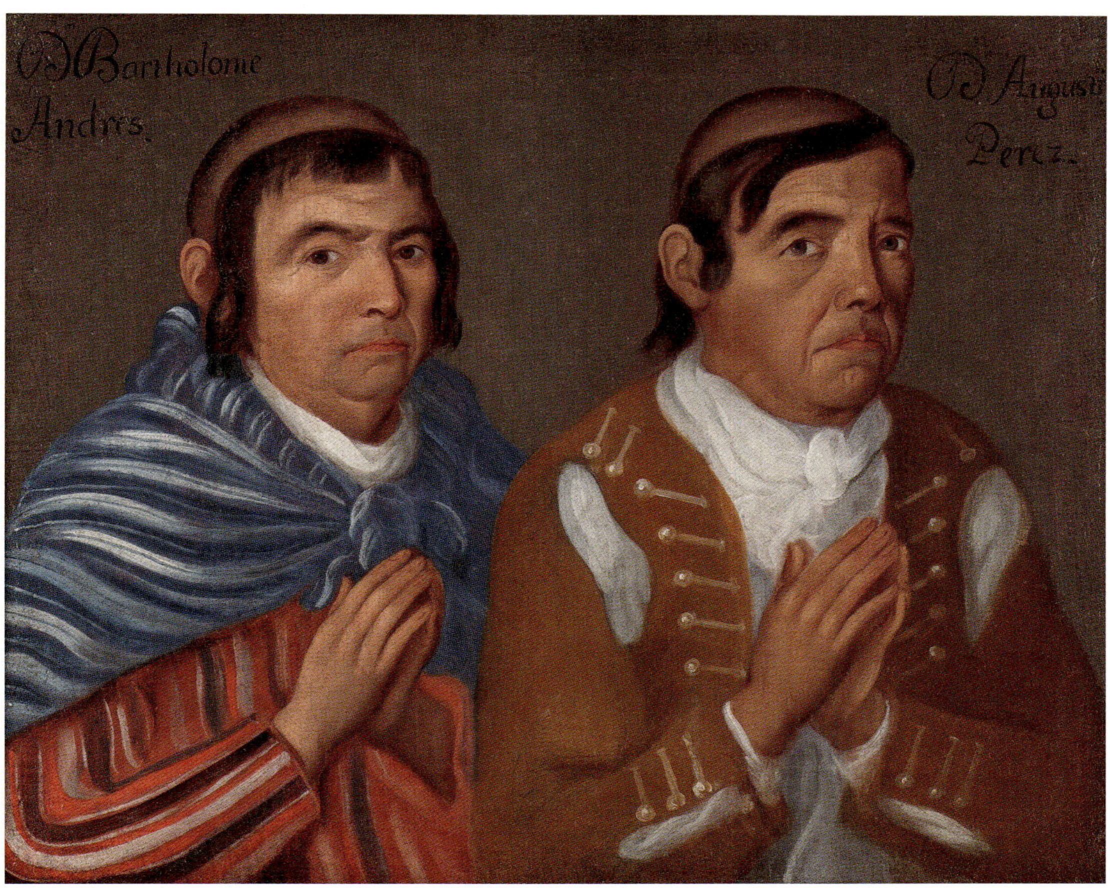

FIG. 2 Unidentified Tlaxcalan painter, *Don Bartolomé Andrés and Don Agustín Pérez*, late 1600s. Oil on canvas, 22.25 × 27.5 in. (56.51 × 69.85 cm). Denver Art Museum, gift of the Collection of Frederick and Jan Mayer, 2014.219. Photography courtesy Denver Art Museum.

on his—purportedly accurate—physiognomic likeness. Depictions of the Jesuit saint are therefore always both portraits and sacred images. Similarly, if the sitter of a portrait was later canonized by the Catholic Church, that image would, by extension, undergo a transition to become an image of a saint. Moreover, royal portraits frequently functioned akin to sacred images in how they were treated and displayed.[6] Other cases, however, were much less orthodox. "Normal" portraits of secular sitters could be repainted, their sitters endowed with saintly attributes that transformed the paintings into images for worship. Likewise, portraits could be altered by their use and simply be treated as if they were religious images, even if no iconographic markers of sanctity were ever added to their surfaces.[7] The portrait, then, was a mutable image type. With the help of their users and viewers, these images voraciously inhabited different artistic categories, challenging, even belying, their promise of stable, static commemoration.

This book's title, *Praying to Portraits*, is therefore intended as more than convenient alliteration. It speaks to the reality of early modern Hispanic—but also, more broadly, Catholic European and colonial—image making, in which the capacity for creating portraitistic likenesses coincided with a religious practice that centered on anthropomorphic representation. Portraits were not only, as has been long claimed, harbingers of secular modernity and autonomous selfhood. Rather, fickle and flexible, portraits were also unique sites for mediating an individual's relationship to the sphere of the sacred. This relationship had never been straightforward or universally applicable, and it became ever more complex with the increasing diversification of the audiences that fell under the Spanish monarchy's aegis. The sacred portrait, which melded the idiosyncrasies of individual likeness with the supposed universality of the religious image, emerged as an arena in which early modern individuals wrestled with what could be known of the divine and how the divine could be experienced. Individuals turned to such images in order to perform their personal or public devotions and, by extension, to articulate their changeable, complex selfhoods, linking the mundane with the sacred, the personal with the universal. For individuals living across the early modern Hispanic world, in sum, praying to a portrait was not an unusual thing to do.

Types of Sacred Portraits

Religious painting and portraiture have long been considered the two most important contributions of early modern Hispanic art, but they are commonly treated as distinct artistic categories.[8] Situated in the vast gray space between them, however, is a constellation of images in which portraiture came into conversation with the sphere of the sacred; I term these works "sacred portraits." These include donor portraits, portraits of sitters in the guise of saints, "true portraits" of recently deceased but already canonized individuals, paintings of saints that merely drew on the conventions of portraiture without being actual likenesses, repainted portraits, and even royal portraits.[9] Some of these image types have been studied individually, but thus far the category of sacred portraiture has rarely been considered as an integrally connected whole.[10] This inattention may derive from the oft-uncategorizable, fluid nature of many of its constitutive image types. No less, there is the long-standing historiographic bias against artworks that do not easily align with modern artistic genres. This impasse is compounded by the fact that the policing of such image types by entities like the Holy Office of the Inquisition could result in their destruction, with their traces intermittently surfacing in the archive.[11]

When examined individually, these images (with the exception of the royal portrait) appear as curious footnotes at the margins of early modern Hispanic visual culture or as unusual variations on the seemingly monolithic categories of portraiture and religious painting.[12] As I argue here, sacred portraits were not marginal at all. Rather they were ubiquitous images, which were variously commissioned, produced, and employed across social tiers and geographies; they lay at the very center of the period's artistic consciousness. Their users and viewers ranged from aristocratic nuns in Madrid to innkeepers in Nahuatl-speaking towns in central Mexico, from Guatemalan bureaucrats to Neapolitan insurgents, and from Bolivian ecclesiastics to the king of Spain himself. That sacred portraits were widespread, perhaps even common, in Habsburg and early Bourbon realms is not to say that they were straightforward: those works could be both orthodox and unorthodox, popular and persecuted, fully normalized and utterly scandalous. In their inherent duality—belonging to both portraiture and religious imagery—they frustrated the stability, legibility, and uniformity of those two most pivotal, theoretically fraught artistic categories of the early modern period.

But their pervasiveness suggests that they were also worth the frustration. A portrait in a sacred picture makes the depicted holy figure actualized and relatable, assisting the Catholic devotional image in its task of moving its viewers.[13] A human face, replete with idiosyncratic features, imperfections, and eyes that seek out those of the viewer, arrests the viewer's attention.[14] Any figure in a multifigural composition that makes direct eye contact with the viewer—a quintessential portraitistic convention—has such an anchoring function, as Michael Baxandall famously noted of the *festaiuoli* (revelers) of quattrocento painting.[15] There was also a second effect. As I hope to make clear in this study, enhancing a portrait with sacred elements transformed it from an image of limited relevance—cherished primarily by the people who had known the sitter—to one that from the point of view of the Catholic Church had ostensibly universal significance. Even though portraits introduced new, often completely irreconcilable tensions into institutional imagery that relied on precedent and tradition, their contemporaneity and relatability, their energetic potential (from the classical rhetorical concept of *enargeia*—to make vivid), created new possibilities for affecting viewers.

Portraiture and the Sacred Image

Because the difficult-to-categorize image types that I have grouped within the category of sacred portraits reside at the intersection of politics and theology, they are, by extension, inextricably linked to the Spanish monarchy's defining projects: first, the aggressive expansion of a polity and its attempts to rule an increasingly diverse set of subjects and, second, the dissemination of a confessional system, premised on orthodoxy, that was more or less uniformly applied to those varied individuals.[16] In the period under examination in this book (the sixteenth and seventeenth centuries), a number of pressures, including encounters with non-Christian populations and Protestant reformist criticisms, led the Catholic Church to become increasingly aware of the need to standardize its policy concerning images and to verbalize the benefits of images to spiritual practice. The Council of Trent, largely convened in order to respond to these Protestant challenges, was famously terse on the subject of creating and using sacred art in accordance with orthodoxy, but in the decades after the council, theologians began to expand on its general recommendations.[17] For instance, the Italian theologian Gabriele Paleotti believed that predication was crucial in teaching and maintaining adherence to Catholic doctrine. In terms of catechetical effectiveness, however, few things could surpass the seeing of a sacred scene. "To hear the story told of the martyrdom of a saint," Paleotti argued, "or the zeal and constancy of a virgin, or the passion of Christ himself—those are things that really hit one inside. But when the saintly martyr practically materializes in front of your eyes in vivid color, with the oppressed virgin on one side and Christ pierced by nails on

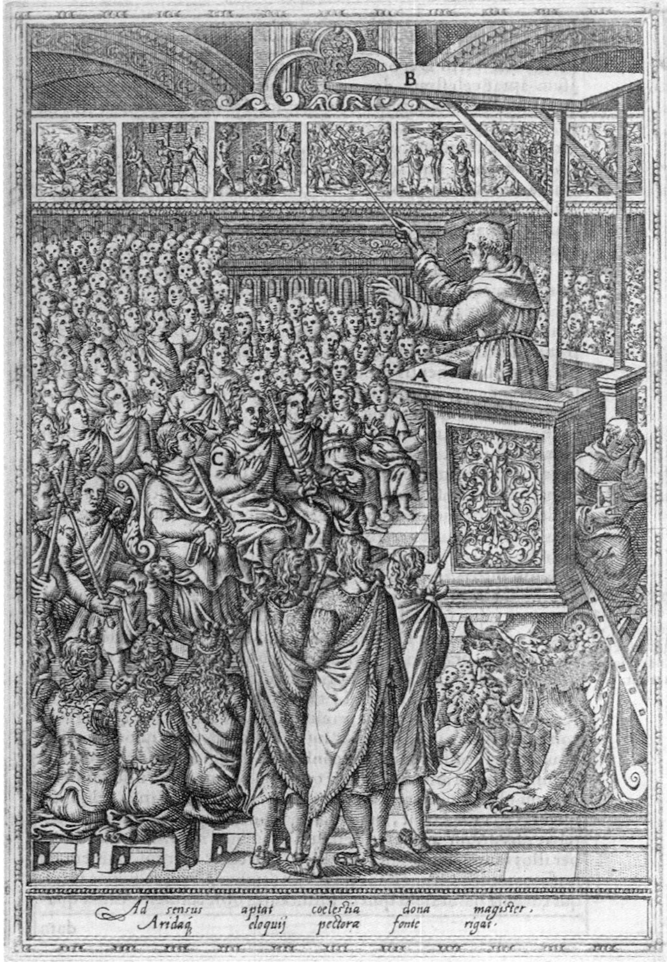

FIG. 3 Attributed to Diego Valadés, *Friar Preaching with Images*, in Diego Valadés, *Rhetorica Christiana* (Perugia: Petrus Jacobus Petrutius, 1579). Engraving on paper. Getty Research Institute, Los Angeles, 1388-209.

the other—one would have to be made of wood or stone not to feel how much more it intensifies devotion and wrenches the gut."[18]

Perhaps nowhere is the capacity of images to "hit" the viewer visualized more explicitly than across two engravings that appear in Diego Valadés's *Rhetorica Christiana*, largely composed in central New Spain but published in Perugia in 1579, three years prior to Paleotti's text. In the first image, a Franciscan friar preaches to a congregation of Indigenous American neophytes (fig. 3). He uses a pointer to indicate a painting from among seven framed vignettes with scenes from the Passion that hang above his listeners' heads. The book's text explains that because the Indigenous congregants could not read, it was the images that "reveal[ed to them] the mysteries of our redemption," which became, in this way, "better affixed in their memories."[19] The second image includes many of the same protagonists, including the preacher, still wielding a pointer, and his congregation (fig. 4). Moved out of the space of the

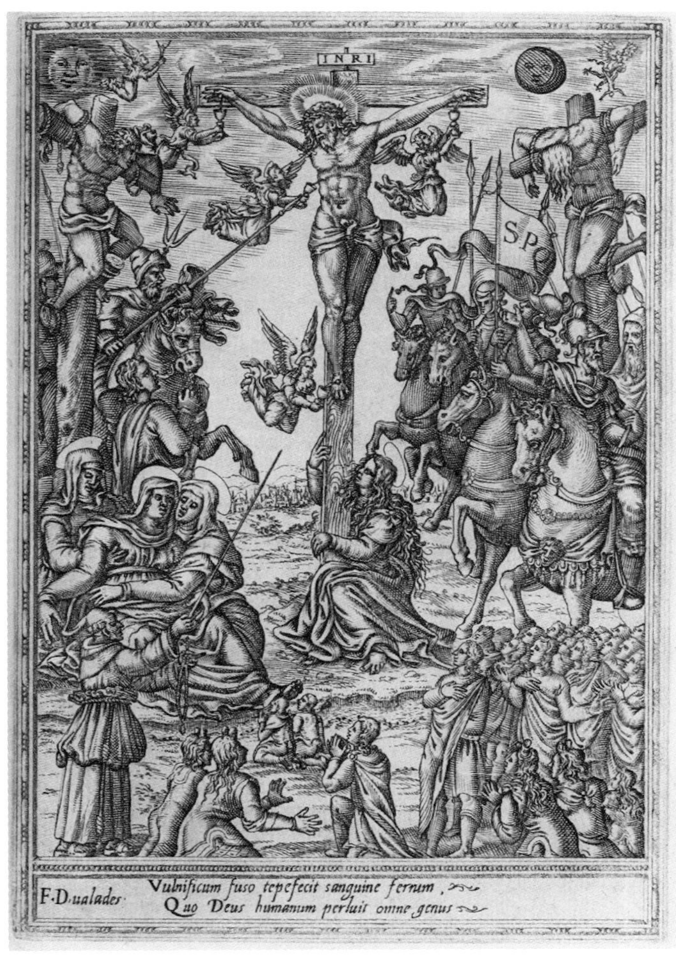

FIG. 4 Diego Valadés, *Friar Preaching Before the Crucifixion*, in Diego Valadés, *Rhetorica Christiana* (Perugia: Petrus Jacobus Petrutius, 1579). Engraving on paper. Getty Research Institute, Los Angeles, 1388-209.

church or atrium, they have now come to inhabit the scene of Christ's Crucifixion (which was the next vignette in the row of pictures from the first engraving). The preacher's rhetoric, combined with the affective capacity of the image, Valadés visually argues, allows the audience to become imaginatively transported into a shared space with the sacred protagonists.[20] The arguments that Valadés's text and its images make can be applied to the use of sacred images in early modern Catholicism writ large. Though I am unaware of whether Paleotti owned or read Valadés's work, he would have likely agreed with the Mexican friar about the affective power that images could wield over those who saw—and meditated over—them.

The meteoric rise of sacred portraits from the fifteenth century onward suggests that, to early modern audiences, the inclusion of a portrait likeness in a sacred image enhanced even further the efficacy with which that image performed its functions or, to borrow from Paleotti, with which it "hit" its viewers. For instance, a moralizing true

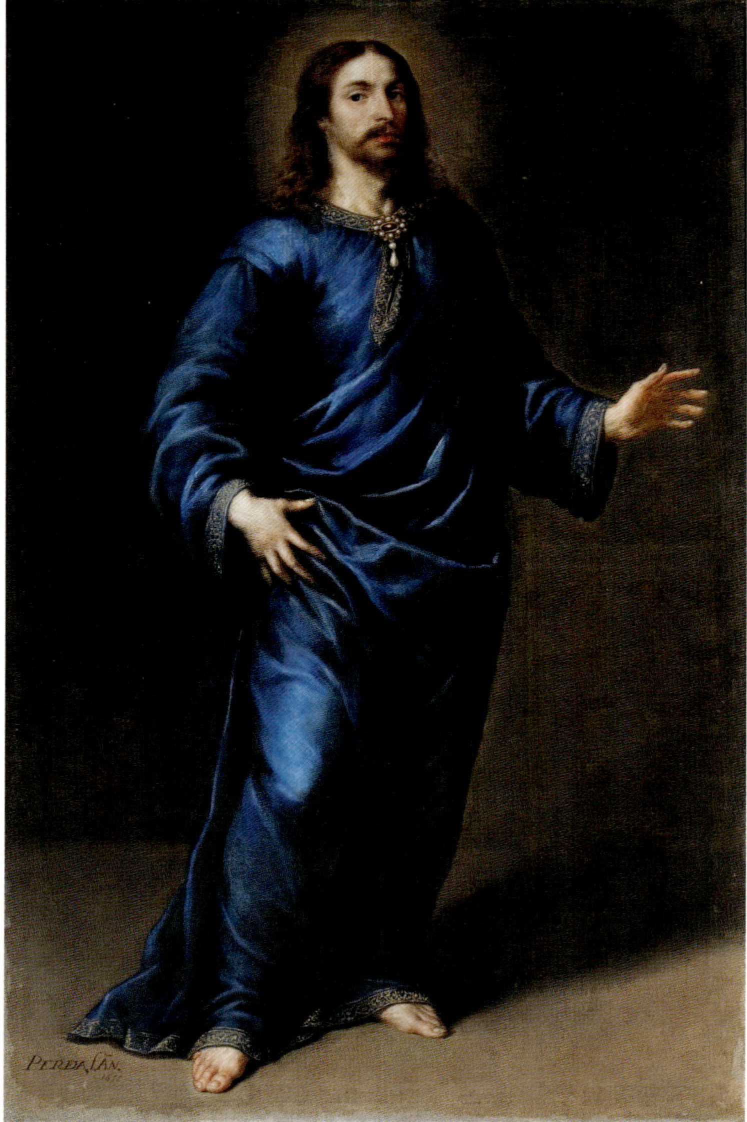

FIG. 5 Antonio de Pereda y Salgado, *Christ as Savior*, ca. 1655. Oil on canvas, 83.4 × 56.3 in. (212 × 143 cm). Long-term loan to the parish church of San Ginés, Madrid, from the ex-Convent of the Discalced Capuchin Sisters, Alcobendas.

portrait of a saint communicated to pious viewers that they, too, could work toward spiritual perfection since a real person had already achieved that goal. Or, when patrons requested that they be portrayed as saints, the emotive potential of the portrait within the devotional image allowed the patrons to—quite literally—see themselves and their familiars inserted into the holy episode they contemplated.

But, as artistic portrayals that were subject to an individual artist's invention and whim, depictions of holy figures and narratives were inherently fallible. Therefore, the insertion of a portrait—with its connotations of eyewitness immediacy and

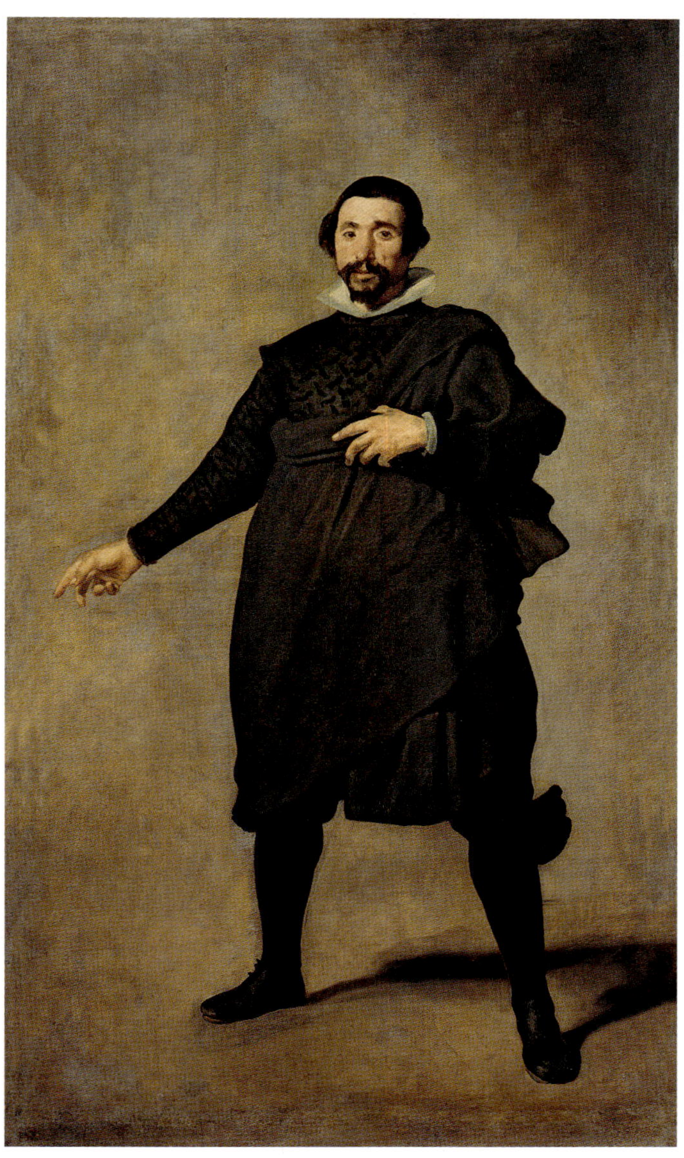

FIG. 6 Diego Velázquez, *Pablo de Valladolid*, ca. 1635. Oil on canvas, 42.9 × 48.4 in. (209 × 123 cm). Museo Nacional del Prado, Madrid. Photo: Museo Nacional del Prado / Art Resource, New York.

veracity—or of portrait-like elements into a religious context could endow the depiction of a holy individual or scene with a sense of reality, contributing to the viewer's acceptance of their validity.[21] For example, the painter Antonio de Pereda's indebtedness to the conventions of period portraiture becomes apparent when comparing his *Christ as Savior* of around 1655 (fig. 5) to Diego Velázquez's portrait of the actor Pablo de Valladolid of 1635 (fig. 6).[22] Both figures gaze out directly at the viewer and stand in dynamic poses, seemingly caught midgesture—blessing and speaking, respectively—and placed in what Javier Portús Pérez calls "absolutely indeterminate space."[23]

The formal parallels are indisputable even if, ontologically, the two images could not be more different. Pereda recombined elements from the court portrait, capitalizing on the instant recognizability of this pictorial language to his audiences, in order to isolate and monumentalize his arresting figure of Christ. In practice, however, portraiture was plagued by the same issues of veracity as religious imagery. When portraits became separated from their sitters, the images could not easily be compared to their prototypes. Their validity had to be accepted on faith. The laboriously constructed authority of images, it turns out, could be easily dismantled.

Nowhere is this more apparent than in the vernacular appropriation of official forms of using and living with images, including sacred portraits. Political and religious images were deployed across great distances and among varied populations and were tasked with maintaining stability and modeling forms of correct behavior. The heterogenous audiences who encountered them, however, were not necessarily invested in universals. Factors including their gender, ethnicity, faith, and economic standing could affect what they thought of images and how they used them. They adapted incoming models to better fit local conditions, often resulting in images that only seemingly adhered to accepted modes of art making. Or, they used images in ways that superficially aligned with established practices but that, when probed, proved to be entirely heterodox. Often, these images and their users were subjected to institutional surveillance and censorship. It is critical to stress, however, that this "misuse" of images was not simply a concern in places that were removed from the seats of institutional power. It was as likely to occur in Madrid and Mexico City as it was in small towns like Algete in central Spain, discussed in chapter 3, and San Martín Texmelucan in central Mexico, examined in chapter 4. Perhaps paradoxically, in all those places, it was the censors who revealed themselves to be some of the most astute viewers and critics of images, both religious and profane. In turn, their struggles to determine the limits of different image types constitute some of the period's richest art-theoretical debates.

Portraiture in the Early Modern Hispanic World

In a 1942 essay on the Baroque, the art historian Enrique Lafuente Ferrari argues that "in Spanish painting, both devout and profane, everything, even the still life, is portraiture," a statement that was powerfully attuned to the breadth of the category.[24] Indeed, in sixteenth- and seventeenth-century Castilian Spanish, the interpretive breadth of *retrato*, or portrait, made space for a range of distinct image types that could fit beneath its rubric. City views, such as Antonio Mancelli's depiction of the main plaza in Madrid; representations of holy relics, like the *santo chiodo* or nail from the Crucifixion held in Milan (fig. 7); and images of animals and plants, particularly those deemed exotic, prodigious, or monstrous were all labeled as portraits, even as true portraits—*verdaderos retratos*—which granted them the cachet of unimpeachable authenticity. As a concept, then, the portrait was a ductile notion characterized, above all, by the credibility that it imparted to things that bore its name.[25]

The portrait's claim to truthfulness was implicit in its etymology. The lexicographer Sebastián de Covarrubias defined *retrato* in relation to the term *retraer*, because the person making the portrait brings or "draws [*trae*] toward him or herself the semblance and figure that is being portrayed," suggesting a physical relationship between the image maker and the model, and, by extension, the experience of being an eyewitness, which was often understood as a guarantee of veracity.[26] Similarly, the painter and art theorist Francisco Pacheco noted that for an image to be deemed a portrait, it had to fulfill two conditions: "The first is that the portrait be very similar to the original . . . and the second obligation is that it be well drawn and painted. . . . But if either likeness or good quality are to be missing, then let likeness remain, since this is the goal of portraiture."[27] According to these distinctions, all an image needed to be a portrait was a real world prototype, with which it bore a connection through resemblance, explaining the wide variety of images, including depictions of animals, religious statuary, and even cities, that fell under this rubric.

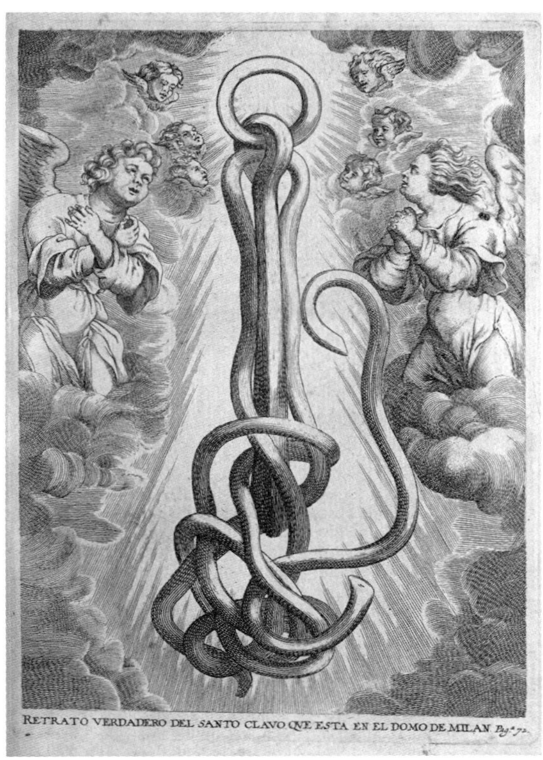

FIG. 7 Marinus van der Goes, after Peter Paul Rubens, *Retrato Verdadero del Santo Clavo que Esta en el Domo de Milan*, in Diego de Aedo y Gallart, *Viaje del infante cardenal don Fernando de Avstria, desde 12. de abril 1632. que saliò de Madrid con Su Magestad D. Felipe IV. su hermano para la çiudad de Barçelona, hasta 4. de noviembre de 1634. que entrò en la de Bruselas* (Antwerp: Jan Cnobbaert, 1635), between pages 72 and 73. Engraving on paper. Julius S. Held Collection of Rare Books, Sterling and Francine Clark Art Institute Library, Williamstown.

The term's breadth notwithstanding, *retrato* was also understood as a depiction of a specific person. Even though there existed nonphysiognomic ways in which a portrait's relation to its prototype could be cemented, including textually and symbolically through inscriptions and coats of arms, there was a growing interest in physiognomic likeness in early modern Spain. In this understanding, a portrait was a rendering of the appearance of a human individual, of a face endowed with specific, even unique, physical features.[28] In rare situations when sitters are depicted multiple times, they should be recognizable from one portrait to the next based on their facial features. Of course, it is impossible to determine accuracy in depictions of once-living individuals, and neither is this a goal here. The images that are of interest are those that *present* as portraits, aiming to convince the viewer that what they depict is a real, (once-)living person.[29] That portraits were understood by a broad cross section of society to be recognizable depictions of specific individuals is demonstrated by their prominence as topoi in period theater.[30] Indeed, even if an individual did not have the wherewithal to commission a portrait, they still understood what kind of image it was and how it functioned. When speaking of portraiture in this book, I have this more constrained but still capacious definition in mind.[31]

A further note on terminology: although the word *genre* was used in the early modern period, I generally prefer the terms *artistic type* or *category*, which respond more precisely to the exigencies of dealing with images that resist clear-cut categorization. Just as we cannot say that early modern religious imagery was a genre, given the breadth of types of images that fulfilled religious purposes, so too, in the Hispanic world, the portrait was not so much a genre as a type of image defined by its claim to truthfully rendering that which is real. The artistic categories under consideration were flexible and extendable, allowing for frequent overlaps and ambiguities of classification.[32]

Historiographically, portraiture has long been understood as one of the two poles that dominated artistic production in the Hispanic world, with the other being religious painting.[33] In part, this conception derived from the fact that the modern understanding of portraiture as the painting of physiognomic likenesses, distinct from the sphere of religious imagery, was already present in early modernity.[34] For example, Javier Portús Pérez has shown that portraits were frequently grouped together in portrait galleries, separately from other types of paintings.[35] Moreover, in Spain painters had to pay the *alcabala* artisans' sales tax for portraits or still lifes but were exempt from it when taking on religious commissions.[36] Perhaps for this reason, in Peter Cherry's words, Pacheco "maintained a strict conceptual division between his extensive practice as a portraitist and his narrative pictures of religious subjects, evidently seen as two entirely different categories of painting."[37] Therefore, notwithstanding the extreme breadth of the concept of portraiture, early modern artists, patrons, censors, and officials also understood the portrait as a highly specific, discrete artistic category: a depiction of a living individual, clearly outside the sphere of the sacred image. As the concept of portraiture evolved, it was precisely this narrower understanding of the category that emerged triumphant from the broader and more fluid set of understandings that I have outlined above.[38] These divisions and hierarchies gradually crystallized even further in the eighteenth century under the influence of burgeoning secularism, Enlightenment theory, and French academic models with hierarchies of genres, which defined what constituted the boundaries of a portrait against those of, for instance, a history painting or a still life. Portraits became cast as not only separate from but as binarily opposed to the sphere of the sacred.

Organization

This book considers together the wide range of ways in which portraiture and religious painting overlapped in the sixteenth and seventeenth centuries. Because similar forms and practices related to sacred portraiture recurred throughout the Hispanic world, precluding a clear organization by chronology or geography, each of the four chapters that follow is structured around a distinct type of sacred portrait. The first chapter examines the phenomenon of artists depicting their patrons in the guise of holy figures, arguing against the interpretations that such images expressed the notion of sacred monarchy or that they revealed the sitters' vanity. For such images to possess even a semblance of canonical correctness, I assert, their portraitistic aspects had to be suppressed.

By performing acts of prayerful, introspective meditation before images of themselves as holy figures, sitters would have attempted to debase, rather than celebrate, their selfhoods. Notwithstanding the pious intentions of their patrons, however, both ecclesiastical censors and satirical sonnetists condemned these images for the ambiguous messages they could impart to other viewers.

The second chapter analyzes the roles of portraiture in the cults of the recently deceased Ignatius of Loyola and Teresa of Ávila, whose physical appearances were known with some accuracy. I suggest that such portrait-based image cults of modern saints arose in indirect response to the increasing popularity of images in which living patrons appeared in the guise of holy figures. Subsequently, institutional patrons insisted on producing increasingly portrait-like images of saints for whom there survived few or no reliable portrait likenesses, like the long-deceased Saint Benedict of the sixth century. In analyzing the testimony of a group of demonically possessed nuns, the chapter shows that period audiences were eager to accept authoritative declarations about the truthfulness of depictions of ancient and medieval saints even if their sources were suspect.

The third chapter considers the afterlives of portrait likenesses and the circumstances that could lead to their transformation into sacred images. The portrait was a labile image type, easily acquiring meanings that were at odds with the goals of its original patrons and intended viewers. The transformation of portraits into sacred pictures occurred when their later owners added to them standardized iconographic markers of sanctity, such as halos or textual inscriptions that identified their sitters as saints. The resulting images were often only slightly divergent from their earlier versions in formal terms—the addition of a halo or a line of text hardly constituted a major overpainting campaign—but drastically different in terms of their ontology, spiritual efficacy, and potential usage. Moreover, given the multiethnic and multilingual audiences of such images, I attempt to elucidate and nuance the culturally bound forms of seeing that were present in the example of the portraits of Juan de Palafox y Mendoza, the bishop of the central Mexican city of Puebla de los Ángeles. As I will suggest, a Nahuatl-informed definition of sacred portraiture not only helps us understand how these images functioned and were understood in Puebla and its surrounding towns, including San Martín Texmelucan, but it can also be read back onto European paintings from the period, further expanding the increasingly capacious definition of the early modern portrait. To paraphrase Steven Nelson's response to "A Questionnaire on Decolonization," we can explore Madrid from the vantage point of San Martín Texmelucan and analyze San Martín Texmelucan in ways that do not center Madrid.[39]

Finally, the fourth chapter focuses on the image of the king, which provides yet another conduit between the categories of religious imagery and portraiture. Royal portraits relied on external elements of display, such as the baldachin, curtain, and dais, for legibility but shared them, as well as the behaviors their viewers were expected to perform before them, with religious images. These elements and behaviors become essential to understanding the implications of an inquisitorial trial from central Mexico, which focused on the unsanctioned cult surrounding Bishop Palafox's portraits. I argue that the royal portrait's functional similarity to religious images accounts for how the controversial cleric's portraits, which I

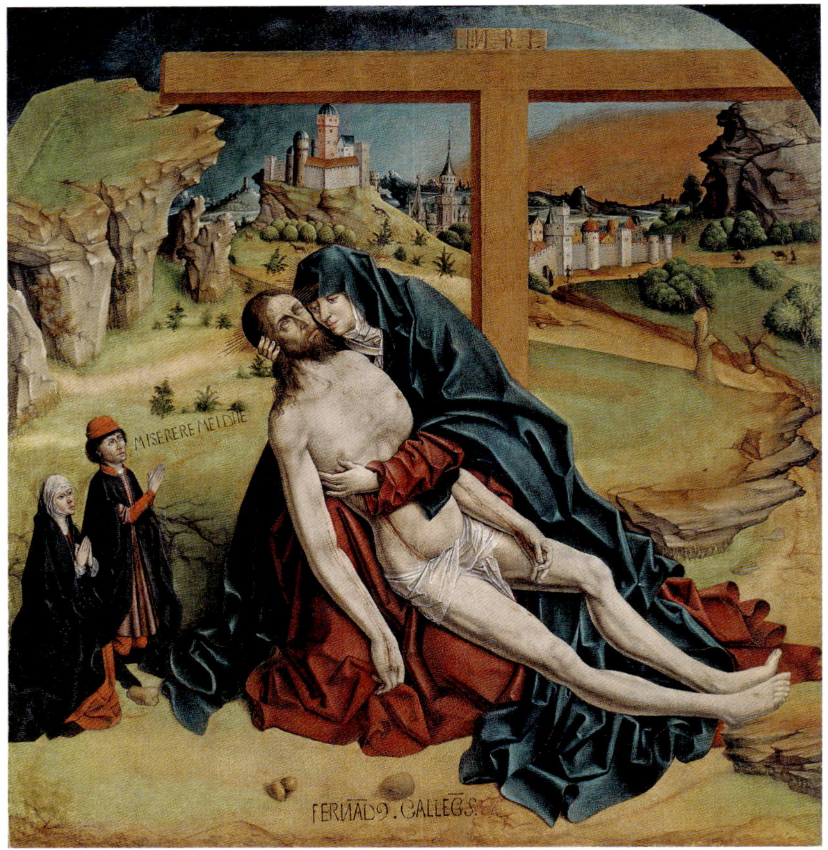

FIG. 8 Fernando Gallego, *Pietà*, 1465–70. Mixed media on pine panel, 46.45 × 43.7 in. (118 × 111 cm). Museo Nacional del Prado, Madrid. Photo: Museo Nacional del Prado / Art Resource, New York.

call omnivorous, could lay claim to the privileged status of both those image types.

Donor portraits (or, to use the more capacious term recently suggested by Ingrid Falque, devotional portraits) are frequent points of reference throughout the book.[40] In these images, the likenesses of a religious artwork's commissioners are included within a holy scene, ossifying the sitters into positions of permanent supplication, veneration, meditative contemplation, or votive thanks and serving for both pious and mundane commemoration.[41] The category, which developed in the Netherlands in the fifteenth century and soon appeared in Spain and its colonial holdings, adopted a wide range of solutions for representing the relationship of the secular person to the sacred protagonists, from marking them as entirely distinct from each other to eliding their differences entirely. Early examples commonly represented miniaturized kneeling donors dispassionately observing a group of larger sacred figures at some remove, as in Fernando Gallego's *Pietá* from the third quarter of the fifteenth century (fig. 8), while in later images, such as in an early seventeenth-century painting attributed to a follower of El Greco, the donor—a man identified as Julián

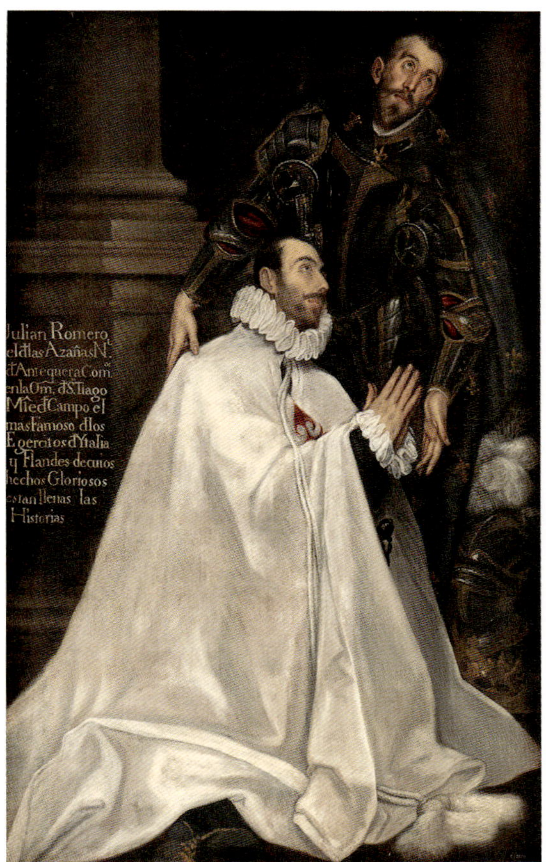

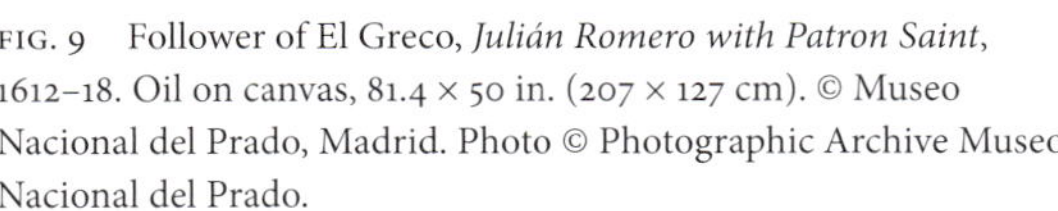

FIG. 9 Follower of El Greco, *Julián Romero with Patron Saint*, 1612–18. Oil on canvas, 81.4 × 50 in. (207 × 127 cm). © Museo Nacional del Prado, Madrid. Photo © Photographic Archive Museo Nacional del Prado.

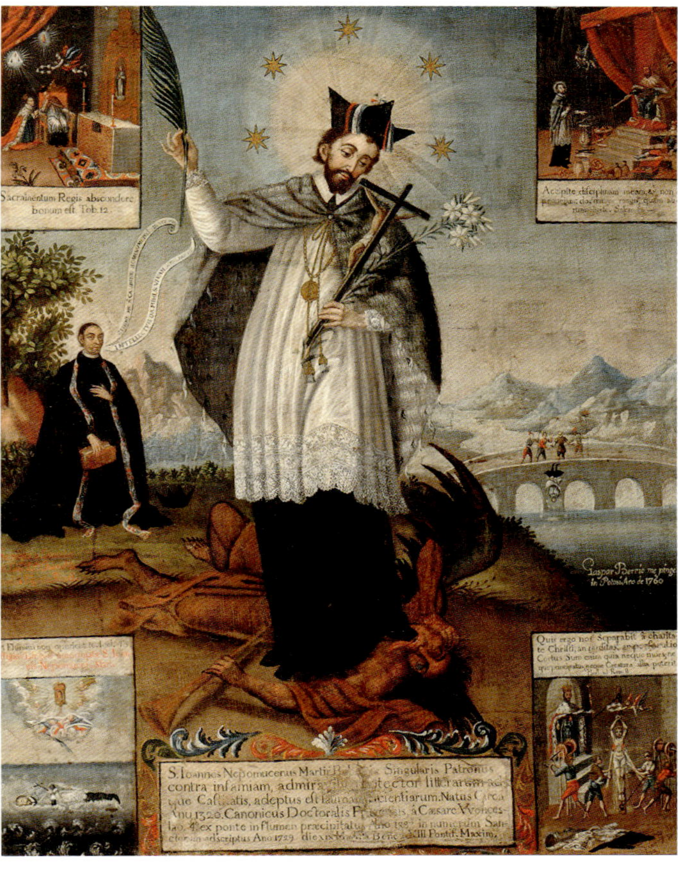

FIG. 10 Gaspar Miguel de Berrío, *Juan Manuel de Elgueta Rocel with Saint John of Nepomuk*, 1760. Oil on canvas, 40.56 × 32.31 in. (103 × 82 cm). Philadelphia Museum of Art, promised gift of the Roberta and Richard Huber Collection, Hub-6.

Romero—is depicted at the same scale and with the same degree of verisimilitude as his intercessor, Saint Julian (fig. 9).

It is important to stress here that there was not a clear teleological movement from greater to lesser overlappings of portraiture and devotional imagery across the period in question, regardless of institutional attempts at creating one.[42] As late as 1760, the Potosí-born painter Gaspar Miguel de Berrío used a similar maneuver to Gallego in a painting depicting the medieval Bohemian saint John of Nepomuk, including a miniaturized donor, named Juan Manuel de Elgueta Rocel, on the left side of the canvas (fig. 10).[43] In both cases, the respective sizes of holy figure and donor correspond to their relative importance. Moreover, the proximity of Berrío's donor to the body of Saint John of Nepomuk is nearly the same—in inches of painted canvas—as is that of Gallego's patrons to the Virgin and Christ, even if Berrío creates

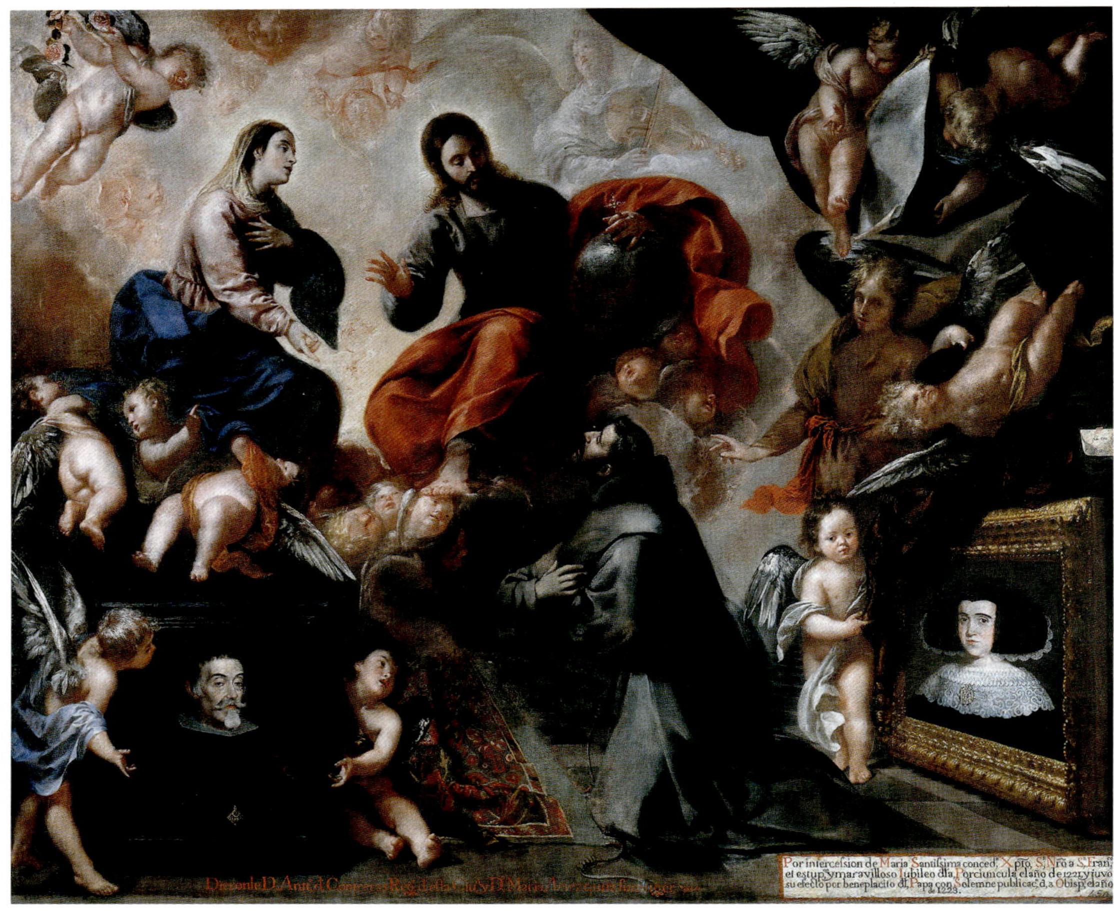

FIG. 11 Francisco Caro, *Saint Francis of Assisi in the Porziuncola with Donors Antonio Contreras and María Amezquita*, 1659. Oil on canvas, 107.48 × 129.92 in. (273 × 330 cm). Museo Nacional del Prado, Madrid; on display at the Museo de Belas Artes da Coruña, A Coruña. Photo: Album / Art Resource, New York.

perspectival depth. The two paintings, separated by three centuries, are clearly of a kind with each other. Similarly, the painting of the woman as Saint Barbara, with which this book opens, was created nearly concurrently and in a similar geographic context as a painting by the Madrid painter Francisco Caro, to be discussed in the book's conclusion, which casts the donor portraits and the sacred scene as not only separate from each other but as entirely, ontologically distinct (fig. 11).

Geographies and Chronologies

Alfonso E. Pérez Sánchez suggests that portraits in which living individuals are purposefully depicted in the guise of saints are "in good part almost exclusively Spanish," while Cherry argues that Florentine examples of such imagery actually may have derived from an influx of Spanish fashions and individuals into Italy in the late sixteenth

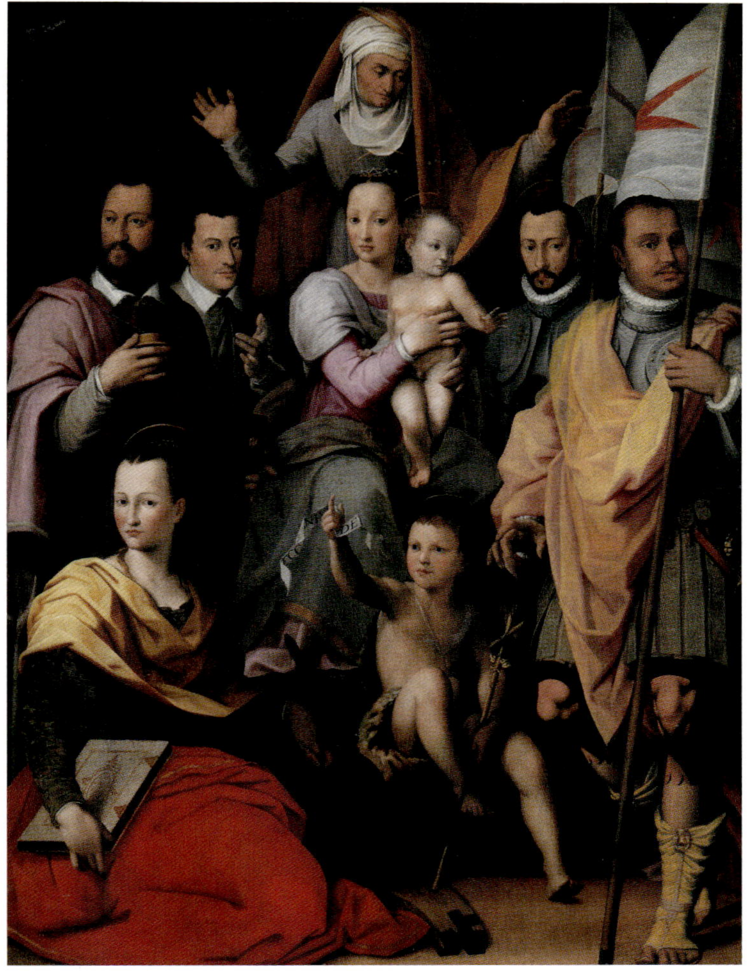

FIG. 12 Giovanni Maria Butteri, *The Family of Cosimo I de Medici as Saints*, ca. 1575. Oil on canvas, 75.5 × 55.1 in. (192 × 140 cm). On display at the Museo della Villa medicea di Cerreto Guidi. Permission granted by the Ministero della Cultura / Direzione regionale musei della Toscana—Firenze.

century. Indeed, a painting like Giovanni Maria Butteri's group portrait of the family of Cosimo I de Medici as saints of circa 1575, in which the Spanish-born Eleonora de Toledo appears as the Virgin Mary, makes it tempting to connect the fashion for such portraits to a Spanish impulse (fig. 12).[44] However, there existed an earlier Florentine tradition of sacred portraits, including the portraits of Medici family members that Giorgio Vasari claimed populated Sandro Botticelli's Uffizi *Annunciation*. Moreover, such images appear across the rest of Italy, as well as in German and Slavic speaking territories, throughout England and France, and, perhaps more than in any other region, in the Low Countries.[45] In many ways, then, nothing about the material examined here is specific to the Hispanic world.

The pervasiveness of such images suggests that, rather than identifying an origin point from whence a fashion for them spread, they should be considered as coetaneous to the rise of physiognomic portraiture in early modernity. In the mid-fifteenth century—and sporadically even earlier—European artists returned to the painting of individualized portrait likenesses (those that depicted their sitters with idiosyncratic facial features and made claims to their verisimilitude) after the art form had nearly disappeared during the preceding millennium.[46] More important, Europe also had a longstanding tradition of creating figural religious imagery. The new category of the portrait as physiognomic likeness quickly made incursions into previously hieratic and standardized depictions of sacred figures, which were often already believed to be their authoritative portraits.[47] Even though *Praying to Portraits* shines a spotlight on the Hispanic world, the deep-rooted tensions and concerns about representation that it identifies as emerging from the intersection of portraiture and sacred imagery apply equally, I believe, to other areas of Europe. Just as the types of images examined in the following chapters appear across Europe and its colonial holdings, so, too, this book's conclusions can be broadly applied to those geographies.

This notwithstanding, the forms and theories of royal and sacred representation that were developed in the Hispanic world differ in crucial ways from those articulated in other European contexts. For example, Spanish kingship was not believed to be divinely ordained, as was the case in France or England. Royal rule was therefore not consecrated through a coronation ceremony or royal unction, and Spanish kings did not possess any distinct material insignia of royal power, such as a crown or scepter. By extension, their portraits are devoid of any material symbols of royal power. Similarly, differences can be ascertained between Italian and Spanish conceptions of the degrees of worship of sacred images. For example, the majority of Italian texts on images maintain the absolute separation between the sacred image and its celestial referent. An author like Paleotti restricted *latria*—the highest form of adoration—to the Holy Sacrament, which was believed to actually become Christ in the process of transubstantiation. Images, he argued, could be the recipients of decreasing degrees of veneration based on whether they represented Christ, the Virgin, or the saints.[48] In a treatise published in Valencia in 1597, by contrast, the ecclesiastic Jaime Prades argued that *latria* was appropriate not only for the sacrament but also for crosses and for images of Christ.[49] Like Prades, Pacheco, who claimed to faithfully translate Paleotti's Italian text for Spanish audiences, actually argued that *latria* was appropriate not only for the sacrament but also for representations of the cross as the quintessential image of Christ.[50] This is seemingly a minuscule distinction, but its significance becomes magnified when considering that both the author, Paleotti, and the translator, Pacheco, claimed to be on the side of orthodoxy. Given that these subtle differences affected the functioning and ontology of royal portraits and religious images in Spain and its colonies, Hispanic sacred portraits also functioned differently than their European counterparts, even if this divergence was not always immediately discernable in their appearance.

The cases examined in this book span a wide geography, with particular attention paid to Spain and the Viceroyalty of New Spain. My intent in deploying a broad scope that grants equal weight to examples from Europe and the Americas is not to discredit the specifically colonial nature of some of the cases described or to elide the differences between colonial and European contexts. Rather, my aim is to show that each city or town in the Hispanic world differed from its counterparts in the rich conglomeration of *local* factors that affected how its inhabitants experienced and understood the visual landscapes that surrounded them. In the multiethnic and multilingual Spanish monarchy, different individuals would have brought distinct arsenals of experience to bear on the same images that they would have encountered in their homes, churches, streets, and squares. Given that forms of seeing were culturally bound, certain image types would have undoubtedly registered as orthodox to some and surprising to others.

Just as the Hispanic world was not a monolith, its constitutive components, like "Spain," "New Spain," or "Peru," were diverse, multilingual places, the complexities of which are too easily elided by a generalizing nomenclature. This is not to say that crucial commonalities did not exist between them. The monarchy's inhabitants, from Madrid and Algete to Guatemala and Tehuantepec, drew on shared pictorial, cultural, and religious practices that informed their behaviors and decisions. Another, perhaps counterintuitive, commonality between these places was that their local conditions inevitably distorted the downwardly imposed universals developed by the Crown and the Church. Thus when universals, which include religious doctrine, the rule of the law, and uniform official imagery, encountered the specificities of local contexts, they were consistently questioned, subverted, and remade. In this perspective, "local" is a more accurate methodological framework than the commonly used term "popular," which implies nonelite subjects.[51] This is because the reinterpretations and variations of orthodox forms and practices related to portraiture and religious imagery occurred in similar ways in both elite and nonelite contexts. They all arose from a culture in which the sphere of the portrait frequently intersected with, drew on, or served as the model for the sphere of sacred image making.[52] This book examines such practices both in terms of the local concerns that drove them and in relation to a bank of shared transcultural motifs, activating a wider set of considerations on the interconnected relationships of the local with the global. What it finds is that images—as well as their audiences—were mutable and nimble, mimicking established forms and practices as often as they created new ones.

The phenomenon of sacred portraiture arose around the fifteenth century and continued well into the nineteenth and twentieth centuries and, episodically, even up to the present day. However, the long seventeenth century, during which the majority of the cases examined in this book take place, represents a particularly rich period for the study of sacred portraits. During this time, the majority of the important artistic texts that expanded upon the Council of Trent's general recommendations about religious imagery—and the largest number of ecclesiastical decrees that tried to control the proliferation of sacred portraiture—were written. It is also in this period that religious orders began to vigorously develop the portraitistic cults of their founders, including Ignatius of Loyola and other Jesuit figures, and the semiportraitistic cults of women saints, including Teresa of Ávila, who, like Ignatius, was canonized in 1622. Additionally, although the conquest of the Americas predates this general temporal frame, the second half of the sixteenth and the seventeenth centuries witnessed the continued territorial expansion of the Spanish monarchy and the stabilization of its hold on its American territories. These efforts led to the diversification of its audiences, who, on paper, were expected to respond to its ostensibly universal devotional images and political portraits in a consistent, orthodox manner.

Furthermore, the proceedings of the Holy Office of the Inquisition from this period form a vast documentary archive that has only recently been tapped by art historians and mined for art-historical inquiries.[53] The careful definition of an art object—its appearance, type, intended functions, and impact on its viewers—is an important element of inquisitorial cases about images, which often delved into the minutiae of what characterized an image type as nebulous as portraiture or of how to assess what constituted a sacred image. These proceedings should therefore be considered within the category of noncanonical art-theoretical texts alongside religious sermons and synodal proceedings.[54] Such writings rarely explicitly announce their investment in image theory but are nevertheless crucial to understanding period debates about art's roles, boundaries, and publics. This said, the Inquisition's trials, which form one of this book's documentary cores and which are a record of institutional attempts to anticipate, surveil, and police image practices that did not align with Catholic orthodoxy, were formulaic, heavily mediated, and often guided by deeply prejudicial agendas.[55] However, when read against their hegemonic viewpoints, they become a—fragmentary, speculative, but still intensely fecund—source for why early modern people did what they did with images.[56]

At the same time, this book challenges the distorted historiographic tradition that has cast the early modern Hispanic world as crushed under the inflexible and ruthlessly efficient machinery of inquisitorial control.[57] In nearly every case examined throughout, the inquisitors confronted the problem of the intermingling of portraiture with sacred imagery by defining the boundaries of each type, only for the same issue to arise a few years later in a different locale. This pattern stemmed, in part, from the inconsistency with which the Catholic Church approached portraiture. Certain branches, like the Jesuits, shrewdly capitalized on the power of likeness in the construction of image cults, while others at different times abhorred its ahistoricity as it encroached upon the authority of ancient sacred narratives. The boundary between the categories of portraiture and religious imagery was permeable; the inquisitorial task of controlling public engagements with the resulting images was Sisyphean.

Drawing on a wide range of both canonical and unstudied images and archival documentation from Europe and Latin America, *Praying to Portraits* offers the first complete account of this key category of early modern image making. Sacred portraiture allowed early modern individuals to balance the needs of selfhood and eschatology and to question how they might access, and even conceive of, that which was sacred. Seen from this perspective, the early modern portrait was not static, clear-cut, and secular. It was malleable, impermanent, and conditional, inhabiting and interacting with distinct artistic categories, including sacred imagery, with ease.

SACRIFICING THE SELF

Chapter 1

Demonic Patrons

The demons' instructions were clear. A priest was to commission paintings on their behalf and in accordance with their specific instructions. The images, six in total, were to depict the guardian angels of different men associated with the Madrid convent where the demons had taken root. Moreover—according to the testimony that the painter, a man of Genoese origin named Giulio Cesare Semini (Hispanicized as Julio César Semín), later delivered before the tribunal of the Holy Office of the Inquisition—the painting of the angel of one of the men, the convent's confessor, "was to bear his likeness."[1] A portrait of a living individual, then, was to be inserted into the depiction of a supernatural being.

This was but one episode within a larger set of events that occurred in 1628, when the Holy Office of the Inquisition was alerted to the fact that a number of the nuns resident in the Benedictine convent of La Encarnación Benita, commonly known as San Plácido, were displaying signs of demonic possession. Among these signs, the inquisitors noted the nuns' glossolalia or speaking in tongues, their uncanny knowledge of past and future events, and their extraordinary physical transformations, which included becoming more beautiful. Eventually, they levied a battery of charges against the nuns, their confessors, and others patrons of the convent, including accusations of sexual improprieties, blasphemous declarations, and alumbradismo heresy. Even though the larger case is relatively well known, little attention has thus far been devoted to the demons' artistic interests, perhaps because mentions of images account for only a small fraction of the many threads investigated in the trial.[2] However, they are by no means unimportant and can serve as an introduction to a larger consideration of the anxieties about the convoluted relationship between portraiture, likeness, and religious art that permeated the period and that will be the focus of this chapter.

The tribunal learned that the possessed nuns, and therefore implicitly the demons themselves, had commissioned artworks and that the nuns' confessor and spiritual advisor, Francisco García Calderón, had fastidiously recorded their declarations in his *cartapacio* (notebook).[3] One of the demons named the six guardian angels, including of the royal secretary and *protonotario* (chief notary) Jerónimo de Villanueva, while another described their appearance and attributes. Then, the demons commissioned the six paintings from Semín.[4] Ultimately, only two of the six were made, and they were subsequently given to the designated men as gifts.[5] When the trial began, Semín stated that he had received very specific instructions from a priest associated with the convent for these paintings and that he understood that the directives had come from García Calderón. He added that "the priest told him that . . . the painting of the angel [of Francisco García Calderón] was to bear his likeness," even though such an instruction had apparently never been recorded in García Calderón's notes.[6] The inquisitors who were examining the painter were curious to know whether "any person had told him the reason for which these angels were painted with such novelty, and where they had come up with it," to which he could provide no satisfying response.[7]

We can only speculate as to why the nuns requested that Semín depict García Calderón as an angel. It may have been their desire to see the prior visually elevated, or it may have reflected the prior's own agenda of self-representation. We can even consider whether the demonic commission of a painting in which García Calderón appeared as an angel could have represented an undercover attack on the fashion for paintings that depicted elite individuals as saints. What is clear is that the demons' request that the prior be represented as an apocryphal guardian angel was actually a perversion of an already unorthodox but widespread artistic phenomenon: the creation of images in which living individuals were depicted with the hallmarks of sanctity. That relatively few such images can be explicitly identified today might suggest that this was a marginal phenomenon. However, this assumption is belied by the fact that every few years, from the late fifteenth century onward, Catholic ecclesiastics in Europe, and later throughout Europe's colonial holdings, railed against these portraits, regularly publishing decrees that tried to definitively prohibit them.

What is more, the wide range of terms that scholars use to describe images in which sitters purposefully impersonated nonreal or historically distant figures further evinces their ubiquity.[8] These expressions include allegorical portrait,[9] composite portrait,[10] moralized portrait,[11] historical effigy or historiated portrait (*portrait historié*),[12] intrusive portrait,[13] performative portrait,[14] disguised portrait,[15] personated portrait,[16] and identification portrait.[17] These are often modified by adjectives such as "sacred" or "mythological," suggesting that these two subcategories of historiated portraiture are closely related.[18] However, at the level of ontology, portraits that depict nonholy individuals as religious figures differ in important ways from other forms of *portraits historiés*. According to Catholic writings on images, when a viewer prays to a painting of a saint, they are actually communicating those prayers to that image's holy prototype: the saint in heaven.[19] The image simply serves as a way for the viewer to focus and better articulate those prayers. A portrait of a living individual *depicted* as a saint, on the other hand, has two referents: the saint and the person portrayed. Such an image could be misunderstood as claiming that the sitter—in many cases, still a living person—was holy, usurping the actual saint's privileged position. Not only was such behavior problematic because the living sitter did not deserve such veneration, but implicitly, it also threatened to misdirect the pious viewer's prayers to a nonefficacious prototype. The doubling of referent, occasioned through the insertion of a portrait of a real, nonholy individual into a devotional picture, muddied the didactic clarity demanded of religious imagery. By contrast, from the perspective of its viewer, a portrait of a living person as a mythological hero (say, as Hercules) behaved in exactly the same way as any other portrait of that person. Certainly, it also had two referents, but neither of them could receive prayers or be the focus of codified spiritual practices, in the mode of an image of a saint.

It is for this reason that I use the terms "sanctified portrait" or "portrait *a lo divino*" (portrait in the divine manner). The latter term was coined by Emilio Orozco Díaz to describe presumed portraits of aristocratic women in the guise of saints, even though he saw them, first and foremost, as images "of ladies with attributes of saints" and not as de facto devotional images.[20] These terms uphold the distinction between sanctified and mythological portraiture, which was less frequent in the Hispanic world than, for example, in France.[21] Nevertheless, both terms—sanctified portrait and portrait *a lo divino*—are imperfect, given the implication that the stable element in these images is the portrait, which is transformed through sanctification. By contrast, I see the portrait in them as highly labile.[22] Furthermore, were such images to have been seen in a public space by a diverse group of viewers, undoubtedly more of them would have recognized the images' religious message than the identities of the nonholy persons depicted within them.

In practice, the claim that a religious painting might contain a portrait is frequently equivocal.[23] Religious images that *appear* to include portraits may have simply been created using live models, with no intention that the figures be recognized as specific individuals but rather hoping to produce a generalized sense of recognition.[24] Similarly, artists may have created idiosyncratic but ultimately invented likenesses to more convincingly represent ancient saints. And finally, images that had, at one point in their lives, been simple portraits could have been transformed into religious images through posterior repainting. Although there do survive artworks where the identity of the sitter, depicted in the guise of a saint, can be confidently established through comparison with their other portraits, these are never, to my knowledge, accompanied by documentary materials that could shed light on the circumstances of their commission. In other cases, there exist trial proceedings, inventories, and even poetic texts that explicitly describe portraits inserted into religious images, but here, in turn, the images themselves do not survive. Speculation, therefore, guides much of what scholars can claim about such images' motivation and intended function.

What, then, are the criteria by which we can recognize sanctified portraits, particularly from within the larger corpus of sacred portraiture? First, the image must contain explicit religious iconographic elements or have been used in a religious context. Second, the image must possess portraitistic features, chief among which is the physiognomic likeness of an individual who is not a saint. Third, the depiction of this individual in

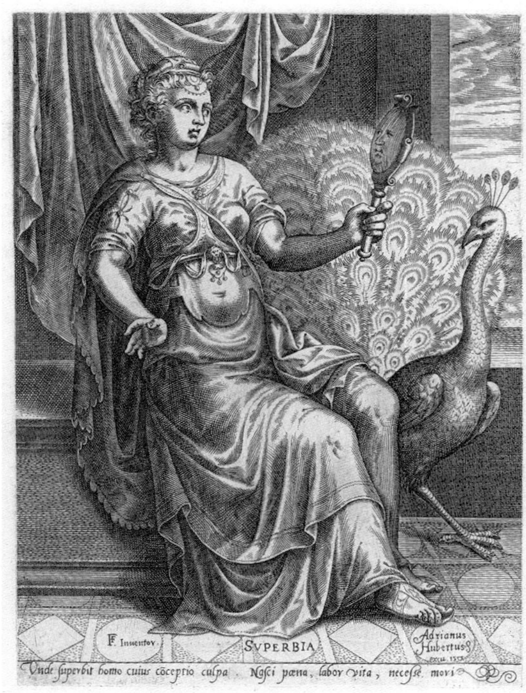

FIG. 13 Unidentified engraver, after Frans Floris I, *Superbia*, published by Adriaen Huybrechts I, 1575. Engraving on paper, 8.6 × 6.3 in. (22 × 16.1 cm). Rijksmuseum, Amsterdam.

the context of the religious image must be purposeful and meant to be recognized as a specific person (as opposed to incidental, which might be said of an artist using a model for a painting a saint). And finally, the painting's portraitistic and religious components must be, as far as we can determine, coeval with each other, which is to say that the painting was not reworked at a later moment.

What these criteria cannot provide, however, is any insight into potential reasons for the creation of such images. Indeed, the complexity of sanctified portraits resides precisely in the wide range of possible motivations behind them, which could change depending on the commissioning person's gender or social status (a royal person represented in the guise of a saint potentially made a different visual argument than did a nonroyal person); their relationship to the depicted person (was it their child or other family member? Their king or bishop? Was it, finally, a portrait of themselves?); and the painting's intended destination and attendant function, as Cécile Vincent-Cassy has shown.[25] Depending on this combination of factors, the resulting images can vary greatly, even if they bear a degree of formal similarity.

To highlight the profusion of sanctified portraits is not to say that they were universally applauded. Writers of satirical sonnets and religious censors concurred in their condemnation of the fashion of representing oneself as a saint, taking particular aim at the sitters' presumed vanity. It is easy to see why. After all, when the sitter and the viewer of a sanctified portrait are one and the same, the patron would gaze upon an image for devotion that looked back at them with all of the idiosyncrasies of their own appearance, just as the beautiful female personification of the deadly sin of pride is often represented as staring transfixed into a mirror, from which her own reflection looks back with equal fascination (fig. 13). But were the motivations for these images really so transparent as vanity and pride? Would a sixteenth- or seventeenth-century Catholic sitter have marshalled the immense powers—and I use the term consciously—of likeness and of religious iconography in such a patently problematic way? If we look to the extensive scholarship on early modern Hispanic social and religious history, including on piety and spiritual practices, this seems unlikely for most of the images that fit this category. I contend, therefore, that we look at portraits *a lo divino* through the lens of period selfhood and spirituality, which abhorred and feared pride, in order to argue that such images—or, at least, *most* such images—were not designed to celebrate or vaingloriously elevate their sitters.[26] Indeed, short-term, mundanely self-centric behaviors would have been understood as hindering, rather than assisting, the long-term eschatological pursuits of the early modern Catholic individual.

My argument, then, is that when in prayer before a sanctified portrait, the sitter's constant reflection in the religious image would have served as a reminder of the inherent fragility of their selfhood. The sanctified portrait would have underscored the sitter's worthlessness rather than achievements. Such dismantling, rather than glorification, of selfhood would have been a desirable goal, possible to achieve only through practices of self-abnegating meditation. Denying the portrait within the portrait *a lo divino*, I contend, was the only way for the image to function with any semblance of doctrinal decorum.

Royal Sanctified Portraits

Historiographically, *a lo divino* portraits of royal individuals—like Juan Pantoja de la Cruz's 1605 portrait of Margarita of Austria and her daughter, the *infanta* Ana, enacting the scene of the Annunciation (fig. 14)[27]—have been the primary focus of scholarly attention, given that they are the best-documented and today best-known examples of sanctified portraits. In studies of royal sanctified portraits from across Europe, these images have most frequently been understood as illustrating the idea that a European ruler's reign was divinely sanctioned.[28] This line of reasoning has extended into studies of Spanish sanctified portraiture, with scholars suggesting that portraits in which royal individuals appear in the guise of saints were politicizations of piety and, as in other geographic contexts, affirmations that the Habsburg dynasty's power had been bestowed upon them by God.[29]

Even though the northern European model of sacred kingship has, at times, been indiscriminately applied to the early modern Hispanic context, the equivalency does not stand up to close inspection.[30] While the Habsburg kings of Spain bore the moniker of "most Catholic," endorsed and embraced certain doctrines and cults with fervor, and even occasionally performed self-sacralizing gestures, they were not anointed, did not wear crowns, and did not typically perform miracles of thaumaturgy, including the curing of scrofula, as was famously claimed of the monarchs of France or England.[31] In part, this "unsacred"—to borrow from Teofilo Ruiz—character of early modern Hispanic royalty derived from the fact that the medieval rulers of Spain's kingdoms had either ignored or irregularly deployed the elaborate rituals (such as anointment with holy oils) and symbols (such as crowns and scepters) that affirmed the divinely sanctioned legitimacy of kings in other European contexts, marking them as something more than human.[32] That the early modern Spanish monarchy was not sacred is further corroborated by the attempts of some early modern Hispanic intellectuals to encourage the king to embrace a more explicitly sacralized form of rule. In the 1580s, two jurists wrote arguments in favor of instating the ceremonies of royal unction and coronation in Spain, but their proposals never came to fruition.[33] Similarly, in the seventeenth century, a number of prominent authors put forth the claim that the Spanish king could not only heal scrofula but also demonic possession, with the poet and historian José Pellicer

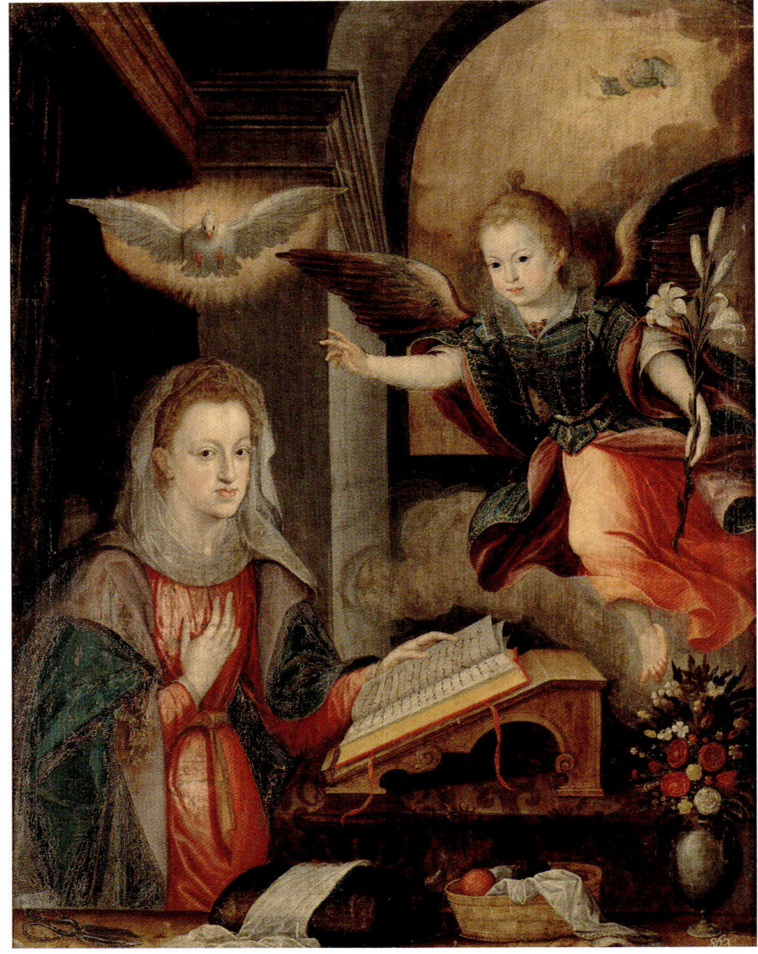

FIG. 14 Juan Pantoja de la Cruz, *Annunciation with Portrait of Margarita de Austria as the Virgin Mary*, ca. 1605. Oil on canvas, 59.84 × 45.27 in. (152 × 115 cm). Kunsthistorisches Museum, Vienna; on display at Schloss Ambras, Innsbruck. Kunsthistorisches Museum Vienna, Picture Gallery. KHM-Museumsverband.

de Salas y Tovar belittling the French monarch by pointing out the "great difference between curing an illness of the body and liberating souls from the power of demons."[34] However, these were not reflections of an established belief system but—ultimately rejected—attempts at constructing a propagandistic program of royal sanctity.[35]

The political claim that Spanish royal sanctified portraiture made, then, was not about *its sitters'* sanctity but rather about their piety and their status as the "most Catholic" of Europe's ruling families.[36] The primary function of royal Spanish portraiture *a lo divino*, furthermore, was not public and propagandistic but intimate and related to personal devotion (which was, nonetheless, both public and propagandistic in the way that—to an extent—all of the royal family's activities were). More important, royal portraits *a lo divino* form only a small percentage of the much larger corpus of all sanctified portraits produced in early modern Spain and its colonial holdings. Any argument that sees royal sanctified portraits as making a claim about divinely ordained kingship or that grants primacy to their political character—as valid as that may be—runs dry when applied to nonroyal images. Of course, portraits of the royal family would have had crucial differences from nonroyal portraits by the simple virtue of whom they represented. Nevertheless, they also shared many similarities. What kind of argument can we develop, then, that sheds light on *both* royal and nonroyal sanctified portraits? Considering these images through a lens of introspection, meditation, and abnegation will allow for an interpretation of royal sanctified portraiture to be extended and applied to the larger category of portraiture *a lo divino*.

Regardless, the forms of, and motivations behind, sanctified portraits were so diverse that I aim to provide neither interpretations for all of them nor a single interpretative paradigm that could easily fit them all. Rather, I focus on one relatively well-documented example of such imagery in order to examine more fully the self-deprecatory function that I contend many of these paintings possessed. Subsequently, I consider how these controversial objects were understood by the individuals who were critical of them, which reveals much about period conceptions of selfhood, social decorum, and the categories and functions of art. I conclude with an argument about the "threat" of portraits *a lo divino* as related to the degree of their visibility, by examining a case that additionally reveals the ramifications of the phenomenon for the Spanish Crown's global aspirations.

The Queen as Virgin

What might the devotional motivations for portraiture *a lo divino* have been? The growing number of depictions of living, recognizable individuals as attendants in religious scenes or in the guise of holy figures, beginning in the fifteenth century and appearing across Christian European communities, has been read in relation to the rise of a personal and deeply introspective spirituality termed the *devotio moderna*.[37] They functioned along any solution that introduced modern settings, accessories, and dress into religious scenes, given that these inevitably shrunk the temporal distance between the biblical episode and the moment in which the image was made or seen. Indeed, such interruptions of the contemporary in historicizing religious scenes became, in the words of Alexander Nagel, "a field for meditation," allowing patrons and sitters to picture themselves in religious scenes, both literally and metaphorically.[38] Because there were numerous ecclesiastical proscriptions against the creation of such images, however, the majority of portraits *a lo divino* were likely created for highly restricted contexts, available only to the commissioners and their closest confidantes. Only later would these images have moved out of their initial settings to acquire new significations that differed from those they had held at their conception. For this reason, it is necessary to distinguish between the motivations behind the original idea inspiring a sanctified portrait and its later responses and uses. Though the latter are often much better documented, they reveal little about why an early modern patron might have initially chosen to be represented in the guise of a holy figure.

Indeed, very few surviving sanctified portraits can be contextualized in any meaningful way, hindering investigation into how they were understood by those who commissioned them. An exception is Pantoja de la Cruz's already mentioned 1605 portrait *a lo divino* of Margarita of Austria and her daughter, the *infanta* Ana, which depicts the two royal women enacting the scene of the Annunciation (see fig. 14). Knowledge of the sitter's identity allows us to reconstruct the context for which the work may have been created and, subsequently, how it may have been used. In the portrait, the queen, unmistakably recognizable by her facial features, including a long, slightly bulbous nose and pouty lower lip, looks directly at the viewer. She wears robes of red and blue, traditional colors for the Virgin Mary, and a gauzy white veil over her head. Her left hand is still leafing through the pages of the book before her, while her right hand, brought up to her chest, registers her reaction to the angelic visitor, who fills the painting's upper right corner. The royal *infanta*, in the guise of the lily-bearing archangel Gabriel, also looks out at the viewer rather than at the recipient of her message, ensuring that the image registers as a double portrait. Above the queen's head appears the dove of the Holy Spirit, while the figure of God is visible in the clouds beyond the *infanta*'s head.

The painting was likely commissioned either before the future Philip IV's birth, or conversely, immediately after, as a talisman or as an ex-voto for a safe delivery.[39] María Cruz de Carlos Varona has analyzed it through the lens of renewal, in which Christ represents the restoration of humankind, and the newborn king represents rebirth for the monarchy.[40] Thus, the association of the royals with holy figures would have also extended to equating the future king in utero with the newly incarnated Christ. In this interpretation, the devotion is practical and quasi-magical, based on a desire for an efficacious form of self-protection, with the portrayed figures permanently benefitting from the religious iconography that surrounds and shields them.[41] The assumption that the painting is votive or thaumaturgic is convincing, corroborated by the frequent insertion of portraits of women into devotional scenes related to childbirth in other European contexts.[42] However, as an object that functioned plurally, its potential status as an ex-voto did not preclude its use for meditation and prayer, which are the purposes that interest me here.[43]

The precise date and destination of the Annunciation painting are unknown, as no documents concerning its commission and early life history have surfaced.[44] However, it is accepted that Margarita commissioned two other sanctified group portraits of herself and her family members, depicting the birth of the Virgin and the Nativity, which survive today, for her oratory in the royal palace in Valladolid. She is also known to have commissioned a now-lost painting of the Expectation, a predominantly Spanish iconography representing the Virgin Mary as pregnant, which may have also potentially been a portrait *a lo divino*. The oratory was a space that her biographer described as "where her heart rested, and rejoiced in God," where she heard mass twice daily, and where she kept her collection of relics.[45] When the court moved from Valladolid to Madrid, the queen ordered that an oratory be designed for her, "and that it was all to be of rich jaspers and stones [and] the best oratory a queen had ever had."[46] At least one of these portraits *a lo divino*, and maybe more, would have undoubtedly formed an important part of the decoration of that new space. It is possible that the Annunciation with the queen as the Virgin would have been the centerpiece; given that the two group portraits of the births of the Virgin and of Christ are thematic pendants, much larger than the Annunciation scene but equivalent in size to each other, they may have flanked the smaller central work.

In the *Birth of the Virgin*, a figure identifiable as Mary of Bavaria, Margarita's mother, is cast as a prominently placed attendant who holds the newborn, while two women identifiable with Margarita's older sisters stand in waiting (fig. 15). Curiously, Pantoja does not depict Mary of Bavaria as the Virgin's mother, Saint Anne, even though the other paintings in the room equate Margarita with the Virgin. Saint Anne herself—visibly not a portrait—convalesces in bed. In the second of the two flanking paintings, the *Nativity*, the scene centers around the manger and a long-haired Margarita-as-Virgin, who crosses her hands over her chest and gazes down at her child (fig. 16). Therefore, even if the *Annunciation* did not form part of the oratory's decoration, the queen would have seen another image of herself—Pantoja's painting of the *Nativity*—in the guise of the Virgin whenever she visited it.[47] Whereas the *Annunciation* includes only two figures: the queen and her daughter, the two larger works are heavily populated by portraits. In them, the figures that look out at the viewer are historical individuals and members of Margarita's closest family: her siblings, husband, and mother.[48] They are witnesses to the successful and desired birth but do not enact the roles of specific holy figures. As part of the framing for Margarita's meditative practices, described below, they would have enhanced the queen's understanding of the context within which each subsequent holy event had occurred.

The Queen's Library

It is worth seriously examining Nagel's claim that these types of images form a "field for meditation."[49] Indeed, once we accept that the queen would have seen the *a lo divino* portrait of herself as the Virgin Mary in her oratory, we still have to reckon with a crucial question: What did she—Margarita—get from seeing her own recognizable face within the larger context of the religious painting that surrounded it?[50] The power of the portrait likeness did not evaporate when inserted into a devotional scene. Rather, I suggest, it came to serve as a perennial admonition of the insidious pleasures of selfhood—in contrast to the selflessness of the holy figure—and the constant labor necessary for its dismantling. In the Saint Barbara portrait *a lo divino* (see fig. 1), discussed in the introduction, for example, the narrative vignette in the painting's background was a reminder of how Barbara's spiritual reward had been achieved: through a willful acceptance of the violent unmaking of her physical body, with all of its incidentals of individualized appearance, to the benefit of the universal, eternal soul. Similarly, individuals portrayed in portraits *a lo divino* had to exert immense mental effort to move past the stage of recognizing themselves in paint in order to deny the individuality that was undeniably part of early modern portraiture and to debase themselves when they saw themselves so clearly elevated: in sum, to ef*face* themselves.

This was the only way for a portrait *a lo divino* to reconcile its dueling doubled referents: the celestial saint and the mundane sitter. This idea is best expressed in the Portuguese cleric Antonio Vieyra's sermon on Saint Francis, which argued that the dismantling of self was the only way to imitate and follow Christ: "This is what Saint Francis did," noted Vieyra, "He negated himself to such an extent that he was entirely no longer that which he had been. But if Francis was not Francis, what was he? He was Christ."[51] Following this model of Saint Francis, only when almost nothing remained of

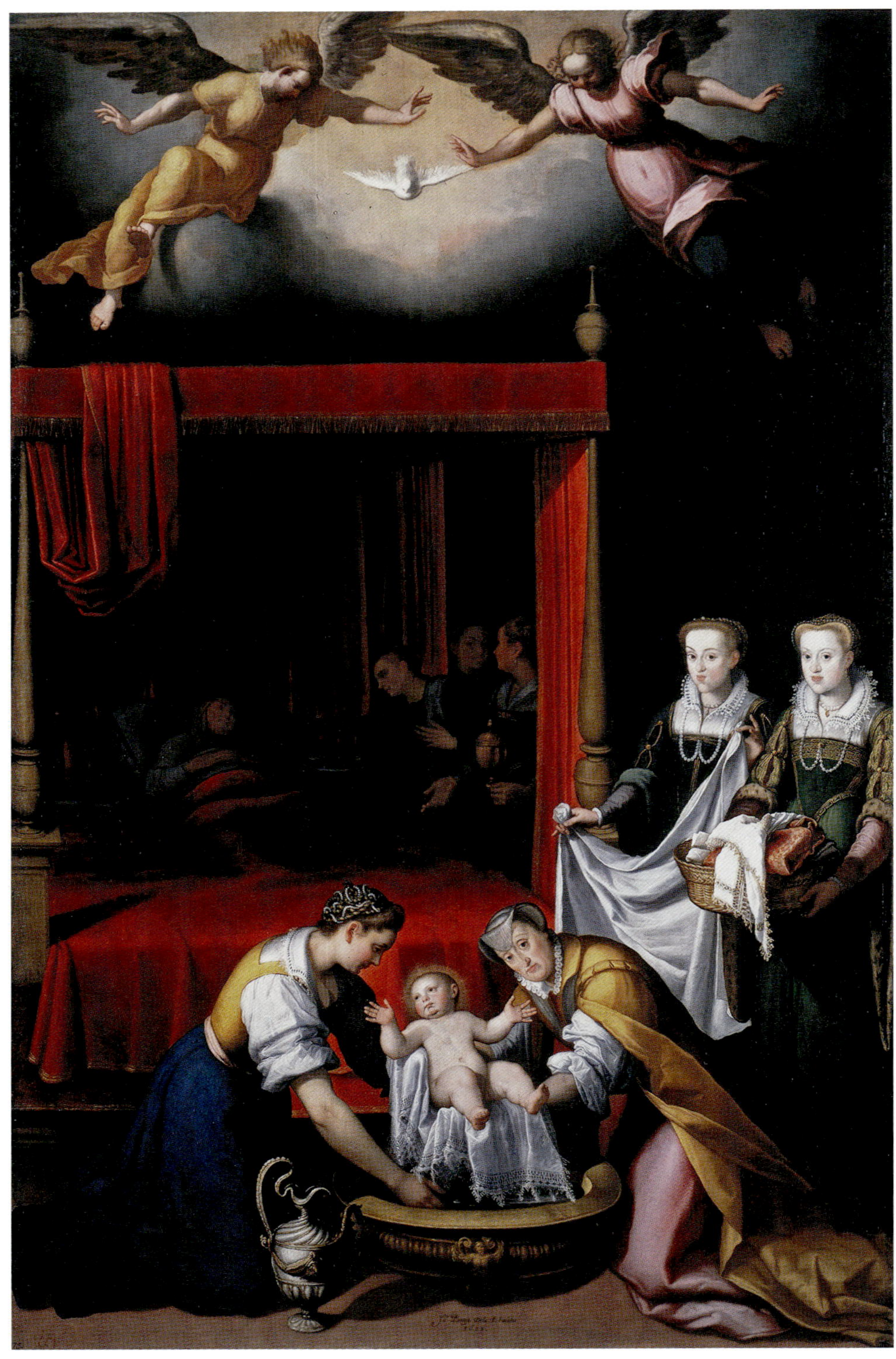

FIG. 15 Juan Pantoja de la Cruz, *Birth of the Virgin with Portraits of Habsburg Royals*, 1603. Oil on canvas, 102.36 × 67.71 in. (260 × 172 cm). Museo Nacional del Prado, Madrid. Photo: Joseph Martin; Album / Art Resource, New York.

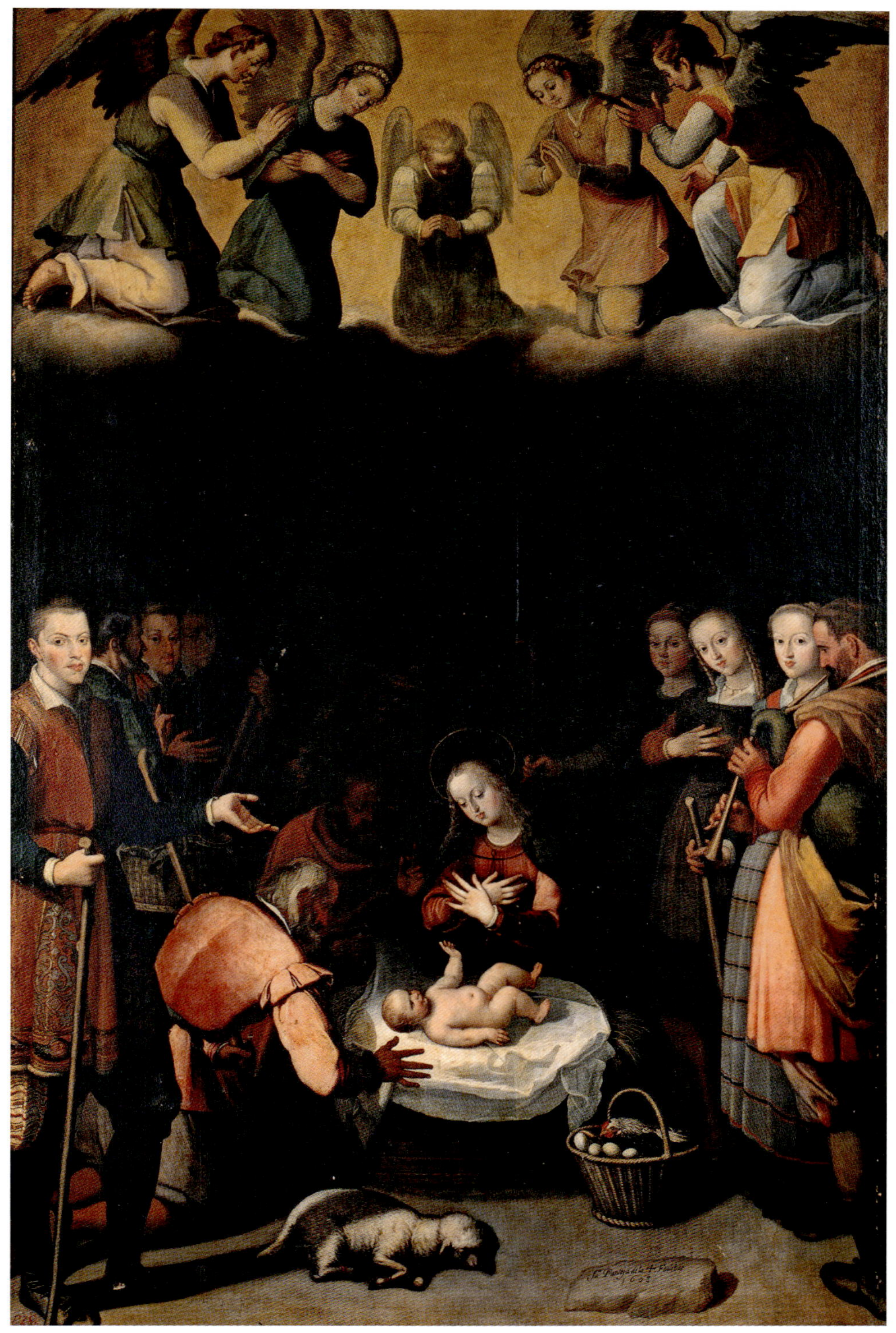

FIG. 16 Juan Pantoja de la Cruz, *Nativity with Portraits of Habsburg Royals*, 1603. Oil on canvas, 102.36 × 67.71 in. (260 × 172 cm). Museo Nacional del Prado, Madrid. Photo: Album / Art Resource, New York.

Margarita, after the painful and always incomplete process of the dismantling of selfhood, could the image be a painting of the Virgin.[52] Most portraits *a lo divino*—those in which the commissioner and the sitter were one and the same—should therefore not be understood as self-celebratory. In fact, it is inconceivable that they could have been.

An important clue in Margarita's biography opens the door to such an interpretation. Upon arriving in Madrid with her retinue in October of 1599, the queen broke with tradition, which dictated that she was to take on a Spanish Franciscan as her spiritual guide. Instead, she retained Richard Haller, a German-speaking Jesuit, as her confessor and confidante until her death in 1611.[53] Diego de Guzmán, the queen's biographer, wrote that Margarita was "so surrendered and obedient [to Haller] that she could tell him what she was feeling as freely as if she were a novice in a religious order."[54] That Haller was a Jesuit is crucial here, as he would have exposed Margarita to period forms of eschatologically motivated meditative practice, likely including Ignatius of Loyola's *Spiritual Exercises*, the subtitle of the First Week of which announces that the goal is for the exercitant—or practitioner—to "vencer à si mismo," to "vanquish oneself."[55]

There is no concrete evidence that the queen ever undertook the *Exercises*, and there was much disagreement in the Society of Jesus concerning whether the *Exercises* should be administered to women at all, and if so, to what extent.[56] However, it seems unlikely that the queen would have been entirely unfamiliar with their content and purpose, given the prominence that someone like Haller had in her retinue and the numerous works by other Jesuit authors, including Pedro de Ribadeneira, in her library.[57] Furthermore, as a royal woman, she may have been permitted to perform more than just the First Week, which is what was typically permitted to laypersons.[58] In this she had the likely precedent of Juana de Austria, a contemporary of Ignatius's and aunt to Margarita's husband, Philip III, who enthusiastically sponsored the Jesuits—an order that famously rejected all attempts at the creation of a female branch—to the point of being admitted into the Society as a scholastic, the only woman ever permitted to do so.[59] Finally, the *Exercises* were meant to be performed with a spiritual director, which means that the queen would have never actually paged through the manual herself, further explaining why the book does not appear in her collection.[60] Haller's role was crucial, as the queen would have undertaken the *Exercises* under his guidance or under the guidance of another Jesuit from his circle, given Ignatius of Loyola's recommendation that the *Exercises* be administered by someone other than a person's confessor.[61]

Margarita was sufficiently well-read to have understood that Ignatius's text drew on earlier traditions of introspective religious meditation and on earlier ascetic publications, many of which already formed part of her extensive library of nearly 360 books, including Thomas à Kempis's *Contemptus mundi*.[62] Thomas advocated a similar rejection of self as did Ignatius: "If you want to know and learn something of benefit, desire that you not be known, that you be thought of as nothing. . . . It is great knowledge and perfection to always think highly of others, while holding yourself and reputing yourself as nothing."[63] Elsewhere, beseeching God, he noted: "Let your name be praised, and not mine. Let your deeds be magnified and not mine . . . Every day my glory and exaltation will be in you: of me there is nothing to glorify and exalt, only my failings."[64] In the Spanish translation of the text that Margarita owned, by frequently repeating the possessives *mi*, *mio*, and *me* (my and mine), while stressing the worthlessness of their referent, Thomas posited a selfhood that was actively sacrificed to a higher instance and in a state of permanent relativity to God.

Cristóbal de Fonseca, another author present in Margarita's library, describes the enjoyment of mundane things as an insatiable hunger: "For although pleasure, games, hunting, and music bedazzle the mundane person, it is like lightning, which passes quickly and leaves them in murky darkness, in a continuous melancholy, and with so much hunger that it seems that it has grown with what they have consumed."[65] To Thomas and Fonseca, sitting for a portrait would likely also fall under the rubric of acts that celebrated the individual. These behaviors—enjoying praise, for instance; focusing on oneself, as described by Thomas; or trying to fill the insatiable, mundane hunger, as described by Fonseca—were a perennial impediment to the stripping away of selfhood that was required to celebrate God's universal timelessness.

The *Spiritual Exercises*, too, aimed to push away such comforts in a process of profound introspection that would benefit the universal, immortal soul. Exercitants declared to Christ their willingness to "imitate [him] in suffering all invectives and all vituperations and all poverty, both real and spiritual" and deployed every sensory and intellectual faculty to come as close as possible to the holy model. Ignatius encouraged the exercitant to begin this process by effectively negating the self through "looking at who I am, [and] diminishing myself through examples; first, how little I am in comparison with all mankind; second, what men even are compared to all of the angels and saints of paradise; [and] third, seeing what all creatures are when compared to God: then, I myself, what can I be?" This meditation concluded by examining one's "corruption and corporeal ugliness" and finally seeing oneself as a "sore and abscess, from which so many sins and so many evils, and such inglorious poison have emerged."[66]

In one of the many directives that were written concerning how to administer the *Spiritual Exercises*, the Spanish Jesuit Duarte Pereyra states that "the purpose of this First Week [of the *Exercises*] is for a person to enter interiorily into self-knowledge," leading to what he calls a "purgative life," which "consists . . . in a loathing for oneself; in a love for contempt of self."[67] Later, Pereyra discusses how such self-knowledge could be achieved, and he invokes the metaphor of looking at oneself "as in a mirror which shows us what is clean and what is dirty."[68] To move from a mirror to a portrait, which, like the personification of vanity, looks back at the viewer, represents a small conceptual leap. We have little reason to suspect that the piety Queen Margarita was known for by her contemporaries was not sincere, if perhaps it was overly stressed following the queen's death.[69] If she indeed performed the *Exercises* under the guidance of Haller or another Jesuit, she would have done so in the space of her oratory, given that Jesuit directives recommended that women be administered the *Exercises* "in church."[70] There, she would have been surrounded by votive portraits *a lo divino* that, like mirrors, looked back at her. Notwithstanding her queenly status, she, too, would have engaged in the self-negating meditation that Ignatius recommended. Disgust—including at oneself—was a powerful tool in the pursuit of salvation.[71]

The claim that the queen would have engaged in introspective spiritual practices is strengthened by the fact that elite women from Margarita's circle are documented as having performed similar religious meditations. For instance, in a manual written for Sor Margarita de la Cruz, a close relative and confidante of Margarita and her husband, Philip III, the use of a first-person narration (implicitly of Margarita speaking to herself) highlighted the dismantling of individuality that any Catholic had to perform for their salvation.[72] In one place, the book's narrator reminds the female reader that "on this day I will take care to distrust myself, and to manifest my defects and weaknesses, in order to further abase myself."[73] In another, the narrator instructs her that "today I will [shed] tears of pain and contrition for the many times that I have caused death to my soul through sins, and I will abstain from any joy."[74] Similarly, the exercises that Margarita de la Cruz performed during the forty days of Advent required an emptying of self and relied on physical and visual aids. "Your interior, soul of mine," the narrator admonishes herself, "is still so indecent . . . that it will be necessary to purify it anew."[75] Each meditation contributed to the mental evacuation of the inherent filth of the soul, cast as an internal room, and its subsequent preparation through furnishings, decorations, and perfume for the arrival of Christ.

In her library, the queen would also have found criticisms of portraiture. The Portuguese Hieronymite Heitor Pinto's *Dialogos de la imagen de la vida christiana* (Dialogues on the image of Christian life) described portraits as empty vessels, void of the spirit found in a person's epistolary writings: "I consider the image that is written on paper to be more expressive and more excellent than the one painted on panel. The [portrait] displays the exterior, the text the interior; [the portrait] shows their features, and the latter their thoughts; one shows color, the other heart."[76] A painted image, no matter how verisimilar, did little to convey the sitter's interior qualities and virtues, and it was those qualities that mattered in friendship—the subject of Pinto's dialogue, as well as in eschatology. Like the painted image, which obfuscated a person's true character (Fonseca called it "a shadow and not the truth"[77]), the enjoyment of mundane things, including the vanity of the portrait itself, blocked one's access to virtue.[78]

Although some early modern theorists of art, such as Paleotti, considered portraiture to be base and arrogant in its focus on specific individuals, others, like Pacheco, argued that it was not always a symptom of vanity.[79] Pacheco points out that certain saints allowed themselves to be portrayed, even if he concedes that, for the most part, "we are unable to understand the goals they have in doing so."[80] For example, he cites Joannes Molanus's account of Pope Gregory the Great, who left a portrait of himself to a community of monks "not out of vainglory and pride" but so that it could serve as a sacred image in the future, should the sitter ever be canonized (as he indeed was).[81] By this, Pacheco suggested that the portrait would serve as a moral exemplar for those who had once known the sitter, even if he implicitly admitted that "vainglory and pride" were the immediate associations of portraiture for many early modern Catholics. In practice, Pacheco himself was a renowned portraitist and devoted significant space in his *El arte de la pintura* (The art of painting) to the practice.[82] The complexity of early modern portraiture resided, at least in part, in its moral ambiguity.

A lo divino Portraiture and the *Spiritual Exercises*

The annihilation that Margarita would have tried to perform when embarking on the *Exercises* was the first step in moving from the limitations of her own self to the universality of the holy figure, akin to Vieyra's analysis of how Francis unmade himself in his contemplation and imitation of Christ. In the progression of the *Exercises*, she would have been instructed by Haller in the contemplation of sacred narratives. This began by first picturing the setting in which the sacred event played out through the "vision of the imagination."[83] For example, in beginning the meditation on the Incarnation, Haller would have tasked the queen with imagining the specific space in which the episode took place, "the house and lodgings of our Lady, in the city of Nazareth, in the province of Galilee."[84] When asked by Haller to contemplate the Annunciation, Margarita would have drawn on a familiar repertoire of images that depicted that episode as tools for her self-effacement, performing what Jeffrey Chipps Smith termed an "individual particularization" of the *Spiritual Exercises*.[85]

In preaching, the practice of using images for making the spoken word more vivid was well established, and the Jesuits were particularly proficient in enhancing sermons through such means.[86] Similarly, there was a longstanding tradition of using images for mental prayer and devotional meditation, and there is evidence that royal Habsburg individuals also performed their spiritual practices in this manner.[87] In Pantoja's painting of Margarita as the Virgin Annunciate, a number of details, irrelevant to the narrative but crucial to its enlivenment, fill the ledge in the foreground, which serves as a threshold between the viewer and the painted protagonists.[88] Feasibly, the queen would have considered each of these in turn. The scissors, thimble, cushion, basket of yarns, and embroidered cloth were quotidian objects that, in the fiction of the picture, were elevated to the status of relics through their incidental presence during the sacred encounter. Just as with the book on the table before the Virgin or the curtain of the bed behind her, Margarita would likely have recognized such objects from her own surroundings, easily recalling the touch and heft of each, thus strengthening the comparison that she sought to draw between herself and the holy figure.[89] Furthermore, early modern Catholic women often engaged in needlework and embroidery as a stimulus for, or in conjunction with, spiritual meditation and prayer. The sewing accouterments that littered the sill before the Virgin may have reminded the queen of these practices, further enhancing the painting's introspective character.[90] Finally, as argued by Carlos Varona, the particular association of these paintings with childbirth and the inclusion of painted elements such as a bed, bath, or vessel may have brought back memories of the queen's own parturition and prompted Margarita to consider the pain of labor as a tangible corollary to the pain endured by Christ, by the Virgin, and by the Catholic martyrs.[91]

Margarita's meditative interactions with her portrait *a lo divino* may be extended to other nonroyal examples of such imagery, particularly given the extreme popularity of the *Spiritual Exercises* and the self-reflective practices it championed among early modern Catholic laypersons.[92] Consider, for example, a mid-seventeenth-century Spanish painting depicting the profession of Saint Clare (fig. 17).[93] Nearly everything in the image derives from period hagiographic texts: the scene takes place at an altar, where the young woman kneels before a bearded Saint Francis, who brings a pair of shears to cut her stylishly coiffed hair.[94] A friar—one of Francis's companions—holds the coarse robes that she will exchange for her richly trimmed gown. The heads of both Francis and

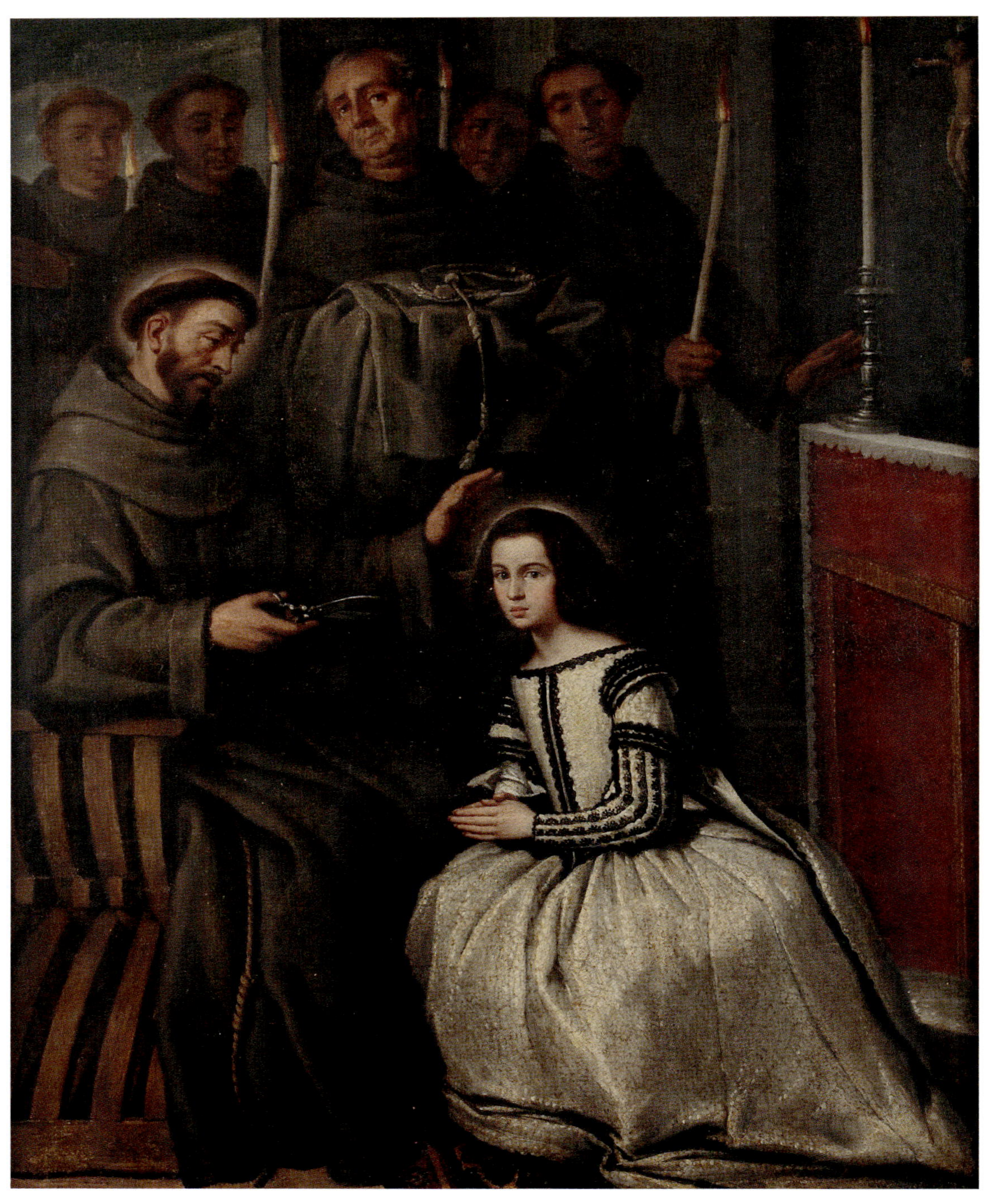

FIG. 17 Unidentified painter (Claudio Coello?), *Portrait of a Young Woman (Margarita de Austria?) as Saint Clare*, mid-seventeenth century. Oil on canvas. Photo © Patrimonio Nacional, Monasterio de las Descalzas Reales, Madrid, 00611985.

Clare—but not of the other friars—are outlined in a golden glow, which the artist used to demarcate their privileged saintly status. Incongruously, the young woman does not look at Francis but turns her head toward the viewer. Her facial features, while perhaps idealized, are idiosyncratic, and her garments and hair resemble fashions recognizable from period portraits (fig. 18).

The painter did not simply base the figure of Saint Clare on a model nor merely depict the historical saint styled in contemporary clothing. Rather, the angle of the face, the direct gaze, the pose, which draws on the conventions of the donor portrait, and the individualized features all ensure that the figure of Saint Clare would be recognizable as a specific individual. At the same time, the glow of the halo and the attendant figures ensure the painting's status as a religious image. A political argument about royal sanctity would shed no light on these choices. The depiction could, feasibly, be votive, expressing thanks to an invoked saint for an overcome illness, or thaumaturgic, enveloping the sitter in a quasi-magical protective guise. However, analyzing it through the lens of meditative unmaking provides a functional interpretation for why the recognizable, individualized portrait likeness was granted such prominence in an explicitly religious painting: something that neither the votive nor thaumaturgic functions would require. Furthermore, the chosen iconography—religious profession—also explicitly addresses the abandonment of worldly comforts and the subjugation of the self to a community and to God.

A lo divino portraits appear to depict women more frequently than they do men, but the images were not the exclusive domain of either group. Indeed, a male figure in Luis Tristán's early seventeenth-century *Adoration of the Magi* is most likely a portrait of the donor, given the portraitistic quality of his depiction, with idiosyncratic features; a direct, penetrating gaze; and peculiar placement closest to the picture plane and the space of the viewer (fig. 19).[95] He appears in the guise of biblical King David, principally identifiable by the inclusion of a harp. Even though David was understood to be Christ's royal progenitor, therefore logically fitting in a scene that was about familial lineage and royal authority, it is unusual to find him included

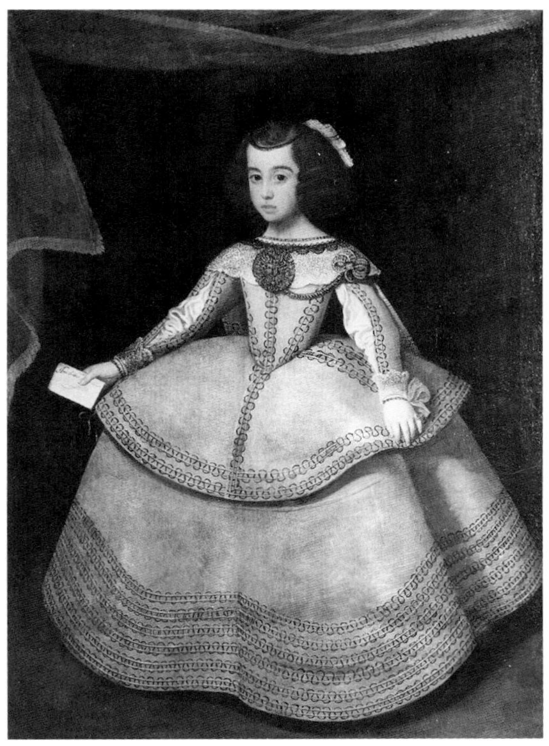

FIG. 18 Unidentified painter, *Portrait of a Young Girl*, mid-seventeenth century. Present location unknown. Photo courtesy of Arxiu Mas, Fundació Institut Amatller d'Art Hispànic, Barcelona. Digital file courtesy of the Department of Image Collections, National Gallery of Art Library, Washington, DC.

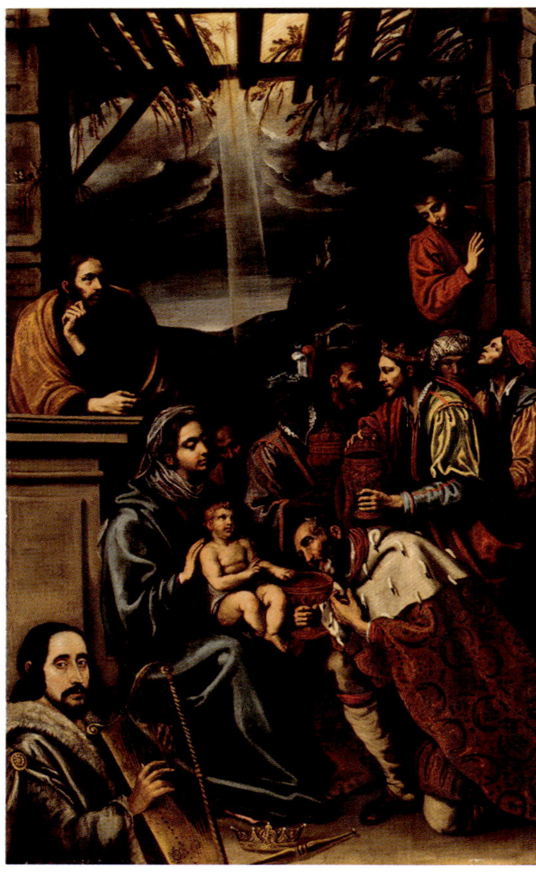

FIG. 19 Luis Tristán de Escamilla, *Adoration of the Magi with Portrait "a lo divino" of Donor as King David*, before 1624. Oil on canvas, 65.9 × 39.4 in. (167.4 × 100.3 cm). Pollok House, Glasgow. Photo © CSG CIC Glasgow Museums and Libraries Collections.

in episodes from Christ's life. The painting's donor could have feasibly commissioned such a painting, including his own portrait as a biblical king, for his home or private chapel. Once there, he could have used it with the same sort of humbling meditative intent that Margarita employed in front of her painting as the Virgin, considering the miracle of Christ's birth and the grand temporal scope of the divine plan. All portraits *a lo divino* challenge a linear conception of time, but the patron's choice to be depicted as King David made this tension particularly acute: the individual was simultaneously a biblical king who preceded Christ by many generations and a modern individual who lived hundreds of years after him. The patron would have been forced to reckon with the insignificance of his own life and lifespan in the face of the centuries that separated him from not only Christ but also David.

When a sitter asked to be represented as a saint, his or her densely networked, relational personhood was subsumed to the even denser universalizing network of the religious image. The conscripted relevance of the portrait, relatable only to those who had known the sitter, was thus subsumed to the generality of the Catholic image, which, from the point of view of the Church, was beneficial to anyone who saw it—Catholic or not.[96] To apply a geopolitical metaphor, the portrait was local; the religious image was global. For the patron, the image would serve as a vehicle for meditative unmaking during his or her own lifespan, but the image's longevity resided in its status as a devotional picture. In contrast to a simple portrait, which was evacuated of meaning once those who had known the sitter themselves disappeared, what remained in a sanctified portrait was an efficacious image that any Catholic could use for religious contemplation. In a portrait *a lo divino* the patron is triply sacrificed: in terms of the word's etymology (*sacrum facere*—to make holy), in the meditative dismantling of the self that I have suggested was the guiding principle for how such images functioned, and in sacrificing the limited applicability of the portrait to the limitless universality of the religious picture. However, a contrary argument could easily be made as well. It was

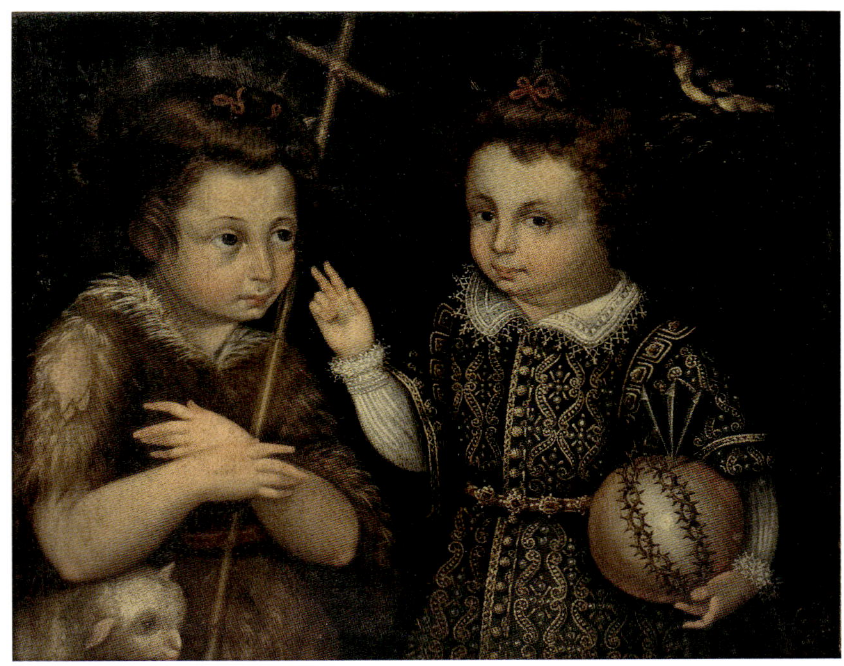

FIG. 20 Luis Rosicler y Carpio, *Saint John the Baptist and the Infant Christ*, 1604–10?. Oil on canvas, 25.5 × 20.4 in. (65 × 52 cm). Convento de San Ildefonso de las Trinitarias Descalzas, in deposit at the Casa Museo Lope de Vega, Madrid. Dirección General de Promoción Cultural; Consejería de Cultura y Turismo, Comunidad de Madrid; Real Academia Española.

precisely portraiture's constrained specificity, its having been made for a very specific place at a very specific time, its eyewitness status, that gave it the significant power that it could then lend to religious imagery. Indeed, religious images that drew on the formal language of portraiture possessed an enhanced degree of authority.

Non-Meditative Portraits *a lo divino*

The hypothesis that portraits *a lo divino* did not glorify but belittled their sitters and that they served as aids in lengthy introspective meditation cannot be uniformly applied to all the extant images that fall into the category. Children were commonly depicted as holy figures (and frequently as Christ, which is not found in any surviving or documented sanctified portraits of adults from the Hispanic world). For instance, there are a number of depictions of royal children as holy figures held at the convent of the Descalzas Reales, including one of the future Archduke Ferdinand represented as the Infant Christ of Prague. Similarly, the painter Luis Rosicler y Carpio portrayed two children, one of whom is thought to be the poet Félix Lope de Vega y Carpio's son Carlos Félix, as Christ and John the Baptist (fig. 20).[97] It is difficult to imagine that these young children could have even begun to understand the meditations that adults like Margarita performed in front of their sanctified portraits. Rather, their depictions in the guise of saints may have instead served to counteract the ancient fear of the *mal de ojo*, or evil eye.

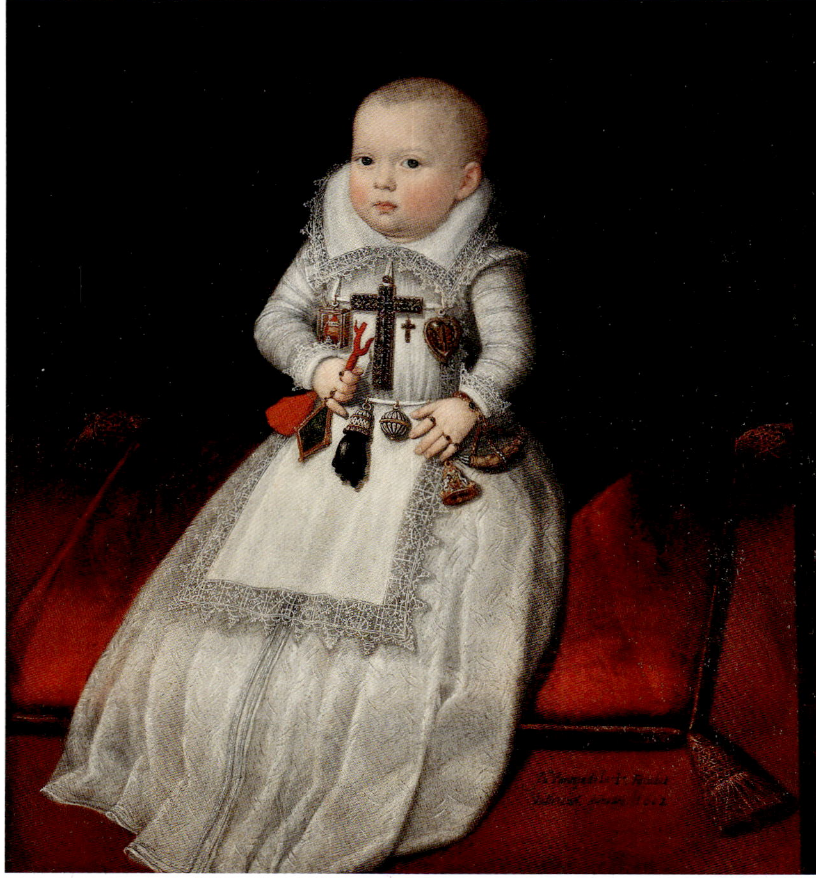

FIG. 21 Juan Pantoja de la Cruz, *Infanta Ana Mauricia de Austria*, 1602. Oil on canvas, 33.4 × 29.5 in. (85 × 75 cm). Photo © Patrimonio Nacional, Monasterio de las Descalzas Reales, Madrid, 00612229.

According to Covarrubias's 1611 dictionary, there existed "people who effect evil simply by looking at another person, especially if they do so with anger or jealousy," and in Spain, "it is suspected that even today there are in some places lineages of people who are infamous for committing such evil."[98] Children were believed to be particularly susceptible to the insidious effects of an ill-intentioned gaze, given that they were "very delicate, and had thin blood."[99] The mere creation of a portrait of a child was a potentially dangerous act, given that the quasi-magical connection of portrait to prototype could feasibly transfer the evil eye back onto the sitter. To counteract this threat, royal children are often portrayed with talismans, including jeweled *higas de azabache* (objects carved from black jet in the form of a hand with the thumb held between the index and middle fingers), crucifixes, pieces of coral, rattles, and bells, as seen in a 1602 portrait of the *infanta* Ana (who would feature as an archangel in the *a lo divino* portrait of her mother as the Virgin just a few years later) (fig. 21). The inclusion of talismans in portraits of royal children demonstrates that this belief—though criticized by some early modern ecclesiastics as superstitious—was widespread at court.[100] The fragile royal body had to be dressed in a protective layer that minimized the risks that the evil eye posed to the individual sitter and, by extension, to the success of the entire Habsburg lineage.[101]

The practice of donning amulets and talismans as well as the portrayal of sitters with such objects posit the individual's body as a base layer that can be transformed and enhanced through the superimposition of additional visual information. Indeed, the role of talismans such as the higa de azabache is to "distract the looker" in order to prevent the visual concentration that is necessary to enact the evil eye.[102] Similarly, the iconographic attributes of sanctity that are a component of a portrait *a lo divino* may be interpreted as apotropaic layers placed onto the base layer of the portrait likeness.[103] Therefore, while the portrait of *infanta* Ana in Pantoja's *Annunciation* may have functioned as a source for meditative engagement for the young girl as she grew, it is equally likely that it shrouded her with this sort of spiritual protection, thus playing a double function.

Similarly, there are a number of early modern Hispanic examples of kings depicted in the guise of saints that do not appear to have functioned as meditative images.[104] For instance, Charles V was commonly represented as one of the three magi coming to adore the infant Christ at the manger in multifigural compositions that may have formed part of larger altarpieces, including in Marco Cardisco's *Adoration* from the Castel Nuovo in Naples, Juan Correa de Vivar's *Adoration* from the church of Nuestra Señora de la Asunción in Meco, and in a panel by Rodrigo de Sajonia from the monastery of Santa María de Sigena (fig. 22). In the first two examples, the monarch's facial features are unmistakable. In the third, a banner with the bicephalic eagle of the Habsburgs visible behind the head of the centrally positioned, standing magus suggests that the artist may have intended for the painting's viewers to identify the man with Charles, even if the painted face is not unequivocally that of the young king.[105]

Many of these images were unlikely to have been commissioned by the monarchs themselves.[106] To wit, a painting attributed to the circle of Juan de Borgoña, in which a recognizable Charles I (likely prior to his coronation as Holy Roman Emperor) is depicted as Saint Sebastian, additionally includes a figure in the standard pose of a donor. Presumably this is the work's patron, but without knowledge of his identity, relation to the king, and the painting's destination, it is difficult to speculate on the motivations behind its making.[107] Similarly, we know little about the commission, context, and usage of the pair of miniature portraits, attributed to Jan van Kessel, where Charles II and his queen, Mariana of Neuburg, are represented as Saint Ferdinand (or as the Emperor Constantine) and Saint Helena or the pair of paxes of Saints Hippolytus and Concordia, where gilded portraits of the same royal pair were inserted into the existing silver objects and enhanced with halos and palms of martyrdom (fig. 23).[108] Perhaps these artworks, all likely produced outside the auspices of the court, should be understood as the material manifestations of the push by numerous theorists and intellectuals, like the aforementioned Pellicer de Salas y Tovar, that the monarchy embrace the propagandistic agenda of sacred kingship, which it ultimately never did.

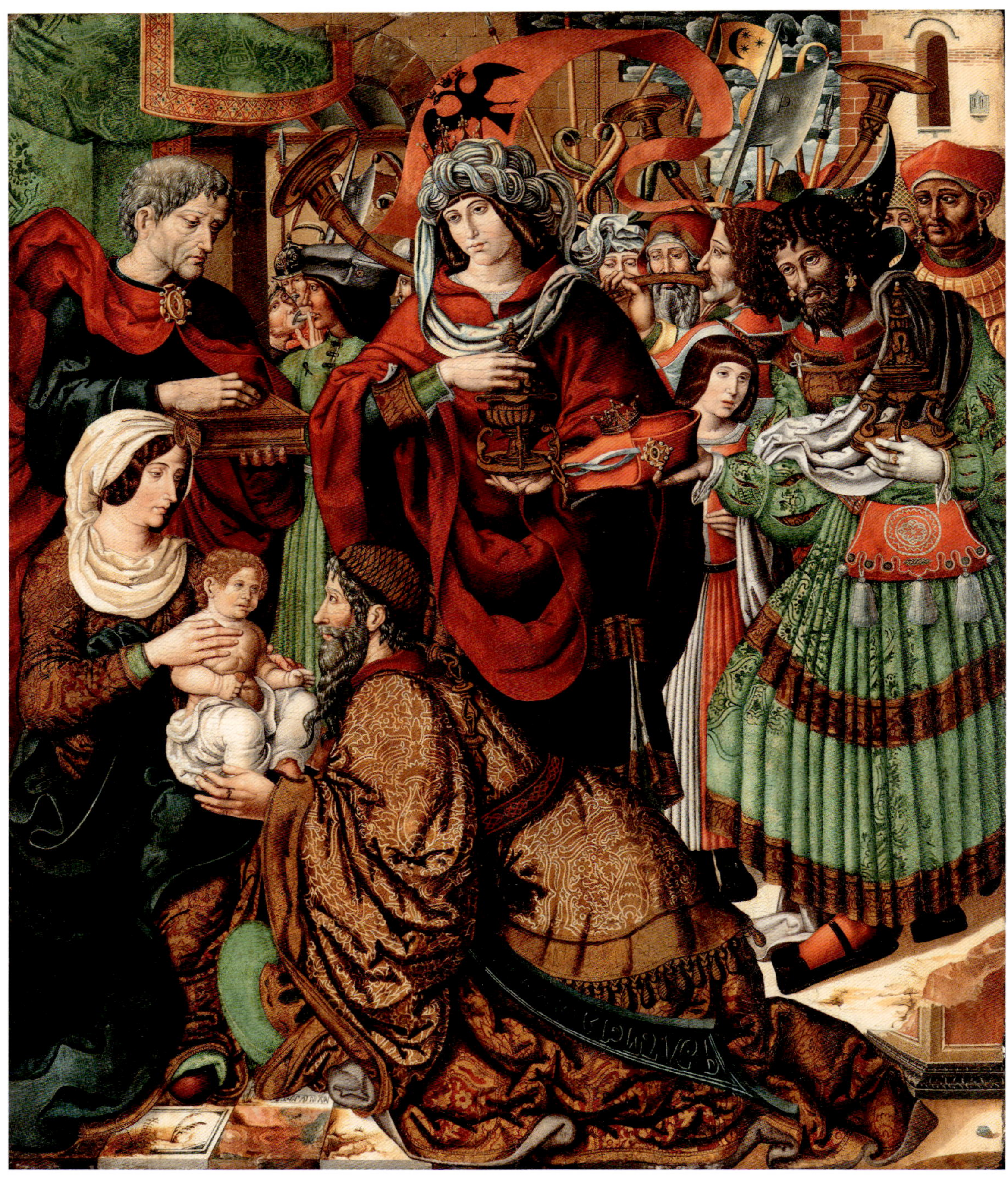

FIG. 22 Rodrigo de Sajonia (called Master of Sigena), *Adoration of the Magi*, ca. 1519. Oil on panel, 61.25 × 51.37 in. (155.6 × 130.4 cm). Meadows Museum, Southern Methodist University, Dallas; museum purchase with funds from The Meadows Foundation, with additional support provided by Susan Heldt Albritton, Gwen and Richard Irwin, and Catherine Blaffer Taylor, MM.2018.06. Photo: Kevin Todora.

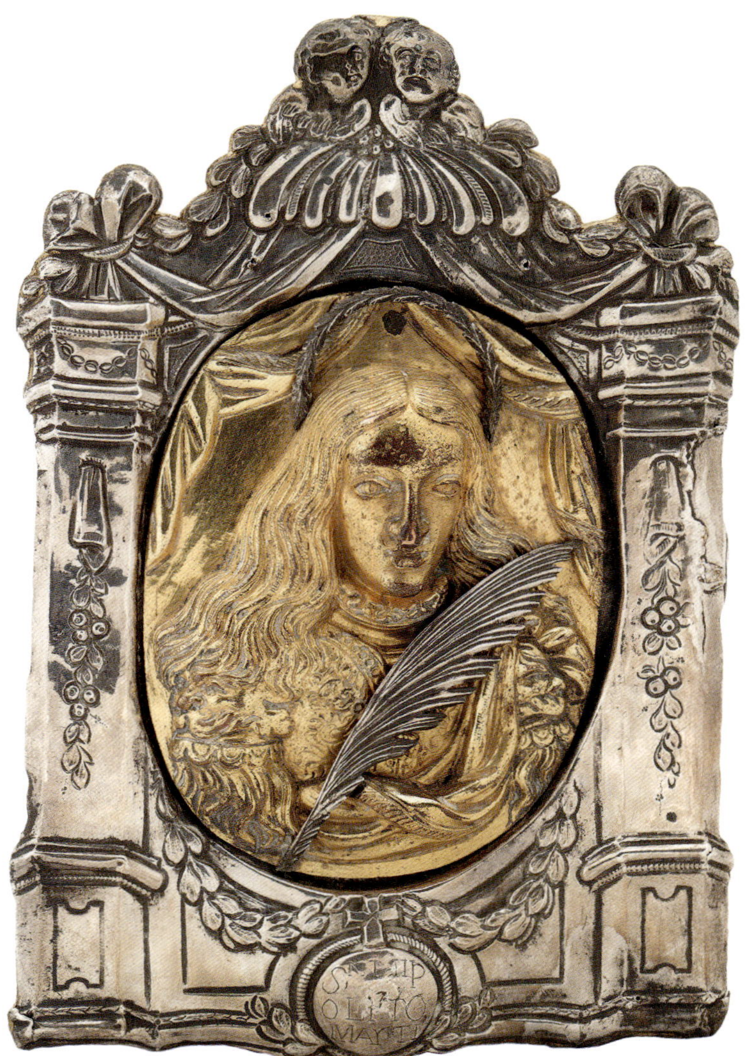

FIG. 23 Unidentified silversmith, pax with portrait of Charles II as Saint Hippolytus, ca. 1691. Museo Nacional del Prado, Madrid. Photo © Photographic Archive Museo Nacional del Prado.

Poetry About Portraiture

There are relatively few images that can be incontrovertibly termed portraits *a lo divino*. However, the fact that typologically similar sanctified portraits appear in a wide range of contexts—including Spain, Mexico, Naples, the Netherlands, and Guatemala—at irregular intervals during the entire early modern period suggests that these may simply be the few survivors of a much larger corpus of images. The ubiquity of sanctified portraits within early modern Hispanic artistic production is further corroborated by the quantity of textual responses, either poetic or legal, that they generated. For instance, Orozco Díaz identified a number of seventeenth-century sonnets that explicitly criticized the fashion for sanctified portraiture, using them to argue that Francisco de Zurbarán's paintings of female saints were actually portraits of noblewomen from Seville masquerading as holy figures.[109] The sonnets, written by men about women, capitalize on the contrast between the sitters' holy appearance and their supposedly less-than-virtuous behaviors, relying on stereotypes about female vanity, false modesty, and promiscuousness, for comedic effect.[110]

For example, the poet Luis de Ulloa y Pereira describes a painting of Saint Lucy, into which a woman, whom he calls "Lesbia," "inserted a copy of her face." Playing on the sitter's purported conceitedness, he notes that she had commissioned the painting in order to "receive yet more adoration," if more for the image's novelty (*novedad*) than for her actual merits. The moniker Lesbia is not accidental here, as this was the pseudonym of Clodia Metelli, whose supposed licentiousness was lambasted by Cicero.[111] Capitalizing on the inherent duality of an image that was both a portrait of a living woman (whose morals he questioned), and a saint, Ulloa y Pereira concludes, "Whether the painting be divine or profane, [the Lady] is too devout to resemble Lesbia, but too little penitent to resemble the saint."[112]

Even if an image, such as the one Ulloa y Pereira ridicules, never existed, the sonnet nevertheless allows us to discern period attitudes toward portraiture *a lo divino*. First of all, the image is described in terms of its *novedad*, defined in the 1734 edition of the *Diccionario de Autoridades* (Dictionary of authorities) as "a mutation of things, which normally have a fixed state, or it was believed that they should [have a fixed state]."[113] The painting of a saint depicted with the recognizable features of a living woman is thus cast as a perverse admixture of seemingly established, fixed image types: the devotional picture and the portrait. Furthermore, the sonnet's very title, "En ocasión de haber puesto una dama la copia de su rostro en una imagen de santa Lucía" (On the occasion of a lady having inserted a copy of her face into an image of Saint Lucy) implied a repurposing of a stable, otherwise immutable religious image, into which a vain woman demanded that her visage be inserted. But the frequency with which portraits *a lo divino* were created (based both on surviving exemplars and on period documentation) suggests that these claims of fixity may have been mere sophistry, aiming to present a desired situation as actuality, based on an understanding of Catholic orthodoxy that saw such images as problematic.

In wavering "whether the painting be divine or profane," the sonnet also introduces the question of how viewers understood the ontology of portraits *a lo divino*. A viewer who recognized the painting's sitter, a woman cast as "too little penitent" for having commissioned such a vain "novelty," would likely have been discouraged from treating the image as a holy one that could serve as the focus of prayer. In Ulloa y Pereira's conceit, the real-life woman's virtue was so lacking that it could never even approximate the saint's.[114] But neither could the painting please the masculine gaze; the author implies that the painting's spiritual layer ("too devout to resemble Lesbia") impeded the male viewer's enjoyment of looking upon the woman of apparently loose morals that it depicted.

Like Ulloa y Pereira, who was never able to see just one of the picture's two layers without thinking of the other, Lope de Vega also identified the internal conflict in an image with multiple, very different referents in a sonnet titled "A una tabla de

Susana, en cuya figura se hizo retratar una dama" (To a painting of Susanna, in whose guise a lady had herself portrayed). The poem's last stanza concludes, "Two are here exhibited as one: the honor of Susanna's matrimony, contrasted with decrepit affection. And yours, fake Fabia, whom I would only call chaste, if I wanted to bear false witness." As the sonnet describes, a portrait *a lo divino* is in a state of permanent tension between the recognized virtue of its saintly referent and the imperfect nature of its earthly one. However, should a person unfamiliar with the patrons have come across either one of these two paintings, they may have noticed the idiosyncrasies of each figure's features but otherwise had no reason to assume that the paintings' function was anything but religious. Indeed, Lope de Vega avers that such a painting's devotional content can only be appreciated as such "if you ignore the truth of the portrait." Only thusly can one "justly adore the holy story, [and] justly admire the sitter."[115]

Returning to the example of Queen Margarita of Austria's portrait *a lo divino* as the Virgin, I have argued that the queen, too, would have attempted to "ignore the truth of the portrait" and "justly admire" the Mother of God in the painting. Notwithstanding her privileged status, however, the image could have also garnered such crudely sexualized, mocking responses. It is easy to imagine a figure like the Duke of Lerma, Philip III's royal favorite who had a troubled relationship with the queen, anticipating the types of sentiments expressed in these sonnets just a few decades later. Lerma could have feasibly expressed frustration or amusement at what he saw as a fundamental incommensurability between the holiest of women and what he really thought of the queen portrayed in her guise.[116] Paradoxically, in criticizing Margarita's vanity or in attacking her character, he may have coincided with the queen's own meditative response to seeing herself in the role of the Mother of God: loathing herself as unworthy of such a comparison.

While these satirical, poetic criticisms of portraiture *a lo divino* confirm its existence and even its popularity, they do little to reveal the actual motivations behind having oneself painted as a saint nor do they say anything about how such images might have functioned and where they might have been displayed. Just as a viewer who did not know the sitters might have approached the images as purely religious, neither should we discredit the actual devotional intent of the "Lesbia" and "Fabia" of the two sonnets (provided that they—and their portraits *a lo divino*—ever did exist). Rather, as described above, they, too, may have been motivated by a desire to engage in set of devotional practices that had little to do with the misogynistically motivated vanity Ulloa y Pereira and Lope de Vega sought to find in them.

"A Horrifying Monstrosity": Ecclesiastical Responses to Portraiture *a lo divino*

Even if a sanctified portrait were driven by true piety—a true desire to annihilate the self—this did little to assuage the threat that many in the Church believed such images posed to those who saw them. Official ecclesiastical censures of images that combined the visages of living individuals with markers of sanctity erased any nuance from the motivations for making and using sanctified portraits. The legal points of reference for the majority of these prohibitions were the decrees that Pope Urban VIII proclaimed in 1625, with expanded reissuings in 1634 and 1642, in response to the ubiquitous early modern problem, in which the Vatican's exclusive authority in bestowing beatitude or sanctity was tested by the proliferation of popular cults.[117] Images, which were often the linchpin in such unsanctioned cults, were of particular concern, and Urban's pronouncements focused on the illicit deployment of codified markers used to identify individuals as saints, including "laurels and rays," or halos.[118]

The papal decrees were widely recapitulated, including in art-theoretical literature. For instance, in an Italian treatise published in 1652, the Jesuit Giovanni Domenico Ottonelli and the painter Pietro da Cortona state that images in which living sitters appear as saints are motivated by the sitters' *capriccio* (whim). They add that, in most cases, there is "dissimilitude" between them and the saints whom they embodied.[119] Urban's edicts, as well as earlier sixteenth-century prohibitions that already addressed the issue in a piecemeal fashion, also formed the backbone of the legion synodal constitutions that were published across the early modern Hispanic, and more broadly Catholic, worlds.[120] Because local ecclesiastical authorities often looked to the same papal sources when administering their provinces, it is not surprising to find similarities between publications separated both by great distance and many decades.[121]

For example, the Venezuelan Synod, celebrated in Caracas in 1687, drew on Urban VIII's decree of 1634 to underline the great benefits that stemmed from venerating depictions of holy figures, "revering in them their holy spirits, which reign in glory with Jesus Christ." At the same time, it stressed the necessity of carefully prohibiting the depiction of figures who had not been beatified or canonized as if they were already saints. The published proceedings stipulated that "no image, or relic of a male or female saint, who is not canonized by the Holy Apostolic See, be placed on the altars of churches for the widespread adoration by the faithful, nor be painted with the rays of light of the Blessed."[122] The 1586 synodal constitutions of the bishopric of Osma in northern Spain required that "portraits of particular individuals not be placed on altarpieces or altars where mass is to be said," while the 1677 constitutions from Huamanga in the Viceroyalty of Peru stated that because "it is not correct that in churches there be profane things that could distract the eyes of the faithful, we prohibit that images or portraits of gentiles, or of other person, be placed in them." However, in Osma all portraits were prohibited, "even [portraits] of the person who paid for the work" (that is to say donor portraits), while in Huamanga in 1677 donor portraits were allowed "but with devout and humble garb."[123]

Proscriptions against the inclusion of portraits of living individuals in devotional scenes fall under the broader set of criticisms of the intermingling of the sacred and profane realms.[124] This becomes apparent in texts that discuss the very term *a lo divino*, which in the seventeenth century applied not to visual images but to literature. In his dictionary, Covarrubias defined the term *coplas a lo divino* (couplets in the divine manner) as, when, in poetry, "a vulgar and secular concept is converted into a spiritual concept, which many times should be avoided, because it retains the memory of what it was. Some think that these [represent] a sharpness of wit, [but] I do not see them as such."[125] Similarly, in his *Discurso theológico sobre los theatros y comedias de este siglo* (Theological discourse about the theaters and plays of this century), first published in 1689, the Jesuit theologian Ignacio de Camargo noted that the proponents and apologists of Golden Age theater often cited the popularity of religious plays as justification for the larger industry. But, he countered, "these plays, which they call 'a lo divino,' have the horrifying monstrosity of mixing the profane with the sacred, of confusing light with shadows, and of uniting the earth with the heavens."[126]

Similarly, in 1625, the Jesuit moralist Bernardino de Villegas criticized the practice of noble families who "[dress] their images like ladies, and their ladies like images."[127] He dramatically stated that painting the "holy virgins so profanely, and with so many trinkets and colorful garments, that the world's most courtly ladies do not wear more" is to "martyr them anew." He also railed against an image of the Christ Child that was painted "wearing shoes of a very festive make, and with an arquebus gun on his shoulder, as if Jesus Christ had been a huntsman at some point, or as if we were to somehow be moved to devotion and reverence by such a gallant and courtly costume."[128] Nearly sixty years earlier, the 1567 Provincial Council of Lima had decreed that "the image of Our Lady, or of any other saint, not be adorned with the dresses and garb of women, nor be painted with oil or the colors that women use; however, they may be given a rich mantle."[129] These excerpts from the Lima Council and the texts by Covarrubias, Camargo, and Villegas speak to the recurring and excessive intrusion of mundane elements into the sphere of the sacred. When the representational repertoires that governed distinct artistic categories, such as portraiture or religious painting, cross-pollinated, viewers with little discernment could easily be misguided. Indeed, it was commonly believed that images were more dangerous than texts because their impact was broader and more lasting. Villegas warned that "heretics [paint] the saints with a thousand indecencies [depraving] many simple Catholics, who by reading these perverse paintings, learn the way to their heresies," concluding with a pseudosynaesthetic flourish: "Through the eyes they drink the poison of these errors."[130] Villegas drew on the widespread notion that paintings were books for those who could not read and identified key concerns related to images. Chief among these was that they had an immediate effect on susceptible individuals who could be dishonestly manipulated by the images, which they could never unsee. Not knowing the truth of what they saw, whether a portrait of a noble lady or a statue of the Virgin Mary dressed in profane contemporary clothes, such viewers would either direct their veneration toward figures that they should not be venerating, such as portraits of nonholy people in similarly opulent garb, or only venerate the materials in which such a figure was dressed or from which the images were made, falling into idolatry.

Much the same was feared of portraits *a lo divino*, regardless of the devotional motivations that may have guided their patrons in commissioning them. Indeed, even though Urban VIII's decrees were above all directed against popular cults, there was a thin line between depicting a living person with a halo because of a misguided belief in that person's sanctity and creating an *a lo divino* portrait that depicted a living person masquerading in the guise of *another* saint. Given this similarity, therefore, sanctified portraits automatically fell under the proscriptions described below and were likely frequently subjected to campaigns of extirpation. The 1671 Synod of Málaga, for instance, would have easily classified such images as possessing "uncertain, superstitious, apocryphal, or unusual elements," by virtue of which they would have been destined to be "burned without delay, and the ashes be thrown into the water, or buried."[131] To the patrons who commissioned those paintings, however, it was precisely the incursions of the mundane into sacred scenes that allowed them to more richly contextualize their imagined experience of those ancient places and events. For example, for Margarita, whom Pantoja depicted in archaizing garb and in the traditional colors of the Virgin, it was not contemporary clothing but elements such as the sewing implements that performed this crucial role.

Problems of Visibility

Due to these proscriptions and attitudes, it is unsurprising that portraits *a lo divino*, particularly those that were publicly accessible, were reported to ecclesiastical authorities. In July 1615, Rodrigo de Villegas, the canon of the cathedral of the city of Santiago de Guatemala (today Antigua), denounced Juan Maldonado de Paz, an *oidor* (judge) of the Royal Audiencia of Guatemala before Felipe Ruiz de Corral, an official of the Holy Office of the Inquisition.[132] Villegas claimed that he "had seen a canvas [painted] in oil, and in it was painted an image of Our Lady and at her feet an image of Saint John the Baptist, and one of Saint Stephen and another of Saint Lucy, and it seems to this witness that the image of Saint John is a portrait, which is face and head [*rostro y caveza*], of the *licenciado* (graduate) Juan Maldonado de Paz, *oidor* of this Royal Audiencia, to whom belongs the canvas with these paintings."[133]

The witness then identified portraits of Maldonado de Paz's son (or nephew) and (illegitimate) daughter in the depictions of Saints Stephen and Lucy and added that "when this witness saw the painting for the first time it seemed to him bad that these people should be portrayed in the guise of saints [*debajo de figuras de santos*], and especially the daughter, being illegitimate . . . and he thought this every time that he saw the painting because it was very normally [*muy de hordinario*] displayed in churches and on altars during processions of the Holy Sacrament, and this witness heard various people whisper [*murmurar*] about these portraits."[134] Villegas made it clear that, in his eyes, the sitters who claimed the saints' identities could not match the virtue of the painting's saintly prototypes, similarly to the satirical sonnets about paintings *a lo divino* described above.[135] The deposition gives no insight into whether Maldonado de Paz and his family members used the painting in the same way that Margarita may have meditated upon her sanctified portrait, though this is certainly not outside the realm of possibility.

The various papal and synodal decrees against depicting nonholy individuals with markers of holiness certainly encompassed portraits *a lo divino* but never explicitly articulated whether the sitters depicted within such images were guilty of any particular sin. Claims that the sitters' characters were incommensurate with the virtues of the saints in whose guise they were depicted would imply that pride or *soberbia* was the primary issue. However, the criticisms may actually be closer to period concerns with blasphemy. According to Javier Villa-Flores, early modern understandings of blasphemy took three forms: "attributing to God any characteristic that does not confirm to his nature," "denying to God attributes that belong only to him," or "ascribing to a creature qualities that conform only to God." Any of these could also apply to attacks on the Virgin and the saints or to any other holy things.[136] Francisco de Quevedo satirized persecutions of blasphemy in his picaresque novel *Historia de la vida del Buscón* (History of the life of the Swindler) of 1626, demonstrating that the general literate public would have understood what constituted blasphemous speech. Don Pablos, the titular character, tricked a woman out of two chickens by terrifying her that she had unwittingly committed the sin: "Don't you recall that you called to your chickens *pío, pío, pío*"—an onomatopoeic approximation of bird sounds—"[whereas] *Pío* is the name of popes, vicars of God and heads of the Church?"[137] The humor of the episode depended on the fact that his readers would have understood that the woman's act was unlikely to have been prosecuted as true blasphemy but approximated it just enough to terrify a gullible individual.

Feasibly, sanctified portraits could have been criticized for "ascribing to a creature," in this case a secular sitter, "qualities that conform only to God" or another holy figure. Or, conversely, by depicting a sinful individual in the guise of a holy figure, such images could have been understood as subtracting from the aura that such a figure normally possessed. Given that blasphemers in colonial contexts were seen as particularly pernicious for affecting Indigenous populations, it is likely that in Guatemala, the inquisitors were particularly concerned about the exposure of Indigenous Guatemalan viewers to an unorthodox, possibly confusing, and potentially blasphemous image.[138] Furthermore, the ambiguous painting was displayed in what was likely the city's most trafficked indoor space—the cathedral—where it could confuse a wide spectrum of the populace, which might make incorrect assumptions about the status of the depicted people. The inquisitors' concerns had real implications for the stability of the colonial system of which they formed part. Indeed, a later case demonstrates that the codified visual language of sanctity could be subversively deployed in resistance to Spanish colonial rule: Juan Carlos Estenssoro has argued that the Andean revolutionary Túpac Amaru had himself depicted in a manner that consciously drew on the iconography of Saint James the Apostle, commonly known as Santiago Mataindios—St. James the "Indian-killer."[139] In the picture, the Indigenous figure was not crushed under the hooves of the saint's galloping horse, as in myriad images of the subject, but was mounted atop it, entirely reversing the established power structure. The result of Villegas's Guatemalan deposition is not known, barring the discovery of further documentation related to the trial, but if the painting commissioned by Maldonado de Paz indeed contained portraits of the *oidor* and his family members in the guise of saints, it is likely that it was repainted, removed, or destroyed.

By contrast to the episode in Guatemala, where visibility was the most likely cause of censure, the surviving double portrait of Queen Margarita and her daughter enacting the Annunciation was likely made for a restricted space within the royal palace in Valladolid.[140] Unlike the Madrid Alcázar, which also housed the king's councils, the Valladolid residence was designed to protect the royal family's privacy.[141] The painting was then transferred to Madrid's Alcázar residence after Philip III moved his court to that city in 1606.[142] The Burgundian ceremonial etiquette of the Habsburg court was highly formalized, with the monarchs largely withdrawn from the public eye.[143] In practice, however, even the most private spaces of early modern royal individuals were quite crowded. If the painting was actually made for the queen's oratory, it would have been seen regularly not only by the queen herself but by family members, elite guests, servants and enslaved workers, singers and musicians, attendants and persons-in-waiting, valets, buffoons, dwarfs, charges, and confessors.[144] These people, too, would have brought their own preconceptions to the image and departed with their own potentially unorthodox ideas about what they had seen. Or, conversely, their thoughts about the painting may have been entirely orthodox and in line with the Church's stance on such images. Indeed, any of the individuals who saw the painting but for whom the painting was not intended could have feasibly perceived a tension between the image's devotional character and its clear portraitistic features.[145] Privately, they may have felt as scandalized as did many early modern ecclesiastics at this mixing of representational repertoires. And yet, the three paintings from the queen's chapel survive to this day. Had they been more readily accessible, they may have been targeted by the Inquisition, their royal patronage notwithstanding.[146]

The known portraits *a lo divino* that were commissioned by royal individuals were not propagandistic in the manner of architecture, state portraits, or processions, all of which were meant to be widely seen. Furthermore, as far as is currently known, there are no known sanctified portraits of the king that were commissioned by him or his family. Rather, all depict either women or children as their primary figures. Even though these images appear to have been produced first and foremost for the private use of royal women, they were nevertheless political in that they contributed to the royal family's own understanding of its status and role in statecraft. When they did speak politically, it was to a restricted group of individuals from society's highest echelons.[147] The absence of sanctified portraits of the king does not, therefore, argue against applying a political reading to this corpus of images. However, they were not simple statements on the royal family's divine right to rule. Rather, more complexly, they were declarations of its piousness precisely through the ways in which its members, too, had to labor at the dismantling of their own, particularly privileged selfhoods. That there are no known portraits *a lo divino* of adult male royals and that, in general, there appear to be fewer such images of men can also serve to corroborate the argument that these images were used to diminish rather than celebrate the self. Broadly speaking, women were already considered to be lesser selves, subservient to men and the home and devoted principally to the concerns and needs of others.[148]

As far as I am able to establish, mentions of portraits *a lo divino* are not common in inventories and artists' contracts from the early modern Hispanic world.[149] This absence may reveal something about how people thought about and responded to these artworks that fall between two pictorial categories.[150] For example, the Annunciation scene with Queen Margarita and the two other *a lo divino* compositions from her oratory do not appear among the items in Pantoja's official billing of the queen's purse for the years from 1600 to 1607. Maria Kusche notes that the queen likely remunerated Pantoja directly for two portraits of the *infanta* Ana Mauricia that are also absent from the invoice rather than going through courtly channels.[151] An awareness that the *a lo divino* portraits could have been criticized for their seemingly unorthodox character may explain their absence from an official invoice that did list other, more orthodox religious paintings made for the queen's oratory, in addition to numerous state portraits, including ones sent in diplomatic gift exchanges.[152]

Conclusion—*A lo divino* Portraiture and the Early Modern Self

Recorded period responses to sanctified portraiture ranged from deeming it a mutation of established precedents, to calling it an "offense to God," to something "bad" that caused much "whispering" among those who saw it. Such testimonies, while crucial, give the skewed impression that sanctified portraiture was uniformly lambasted in the early modern period. A rare uncritical description appears in an account of the Escorial by the Hieronymite monk Francisco de los Santos, who writes that the painter Juan Fernández Navarrete, "put a portrait of his father [into the figure of one of the Apostles], and they even say that he put a portrait of his mother as the face of our Lady, because she was very beautiful . . . the painting is all well finished."[153] The very fact that the cleric made note of this, perhaps apocryphal, episode suggests that the artist's behavior was worth mentioning for having pushed the boundaries of an established norm. However, the lack of any accompanying censure implicitly normalizes the image within Santos's larger litany of ekphrastic descriptions. Moreover, other individuals—those who commissioned sanctified portraits in the first place—felt that such images were perfectly appropriate. Rather than heretical or heterodox perversions, they clearly understood them as artistic forms that fell well within the boundaries of acceptable Catholic image practices.

Nevertheless, modern scholarly diagnoses of sanctified portraits frequently deem these images as "strange,"[154] "surprising,"[155] "beyond the normal confines of the genre,"[156] and call the phenomenon an "almost blasphemous audacity"[157] that is "striking to notice."[158] These descriptions indicate that our understanding of the modern portrait still has difficulty making space for sanctified portraiture as anything more than an outlier, even though it was, in actuality, part and parcel of portrait making in early modern Europe and its colonial holdings.[159] In part this stems from the still-prevalent notion that modern portraiture "began" in the Renaissance and therefore was the most visible manifestation of a Renaissance selfhood that was, in broad terms, individualistic, humanistic, and secular.[160] Certainly, such characteristics were beginning to manifest sporadically in how European, and later colonial, individuals thought of themselves between the fifteenth and eighteenth centuries. However, a number of scholars have argued that early modern selfhood was, above all, relational, with the early modern European person's sense of self dependent on how they fit within the larger communities they inhabited.[161]

This relationality can already be discerned in early modern ideas of portraiture. In Leon Battista Alberti's definition of painting, and by extension of portraiture, as a memory tool that "makes the dead seem almost alive" and that "makes the absent present," the identity of the sitters is always cast in relation to those who were or are around them; the role of the portrait defined by those who would view it.[162] The person, then, is not only intensely relational but also constrained in relevance by the extent of those relationalities: the more people one interacts with, the wider one's relational networks. Much the same can be said of one's representations. What seems clear is that the early modern idea of selfhood was in flux: at times it was relational, collective, dependent on the communities around it, and subsumed to religious priorities, while at other times it was individualistic and even secular.[163] This ambiguity is similar to portraiture's position relative the sacred. Sometimes, it stood opposite devotional imagery, while at other times it was closely connected to it. Far from being something "strange," then, portraiture *a lo divino* was a quintessential manifestation of this evolving, fluctuating character of European, and later colonial, selfhood.

When the viewer of a portrait *a lo divino* was also its sitter, the image would have required a debasing of self, not a celebration. When the viewer was an ecclesiastic or an inquisitor, however, the valence of the painting shifted considerably. Readily classified by critics as perversions of established image types, sanctified portraits were deemed vainglorious novelties that were insidious to their viewers, who might make improper inferences regarding the status of the sitters who were represented as saints. Indeed, if we look back to the case of the possessed nuns of San Plácido, with which this chapter opened and which will be considered in further detail in the next, we might see the request that the convent's confessor be depicted as an apocryphal angel as a veiled criticism of the fashion for sanctified portraiture or perhaps of the confessor himself. In another scenario, the demonic possession could be interpreted as a fully conscious attempt by the nuns to remove the men associated with their convent, including García Calderón, from positions of power by deploying the dangerously flexible, seemingly celebratory category of portraiture *a lo divino*, which was bound to garner inquisitorial attention. What the sheer quantity of ecclesiastical prohibitions, recurring inquisitorial trials, and even poetic satires reveals is that portraits *a lo divino* were not only common, but they were a central connecting node between the primary areas of early modern Hispanic artistic practices.

In some ways, the appearance of sanctified portraits, and of sacred portraiture more generally, appears to have been inevitable in a cultural tradition that both had the desire to create verisimilar depictions of individual human beings and that relied on figural representation for its devotional art. Indeed, the meteoric rise of idiosyncratic portraits of nonholy individuals in the Renaissance quickly troubled established religious image types. Artists increasingly turned to the conventions of portraiture, with its immediacy, directness, and truth status, for their renditions of holy figures or devotional narratives. These images came to number among perceived intrusions of the profane into the sphere of the sacred, which generated institutional concern with how images could be used for religious purposes. Implicitly, this also led to anxieties about the ontology of images writ large and a mounting preoccupation with classification, including the designation and separation of artistic types, in order to categorically demarcate what was, was not, or could not be an image for devotion or a portrait. That very similar responses were articulated in different places and at different moments between the fifteenth and eighteenth centuries suggests that this seeming irreconcilability between the portrait, with its connotations of presence and contemporaneity, and the timeless devotional image was one of the defining representational tensions of early modernity.

TRUE PORTRAITS, LYING PORTRAITS *Chapter 2*

Theorizing True Portraiture in the Seventeenth Century

Is one egg a portrait of another egg? After all, eggs do look, more or less, alike (as they certainly do in Luis Egidio Meléndez's earthy kitchen scene) (fig. 24). According to the Andalusian cleric Juan de Acuña del Adarve, whose *Discursos de las effigies y verdaderos retratos* (Discourses on effigies and true portraits) of 1637 represents one of the most comprehensive early modern analyses of the concept of "true portraiture," for an image to be a portrayal, it had to fulfill two basic conditions: that of likeness and that of intention.[1] Although one egg might perfectly resemble another egg, thereby fulfilling the condition of mimesis, the former egg had not been made with the purpose of representing the latter egg or any ur-egg. Both were simply eggs.[2]

Using heuristic rules such as these Acuña del Adarve discussed the numerous portraits of Christ, as well as other miraculous images. The most important ones of these were *acheiropoietoi* or *imagines non manu factae*—images not made, in Acuña del Adarve's words, by "the limited virtue of a man, which tends to be defective in that which it spawns,"[3] but rather by divine means. Acheiropoietoi became key points of reference in debates over the validity of using images in Christian practice. To early modern Catholics, the very existence of these divinely made objects constituted tangible evidence that God approved of images for, among other uses, prayer and predication and, furthermore, that there was a long tradition of doing so in the Christian church. For both of these reasons, acheiropoietoi possessed an impeccable truth value.[4] Preempting criticisms that true portraits of Christ were merely apocryphal and not explicitly mentioned in holy scripture (indeed, most of them are not), Acuña del Adarve argued, "It is as if one who has not seen Toledo or Lisbon were to negate that these

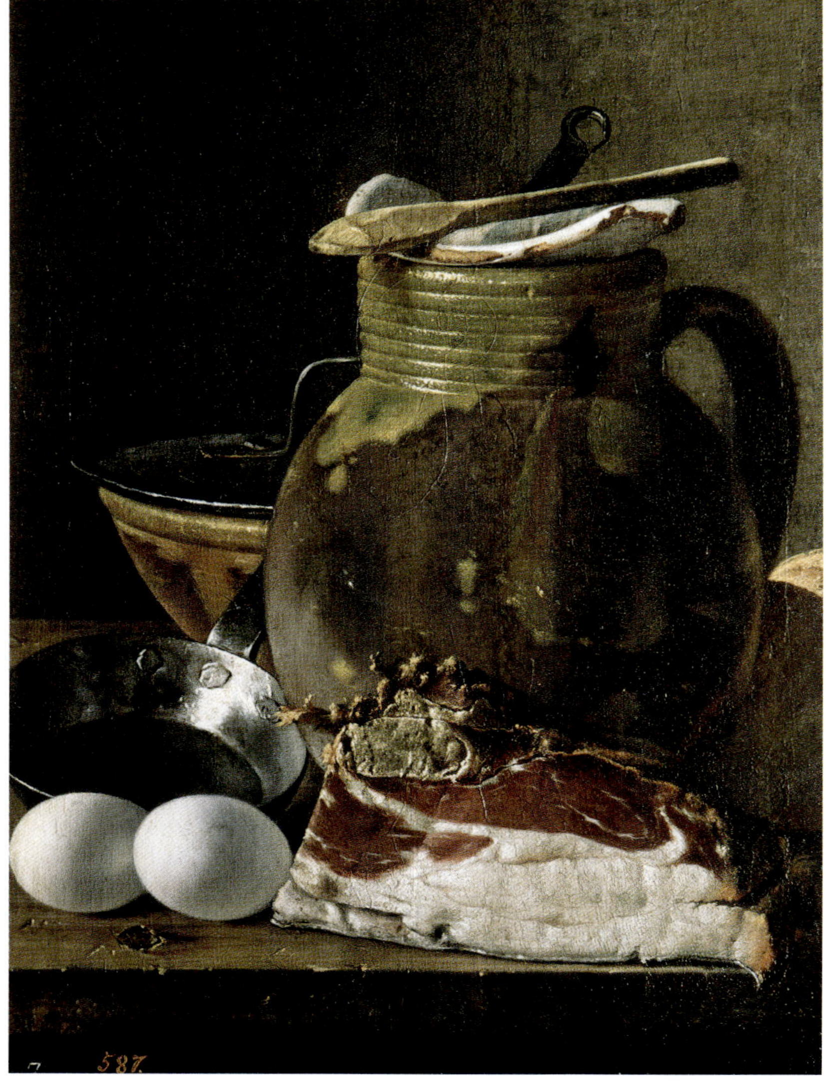

FIG. 24 Luis Egidio Meléndez, *Still Life with Ham, Eggs, and Dishes*, third quarter of the eighteenth century. Oil on canvas, 19.29 × 14.5 in. (49 × 37 cm). Museo Nacional del Prado, Madrid. Photo: Album / Art Resource, New York.

cities exist in the world, because they are not described in the Holy Writ."[5]

True portraiture possessed numerous subdivisions, based on the conditions under which the images had been made, as well as their proximity to divinity. For instance, the Mandylion of Edessa—a portrait that Christ was said to have sent to the ruler Abgar—was among the true portraits valued most highly because it was believed to have been the result of a direct and purposeful imprinting of Christ's face onto a piece of cloth.[6] In turn, this portrait was miraculously copied onto other pieces of canvas, resulting in images that were still *non manu factae* but that did not possess the same value as did the unique matrix from which they had been perfectly reproduced.[7] The image of

Christ's bloody face on Veronica's veil—another of these most highly valued contact relics, the cult of which developed in the twelfth and thirteenth centuries—"was effigied with sweat and blood, colors that are . . . necessary for the painting of a human face."[8] In Acuña del Adarve's reading, such an image was doubly true: not only was it an indexical imprint, taken directly from Christ's face, but it was also rendered in the very substances that artists strove to represent, the blood and sweat that pigments could only imitate. By extension, a *painting* that depicted the veil of Veronica was doubly fictive insofar as it was an illusionistic representation of an indexical image *and* rendered in pigments that merely imitated its corporeal substances.

Lower than these acheiropoietoi of Christ stood non-Christological images. For instance, the miracle of the angelically made "true portrait" of the Virgin that was given to the future saint Ferdinand III of Seville hinged on the fact that angels produced the portrait "more quickly, and with greater perfection" than might have been done otherwise, but using earthly materials.[9] This was an image that was true and not made by human hands, but it was not as proximate to the divine prototype as the imprints made from Christ's face. Although depictions of saints were not the focus of Acuña del Adarve's treatise, they also formed part of the debates about true portraiture in the early modern period. Indeed, there existed numerous accounts that aimed to prove that the likenesses of some ancient and medieval figures were taken from life: for example, an image of Saint Dominic in Madrid was supposedly "taken very accurately from his face."[10] Finally, paintings and prints that depicted venerated miracle-working statues were frequently also described as being true portraits of those objects. The inclusion of text became crucial to announcing and cementing the status of all these images as *verae effigies* or *verdaderos retratos* rather than as artistic inventions, showing them to be of a kind with the unimpeachable true portraits of Christ.

Acuña del Adarve criticized modern painters for taking excessive liberties with holy scenes, noting that "as Cicero says, we know the gods by those faces which painters wanted to give them."[11] He translates Cicero's statement nearly verbatim: "A parvis . . . deos ea facie novimus, qua pictores fictoresque voluerunt"(from a young age we got to know the gods by those faces that painters and makers [sculptors] wanted [to give them]),[12] but he changes the context. Cicero was not making this claim in order to attack painters, but rather, he was formulating a larger hypothetical argument about the physical forms that deities might take and whether those forms approximated the human body. To Acuña del Adarve, the authoritative invocation of Cicero serves as a way to bolster his own aspersions against artistic excess in the making of religious artworks. When subjected to excessive interference by painters, he claims, religious images lost the authority that derived from their being descended from the miraculously created, miracle-working images of Christ. It was those images, the original *verae effigies*, that stood at the head of the category of true portraiture and were its most prestigious exemplars.

Truth in the Early Modern Hispanic World

How can we chart the relationship between portraiture and the idea of the truth in the early modern Hispanic world? One interpretation might be that the growing importance of the portrait as an image type in Spain from the sixteenth century onward led to an increased interest in truth. But it is more likely that portraiture, and more specifically true portraiture, were simply the visual manifestations of a broader cultural turn that centered on veracity. Indeed, it is this period that witnessed the exploding popularity of the literary category of "true history" as well as of first-person writing, which emphasized the personal experience of witnessing as a guarantor of truthfulness.[13]

Only in the second half of the seventeenth century, however, does the notion of *verdad objectiva* (objective truth), rather than subjective, experiential truth, appear to gain traction in the Hispanic world. With the exception of Christological texts that took up the notion from the Gospel of John 14:6 of Christ as the one truth, the idea of a single truth was, until that point, uncommon. A concrete definition of the term emerges in a text written in 1695 by the theologian Bernardino de la Cueva, in which he lambasted the historical legitimacy of the writings of the bishop of the central Mexican diocese of Puebla, Juan de Palafox y Mendoza (who is one of the protagonists of chapters three and four of this book):

> In a historical text, it matters little that the historian not lie and that he write with moral truthfulness [*verdad moral*], that is to say, according to his judgment, if that which he writes did not happen, and if he lacks objective truthfulness [*verdad objectiva*], or a conformity with how events occurred in reality. I do not doubt, that Lord Palafox wrote according to his judgment, but I do have a major suspicion that he wrote many things that did not occur as he tells them, driven by affect, or deceived by others, or by the vehemence of his imagination, or by his greatly speculative temperament.[14]

From Cueva's text, it becomes clear that a subjective judgment made in good faith (moral truth) was not yet sufficient to prove the objective truth of a historical event.[15] Unsurprisingly—this a harbinger of later notions of scientific objectivity—medical texts are another category in which the notion of a single, rather than subjective, truth began to be articulated in this period. For instance, the medical doctor Tomás Longás wrote in 1689 that "contrary opinions about an issue can [all be] probable, but there is only one true one, because although . . . understanding generates a formal truth [*la verdad formal*], the act has to be in conformity with the objective truth, of which there is only one: and therefore, only one is true."[16] Many of these seventeenth-century authors would have likely agreed that the "formal truth" of an individual's subjective opinion could have very little to do with the objective truth of a given matter: opinions, in sum, were not facts.

Concurrently, a fatalistic acknowledgment of the instability of truth permeated early modern Hispanic society.[17] A passage from José Camerino's novel *La dama beata* (The blessed lady), written between 1654 and 1655, perhaps best summarizes this idea: "Falsehood is a portrait / of truth, [that is] so lifelike, / that the greatest expert / cannot recognize it from its original."[18] Camerino's use of the term "portrait" to describe a fiction that is so accurate as to be undiscernible from reality sets the stage for the investigation of the relationship of truth to portraiture and of the larger category of true portraiture, which I will explore in this chapter. It also hints toward the widespread understanding among early modern individuals that images were deceitful by their very nature: they employed ground pigments, bound in oil and bedaubed on wood or canvas, to create illusions of spatial depth on flat surfaces or to depict persons as if they were physically present when they were not.[19] Even when a portrait presented a sitter as real, it was commonly understood that the identities of portrayed individuals could be forgotten, embellished, or confused, while the artworks themselves could comfortably inhabit distinct artistic categories or mutate as they traversed time and geography—they had, in sum, the potential to lie. And finally, differences of language, religious system, and worldview across the Hispanic world had the potential to challenge the commensurability of truth across cultures.[20] In actuality, then, when the adjective *verdadero* was appended to the term *retrato*, this rhetorical flourish amounted to little more than a strained attempt to deny the inherent falseness, uncategorizability, and mutability of images.

If falsehood could imitate the truth so precisely as to become an indistinguishable portrait of it, why did individuals living across the Hispanic world in the early seventeenth century set so much stock by this category? Who had the authority to declare truth to be *obiectiva* rather than *moral* or *formal*?[21] And why, in spite of these challenges, did images and texts that used truthfulness as a guarantor of their authority proliferate in this period? These questions underlie each of the three cases analyzed in this chapter, which examine the truth of the true portraits of Saints Benedict, Ignatius, and Teresa. In each case the images' makers and, by extension, the images themselves attempted to assure their viewers of their trustworthiness. In each case inconsistencies—of how the images were motivated, created, disseminated, or used—challenged their efficacy, even resulting in the artworks being censured by ecclesiastical authorities. Nevertheless, the larger conceptual category of true portraiture appears to have been so robust and so appealing to the early modern Catholic establishment that these shortcomings did little to destabilize it. Indeed, the production of true portraits continued unabated throughout the early modern period and across the Spanish Crown's European, American, and Asian territories because the category of true portraiture promised its viewers something elusive: that what they saw and experienced was real.

"It Is He": True Portraits of Saint Benedict

Chapter 1 introduced the 1628 case of demonic possession in the Benedictine convent of San Plácido, where the nuns—and implicitly the demons who controlled them—commissioned a number of paintings of male ecclesiastics depicted in the guise of apocryphal archangels. At least some of the individuals involved in the trial accepted that the nuns' declarations were actually those of the demons that the nuns claimed had possessed them. Indeed, some early modern Europe thinkers claimed that demons had access to supernatural knowledge—and to the truth—and that they would occasionally share it.[22] Others thought that the possession might have been fabricated entirely. As in chapter 1, my goal here is not to evaluate what it meant to claim or believe in demonic possession within the early modern convent, which has often been interpreted as a space for female agency in an otherwise deeply misogynistic society.[23] Rather, the San Plácido trial—and its few but remarkable mentions of images and material culture—can serve as a litmus test of the anxieties about whether received and conventionally accepted knowledge was, in fact, correct; about the temptations of accessing objective historical truths, even when they stemmed from a suspect source; and about how portraiture participated in the construction and legitimation of the truth in early modern Spain.

The arrival of the demons at the convent inaugurated a process of examining and evaluating the objects that the nuns used in their daily lives, beginning with the most prosaic, so that the inhabitants of the convent might compare how monastic life in seventeenth-century Madrid differed from that of the order's distant historical origins. One of the witnesses noted that "regarding the [nuns'] sandals the demon . . . described the form that they were to have," drawing—we infer—on the types of footwear that had been used centuries prior, in the times of Saint Benedict. The witness recounted, "The Prior [García Calderón] brought a book in which the sandals were painted . . . and it seemed that the more honest form was that which the demon had indicated, and they were made in that way."[24] Furthermore, "regarding the plates and bowls, the demon also told [them] about the kinds that had been used in the times of Saint Benedict, and they got rid of those that they had in the convent; and the truth is that those plates had always been disliked."[25] The authority of the demons' insight into the past took precedent over the knowledge conveyed in illustrated historical texts or in established quotidian practice, and it resulted in the immediate adjustment of the nuns' footwear and dishes to demonic specifications.

These anecdotal snapshots appear to reveal a desire—on the part of the nuns and their demons—that the convent be filled by historically accurate objects from the time of the order's founder, Saint Benedict. But there is a larger picture to be discerned if we focus on what the nuns' utterances might reveal about *why* such historically accurate objects were important and desirable. Beginning in the late fifteenth century, the Spanish monarchy embarked on a project of painfully transforming its dominions—in Iberia, in northern Europe, in the Americas, and in Asia—from multi- to uniconfessional. For all of its assurances of stability, however, early modern Catholicism in the Hispanic world was hardly monolithic, instead resembling a veneer of uniformity overlaid atop infinite local variations of spiritual practices. In some individuals, especially those within the ecclesiastical establishment, these recurring cases of unorthodoxy produced no small amount of anxiety, resulting in what Felipe Pereda terms "the desperate search for certainty" in Catholic spirituality of the early modern period.[26] One of the ways in which those individuals sought to secure their system of faith and, by extension, their place in the world was through anchoring their seemingly unstable present to a seemingly stable Christian past.

The nuns' interest in authentic plates and sandals resembled the manner in which they also cross-examined the convent's holy images of ancient and medieval saints for their truth value. Indeed, the inquisitorial tribunal learned that the demons had critiqued existing paintings that belonged to the nuns of San Plácido, communicating their insights to the convent's confessor, García Calderón, who noted their statements in his *cartapacio*. For example, one of the witnesses examined during the trial recalled that "when the prior Francisco García Calderón was shown a painting of the glorious patriarch Saint Benedict," he behaved as if he had actually seen the face of the medieval saint, which had been implicitly conveyed to him by the demons in a vision. The witness recounted, "Upon seeing the portrait he [García Calderón] declared: 'It is he [St. Benedict] [*el es*] . . . but he was older, and we never had someone there who would know how to portray him.'"[27] The prior drew on supernatural knowledge to declare that the convent's painting was, in actuality, a depiction of Saint Benedict. However, there were inconsistencies in how the convent's image represented its saintly prototype. The Benedict that García Calderón had seen in his vision was older than he appeared in the painting, and moreover the image was lacking in either accuracy or artistic skill. By claiming to know what long-deceased saints had actually looked like, the nuns—and demons—declared whether paintings, such as the convent's depiction of Saint Benedict, were "true portraits" (such that might fit within Acuña del Adarve's classification) or merely artistic interpretations of the saints that the images claimed to accurately depict.

Driven by this desire for accuracy, García Calderón also commissioned new images of the convent's saintly founder, drawing on demonic insight. Sister Juana, a nun resident in the convent, declared that "it was publicly known that the demon of sister Anastasia described the features and face [*facciones y rostro*] of the glorious Saint Benedict" and that the prior had a painter named Julio César Semín make drawings of the saint following these instructions and bring them to the nun. When García Calderón "asked Anastasia whether any of them were in accordance with the face of the saint, her demon responded that they were not."[28]

Reading this, a seventeenth-century participant in the events would be justified in assuming that the demons—and thanks to them, the nuns and their confessor—knew the true appearance of the saint, that is to say, what he had looked like in person, at a specific moment in his life. At one point, García Calderón had drawn on some form of demonic insight in order to evaluate the appearance of an extant painting of Saint Benedict, deeming it true to its model (even if it did differ in certain details). At another, a different demon described the saint's appearance to an artist who was then not able to render it to the demon's satisfaction. This was not an evaluation of the artistic quality of the drawings. Rather, it suggests that the artist was unable to render the physiognomy of Benedict in an accurate manner based on the demon's verbal description.

In the trial's papers, there is a simple drawing on a loose sheet, which appears to be the case's only surviving image (fig. 25). Like many pictorial materials included in inquisitorial cases, it was separated from the file at a later date, making unequivocal identification of its subject matter difficult. Archivists have catalogued the image as a portrait of the García Calderón.[29] However, it is more likely a representation of either the existing painting of Benedict evaluated by García Calderón or of one of the unsatisfactory drawings made by the painter Semín following "demonic instructions," which were brought into the inquisitorial chambers as evidence. Given the drawing's amateur technique, however, it is unlikely that it came from Semín's own hand. Rather, it appears to be the work of a notary who rendered not only the appearance of the image but also its frame and even the loop on which it is suspended from a small nail in the wall of the inquisitorial chamber. These details grant the drawing evidentiary character because

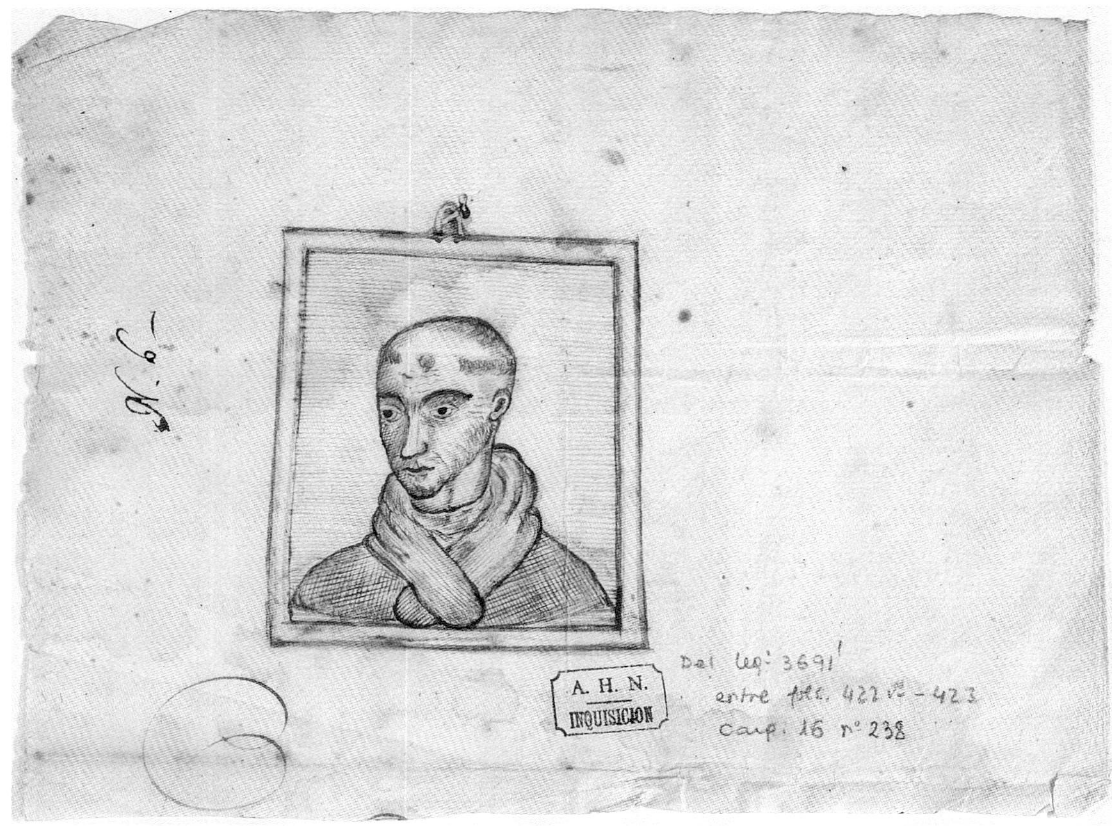

FIG. 25 Unidentified artist, after Julio César Semín, *Saint Benedict*, 1628. Pen and ink drawing on paper, 6.49 × 8.34 in. (16.5 × 21.2 cm). Ministerio de Cultura y Deporte, Archivo Histórico Nacional, Madrid, Inquisición. Mapas, Planos y Dibujos 238.

they self-consciously render the inquisitor's experience of seeing the image qua physical object, as it hung before him. In its subtle yet exacting focus on context, the image becomes a true portrait of the purportedly "true" portrait that was brought in to be examined during the trial.

The drawing undoubtedly depicts a Benedictine monk, as it shares certain characteristics with, for instance, El Greco's painting of Saint Benedict, including the order's tonsure, habit, and hood (fig. 26). In both El Greco's painting and in the notarial drawing, we see clear attempts at individualization, revealed in part by the aging of the faces with wrinkles on the foreheads and around the eyes. In contrast to the half-length figure in El Greco's painting of Saint Benedict, however, the drawing is sharply cut at the bust. This format suggests that the "true portrait" of Saint Benedict examined in the trial may have been designed to evoke contemporary paintings of the so-called modern saints. Saint Ignatius of Loyola's portraits are a good corollary here, as the Jesuits widely disseminated prints, paintings, and wax and plaster casts of the saint's face to serve as models for further images. The image of Ignatius held by Ribadeneira in Theodore Galle's print after Juan de

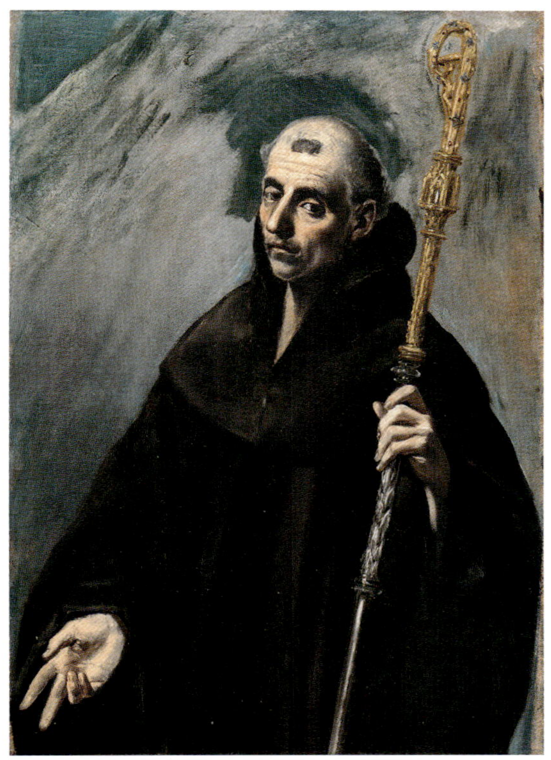

FIG. 26 El Greco (Doménikos Theotokópoulos), *Saint Benedict*, 1577–79. Oil on canvas, 45.6 × 31.8 in. (116 × 81 cm). Museo Nacional del Prado, Madrid. Photo: Museo Nacional del Prado / Art Resource, New York.

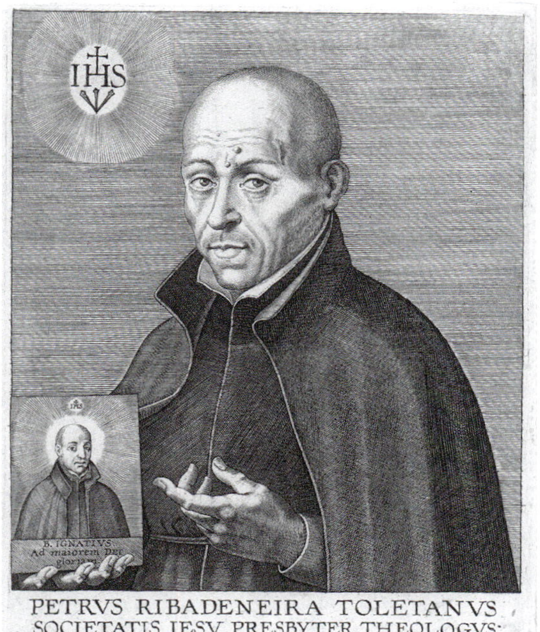

FIG. 27 Theodor Galle, after unidentified engraver, after Juan de Mesa, *Pedro de Ribadeneyra with a Portrait of Ignatius of Loyola*, after 1611. Engraving on paper, 4.8 × 6.9 in. (12.2 × 17.6 cm). Rijksmuseum, Amsterdam.

Mesa demonstrates one from among the numerous portraits of the future saint that circulated throughout the early modern Catholic world, which were often explicitly announced as *verdaderos retratos* (fig. 27). The inquisitorial drawing of Saint Benedict looks to, and models itself after, this type of true portrait, which is informed, in turn, by the ancient tradition and legitimacy of acheiropoietic images of Christ. The true portrait was the most historically authoritative type of holy image in post-Tridentine Catholic visual culture. In its vocal announcing of its truthfulness, however, it was also—paradoxically—quintessentially contemporary.

Ancient Saints

In early modern Catholic polities, various institutions—from religious orders, to municipal administrations, to the royal court—sought to portray virtuous individuals during their lives or soon after. They aimed to ensure that these images might serve as the stable basis for their future cults, should the individuals ever be elevated to sainthood by the Holy See.[30] At the same time, numerous ecclesiastical decrees forbade that depictions of individuals who had not been officially recognized by the Church should approximate depictions of actual saints. One way to circumvent such regulations and the subsequent threat of censorship was to insert the likenesses of noncanonized but already venerated individuals into the iconographies of actual saints, resulting in composite images that were formally akin to portraits *a lo divino* but differently motivated. These depictions covertly presented their protagonists—likely recognizable only to local audiences—as faithful imitators of the holy men and women who came before them.[31]

Patrons—both individual and institutional—also developed portrait-centric programs for the representations of already-canonized saints. Such a project was explicitly outlined in the 1576 contract signed by the painter Juan Fernández Navarrete, whom Philip II commissioned to create paintings of holy figures for the newly constructed basilica at the Escorial. The document states that "should one of the saints have a portrait from life, their painting shall be painted in conformity with that portrait, which shall be sought out with diligence wherever it may be."[32] Similarly, Pacheco insisted that "when there exists a true portrait of a given saint that has been made in death, or from life, or in some way, or when the features of their face are known through history, or through the information of someone who knew them, it must be given more credit than to a [portrait] made by the imagination. And therefore, it is a great consolation to follow the many portraits of the saints of our days that are venerated."[33] The physiognomic likeness possessed an aura of unmediated authenticity. By extension, images of saints that were based on portraits were prized for the believability and relatability that they conveyed to their audiences.

However, an image of an ancient figure, of whom no portraits survived, could hardly compete in veracity and vivacity with images of the modern saints. For this reason, Pacheco cites the Italian theorist Lodovico Dolce regarding images of Christ or of Saint Paul: "Whoever sees them should feel that they are seeing a true portrait."[34] Even those figures from whom portraits could not be taken, then, including long-deceased holy figures, were supposed to convince their viewers that their likenesses had been taken from life. This crucial requirement, common among early modern patrons and painters, provides a clue for the recurring mentions of Saint Benedict's true portrait in the San Plácido trial, especially if we attempt to read past the inquisitors' concern with demonic possession and speculate on the nuns' motivations. The focus on Benedict's likeness may have been undergirded, however implicitly, by the nuns' desire to see their order's ancient founder granted a similarly legitimate and real status as that possessed by various modern saints. Although closed away in the convent, the nuns would not have been impervious to the fascination with true portraits of saints that permeated early modern Hispanic society.

Catholic culture at this time generally adhered to the belief that things that were established and widespread were legitimate.[35] When individuals made or used images, they often did so by citing or reutilizing existing objects and practices. However, sometimes even small transformations of a common practice that occurred under the aegis of tradition could irreversibly push it from being sanctioned under the shelter of orthodoxy to being unsanctioned and threateningly unorthodox. The demons' evaluations of the verisimilitude of the convent's holy images against the "true" appearance of their models, as well as the drawings that were created following their specifications, were manifestations of an adherence to traditional image-based practices. However, they garnered the attention of the Inquisition for the extent to which they distorted those sanctioned models. The demonic perversions of images reveal the fragility of a number of foundational tenets of early modern Hispanic visual culture. These included the accuracy of historical images, which was challenged by the paintings and drawings of Saint Benedict, and the authority of sacred pictorial models, such as true portraits, which was enticingly enhanced and then threatened by demonic assessments of their accuracy.

Truth Authorized: The Portraits of Ignatius of Loyola

Acuña del Adarve was primarily concerned with Christological acheiropoietoi and, by extension, with the historical authority of the true portrait as an image type. However, as I have suggested above, the true portrait was also a very modern image. Beginning in the fifteenth century, the tradition of making *verae effigies* was self-consciously redeveloped for representing virtuous individuals. The corpus of Sienese depictions of Bernardino of Siena constituted some of the earliest "modern" true portraits, based, as they likely were, on the saint's death mask.[36] But it was not until the mid-sixteenth century that the Jesuit Order, as well as other primarily male religious orders, deployed the project of modern true portraiture on a global scale.[37] For the Jesuits, this effort was centered around the true portraits of its founder, Ignatius of Loyola, whose prospects for official canonization were deemed especially promising, even while he was still alive. The complex early history of Ignatius's portraits and the contentious debates they generated were fastidiously documented by at least one Jesuit chronicler, Cristóbal López, in an account titled *Relación de la forma que se tuvo en hazer el retrato de N.S.P. Ignacio de Loyola* . . . (Relation of the model that was used in making the portrait of our holy father Ignatius of Loyola . . .). The text, which remained unpublished until the nineteenth century, was originally written as an addendum to a 1612 autobiography of Ribadeneira. Should Ribadeneira himself have eventually become a candidate for sanctity, as many of the early Jesuits did, López's account would have become important evidence supporting his elevation to sainthood.[38] These debates provide a rare insight into how sixteenth- and seventeenth-century individuals conceived of the true portrait as a crucial tool in the articulation of early modern sanctity.

It may seem paradoxical, but—according to this and other accounts—it was only when Ignatius of Loyola died in 1556 that his admirers were finally able to portray their order's founder. While he was yet alive, Ignatius had repeatedly refused to sit for a portrait. Faced with Ignatius's disavowal of the medium, his followers had repeatedly engaged in surreptitious attempts to capture the future saint's likeness. Nevertheless, the man's countenance somehow always resisted translation onto paper or canvas.[39] As López recounts, the unhappy painter who tried and failed to represent the saint eventually "cast away his brush and declared: 'I have lost my art; God does not wish that this his servant be portrayed.'"[40] This story became a fixture in the saint's later hagiographies, with another text recalling that when the painter looked upon Ignatius's face, "he discovered so many different faces in it . . . and could not paint the portrait of our saint."[41] Ignatius's rejection of portraiture stood metonymically for his humility, and by extension, it acted as an implicit criticism of the vanity inherent to all portraiture, as analyzed in chapter 1.

The Jesuits were often considered to have been particularly (even threateningly) successful in using images in premeditated ways that, in later historiography, became synonymous with the expansive, universal power of the Catholic Church following the Council of Trent.[42] In this interpretation, in the decades following his death, Ignatius's true portrait became emblematic of the Society of Jesus's investment in a concerted image politics. Let us accept, for the moment, the claim that the Jesuits were more concerned with visual culture than most other early modern entities, leading them to formulate this supposedly exceptionally cohesive visual language. Although clearly too simplistic, such a platform allows us to inquire into the seeming inconsistencies in López's narrative about the "true portrait" of the Jesuit Order's founder. *Relación de la forma* is punctuated by indecision and disagreement regarding Ignatius's actual appearance in life and about the validity of his later representations. Moreover, the nearly legalistic focus on experiential eyewitness testimony demonstrates that, in López's account, the truth of Ignatius's true portrait was actually established and cemented through the emotional response and subjective judgment of the actors involved. Without supernatural evidence (of the kind provided by the San Plácido demons, for example), "truth" reveals itself to be a heavily mediated construct.

López first described the death mask that was taken from Ignatius's face immediately following his demise: "They bring a craftsman who understands [the process] and they have him cast a plaster model from the features of the deceased saint, in order to extract the most that they possibly might from his features. And it was done thusly."[43] There is in this description a fleeting admission of the fallibility of even this most indexical form of portraiture: the phrase "the most that they possibly might" (*lo más que pudieren*) reveals that there always remained something ineffable that was impossible to capture and that was perhaps permanently effaced by the transition from life into death, and from flesh into plaster.[44] Indeed, the death mask elided numerous important qualities of the person, chief among which was his or her enlivenment, and it presented the subject at a very specific moment of life—at its close—and not necessarily as he or she had been remembered. Once completed, Ignatius's mask served as the model for numerous other casts in both plaster and wax and for innumerable painted, drawn, sculpted, and engraved portraits. López himself bemoaned the diversity of images that this seemingly reliable matrix produced noting that "from this [model] [*patrón*] some portraits have been made that circulate, and they are so varied and different, and some of them so indecorous [*indevotos*] that it is a pity."[45]

The first of these portraits, by Jacopino del Conte, was painted in 1556 following Ignatius's death, and it served as the prototype for numerous paintings and prints (fig. 28).[46] A copy of Conte's portrait was brought to Madrid where it was seen by Ribadeneira, Ignatius's early friend and colleague. Echoing López's distress at many of the portraits, as López himself recounts, Ribadeneira deemed the painting greatly unsatisfactory, declaring that "this portrait is not a portrait of our Father; rather, it appears to be some comfortable, chubby cleric, or some laborer."[47] The issue appears to have stayed at the back of Ribadeneira's mind. Nearly thirty years after Ignatius's death, in 1585,

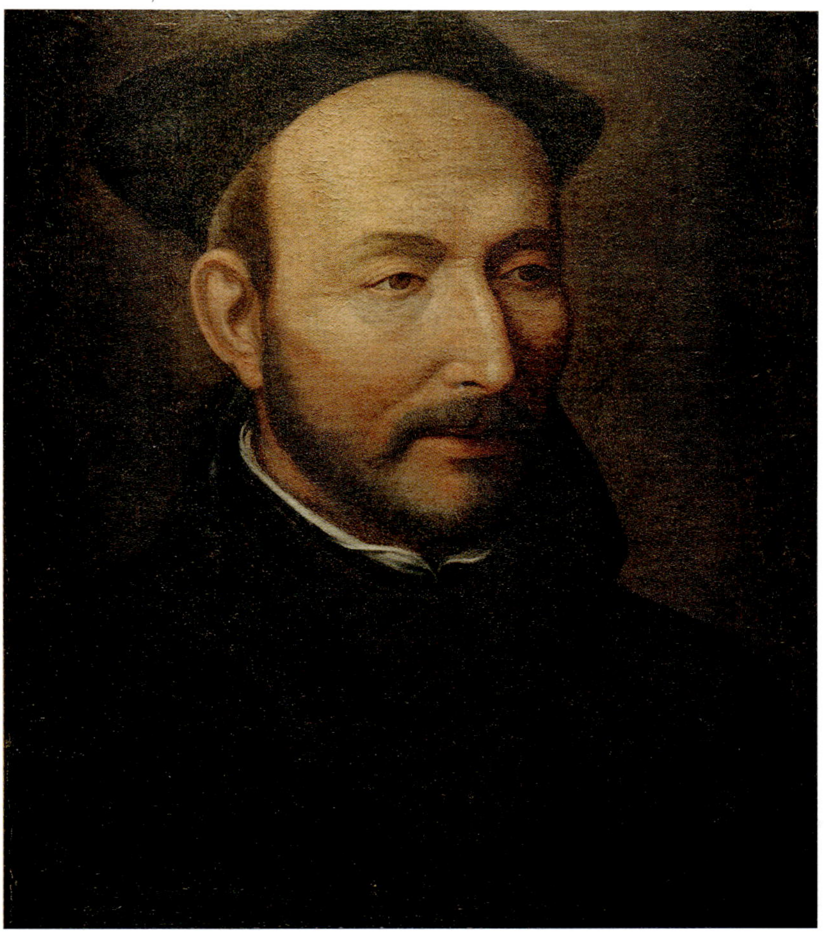

FIG. 28 Jacopino del Conte, *Ignatius of Loyola*, 1556. Curia Generalizia, Rome. Photo: akg-images.

he commissioned another likeness from Alonso Sánchez Coello, painter to King Philip II, based on a wax copy of Ignatius's death mask (fig. 29). Before he began work, the artist entrusted his labor to divine protection declaring: "I offer to do whatever possible on my part, and I place faith in God and in the intercession of his blessed saint [Ignatius] that he help me to do this so that it might be a good thing."[48] Such an invocation of supernatural assistance conceptually approximates the origin stories of images that had been made without human intervention and were therefore irrevocably true.

Like Conte's portrait, Sánchez Coello's painting also spawned numerous copies: for example, a small painting on copper depicts the saint with his recognizable physical features, including a bald head and pronounced nose; standardized attributes of holiness, including a halo; and a textual inscription that promises that this is the saint's *vera effigies*, or true likeness (fig. 30).[49] Additionally, the iconic format has been narrativized into a scene of penitential reflection and visionary experience through the addition of tears falling from the saint's eyes, which gaze up at a golden light that descends

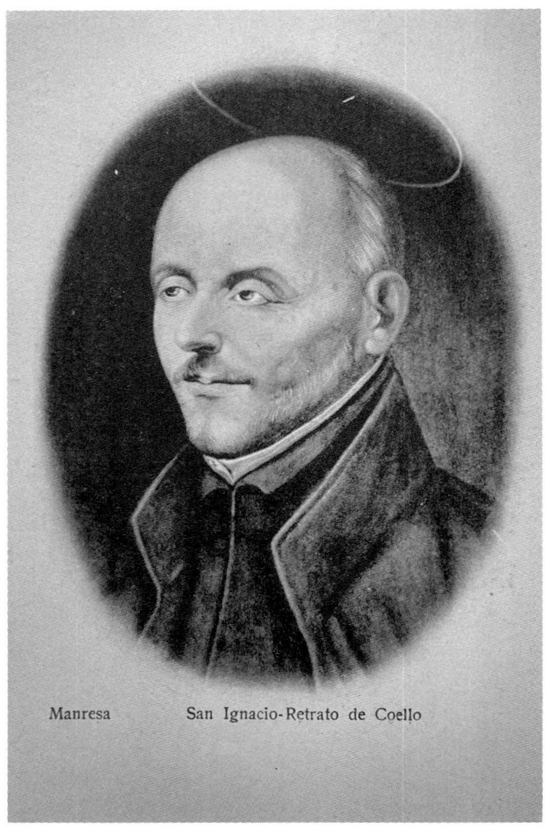

FIG. 29 Postcard with image of *Portrait of Ignatius of Loyola* by Alonso Sánchez Coello, 1585 (original destroyed). Formerly Jesuit College, Madrid. Photo: author.

from the upper left corner of the picture. Nevertheless, when another version of Sánchez Coello's portrait was sent to Rome, it met with the displeasure of, among others, Claudio Acquaviva, the order's general at the time, who criticized its failure in achieving verisimilitude. He noted that "those who knew our Father . . . say that it is not alike."[50]

The back and forth between Ribadeneira, Acquaviva, and various other members of the Jesuit order around the portraits made by Conte and Sánchez Coello reveals the difficulty of ascertaining a "true" likeness, even of someone who was relatively recently deceased and still remembered by many. Perhaps it was this very fact—that so many individuals who had known Ignatius in different moments of his life declared that they, too, remembered the future saint's appearance—that generated inevitable discrepancies. However, a seventeenth-century Catholic may not have been surprised by these disagreements over the future saint's "true portrait." Recall the hapless painter who seemed unable to capture the future saint's likeness. While alive, Ignatius had made it clear enough that he did not wish to be portrayed.

When faced with the uncertainty of where the truth lay, chroniclers like López had to turn to other means of ascertaining and conveying legitimacy. One effective way of doing so was invoking the vocabulary and turns of phrase common in legal proceedings. López rhetorically asks, "What certitude and testimony do we have that it resembles him and that it be a definite and true [*cierto y verdadero*] [portrait] of Our Saintly Father, and that might plainly be said: is this the true one?"[51] To this he responds by listing the reactions of viewers who had seen the portrait. These closely resemble the declarations from the inquisitorial trials discussed throughout this book, such as the trial from Puebla de los Ángeles, which will feature in chapters 3 and 4, where a witness legitimizes his declaration by saying that he "experienced, and publicly saw and heard" everything that he had just described.[52]

Indeed, the literary scholars Nicholas Spadaccini and Jenaro Talens note that "the rhetorical first person"—similar to the testimonial character of the enthusiastic declarations from López's account—"has two distinct and articulated functions: to construct a self and to use this construction for the

FIG. 30 Unidentified painter, *Saint Ignatius of Loyola*, mid- to late 1600s. Oil on copper, 7.625 × 5.5 in. (19.36 × 13.97 cm). Haggerty Museum of Art, Marquette University, museum purchase, gift of Marquette University Jesuit Community, Collection of the Haggerty Museum of Art.

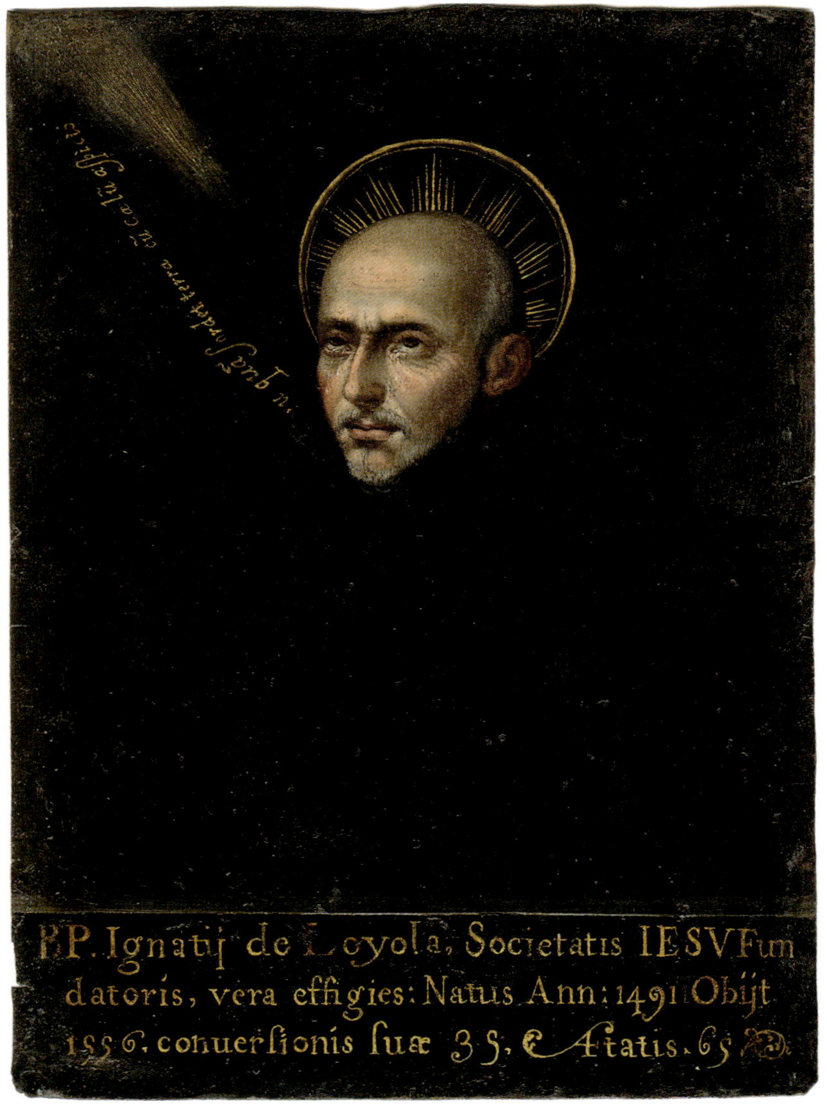

validation of truth."[53] Some scholars have shown that the Spanish Inquisition was unique in its focus on individuals providing extensive autobiographical details in their testimonies (and that this may have been a catalyst for literature written in the first person in the Hispanic world) while others have connected the performance of affect on theatrical stages with the veracity of witness declarations on inquisitorial stands.[54] The multisensory, affective, subjective, and experiential character of such declarations appealed to the notion of truthfulness—granting the readers of such texts or the inquisitorial audiences of such declarations—a sense of certainty in what they were being told, rather than necessarily conveying the absolute truth itself.[55]

In the 1587 López text, one of the first responses to the finished portrait by Sánchez Coello is that of a friend of Ignatius who, upon seeing the image, seemingly spontaneously "stood up from his chair, took off his cap, and made a great and low bow [*grande y profunda inclinacion*] with his entire body" and then proceeded to describe how well he had known the sitter.[56] Such an obeisant reaction from the man, the reader infers, would have been unlikely if the portrait of Ignatius had not captured its sitter's likeness extremely accurately. Furthermore this response corresponds to Acuña del Adarve's belief that the impact of true portraits on their viewers was supposedly distinct from that of other types of images: "In sacred effigies there is a grandeur and majesty that, when seen, moves, affects, and obligates [their viewers] to greater veneration and adoration . . . which we do not see in those who look at other similar painted images, even when they are of much devotion."[57] Another witness of Ignatius's image is described as having "seen Our Father, and known him," declaring about the portrait: "This is Father Ignatius, there is no doubt."[58] Rather than providing concrete proof of truth, these declarations created the impression of truthfulness by marshaling descriptions of seemingly precognitive emotional reactions that the portrait produced.

In 1585, Ignatius had been dead for nearly three decades. Only supernatural knowledge could bolster fallible human memory in order to confirm the saint's features. To that end, López declared the portrait to be a fully collaborative endeavor, made with "the care and assistance of Father Ribadeneira, the desire and labor of Alonso Sánchez, and primarily the grace of God, and the intercession of his saint [Ignatius]."[59] Aside from López's wishful intentions, however, he could do little to prove that the portrait actually possessed divine approbation. Therefore, he turned to the king as the next most significant source of authority in the early modern Hispanic world. In López's telling, when Philip II saw Sánchez Coello's portrait of Ignatius, whom he immediately recognized from the painting, he asked the painter: "¿Pues cómo de aquel muerto le podistes vos hazer al vivo?," which can be translated as "How were you able to make this dead [man] alive?" or "How were you able to take this dead man's portrait from life?" When the painter explained how he and Ribadeneira had collaborated to enliven and add veracity to the information they had gleaned from the cast of Ignatius's face, the king declared, "I knew Father Ignatius; this is his face."[60] In doing so, the truth of Ignatius's portrait became doubly legitimized: both through the authority of the royal word and through the king's eyewitness experience of having seen Ignatius's face.

Although the disagreements over the *verdadero retrato* of Saint Ignatius show just how highly subjective truth was, the notion of *lo verdadero*—the truthful—was nevertheless consistently deployed in the articulation of the sacred in early modern Catholicism. López's own biases must also be taken into account, considering that he was secretary and companion to Ribadeneira for many years. Even though he acknowledged that important figures like Acquaviva criticized Ribadeneira's portrait, López appears to have sided with his superior's view on the matter, presenting Sánchez Coello's portrait as the authoritative version. In the account of Ignatius's portrait, Ribadeneira and López ensured that its truthfulness derived from three distinct sources, which, when mutually present, enshrined it as irreproachable. First, the truth of the portrait was confirmed by the subjective experience of the individuals who saw it and had visceral reactions to it, as occurred in the case of the ecclesiastic who was compelled, seemingly unconsciously, to bow before the image upon first seeing it. Second, the truth of the image drew on institutional power. When the king declared the image to be surprisingly lifelike, he placed the weight of his authority behind the image's claim to being the definitive likeness of the future saint. Third, the truth of the image rested on tradition. By simply describing the portrait of Ignatius as *verdadero*, or truthful, the text implicitly compares it to holy images of Christ, such as the Veronica, that stood at the head of a long tradition of using images in Christianity.[61] Moreover, the iconic format of the saint's portrait connects it to ancient images that, through their presumed age, were deemed to be unmediated. Alexander Nagel and Christopher S. Wood argue that "the strangeness of the Eastern icons read in the West not as conventional, but as truth itself."[62] The reception of Byzantine icons in quattrocento Europe generated a number of experiments with painting images that would replicate these icons' truncated form and "intimate 'zoom' effect," as characterized by Nagel and Wood.[63] These are precisely the features that define the various true portraits of Saint Ignatius and that we also recognize from the inquisitorial notary's drawing of the demonically inspired image of Saint Benedict. To an early modern individual, each of these three sources of authority would have likely represented a compelling certification of the portrait's authenticity.

The notion of the divine (or demonic) origin of a true portrait that is explored in both Acuña del Adarve's 1637 book and in the inquisitorial trial of the nuns of San Plácido in the late 1620s was already present in López's 1587 account of the true portrait of Ignatius of Loyola. Indeed, his description of that portrait as a collaborative endeavor between human and divine actors brings it into conversation with the acheiropoietic tradition of images not made by human hands. Furthermore, López's mention of Philip II's authoritative exclamation when confronted with Ignatius's true portrait ("I knew Father Ignatius; this is his face") closely resembles García Calderón's equally authoritative declaration about the portrait of Saint Benedict: "It is he." The king's authority stemmed from his privileged status as "most Catholic" ruler, while García Calderón drew on supernatural sources of information that, we infer, allowed him to compare the image with its sacred model and opine on its verisimilitude. Although neither image was *non manu facta*, thereby falling into the lowest category of true portraiture, they were both elevated out of their lesser position by privileged, authoritative declarations concerning the extreme degree of faithfulness with which they captured their subjects' likenesses.

Ignatius's Ugliness and the Virtue of Imperfection

In paintings that aspired to the truthfulness of the *vera effigie*, it was logical for artists to carefully render a saint's appearance, including their imperfections, which further enhanced the impression of verism.[64] Indeed, a lack of idealization was stressed in some early modern art-theoretical writings as desirable in portraiture.[65] With time, however, these idiosyncratic characteristics assumed the function of standardized attributes, like the physical objects, including keys, swords, books, or animals, that were used to identify ancient and

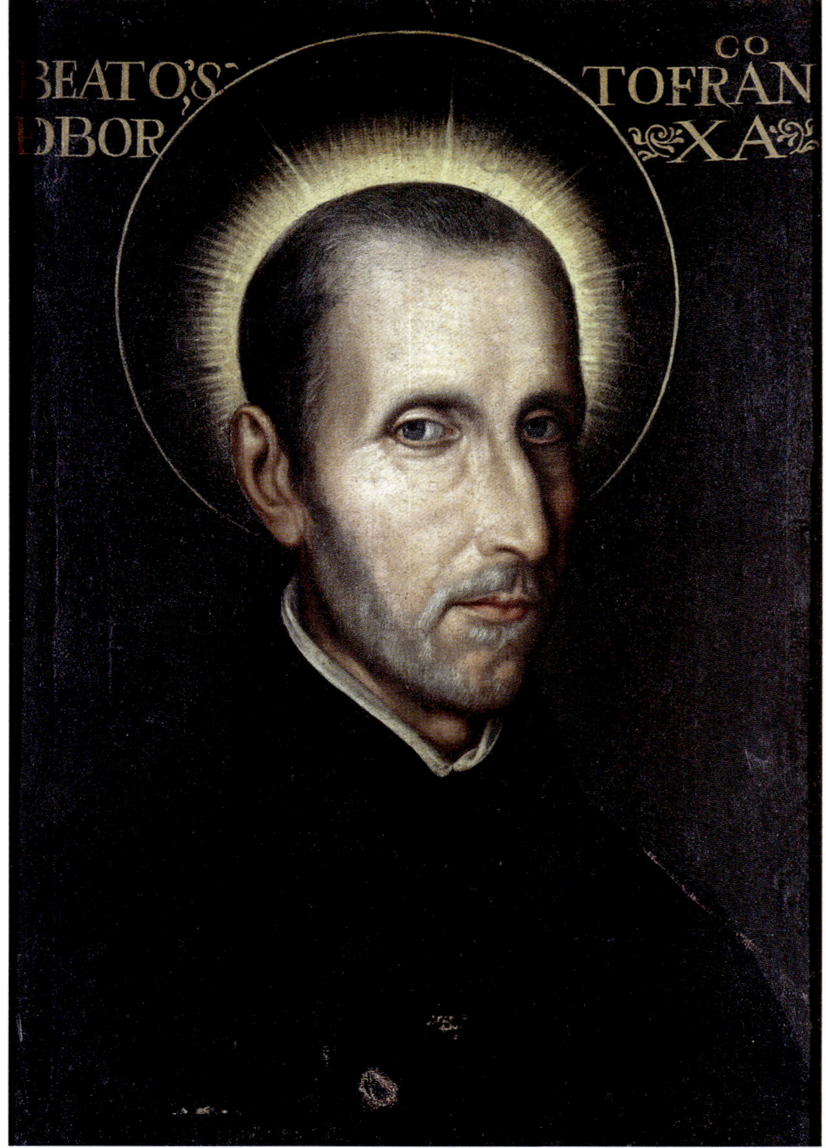

FIG. 31 Unidentified painter, *Saint Francisco de Borja*, seventeenth century. Monasterio de las Descalzas Reales, Madrid. Photo: Album / Art Resource, New York.

more established holy figures. Reduced to the role of attributes, such physical features nevertheless maintained an aura of authenticity, even when they were appended to otherwise entirely generic countenances. Such a deindividualization of the portrait likenesses of saints often—but not always—happened when the images were made at a geographical or temporal remove from the saint's originating context.

In chapter 3 I argue that the desire for portrait-like sacred pictures may have been one of the motivations behind repainting extant portraits with religious attributes, making a representation of an ancient saint like Sebastian as present and believable as that of any living individual. But were there other reasons for stressing verisimilitude in representations of new saints, including Ignatius Loyola or his fellow Jesuit Francisco de Borja (fig. 31)? Why did it matter that they have standardized physical appearances? Could they not simply be recognized by their attributes, as had traditionally been the case? Beyond the growing interest in physiognomy and its relation to virtue, in an image of a saint, I suggest, portrait-like "realness" preempted that image's misuse.[66] The emergence of the portrait *a lo divino* in the fifteenth century, in which secular individuals commissioned portraits of themselves in the guise of saints, had opened up sacred imagery to the problematic appropriation by any living person. Anyone with means could demand that they be depicted as a Saint Sebastian or Saint Lucy, both of whom had no surviving likenesses.

In contrast, a saint who already had a more or less recognizable likeness—like Ignatius or Francisco de Borja—could not, at least in theory, be commandeered for the advancement of an individual's or family's agenda, even if that agenda was the meditative unmaking of the self discussed in chapter 1. Should someone else's face have been inserted into an image of Ignatius, that image would arguably cease being a representation of Ignatius. To those who had at least once seen a representation of the saint, it would be impossible to extract his portrait from the category of sacred imagery—so imbricated were his iconography and his cult with an idea of what he had looked like. By relying on the portraits of their founders and other venerated members—and demanding uniformity in their deployment—the Jesuits and other male religious orders, including the Oratorians, Dominicans, Carmelites, Mercedarians, and Franciscans, had shrewdly designed a new form of religious image.[67] They had also, however subconsciously, replicated the interconnected early histories of portraiture and religious painting, wherein sacred icons were understood to be portraits of holy figures.[68] In doing so, these orders crafted some of the most stable image cults of early modernity. In the case of Ignatius, his images remained legible as sacred because of the order's uniform reliance on the saint's likeness (even though, paradoxically, that likeness was highly disputed). Ignatius's images, moreover, retained their sacrality not only when they were recognizably rendered as sacred pictures with halos and other codified attributes but even when they were simple portraits, as in the prototype painted by Sánchez Coello.[69]

Idiosyncratic facial features, including imperfections, came to play an attribute-like function in portraits of modern saints. However, premodern physiognomic theory often posited that external imperfections potentially mirrored internal ones.[70] Such is the tension that emerges in portraits of Ignatius of Loyola, in which baldness is a prominent and recurrent feature. In early modernity, baldness could hold negative connotations, as made patent in a hagiography of Ignatius published in Madrid in 1685. The text refers a case from Modena, in which a priest affixed a printed portrait of Ignatius in the home of four sisters who had been possessed by demons. In response, "the demons began to scream horribly, saying: 'this image is [a portrait] of Saint Ignatius, Founder of the Company [of Jesus], by which we are gravely tormented.' And with rabid fury they insulted the saint calling him 'skinned [*pelado*], lame, and cross-eyed.' When asked why they called him this

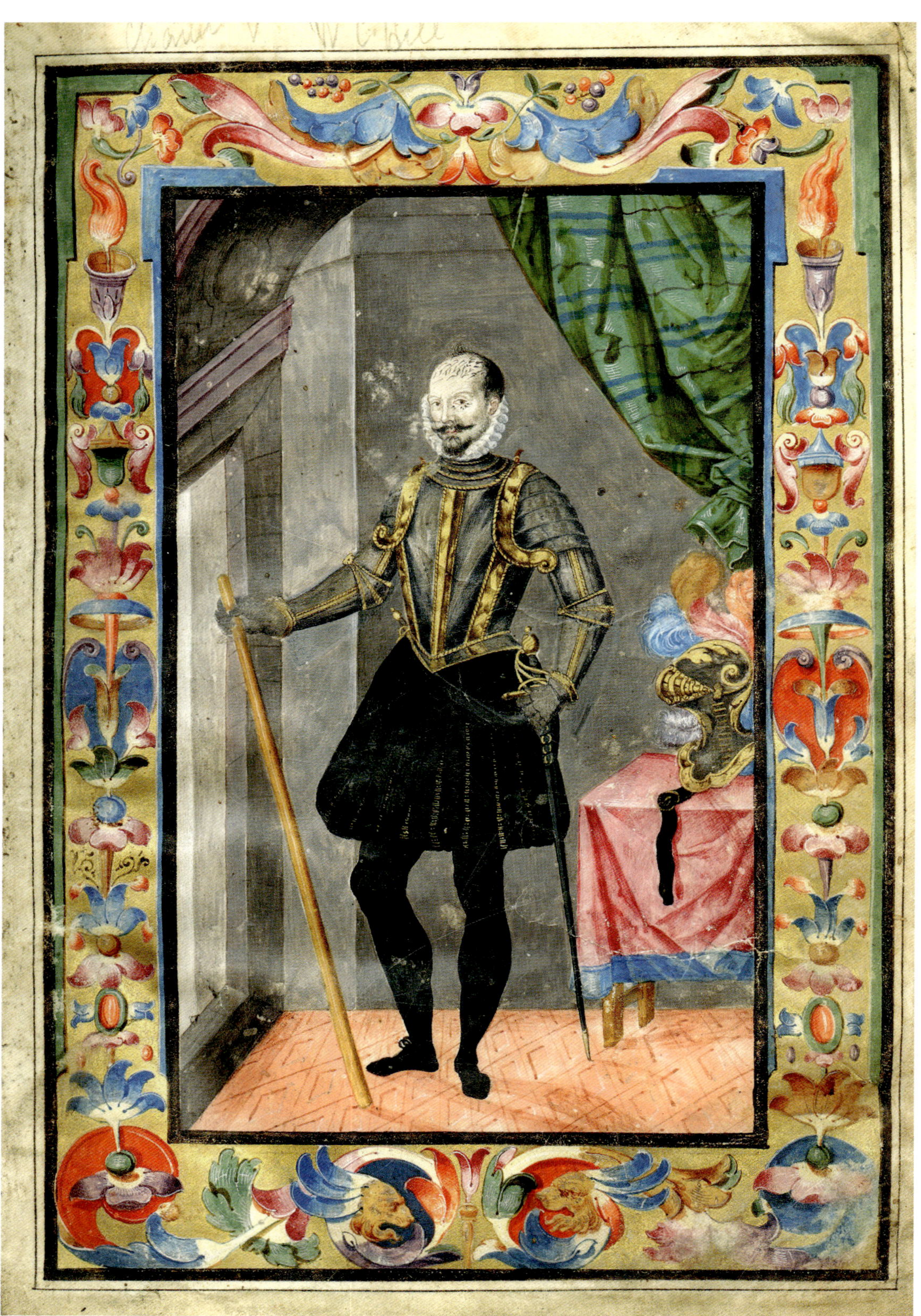

way they responded that he was bald and did not have much of a beard, and his legs were uneven, and one was broken, and that they called him 'cross-eyed' [*vizco*] because he had been at risk of losing his sight for the abundance of tears [he cried]."[71]

The demons targeted the saint's physical imperfections, in particular his "skinned" baldness, in order to mock him. Indeed, hair loss was, in early modern medical texts that drew on Galen, considered to be a medical condition associated with humoral imbalance. One text claimed that baldness derived from "an incurable passion" and was implicitly associated with lust (it did not affect castrates and, surprisingly, stutterers).[72] Baldness, we can also infer, was considered to be a visual imperfection. In a *carta ejecutoria* (nobility patent) issued in Granada in 1533, there is an illuminated page, likely inserted into the volume at a later date, with a portrait of a male sitter, which was subjected to a clumsy later attempt to obscure the sitter's baldness with dozens of quick pen strokes (fig. 32).

However, the "imperfection" of baldness could also signify honesty, given the period association of wigs with deceitfulness. Covarrubias notes that "in vile people, the wig is suspicious, because those without ears [*desorejados*, i.e. those punished through auricular mutilation] use it to cover that [which they] lack."[73] Furthermore, there were important precedents of saints being represented as aged and balding, the most notable being Saint Peter and the numerous ascetic saints, including Jerome and Paul the Hermit. In portraits of Ignatius, the saint's "honest" baldness became more than only an identifying attribute; it could as be read as a virtuous imperfection, and it may have served as a reminder of the saint's indiscretions from a youthful time, now long past, in which his actions had indeed stemmed from the humoral passions that he had successfully overcome. Helen Hills notes that in early modern Neapolitan portrait frontispieces, future saints were cast "as self-conscious shapers of their holy experience, rather than as arbitrarily afflicted by an imponderable deity from without."[74] Similarly, Ignatius's lack of hair could have reminded the viewers of his portraits about the redemptive, if perhaps not fully physically restorative, potential of one's self-conscious commitment to Christ at a later point in life.

FIG. 32 Unidentified painter, *Portrait of a Nobleman*, from *Carta executoria a pedimento de Garcia Gonçalez hidalgo vecino de villa de Alanis*, after 1533. Watercolor on parchment. Hispanic Society of America, New York MS Ex 1633 Gr. Photo courtesy of the Hispanic Society of America, New York.

Gradations of Verisimilitude: True Portraits of Saint Teresa

Just as Ignatius became an emblematic figure for the Society of Jesus, his near-contemporary Teresa of Ávila became a major iconographic source in the image politics of the Carmelite order, of which she was a reformer. In the case of the vast majority of depictions of Ignatius of Loyola, the saint's wrinkles and balding head corresponded with a modern ecclesiastical sensibility that promoted naturalism, while rejecting the simplistic association of that which was beautiful with that which was good. The corpus of images based on Teresa's true portrait looked very different from that of Ignatius, and this in spite of the fact that Teresa had agreed to sit for a portrait from life, which Ignatius had refused.[75] Teresa's likeness was painted by a friar and amateur painter named Juan de la Miseria at the behest of her confessor, Jerónimo Gracián

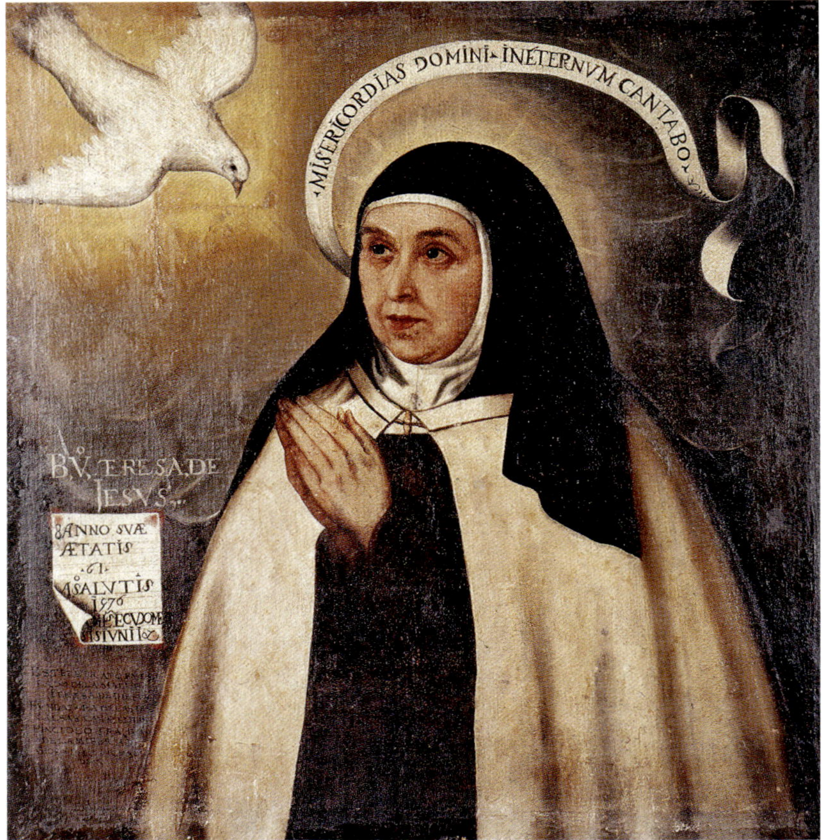

FIG. 33 Juan de la Miseria (Juan Narduck), *Saint Teresa of Ávila*, 1576. Oil on canvas. Monasterio de San José del Carmen, Seville. Photo: Album / Art Resource, New York.

(fig. 33).[76] According to one early eighteenth-century biography of the saint (one of many where the episode is recounted), Teresa saw the finished painting and "recognizing how little she resembled it she said with good humor . . . : 'God forgive you, friar Miseria, that you have already made me suffer here that which God knows, and on top of that you have painted me ugly and rheumy.'"[77] Luis Méndez Rodríguez suggests that this description ("you have painted me ugly") was a complaint on the part of the future saint, but the matter is likely more complex.[78] The author of the text notes that the sitter not only deemed her depiction to be unflattering but also points out "how little she resembled" the painted image. By virtue of being painted from life, the portrait possessed authority as a "true image," but Miseria had failed to achieve likeness, producing an image that falsely laid claim to the implied truthfulness of portraiture. Nevertheless, the painting served as the originator of a vast corpus of images.

According to Teresa's possibly apocryphal declaration, the portrait depicted her in an unattractive manner, but the saint's followers disputed that she had been anything but comely in life. For instance, Francisco de Ribera, Teresa's early biographer, noted that "in her youth she was lovely and even after becoming old she looked very good."[79]

Gracián remarked that "our Blessed Teresa was not, in her time, ugly in the face. And although some of her portraits that circulate around here do not show much beauty, that is because she was portrayed already being sixty years old,"[80] while the Discalced Carmelite María de San José wrote of Teresa that "she was in all ways perfect."[81] San José's glowing judgment of the future saint's appearance was not diminished by the three "little warts" [*verrugas pequeñas*] that Teresa had on her upper lip, even though the word was consistently used in period sources as a marker of shame and ugliness.[82] Perhaps this is why other authors used the term *lunar*, or beauty spot, instead of *verruga* to describe Teresa's face.[83] In any case, there is a discrepancy between the portrait painted by Miseria and the perceptions by Teresa's contemporaries of her appearance in life. Ribera praised Gracián for commissioning the portrait from Miseria in the first place but lamented that he had not "looked for the best painter in Spain for it, to portray such an illustrious person with even more lifelikeness [*mas al vivo*], for the consolation of many."[84]

Teresa's canonization in 1622 marked the beginning of a significant increase in artistic representations of the saint, with many of these copying Miseria's portrait closely. For instance, seventeenth-century Spanish painter Antonio Bisquert remained faithful to Miseria's prototype but inserted it into narrative or multifigural scenes, playing with temporal distance and crafting complex metapictorial conceits. For a painting of Teresa writing in her study (fig. 34), Bisquert relied on Miseria's model, adapting and expanding it to depict the saint in the moment of receiving divine inspiration.[85] By including two secular figures who kneel before her, Bisquert played here with the division of profane and secular space that was familiar from contemporary imagery, including from *cartas ejecutorias*. Newly nobilitated families commissioned artists to decorate these documents with portraits and religious images, highlighting their lineages and their piety. In an example from 1618, the family members of Diego Jusepe de Montoya, the successful petitioner, pray before Saint Anthony of Padua (fig. 35). The image is purposefully ambiguous. Are they praying before a painting or a highly lifelike sculpture, set into a niche decorated with landscape painting? Aside from the carefully rendered altar frontal with a scalloped border, little suggests that the depiction of Anthony is actually an image. Diego's relatives thereby inhabit the same space as the saint, who is as "real" as they are. Similarly, in Bisquert's painting, the nun and ecclesiastic pray before Teresa herself (her bare foot emerges from beneath the green tablecloth on the composition's central axis) just as much as they pray before an *image* of Teresa. Bisquert paints the saint in close accordance with Miseria's true portrait, which flexibly adapts to the narrative needs of his composition. The early modern portrait, including the true portrait of a saint, was tractable rather than static, dynamically inhabiting new contexts unto which it bestowed the legitimacy of its prototype.

Regardless of the care that a painter like Bisquert took in referencing the true portrait of the saint, others departed from it drastically, as evinced by images of Teresa painted by and after José de Ribera. In one such version from Seville, Teresa's face is youthful, with rosy cheeks, full lips, and improbably large eyes (fig. 36). Gone is the slightly jowly and wrinkled countenance from Miseria's portrait, and gone are the characteristic warts around Teresa's lips. Such images of a young Teresa can be explained as occurring in an earlier moment

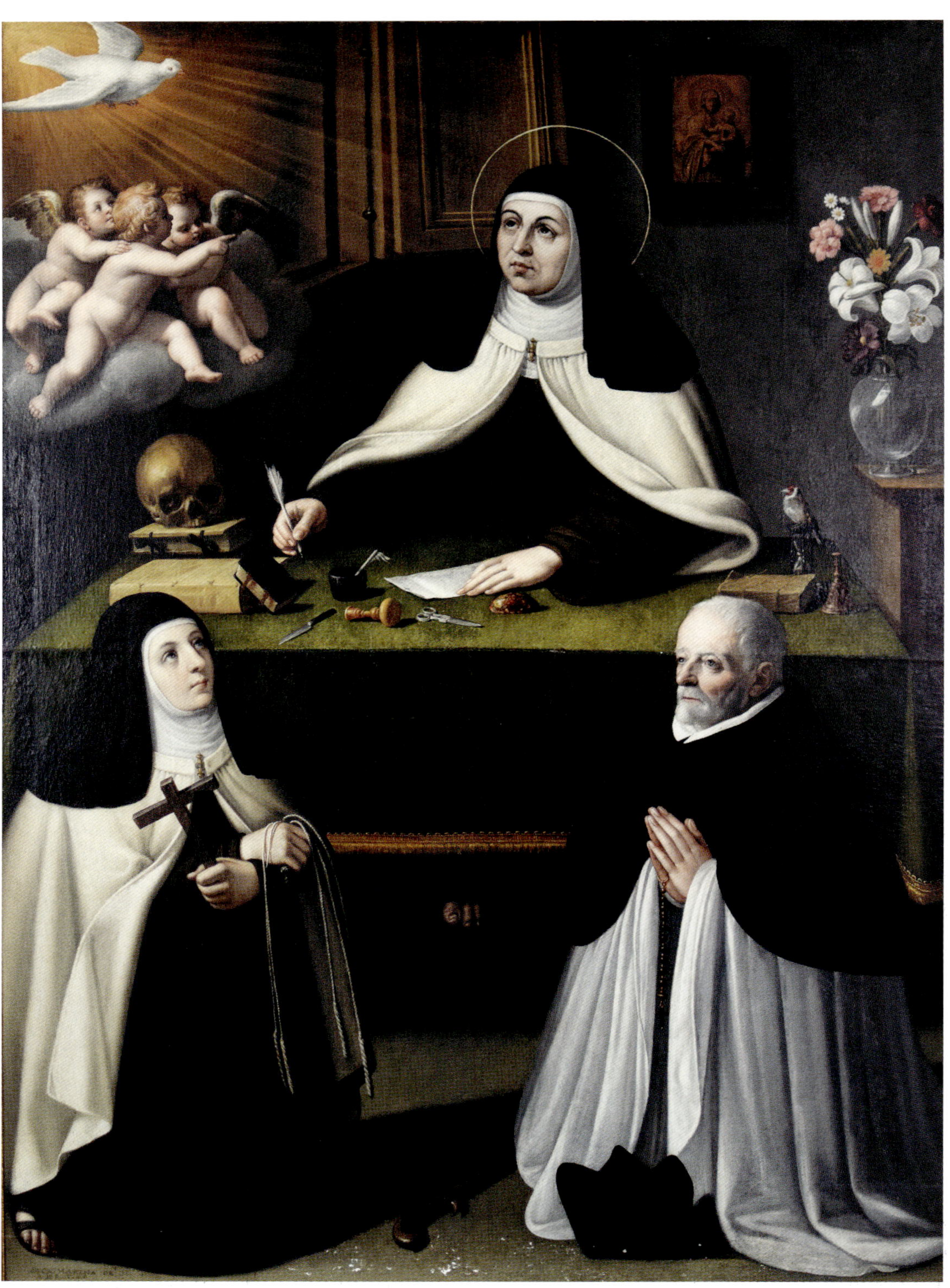

FIG. 34 (*opposite*) Attributed to Antonio Bisquert, *Saint Teresa Writing*, 1628–31. Oil on canvas, 76.3 × 55.1 in. (194 × 140 cm). Museo de Arte Sacro, Teruel. Photo: Belén Díez Atienza.

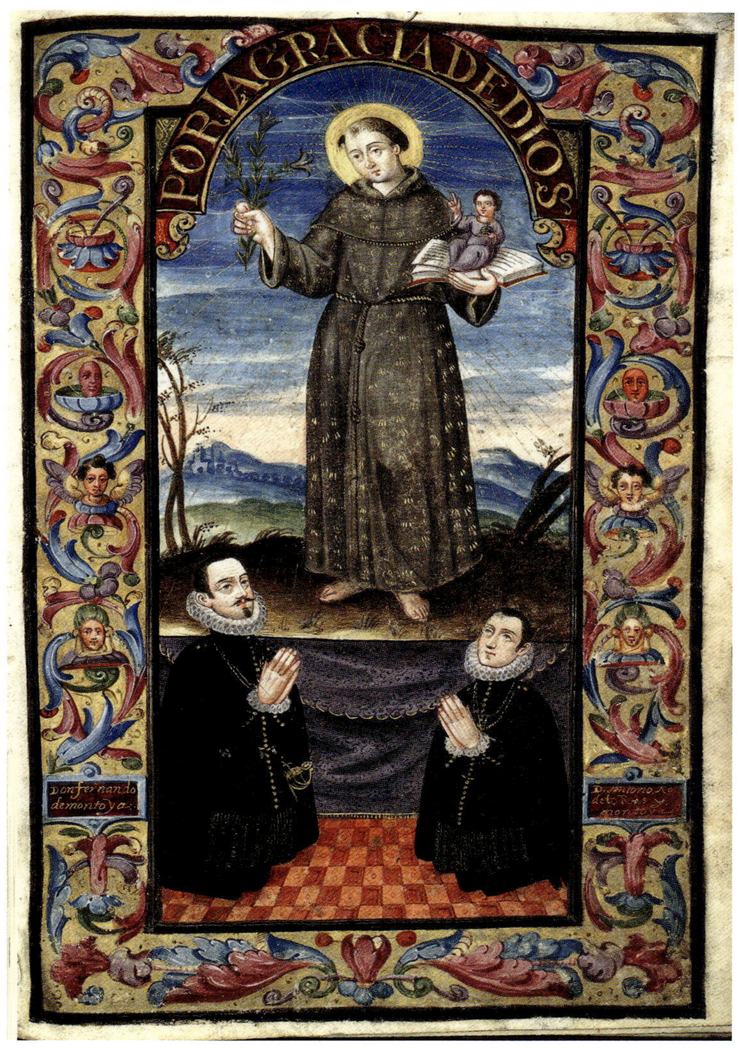

FIG. 35 Unidentified painter, *Illustration from Nobility Patent of Diego Jusepe de Montoya*, 1618. Tempera and gold leaf on parchment, 12.2 × 8.2 in. (31 × 21 cm). Biblioteca Histórica de la Universidad Complutense de Madrid, BH MSS 297, fol. 2r.

of her life or as reflecting the extreme beauty that her face took on during her visionary experiences, which was how the Mercedarian theologian and art theorist Juan Interián de Ayala recommended that she be painted.[86] Recalling the ambiguities surrounding the "true portrait" of Ignatius of Loyola, here, too, we observe that accuracy could have gradations. Perhaps it is because of the early criticism of Miseria's so-called true portrait of Teresa from 1576, including by the saint herself, that there is little sense that her representations uniformly adhere to that painting as a model.

Ribera's painting reveals that Teresa's three warts were inconsistently included in her portraits. When they did appear, they were often added to an otherwise entirely generic face, becoming,

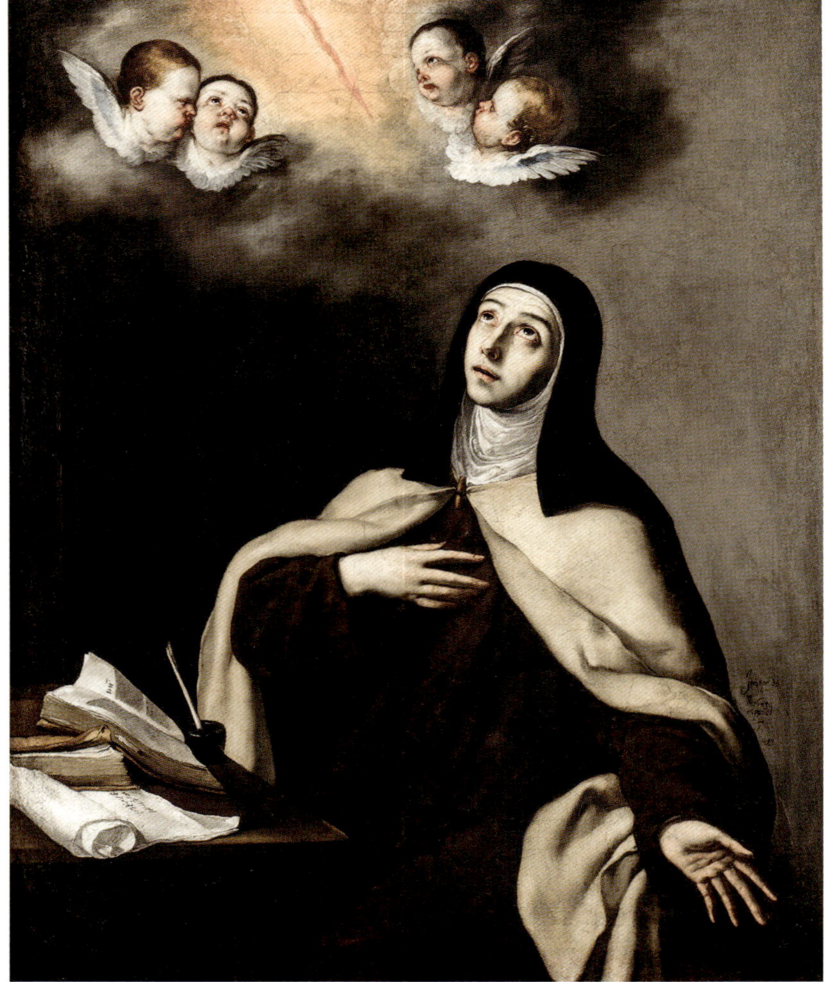

FIG. 36 José de Ribera, *Saint Teresa of Ávila*, 1630. Oil on canvas, 51.625 × 41.625 in. (131 × 106 cm). Museo de Bellas Artes de Sevilla, Seville. Photo: Pepe Morón, provided by Archivo del Museo de Bellas Artes de Sevilla.

like Ignatius's baldness, what Irene Winter calls a "signature trait": a diagnostic characteristic—and, more important, an imperfection—that served to identify the saint.[87] But as often as not, Teresa's countenance was left unblemished by warts. Similarly, it is difficult to discern much, if any, individualization of facial features in the enormous corpus of representations of another seventeenth-century woman saint, Rose of Lima. Although there survives a portrait that the Italian painter Angelino Medoro was said to have painted while the saint was on her deathbed, which spawned numerous copies (fig. 37), Saint Rose is frequently represented with an entirely generic face.[88] Nowhere is this more clear than in a painting by Juan Rodríguez Juárez, which includes a portrait of a female donor in prayer to a scene of Rose receiving a vision of the Christ Child, who hands her an eponymous rose (fig. 38).[89] Whereas the youthful Mexican donor would likely be

FIG. 37 Angelino Medoro, *Saint Rose of Lima*, n.d. Museo de Arte Religioso y Catedral de Lima, Lima. Photo: Daniel Giannoni Succar.

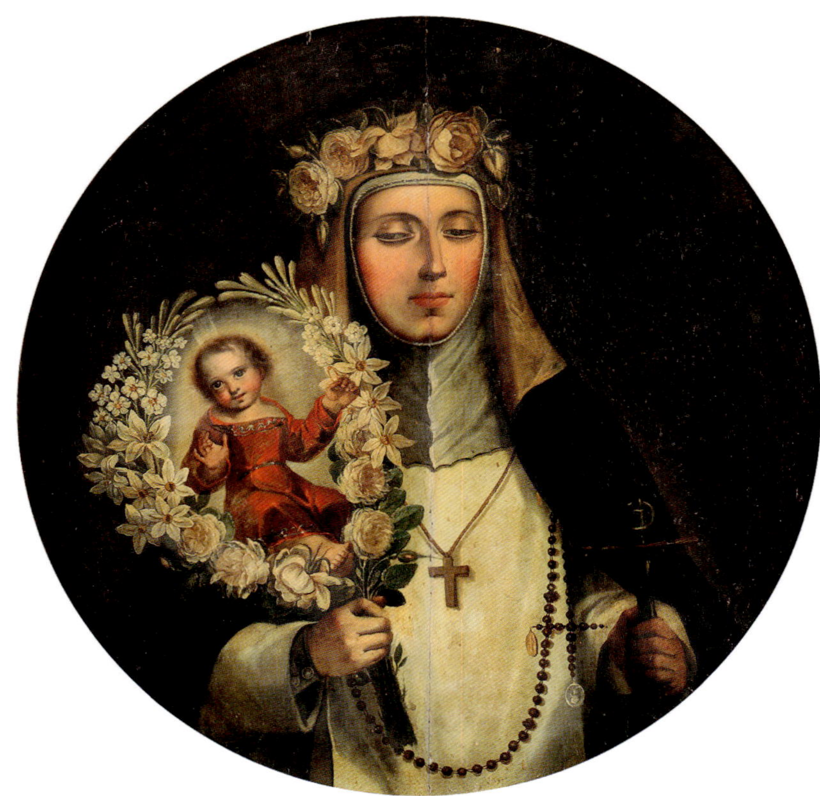

unmistakable from a lineup of other women her age, based on the care with which Rodríguez Juárez rendered her idiosyncratic facial features (not to mention her spectacular garments and jewelry), the saint's face is unmemorable and evacuated of all specificity.

Why, in a period of increasing focus on individualized likeness did Teresa's and Rose's depictions often tend toward the generic, particularly when compared with those of male saints like Ignatius or Francisco de Borja, who were usually represented with some portraitistic features? Perhaps it is because Teresa was nearly always shown in the robes of the Carmelite order, which represented a sufficiently codified, recognizable, and exclusive marker of her saintly identity, at least until the 1669 canonization of the Florentine Maria Maddalena de Pazzi, who was the only other female Carmelite to be recognized as a saint in the seventeenth century.[90] What is more likely, however, is that a gendered concept of beauty may have interfered in attempts to craft for Teresa, as well as for other women saints like Rose, a standardized, veristic representation, based on their actual appearances in mature age or at the time of their deaths. As the example of Rodríguez Juárez's painting makes clear, it was not a lack of interest in portraiture that led to the vagueness of these holy women's faces, considering the incisiveness of his depiction of the donor in prayer before Saint Rose.

In representations of saints, what I term the "virtue of imperfection" challenged the correlation

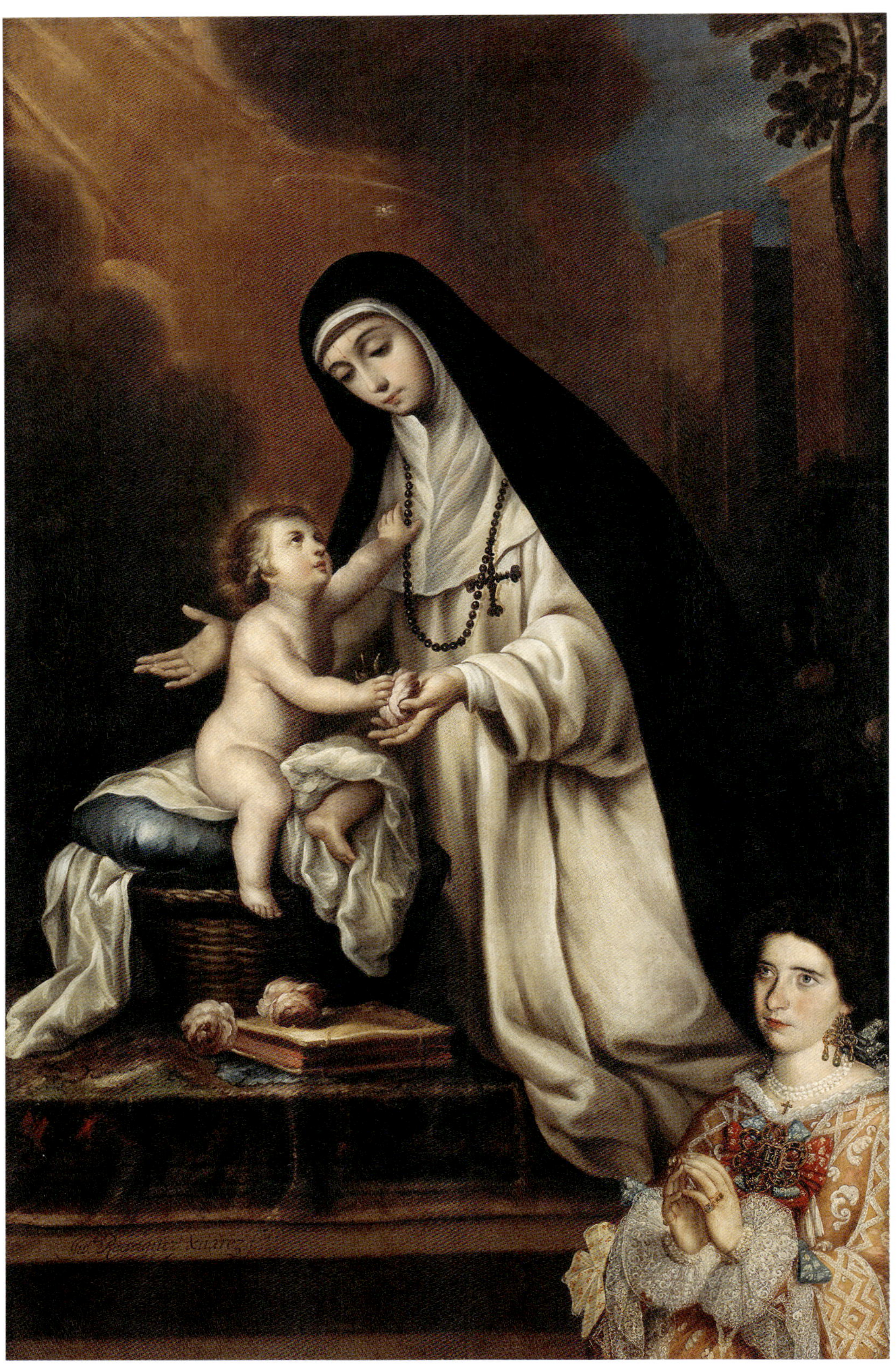

between virtue and beauty, particularly because the latter could be associated with deceit and malicious intent. A stanza from a sonnet that appears in Camerino's 1655 novel *La dama beata* deploys this common topos: "The devil often transfigures / the face into a divine thing, / the woman lies by her face, / as do many who are lovely."[91] Indeed, pictorial depictions of elderly male saintly hermits like Jerome and Anthony being tormented by visions of lustful, merry, and beautiful young women proliferated in early modern Spain and Latin America. Furthermore, future or would-be saints privileged a denial of self, including through bodily mortification and denial of sustenance. These practices challenged the body's predisposition to comfort by exposing it to extreme situations, such as pain, discomfort, hunger, or thirst. The product of these practices was also, inevitably, a body that was damaged, decrepit, and derelict—in a word, a body that was ugly. As I argue in relation to Ignatius's baldness, physical ugliness could coexist as a counterpart to, and even register of, spiritual perfection, and artists eagerly took up the possibilities it presented for early modern representations of sanctity, as evinced by Francisco de Borja's gaunt face or Pedro de Alcántara's massacred body. Regardless of the unstable status of beauty as a signifier of virtue, however, images of saintly women, including Teresa and, to an even greater degree, Rose of Lima (who was known for her self-mortification), appear to have still been expected to conform to norms of female representation, eliding ugliness in favor of a generically pleasing physicality.

FIG. 38 Juan Rodríguez Juárez, *Saint Rose of Lima with a Donor*, ca. 1700. Oil on canvas, 66 × 42 in. (167.64 × 106.68 cm). Denver Art Museum, gift of the Collection of Frederick and Jan Mayer, 2014.216. Photo courtesy Denver Art Museum.

St. Teresa's Fungible Portraits and the Logic of Seriality

If the recognizability of Teresa's images was not indelibly linked to her portrait likeness and if consistency existed only in depicting the saint in the habit of the Carmelite order, any face could feasibly stand in for hers. The 1639 trial of Juan López Martínez, a priest from the town of Arjete (today Algete), north of Madrid, and Eugenia de la Torre, a *beata* accused of false visions, is a case in point.[92] A witness appeared before the inquisitorial tribunal and declared to have visited the house of López Martínez, where he saw a painting of Saint Teresa of Ávila. However, even though he was able to recognize it as an image of the saint, he noted that the painting bore Eugenia's—and not Teresa's—features. It was especially noteworthy, according to this witness, that the artist who created the painting did not know Eugenia, which implied that he had somehow painted her features into the image with supernatural assistance. Even more strangely, continued the declaration, López Martínez "twice ordered the face erased," based, we infer, on its impropriety, but "each time the painter again painted Eugenia more perfectly." In the end, the priest decided to keep the painting of Saint Teresa as it was, bearing Eugenia's features, as this seemed to him "a miraculous case."[93] The witness also confirmed that the portrait had *resplandores*, in this case likely a halo or rays. While these were fitting for a painting of Saint Teresa, who had been canonized seventeen years prior, they were not only indecorous in a painting of a living woman but also explicitly prohibited by various papal decrees. A case was opened against López Martínez, who was detained and brought to the Inquisition's prison in Toledo.

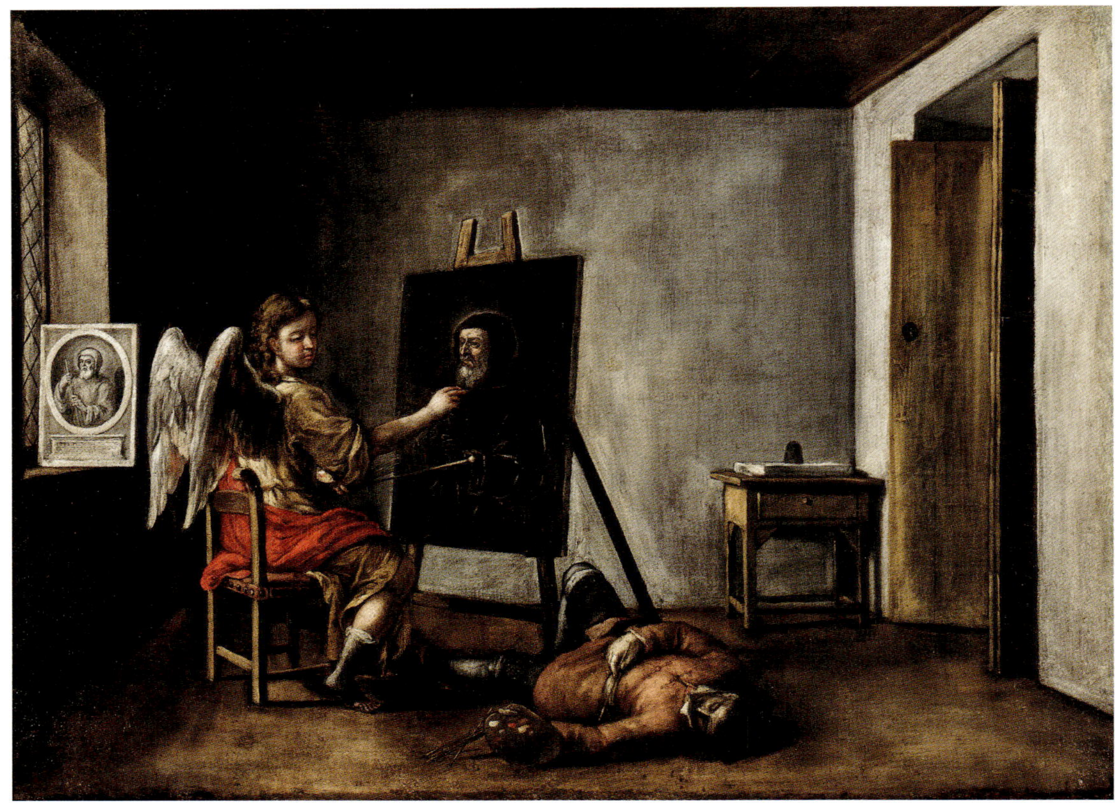

FIG. 39 Lucas Valdés, *The Miracle of the Portrait of Saint Francis of Paola*, ca. 1710. Oil on canvas, 31.85 × 42.9 in. (80.9 × 109 cm). Museo de Bellas Artes de Sevilla, Seville. Photo: Pepe Morón, provided by the Archivo del Museo de Bellas Artes de Sevilla.

During the course of the trial, the *fiscal* (prosecutor) described the painting in more detail, noting that it represented Eugenia "from the upper half of the body," with the rest showing "the holy mother Teresa de Jesús."[94] He then beseeched that the inquisitors have the painting, together with any others, brought to the tribunal to be examined, based on its impropriety and on the fact that Eugenia's face had supposedly reappeared in place of Saint Teresa's on multiple occasions. Although the *fiscal* did not directly state this as a cause for concern, it was commonly understood that such occurrences could actually be the result of demonic interference, as had occurred at San Plácido just a few years earlier. The claim that the painter had repeatedly painted portraits of the *beata* Eugenia into his image of Teresa hinted toward well-known narratives about sacred images being finished, perfected, or transformed with supernatural assistance. An early eighteenth-century painting by the Sevillian painter Lucas Valdés dramatizes precisely such an episode (fig. 39).[95] An angel has descended from heaven to assist a painter, who, having fallen ill, lies on the ground unable to finish his work on a canvas depicting Saint Francis of Paola. In completing the painting in the painter's stead, even holding a maulstick, the angel elevates the still-incomplete canvas from the lowest tier of true portraiture—a simple painted copy after an authoritative print (which was, in turn, purportedly based on the saint's death mask)—to an acheiropoietic image made with supernatural assistance.

Feasibly, López Martínez hoped for the inquisitors to imagine precisely such a scene following his declaration about the wondrous character of Eugenia's portrait. However, when the final accusation was brought against the cleric in October 1640, the inquisitors showed themselves as deeply skeptical of any supernatural occurrences. Accusing López Martínez of having a "sensual correspondence" with Eugenia de la Torre, they declared that his affection for her was "so excessive" that he had had her portrayed in a "mock painting" of Saint Teresa. "The face was that of the aforementioned Eugenia," they stated, "and the body and garb was that of the saint, and with this design and conceit [*traça y invençion*] he kept the portrait in his home."[96] Furthermore, the inquisitors highlighted the falsity of the portrait's purported resistance to repainting, noting that López Martínez's claim that it quasi-magically returned back to a portrait of Eugenia, no matter the painter's attempts at correcting this impropriety, was nothing more than a "lie and fiction [*mendaçio y invençion*]."[97]

Similarly to present-day scholarly disagreements about the original motivations of images that challenge the portrait-icon boundary (were they commissioned as such or were they repainted?), here, too, the inquisitors were unsure of the stages of the painting's life. One visitor to López Martínez's house claimed that "the face of [Eugenia] had been painted in the painting of Saint Teresa," implying that a finished holy picture had been repainted with the features of a living secular woman. But when López Martínez was allowed to defend himself, he declared that although the painting in question did, in fact, resemble Eugenia de la Torre, "he did not order such a portrayal nor was this ever attempted."[98] He even argued against the supposedly supernatural character of the painter's multiple unsuccessful attempts to remove Eugenia's face and replace it with Teresa's, noting that he considered this not "as a miracle but as a natural occurrence."[99]

A year later, in October 1641, the tribunal ruled that López Martínez was to be imprisoned for six months and charged fifty ducats to pay for the trial expenses. In addition, the inquisitors ordered that the portrait "that one witness says he had of Eugenia de la Torre in the guise of a saint" be taken from his home. The inquisitors decided that even the slightest possibility that the sacred image actually bore Eugenia's likeness was reason enough to sequester it. If this had been a mere portrait of Eugenia, it would not have garnered the inquisitors' attention. But the painting apparently made claims to being both a portrait and an icon, recognizable simultaneously as a painting of Saint Teresa, based on her codified clothing, and a portrait of a living woman who was not Saint Teresa.

Even in a culture in which such sacred portraits were highly common, the painting of Teresa / portrait of Eugenia exceeded acceptable norms for image making, likely based on a combination of factors. While *a lo divino* portraits of elite individuals were typically restricted in terms of who had access to them, Eugenia was not an elite individual and the image had been widely seen, as demonstrated by the range of people who testified on this matter against López Martínez. Furthermore, the portrait was the lone tangible manifestation of a larger set of concerns to the inquisitors, which lay at the intersection of sexual transgressions and

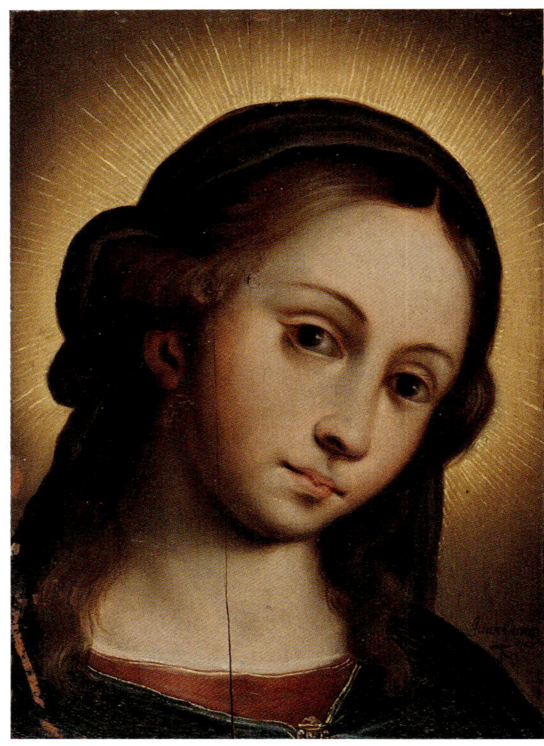

FIG. 40 Juan Correa, *The Virgin Mary*, ca. 1700. Oil on panel, 8.37 × 6.12 in. (21.3 × 15.6 cm). Philadelphia Museum of Art, Dr. Robert H. Lamborn Collection, 1903, 1903-877.

threats to the ecclesiastical status quo, as so often happened in the cases of women who claimed to have visions. These concerns included Eugenia being deemed a "false demoniac" rather than a visionary, supposedly engaging in adulterous relations with López Martínez as well as receiving popular veneration as a living saint, when, in fact, "she was not that but a blundering, lascivious woman of ill repute."[100]

In ordering that the portrait be sequestered, the inquisitors in the Algete case revealed themselves to be finely attuned not only to the flexibility of the portrait as an image type but also to the dangers that this could bring to the stability of an institution like the Church, which relied on dogmatic uniformity of both its tenets and its images. There were situations when a portrait could be repainted and become a sacred image "officially": the example of Philip II's reappropriation of an existing portrait discussed in the following chapter shows that this happened even at the highest echelons of society. But repainting could be unwelcome, particularly when a portrait encroached on, or claimed the privileged status of, a sacred image. The case of the painting of Saint Teresa is ambiguous, as it is never clear whether the painting was actually repainted or not, and if so, the direction of the repainting appears to have moved from sacred image *to* portrait rather than the other way around. The inquisitors' order that the painting be taken away from its owner reveals a distinct awareness that the ways in which portraiture and sacred imagery had blended and overlapped in this case were deeply improper.

The trial of López Martínez resembles a similar case brought to the attention of the Inquisitorial Tribunal in Venice in 1665, in which a woman named Cecilia Ferrazzi ordered two portraits of herself repainted: one with the saintly attributes of Saint Teresa and the other with those of the Madonna of the Seven Sorrows.[101] Ferrazzi's transgressive acts toward devotional pictures were only one of the many reasons for her vigorous inquisitorial prosecution and punishment. However, as Anne Jacobson Schutte points out, the two suspect images were a crucial element of the case, given that they enhanced the woman's claims to a saintly identity in a tangible manner.[102] What is more, they simultaneously devalued the images of Saint Teresa and the Virgin, likely contributing to the inquisitors' disquiet about the destabilization of religious images more generally.

In his defense, López Martínez claimed that the artist who created his painting of Saint Teresa had simply rendered the saint's likeness in such a way that it happened to resemble Eugenia. Within this statement is embedded a key point: the reason why secular women (like Eugenia de la Torre and Cecilia Ferrazzi) could masquerade as saintly women (such as Teresa or the Virgin Mary) was because, even though there existed "true portraits" of these holy women, few depictions—if any—represented them with any degree of facial specificity.[103] To cite one of many possible examples: the portraitistic features of a New Spanish painting of the Virgin by Juan Correa, including its closely cropped format and Mary's direct gaze, suggest unmediated authenticity, but the facial features are entirely generic (fig. 40).

If Saint Teresa could look like Eugenia or if Eugenia's features could convincingly stand in for those of Teresa, then the saint's appearance was malleable. By contrast, the development of portrait-centric cults for the founders of male religious orders ensured, in part, that men who sought to be represented as saints in portraits *a lo divino* would not turn to those individuals for their potentially problematic portrayals (regardless of how piously motivated those might have been, as I argue in chapter 1). It is no surprise, then, that contemporary male sitters who commissioned portraits *a lo divino* appear to have typically been represented as ancient saints of whom there were no surviving likenesses. For saintly women, however, the development of coherent portrait-based image cults may have been impeded by standards of generic female beauty. In turn, this made their representations susceptible to misappropriation.

Early modern religious and political imagery depended on a logic of seriality, where the legitimacy of an entire corpus of images depended on each image's adherence to the conventions of that corpus. This logic applied to a range of seemingly disparate images, from royal portraits, through images of saints, to cultic representations, like the Virgin of Guadalupe. The workshops of both court artists and painters who specialized in religious images were well versed in techniques that allowed for the seamless and accurate transfer of images from one canvas to the next, such as tracing or pouncing.[104] Outliers to any such corpus demonstrated the inherent uncontrollability of images both at the stage of their initial creation and, even more troublingly, once they emerged into the world, often acquiring completely new lives. The image from Algete implicitly devalued other images of Saint Teresa because it tested—and exceeded—the acceptable boundaries of the larger category to which all images of Teresa belonged.

The images that were the focus of inquisitorial trials in the early modern Hispanic world were rarely particularly innovative or unusual. Instead, time and again, the trials focused on perversions of existing forms of interacting with images, be it in how the suspects made or remade the images or the kind of behaviors they performed in front of them. Both at San Plácido and in Algete, the actors' extraordinary actions toward images and their statements about them did not arise ex nihilo; they were a response to contemporary artistic practices, which also limited their scope. The debates over how portraits were supposed to function in secular and sacred contexts were at the root of the adulterations—both demonic and human—examined here. Implicitly, the inquisitors' careful evaluations of images in these cases participated in the larger period discourse that, across the Hispanic world, debated questions of representation, images, and art not only in artistic treatises but also in noncanonical forms of textual production.

Conclusion: Mutable Truths

Each of the cases discussed in this chapter—the authoritative portrait of Saint Benedict; the "true" portraits of Saint Ignatius; and the pliable images of Saint Teresa, only some of which adhered to her true portrait—reveal both the flexibility of the truth and the fundamental desire to have the truth congeal into a reliable, objective form. To that end, early modern Hispanic individuals turned to a range of solutions. In descending order of authoritativeness, these were truth as derived from institutional sanction (first sacred, then political); truth as derived from tradition and precedent; and truth as derived from, or bolstered by, individual subjective experience. With any one of these categories fulfilled, it seems, an early modern inhabitant of the Hispanic monarchy was at least partially satisfied that the visual information they received from an image was sufficiently trustworthy. Nevertheless, were a stronger proof of authenticity to surface or a more authoritative description, it could feasibly supersede existing sources of authority, forcing extant images and the practices surrounding them to adapt.

Most desirable (though most difficult to ascertain) was when the truth was bolstered by divine assistance. For example, Diego de Yepes, in *Vida, virtudes y milagros de la bienaventurada virgen Teresa de Jesús* (Life, virtues, and miracles of the blessed virgin Teresa de Jesús), first published in 1606, illustrated the extent to which the not-yet-canonized Teresa had access to divine knowledge:

> The Saint had come to have such a great knowledge of the saints of heaven, as if she had lived her entire life there. And many times when she saw some portrait of some saint, painted in a lifelike style [*que fuesse al natural*], she would typically say in praising them (especially if she was speaking with people with whom she was not guarded), that they reminded her of [the original] that was in heaven. Not because they had bodies here, but because the Lord represented them to her through the vision of her imaginary [*por vision imaginaria*], with the same faces that they had here on earth.[105]

Such episodes were not without precedent. The twelfth-century southern Italian abbot Joachim of Fiore had prophesied the foundation of two great religious orders, which in later exegeses were identified with the Franciscans and the Dominicans. Fiore was believed to have known the appearances of the two founders, Saints Francis and Dominic, and to have commissioned mosaic portraits of them for the Venetian basilica of Saint Mark.[106] As a result, some early modern Catholic authorities accepted that there existed authoritative portraits of the two saints. A large canvas attributed to Santa Fe de Bogotá–based painter Gregorio Vásquez de Arce y Ceballos dramatizes Fiore's prognostications, depicting the moment in which he first displayed the icons of Francis and Dominic to a reverent crowd (fig. 41).[107] Here, the icons' medium has been modernized. Rather than mosaics, the abbot holds two canvases, positioned at a slight angle that reveals their side and bottom edges, which are tightly stretched and held in place by small nails. A number of smaller bust-length paintings of those same two saints are also attributed to Vásquez, and they resemble formally the authoritative true portraits that he depicted Fiore holding (fig. 42). Vásquez's large painting

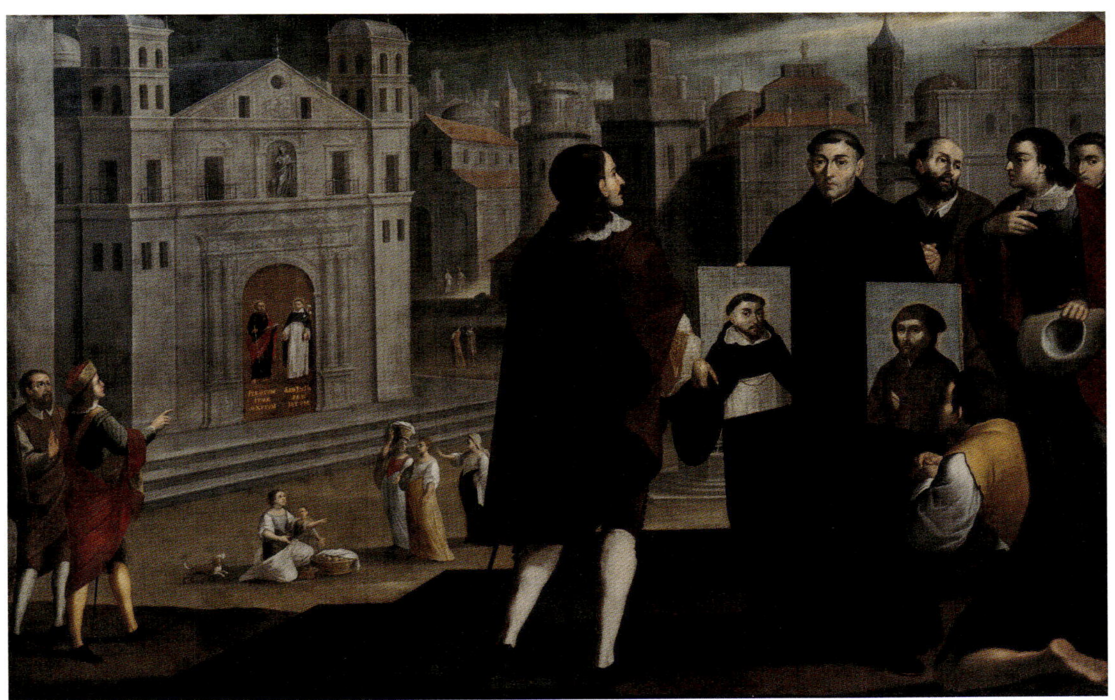

FIG. 41 Attributed to Gregorio Vásquez de Arce y Ceballos, *The Abbot Joachim of Fiore Presents the Prophesied Portraits of Saints Dominic of Guzmán and Francis of Assisi*, ca. 1680. Oil on canvas, 81.8 × 124 in. (208 × 315 cm). Museo Colonial y Museo Santa Clara, Bogotá. Photo © Museo Colonial y Museo Santa Clara / Oscar Monsalve.

thus not only visualized the origin story of the two portraits, but it also legitimized the numerous stand-alone paintings of Francis and Dominic that he produced as divinely sanctioned and true. On the door of the church in the background are visible the two paintings as installed in the basilica. Incongruously, Saint Francis has here been replaced with Saint Paul. This is how the episode was related by the fifteenth-century Dominican bishop and saint Antoninus of Florence and may therefore suggest a Dominican patronage for the painting.[108]

The portraits that Fiore holds in Vásquez's painting, it bears stressing, derive from the myriad printed and painted depictions of the two saints that were in circulation in the early modern world. For instance, Jacques Callot created a print of the Saint Francis icon, which is replete with portraitistic features, including a bust-length format, a direct gaze, and frontal positioning. Lest there be any doubt about its legitimacy, Callot also included a textual description that assured its viewers that the image was a *vera effigies* (fig. 43). In Vásquez's painting, the portraits of Francis and Dominic are not bolstered textually but narratively. In the right foreground, a man falls to his knees before the images and clasps his hands, seemingly spontaneously, performing the standard choreography of veneration before a sacred image. Moreover, the visible lower edges of the two icons that Fiore

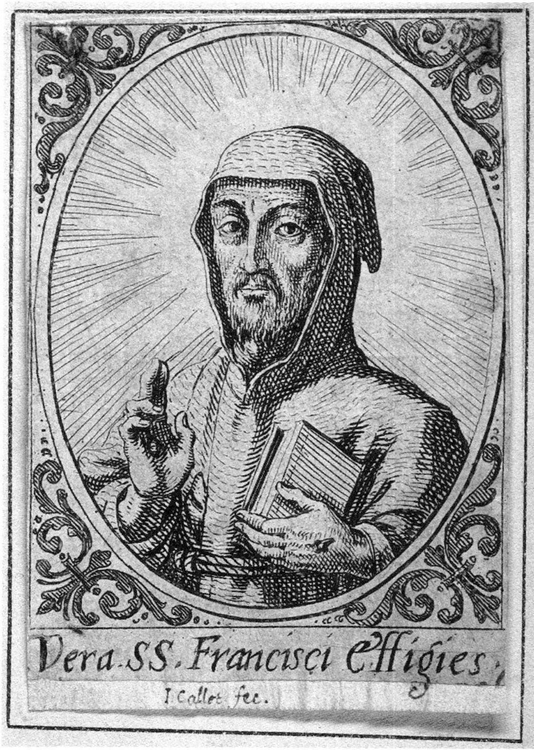

FIG. 42 Jacques Callot, *Saint Francis of Assisi*, ca. 1620–21. Etching and engraving on paper, 2.3 × 1.7 in. (5.9 × 4.5 cm). Wellcome Collection, London.

holds suggest that viewers of the Vásquez painting should mirror the kneeling man by supplicating themselves before the images and adopting a lower viewpoint. Given that, within the timeline of the painting, the two holy men had not yet been canonized, nor even born, Vásquez shows that the kneeling man's reaction of wonderment was produced by his acceptance of divine intervention in the images' ideation. Others were even more explicit in deeming the two portraits as acheiropoietoi. For instance, in describing the two Venetian mosaics depicting Francis and Dominic, the theorist and painter Antonio Palomino notes that "there is the opinion that they may have been created by angelic paintbrushes," a trope that was depicted nearly contemporaneously in Valdés's painting of the true portrait of Saint Francis of Paola (see fig. 39).[109]

Even though Fiore himself was not a saint and even though there appears to have been only one printed image of him—a rather crude woodcut with hardly any individualization—in circulation in the seventeenth century, Vásquez's painting depicts the abbot with all the hallmarks of a *verdadero retrato*.[110] The gaunt cheeks, thin lips, and narrowing chin combine to depict a specific person. This impression is heightened by the abbot's direct gaze toward the viewer, which it shares with the two true portraits of Dominic and Francis. Furthermore, the portraitistic frontality of Fiore's face is all the more apparent when compared to the obliquely positioned faces of the two men behind him. The depiction of Fiore as an invented but convincing portrait lends further legitimacy to the "real" anticipated portraits of the two mendicant saints. All this explains why, until Hector Schenone's identification of the scene's esoteric iconography, the figure of Fiore was long taken to be a self-portrait of Vásquez, shown in the act of presenting two of his paintings to a patron.[111]

And yet, for all their similarities, the three true portraits—of Francis, Dominic, and Joachim—are subtly different, pointing to a variation of ontology. The surface of Vásquez's painting is abraded but the contrasts of light and shadow that play on Fiore's sunken features grant his face three-dimensionality. By comparison, the painted features of Francis and Dominic are evenly illuminated, flat, and pressed up to the surface of their canvases. Within the fiction of the painting, one of these figures is

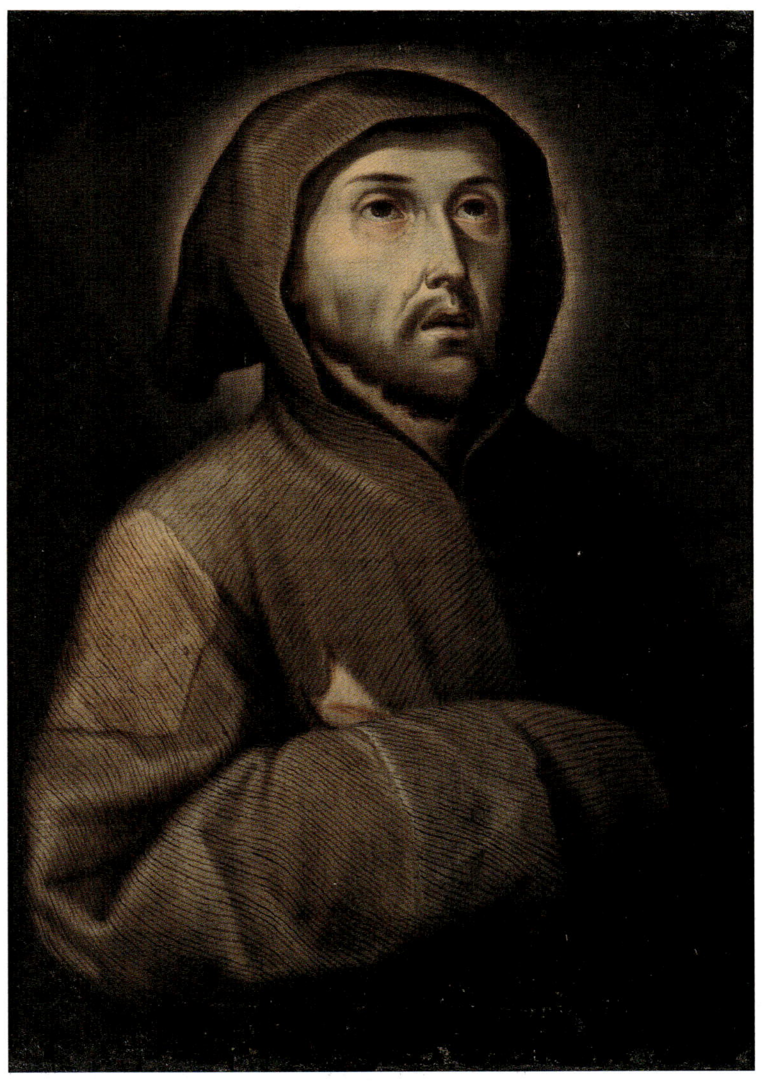

FIG. 43 Attributed to Gregorio Vásquez de Arce y Ceballos, *Saint Francis of Assisi*, second half of the seventeenth century. Oil on canvas, 30.3 × 24 in. (77 × 61 cm). Museo Colonial y Museo Santa Clara, Bogotá. Photo © Museo Colonial y Museo Santa Clara / Oscar Monsalve.

"real," possessing flesh and form, while two are mere images. They are not yet indexical but merely prognosticative. Indeed, the two portraits augur the ideal form that the bodies of Saints Francis and Dominic will take, as if the twice-painted images in Vásquez's canvas were the matrix according to which those bodies would eventually be formed or against which they would be measured. One object in the painting—the beige hat held by the red-cloaked man on the right, with a crescent moon of white paint marking its recession into the canvas—obliquely plays a similar role. The hat, perhaps made of felt, was first mere flat surface, which was molded and formed into the negative of the human head. In its three-dimensionality, then, it implies that, when the prophesy is fulfilled, Saints Dominic and Francis will not only *look* like their images, but they will also have the plastic bodily form of Joachim. And moreover, the fleshed-out, three-dimensional bodily forms that the saints will one day come to inhabit will themselves be forms from which, in turn, casts might be made: the indexical objects that recorded for posterity the shape and image of individuals reputed of sanctity. The hat subtly mirrors the physicality of the death mask, which was the indexical tool for creating true portraits: both are soft, moldable, applied by hand, and fitted to a specific human body.

Divinely inspired, Fiore was able to create authoritative portraits of Saints Francis and Dominic before they were even born. So, too, Saint Teresa confessed that she knew what ancient saints had looked like in life, to the point of being able to compare them against their modern painted images. In much the same way, García Calderón, the prior of the convent of San Plácido, was able to compare the true appearance of Saint Benedict to how he appeared in a painting. Although it is impossible to directly correlate these episodes, it is certain that they were all articulating a deep-seated concern about the potential fallibility of sacred images. Like Saint Teresa's interlocutors, who must have been delighted that the saint's visions granted her a privileged insight into the accuracy of the sacred pictures that surrounded them, and like Fiore's astounded companions, who were presented with anticipated true portraits, so, too, the inhabitants of San Plácido may have celebrated—however briefly—the assurance that their convent's painting of Saint Benedict, their holy founder, was truly a true portrait.

REPAINTING PORTRAITS *Chapter 3*

Palafox's Portraits

In 1651 a witness from the central Mexican city of Puebla de los Ángeles alerted the Inquisitorial Tribunal to a "grave and dangerous matter": a proliferation of unusual portraits of the controversial, recently departed bishop of the city, Juan de Palafox y Mendoza.[1] In one case, the inquisitors learned, a painter by the name of Gaspar Conrado had "made a portrait of the Lord Bishop Juan de Palafox painted with the wings of a seraph."[2] The painter was called before the tribunal and, during the course of his testimony, admitted to having painted eleven portraits of the bishop, including one that had been commissioned by Palafox himself to be sent to the Philippines.[3] As far as is known, none of these portraits survive, but at least some of them may have resembled the official episcopal portrait of Palafox by Diego de Borgraf that is still held in the cathedral of Puebla—or the eighteenth-century versions that look back to it, such as the 1768 painting by Andrés de Islas reproduced here (fig. 44).

The owners of the remaining ten paintings included a local silversmith, a merchant, and the nuns of the convent of Saint Catherine, who displayed their portrait behind the main altar of the monastic church.[4] This output notwithstanding, Conrado denied ever having created a portrait of the sitter with seraphic wings. He suggested that while this might have simply been an issue of misattribution, with the witness having mistakenly assigned another painter's work to him, it was equally possible that "another painter could have added the wings at the command of his masters" to one of the many portraits he had painted "for the profound love that they bear him."[5] Conrado's remark—that someone may have amended his finished portraits—reveals a crucial but largely ignored aspect of early modern artistic production: audiences at the time were accustomed to transforming and manipulating "finished" images.

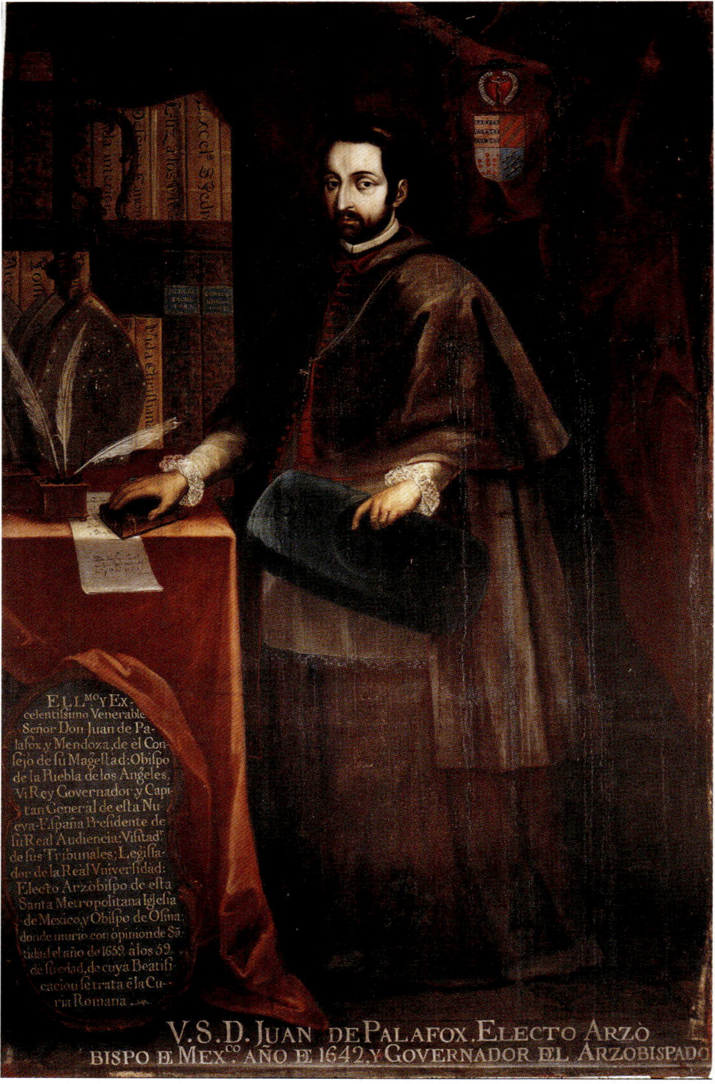

FIG. 44 Andrés de Islas, *Juan de Palafox y Mendoza*, 1768. Oil on canvas, 82.6 × 54.3 in. (210 × 138 cm). Museo Nacional del Virreinato, Tepotzotlán. Courtesy of the Instituto Nacional de Antropología e Historia.

Portraiture was the most mutable art form and, as I will demonstrate, particularly susceptible to targeted repainting, belying its promise of stability and long-term commemoration.[6]

The amending of portraits of secular figures with saintly attributes at a later moment in the images' lives was a widespread cultural phenomenon. Such repainting could happen, I contend, because of the permeable, inchoate boundary between the sacred and secular in early modernity in general and because of the lengthy, imbricated histories of icon painting and portraiture in particular, as demonstrated by scholars like Rona Goffen, Alexander Nagel, and Christopher S. Wood.[7] Furthermore, as discussed in chapter 2, the fifteenth, sixteenth, and seventeenth centuries witnessed the appearance of ecclesiastically sanctioned portrait-centric religious cults, like those of Saint Bernardino of Siena, Saint Ignatius of Loyola, and, in a more irregular fashion, Saint Teresa of Ávila. This meant that the portrait—a more or less accurate depiction of a real, often recently deceased individual's physiognomy—became a crucial component of early modern Catholicism's turn to a more experiential, image-centric, and sensuous religiosity. It was, in sum, not unusual to worship a portrait.

As a result, early modern individuals frequently repainted existing portraits in order to align them with the category of sacred imagery. They produced images that are very similar to one another in general appearance—combining an idiosyncratic likeness with some iconographic or textual marker of sanctity—but they did so for very different reasons. This chapter is therefore organized by motivations—or presumed motivations—for later interventions into finished portraits. Repainting could range from being merely a form of utilitarian reuse to constituting an ecclesiastically condemned form of celebrating a nonholy individual through the codified language of saintly iconography. In some cases, the images' life histories were unclear, even to their contemporaries. In addition, the contexts in which repainting occurred stretched from the most privileged echelons of Hispanic society to some of its least. The complexity of repainting also varied greatly, as sometimes a simple line of text was sufficient to bestow upon a portrait a completely new meaning, producing the same effect as endowing it with a bevy of codified iconographic attributes. Finally, the range of cases under examination spans from poorly documented examples, where the only evidence for repainting lies in visual hints on the surface of the image, which may itself only be known from photographic archives like the Institut Amatller d'Art Hispànic, to cases in which documents with exhaustive descriptions of the act of repainting abound but the images themselves do not survive.[8]

Although repainted portraits accrued layers with time, they are not palimpsests in the word's traditional paleographic meaning; the accumulation of additional signification on their surfaces did not happen at the cost of erasure.[9] Like true palimpsests, however, repainted portraits are characterized by the temporal delay between the objects' initial creation and the secondary intervention into their surface and appearance, as well as by the infusion of those objects with new meanings. What is more, in contrast to nearly all other types of repainting or overpainting that occurred in early modernity, sanctifying additions to portraits subjected them to drastic ontological transformation. Indeed, the repainting of portraits with religious attributes effectively produced entirely new images, based on what those images were believed to be able to do and how. The portrait (just like the individual) had relevance to only a few people, while the superior category of the devotional picture (as well as the saint) could positively affect many more. Repainted portraits of nonholy individuals could begin to receive and communicate prayers, catalyze penitential reflection, and, in theory, occasion the strengthening or even awakening of a Christian conscience in anyone who saw them. The conversion of portraits, in effect, made them into images that could convert.

When portraits were transformed into sacred icons through repainting, they came into alignment with the numerous image types that both possessed religious significance and that relied on the use of the individualized portrait likeness, and

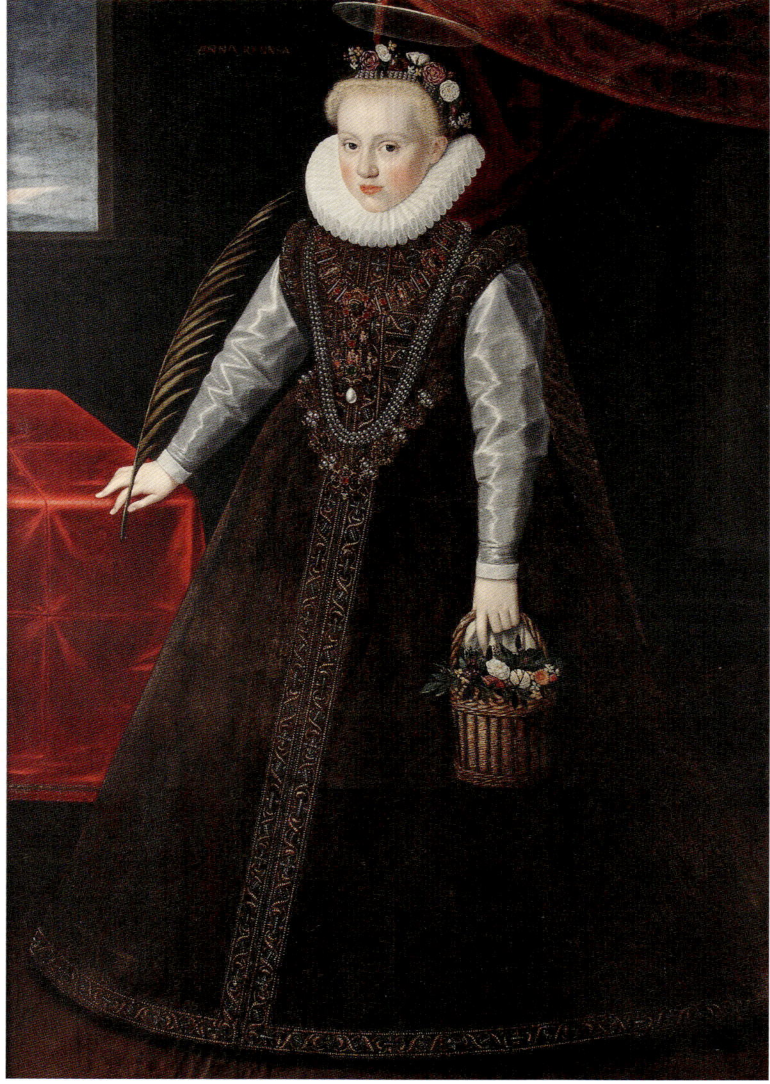

FIG. 45 Attributed to Jakob de Monte, *Anne of Austria as Saint Dorothy*, ca. 1582. Oil on canvas. Monasterio de las Descalzas Reales, Madrid, 00612208. Photo © Patrimonio Nacional, Monasterio de las Descalzas Reales, Madrid.

which are this book's primary foci. These include portraits *a lo divino*; *verdaderos retratos* or "true portraits" of saints, which often served as the basis for the (more or less uniform) corpus of those holy individuals' pictorial representations; paintings of saints that draw on the conventions of portraiture; and even donor portraits.[10] Many of these different types of images are deceptively similar, making it difficult to establish their original appearance and intent. For instance, there is, as yet, no verdict as to whether the portraits of Habsburg princesses that are attributed to Jakob de Monte and Hans von Aachen and held at the Madrid convent of the Descalzas Reales were initially designed as *a lo divino* paintings, which purposefully cast their sitters as saints, or whether they were subjected to posterior repainting that transformed them into the devotional images we see today (fig. 45).[11]

A conclusive answer will be impossible without technical analysis, including X-radiography to identify potential compositional changes and infrared reflectography to compare the underdrawing (if any) with the pictures' present state.[12] Similarly, paint sample analysis could establish whether any grime had accrued or varnish been applied between layers of paint, thereby implying a temporal lapse between the works' initial creation and potential later repainting. In certain cases, immediately noticeable stylistic incongruities corroborate the prolific archival evidence for the practice of repainting in the early modern period, but they cannot reveal when the interventions might have occurred. Nevertheless, just as Michael Camille argued for the importance of studying forms of selective iconoclasm in illuminated medieval manuscripts regardless of the frequent impossibility of their precise dating, here, too, posterior reworking is pertinent to reconstructing not only the afterlife of a particular object but also the diverse beliefs about what images did and how.[13] Although portraits were commonly commissioned with posthumous commemoration in mind, they promised, but could not guarantee, permanence: sitters' identities could be forgotten, their position and status mistaken or confused, and the images themselves cut down and reworked. To an early modern European and colonial individual, the portrait was a fundamentally unstable image type.

"Stupid or Ill-Intentioned" Repainters

Palafox's repainted portraits represent a small facet of a much larger trial, during which the inquisitors realized that the beloved, still-living bishop was surrounded by unwarranted veneration. This reverence approximated the behavior typically directed at a saint, including the collecting of contact relics and the attacking of "nonbelievers." Nevertheless, from the inquisitors' point of view, the portraits were a particularly worrying manifestation of this unsanctioned cult. That Palafox himself discussed the portraits in a letter cited in Antonio González de Rosende laudatory posthumous biography of the bishop, the *Vida i virtudes del Illmo i Exc^mo^ Señor D. Juan de Palafox i Mendoza* (Life and virtues of the most illustrious and most excellent señor Don Juan de Palafox y Mendoza) of 1666, suggests that both Palafox and his biographer were concerned about the lasting impact of this episode and its damage to the bishop's reputation. Like Conrado, who was eager to displace responsibility for the repainted images, Palafox rejected the idea that the portrait's sitter should be at fault when a "stupid or ill-intentioned individual adds whatever he pleases to a few portraits" from among the thousands of his likenesses that were supposedly created in Puebla at that time, including the addition of such elements as "angels, resplendent glories [*resplandores*], or other such foolishness."[14]

As Conrado's and Palafox's comments make clear, repainting was to be expected as part of the artistic process, though no less frustrating for it. While to Conrado it was perfectly natural that some of his paintings should have been modified, Palafox, calling repainters "stupid or ill-intentioned individual[s]," presented a far less charitable view of the practice.[15] In this statement, the bishop suggested two possibilities about the repainting. In the first scenario, the repainter was an ignorant man or woman, whose love for the bishop drove

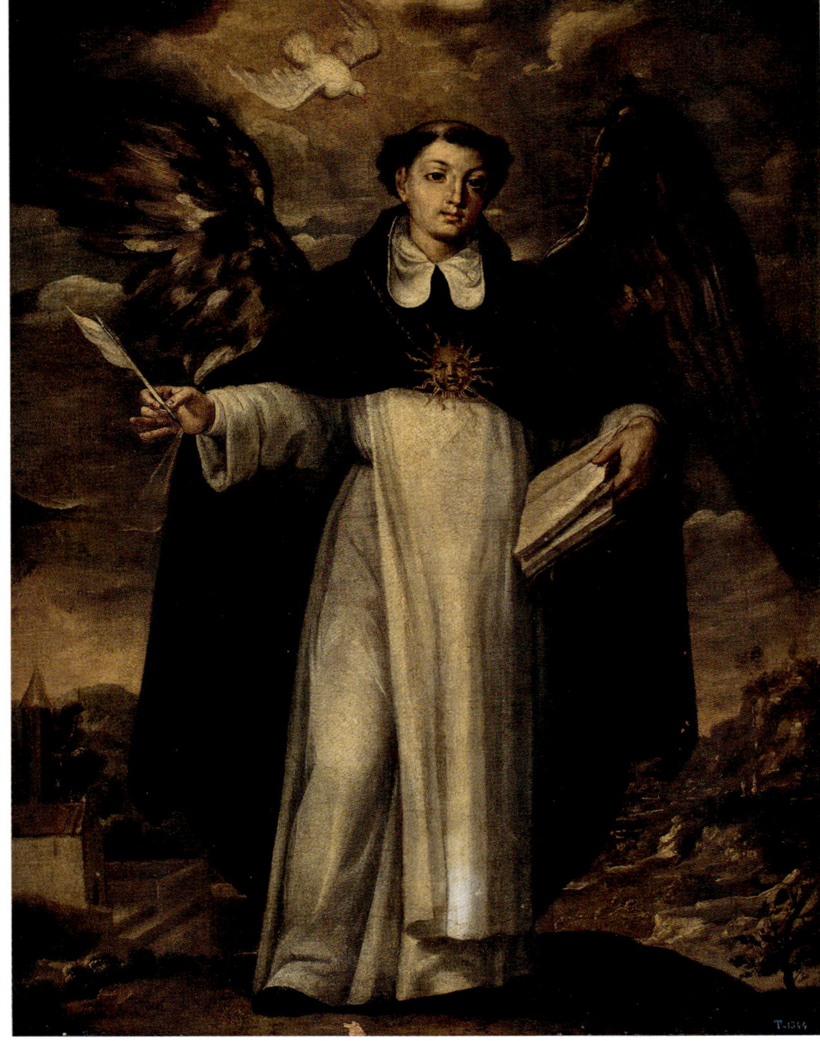

FIG. 46 José Risueño, *Saint Thomas Aquinas as Seraphic Doctor*, ca. 1700. Oil on canvas, 42.5 × 32.2 in. (108 × 82 cm). Museo Nacional del Prado, Madrid. Photo © Photographic Archive Museo Nacional del Prado.

him or her to enhance his depiction, making use of a familiar visual language for the representation of privileged figures, but who was unaware of its impropriety. The second option was more insidious: this repainter's goal was to imply that Palafox vainly supported his own sanctification in pictorial terms, even if the way that this had been achieved was not in explicit contravention of papal prohibitions against such activity.

Indeed, the adding of wings to a portrait did not constitute a breach of Urban VIII's 1642 decree on saints, discussed in chapter 1, which prohibited depicting ecclesiastically unrecognized individuals with the hallmarks of sanctity, such as halos.[16] In the Puebla trial, there is no mention of amending Palafox's portraits with halos, even though they would seem to be the least labor intensive of all painterly interventions and the most explicit in their symbolic charge. Angelic wings, on the other hand, were neither a requisite nor even a common hallmark of sanctity in early modern Catholicism. Nevertheless, they were particularly popular in early modern Spain and Latin America, and they clearly connoted an individual's supernatural status, in this case casting Palafox in a manner similar to Saints Francis, Thomas Aquinas, Vicente Ferrer, or Francisco Solano, who were all sometimes depicted with wings, as seen in an early eighteenth-century picture of Thomas Aquinas by José Risueño (fig. 46). This painting most closely approximates what I imagine Palafox's winged portraits to have looked like, based on the scale and format of the figure, his ecclesiastical garb, and the portraitistic quality of the saint's facial features.[17] The deployment of wings by a "painter . . . at the command of his masters" was a clear attempt at elevating the sitter out of the range of the mundane and, simultaneously, of pushing the affected image out of the confines of the category to which it had previously belonged. The inquisitors in New Spain judged that the effect of adding wings to a portrait was the same as that of the "laurels and rays" that had preoccupied Roman authorities. Even though "the wings of a seraph" were not explicitly mentioned in Urban's decrees, they were judged to require analogous intervention.

The Portrait Beyond Alberti

The repainting that occurred in Puebla, which formed part of a larger cultic veneration directed at a specific individual, was a variant of a widespread practice. In the majority of examples in which we observe the transformation of portraits into devotional images through repainting, however, seemingly simple pragmatism may have been the most important motivation. Indeed, the efficacy of portraits, as objects meant to communicate well into the future, depends on their unchanging nature. At the same time, as depictions of actual individuals commonly endowed with recognizable and idiosyncratic features, they are supremely context-specific, both chronologically and geographically. What happens, then, when the people for whom the portrait acted as a substitutional presence and as a device for remembering (both functions designated for this type of image by Alberti) are gone, either because of the passing of time or the crossing of space?[18] Artists could, of course, bolster likeness with other solutions, including textual inscriptions and symbols, to ensure that their sitters be identified, but these, too, were subject to the vagaries of distance across space or time.[19] Furthermore, being told a sitter's name or age or profession mattered little if they did not hold high rank or office, which could have contributed to their recognition. This is why Jennifer Roberts terms portraits "terminal commodities," given that they were too specialized to effectively communicate when extracted from their originating habitat.[20]

When portraits could no longer be recognized, they became blank slates, evacuated of signification and transformed from specific to generic. From the representation of one person, such portraits became representations of undefined personhood, the sitters' individualities subsumed to universality (even if still bound by the characteristics of gender, age, and social status, which the images could still convey). The later viewer of such a portrait could contemplate its aesthetic qualities but was otherwise left with an uncanny sense of presence that could not be satisfyingly resolved through recognition.[21] It is in that moment that the anchorless portrait, revealing itself not to be static at all but among the most mutable art forms in early modernity, became ripe for resignification. The most effective way to refill such a portrait of a forgotten sitter with meaning, it seems, was to transform it into a religious image.

The interpretive and historical richness of the practice of repainting is exemplified in a picture of a veiled woman at prayer, held at the Escorial (fig. 47). On the one hand, this is clearly a portrait, the "dramatic close-up" of which forces the viewer into direct confrontation with the commanding sitter.[22] The artist has made no attempt to obscure the imperfections of her severe face; she is lined, jowly, and has a wart on her left cheek. However, there are elements in the painting that contrast with its relative naturalism, suggesting the presence of multiple hands at work. For instance, the gauzy veil that frames the woman's face is weighed down by an ornate crown, outlined in thick black lines. Along the receding left and right edges of the crown appear rough crosshatched marks—horizontal striations intersecting with increasingly frequent vertical lines—as if taken from a draughtsman's toolbox for producing a sense of depth. In the lower right corner of the painting, three large iron nails protrude from between the woman's hands, which touch gently in a gesture of prayer. The nails lack heft, balancing weightlessly between her fingers. Finally, incongruously, a string of dark beads cuts vertically across the woman's hand: too close to the fingers to be a bracelet but with no other apparent function or connection to the rest of the picture. It is these inconsistencies within the painting—the crown's crosshatching and flatness; the weightless nails; the disappearing beads, which likely once formed part of a rosary—that reveal the image to have moved beyond its initial identity as a portrait.

There is a paper trail to follow that addresses the painting's duality. Bonaventura Bassegoda has connected the image to an entry in a 1577 inventory of the belongings of one Friar Lorenzo, who was, in all probability, Lorenzo Grillet, a French embroiderer from Besançon whom King Philip II met at the Catalan monastery of Montserrat and invited to the Escorial to head the embroidery workshop there.[23] The entry lists "a portrait of his mother of/by Friar Lorenzo," which given the ambiguity of the Spanish preposition "de," either belonged to or was painted by the friar.[24] By capturing the woman's likeness and character, the image fulfilled portraiture's traditional commemorative functions, which extended the presence of the represented person across time and space. But when Lorenzo died in 1576, he was likely the only one at the Escorial to know what his mother—perhaps even then still living in faraway Besançon—looked like.[25] Suddenly, the image became meaningless and, in its meaninglessness, vulnerable. It is therefore unsurprising that the principal entry in the inventory is annotated in the margin with the words: "This portrait was changed [*se mudo*] into the figure of Saint Helena by order of King Philip our lord."[26] This line of text unequivocally confirms that the nails and the crown, which are now legible as iconographic attributes of Helen, the saint said to have found the relic of the True Cross, are posterior additions to a finished painting.

Further documentary evidence sheds light on when in the picture's lifetime its repainting occurred. A receipt from 1577 notes that the painter Rodrigo de Holanda painted [*pinto*] "ten thousand leaves and one thousand orange flowers and lemons for the artificial trees for the fountain at

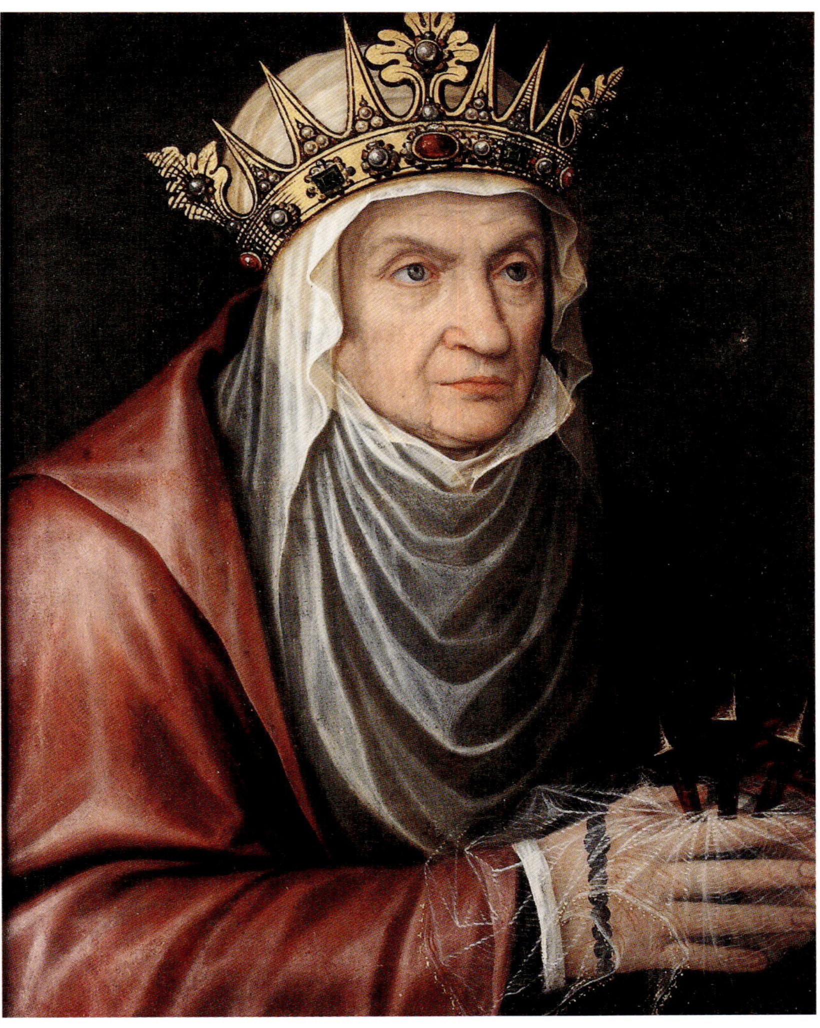

FIG. 47 Unidentified painter and Rodrigo de Holanda, *Portrait of Fray Lorenzo's Mother Repainted as Saint Helena*, before 1577 with later additions. Oil on canvas, 29 × 23.625 in. (71 × 60 cm). Real Monasterio de San Lorenzo de El Escorial, 10014407. Photo © Patrimonio Nacional, Real Monasterio de San Lorenzo de El Escorial.

La Fresneda, as well as the trunks of those trees, seventeen cranes, eight windows, two iron grates, the cross of a marble Christ, a canvas by Titian, and a figure of Saint Helena."[27] This same inventory of objects reappears in another receipt, in which Holanda is described as having "repaired [*reparó*]," rather than painted, the cross, the painting by Titian, and the figure of Helena.[28] Given that Titian's authorship of the first painting is clearly stated, we can infer that Holanda's task was only to clean and retouch it and that his work on the "figure of Saint Helena" may have taken much the same form: retouching and minor repainting.[29] The fact that the painting is first listed as a portrait of the artist's mother in the main body of the inventory and is identified as having been repainted in the margin, as well as the fact that the payment to Holanda was made nearly two years after Lorenzo's death, all suggest that the actual act of repainting also occurred after the friar had died.

The portrait of Lorenzo's mother, whose memory died with the friar, was repainted with a number of codified attributes, resulting in an image of Saint Helena. To Philip II and to those at his court, the narrative of a saintlike Helena was held as irrevocably true. Now, the image of the saint herself, which carried all of the most desirable characteristics of a portrait, could be easily visualized as tangibly real. All religious images had to be consecrated by blessing before they could form part of Catholic practice. Repainted portraits, too, were undoubtedly often blessed in order to cement their newfound role as images of devotion; we can easily imagine that Philip II would have required that the portrait of Saint Helena be consecrated, and he would have certainly had the wherewithal to achieve this.[30] However, it is feasible that in certain cases, particularly outside the confines of orthodoxy, the act of repainting itself stood in for the act of consecration, in its elevation of a selfish record of the individual to the loftier category of universally efficacious sacred picture.

Why were portraits particularly attractive candidates for a posteriori interventions that amended them with sacred attributes? So-called true portraits of recently deceased saints, which granted portraiture particular prestige within Catholic image politics after the Council of Trent, are an important point of reference here. Saints like Ignatius of Loyola and Francisco de Borja were depicted more or less uniformly across all of their representations. In the case of Ignatius, these were based on an interpretation of his appearance derived from a widely disseminated death mask. In these cases, standardized iconographic attributes (like Saint Catherine's sword and Saint Anthony's pig) became secondary to the saints' recognizable physical characteristics, such as Ignatius's balding head and aquiline nose.[31] In contrast to these sixteenth-century individuals, there were no extant portraits or death masks of ancient and medieval saints like Sebastian, George, or Bonaventure. Although this did not mean that there were fewer prescriptions for how such individuals should be represented, artists had to use living models and no small amount of inventiveness to endow their depictions of these saints with the naturalistic impact that the true portrait of an individual like Ignatius had by design.[32] When a portrait that had been uncoupled from its original referent was repainted with a halo, identifying text, or any other attribute of a chosen saint, the revivified image entered into a shared space with the *verdaderos retratos* of recently deceased figures like Ignatius and Francisco de Borja. Once transformed into sacred images, repainted portraits had the potential to affect their viewers with greater immediacy than more generic representations of saints, as they acquired an attractive plausibility and "presentness" familiar from the true portraits of modern saints.[33] Ruth Webb's definition of the rhetorical concept of *enargeia*—that what is sought in representation is "not so much an object, or scene, or person in itself, but the *effect* of seeing that thing"—seems applicable here.[34] That repainted portraits were entirely fictitious renderings of what these ancient saints might have looked like did not obstruct their efficacy as religious objects.

Consider, for instance, a painting of a young man that appears typical, at first glance, of Spanish and Italian portraits of the early to mid-seventeenth century (fig. 48).[35] Depicted *en buste*, his dark garment difficult to distinguish from the background (although this may be due to the available photograph), the sitter, turned slightly to the right, looks over to glance at the viewer. A soft white *golilla* collar worn over a supporting *valona*, which gives it its form and height, frames his face.[36] However, the addition of a few letters—*S. ‘F ‘P,*^{e} *NERI*—slightly clumsy in their flourishes, retitles the image. The text identifies the sitter as Saint Philip Neri, the founder of the Oratorian order, who was canonized in 1622 by Pope Gregory XV. Neri’s likeness was preserved in a death mask as a model for later depictions, and he is typically depicted as a bearded and grayed older man.

The portrait examined here was clearly not painted as a depiction of Neri, as it neither resembles the typical “look” that Neri’s followers would have expected to see in his depictions nor does it stylistically align with the type of portraiture prevalent during Neri’s youth in the 1530s and 1540s, when he would have potentially resembled the young man in the portrait. We can assume, then, that the painting was made in the second quarter of the seventeenth century as a secular portrait of a nobleman. A decision was made about its utility at an unspecified later date that resulted both in a change of format, from an arched to a rectangular frame, and in the addition of the descriptive text. This simple act of writing on the canvas and identifying the sitter as an Italian saint transformed the image from a relatively straightforward secular portrait to a multivalent painting with both religious and portraitistic layers. Indeed, by relying on text, this rebranding remained legible only to some, that is, only to those who could read: a literate viewer now cannot see the image without also receiving the information that the person depicted therein is named Philip Neri and is a saint.

By contrast, a relatively formulaic portrait of an armored man appears to have been later repainted not only with the inscription *S Jorge* (Saint George) but also with a codified iconographic symbol:

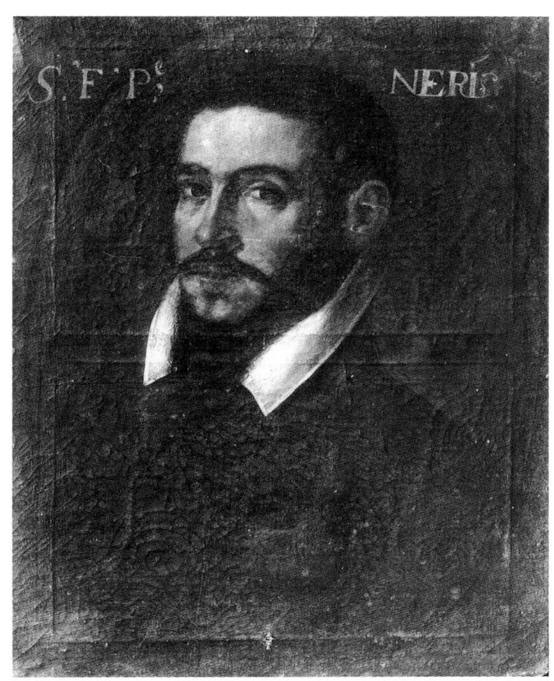

FIG. 48 Unidentified painters, *Portrait of a Man Repainted as Saint Philip Neri*, second quarter of the seventeenth century with later additions. Oil on canvas. Museo de Arte Sacro, Alquézar. Photo courtesy of Arxiu Mas, Fundació Institut Amatller d’Art Hispànic, Barcelona, E-18593. Digital file courtesy of the Department of Image Collections, National Gallery of Art Library, Washington, DC.

the saint’s characteristic cross upon the breastplate (fig. 49). Similarly, and most explicitly, in a likely repainted canvas of a friar, the sitter’s new identity as a saint is marked by the letters that take the shape of a halo around his head, functioning not only as legible text, which reads *S. Buena bentu-rad.* (either Saint Bonaventure, or Blessed Saint), but also as an easily legible attribute of sanctity (fig. 50). These examples provide insight to the range of individuals who amended the portraits with various attributes of sanctity like wings and halos. While Holanda was a professional painter in the service of the court and acting on the king’s

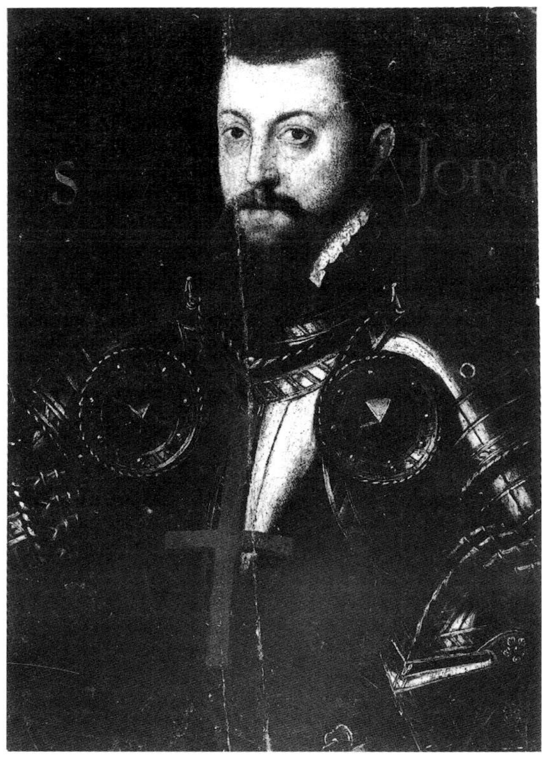

FIG. 49 Unidentified painters, *Portrait of a Man Repainted as Saint George*, sixteenth century with later additions. Oil on canvas. Photo courtesy of Arxiu Mas, Fundació Institut Amatller d'Art Hispànic, Barcelona, C-10448. Digital file courtesy of the Department of Image Collections, National Gallery of Art Library, Washington, DC.

orders, the economy of means with which the changes were made in the portraits of saints Philip Neri and George suggests that their repainters were unlikely to have been professionals.[37]

Portraits appear to have been more frequently subjected to modification than other types of images, as exemplified by the changes made to a large altarpiece painted by Francisco de Comontes for the convent of Santa Ana in Toledo.[38] Barely noticeable among its eighteen panels are portraits of Philip IV and Mariana of Austria in typical donors' poses, inserted into the Adoration of the Magi and the Nativity, respectively (fig. 51).[39] The portraits of the king and queen are palimpsests. Added to the altar over one hundred years after its completion, they obscure the portraits of its original commissioners. It is not clear why the donor and his wife were covered up, but perhaps the income they promised to the convent had ceased or a gift from the royal couple had necessitated their commemoration at a minimal expenditure. The repainting, which reveals the fragility of portraiture, regardless of its claims to eternal remembrance, focused only on the donors and consisted of rather crudely obscuring their garments in black paint and adding a few details, such as Philip's Order of the Golden Fleece.[40] The symbolism of placing a portrait of the ruling monarch in a scene of the Adoration of the Magi would not have been lost upon a seventeenth-century viewer. Philip's patronage of the convent, which housed a community of Christ's betrothed, mirrored the gifts the magi brought to the infant Christ. Moreover, the one-to-one association of ruling and biblical monarchs had numerous precedents in central Spain, including portraits *a lo divino* that depicted Philip IV's predecessors as ancient kings, additionally serving as a reminder of the interrelatedness of different forms of sacred portraiture (see fig. 22).

Repainted Portraits and Their Audiences

The economical reuse of supports for pictures, the resignification of images of forgotten sitters, and the demand for more images are the most obvious reasons for repainting portraits, but simple pragmatism is not an exhaustive motivation for the images examined here.[41] Rather, the act of

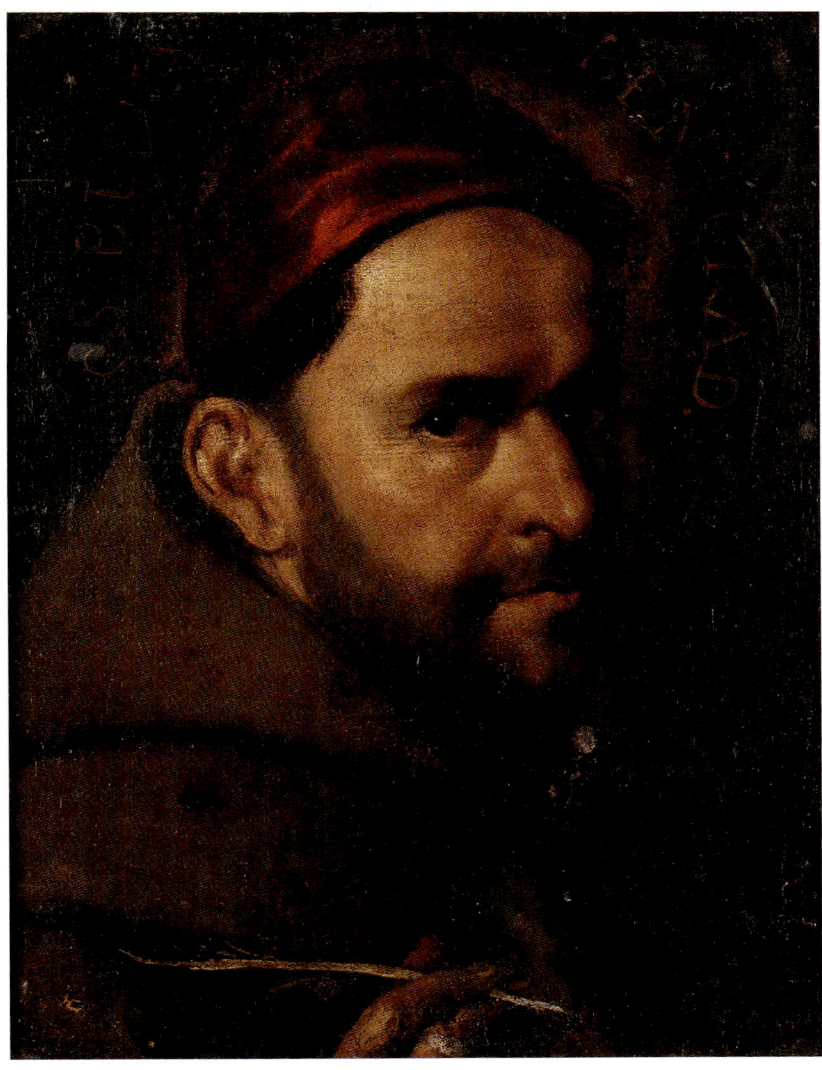

FIG. 50 Unidentified painters, *Portrait of a Friar (Repainted as Saint Bonaventure?)*, seventeenth century with later additions. Oil on canvas, 20.25 × 16.25 in. (51.4 × 41.275 cm). Private collection. Photo: Leland Little Auctions.

amending a portrait with saintly attributes could improve not only its appearance and currency but also the type of image it was. Consider the patron of a painting of Venus and Cupid by Parmigianino. When he decided to gift the work to the pope, he ordered that the painter transform it into a painting of the Virgin and Child for the sake of decorum.[42] This was a common recommendation for dealing with "lascivious" mythological imagery: the Jesuit Cristóbal de la Vega noted that "such paintings can be easily, and without great loss, transformed into others: a Venus into Saint Mary Magdalene, a Diana into Saint Mary of Egypt."[43] This phenomenon did not remain a merely theoretical concern nor was it restricted to the Hispanic world. A painting of Cleopatra holding a lethal asp to her breast by the Florentine Domenico Puligo was transformed at a later moment into a

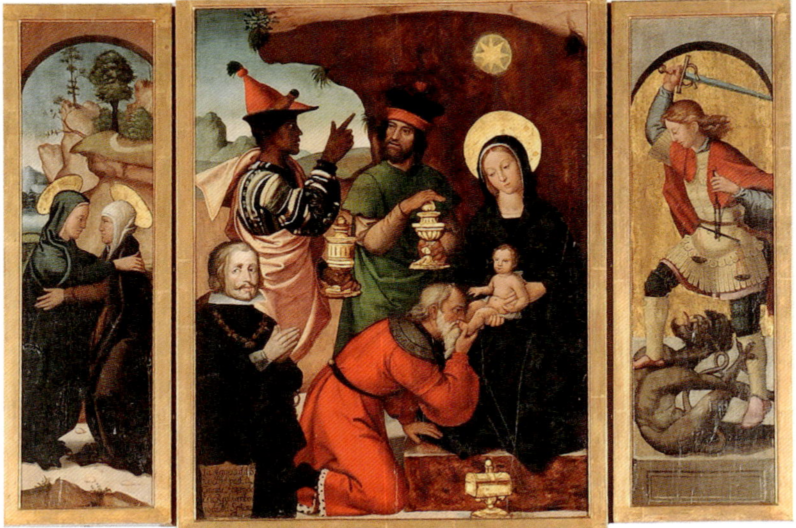

FIG. 51 Francisco Comontes and unidentified painter, *Altarpiece of Saint Ann and Saint Michael* (detail with portrait of Philip IV), 1530–39, with later additions between 1649 and 1665. Oil on panel. Museo de Santa Cruz, Toledo. Photo: HIP / Art Resource, New York.

depiction of the repentant Magdalene through the addition of a halo and the transformation of the serpent's head into the base of the saint's ointment jar.[44] Similarly, in Valencia, the marble-and-bronze portrait busts of Roman emperors in the collection of the city's archbishop Juan de Ribera were "moralized" through the addition of polychromed decoration, including copiously bleeding wounds, which transformed the emperors into early Christian martyrs.[45] From the point of view of a Catholic ecclesiastic, these images were new—and improved.

In the largely implicit hierarchy of image types in the early modern Hispanic world, the representation of a holy figure undoubtedly stood higher than all others, including both portraits and mythological images. In the sixteenth and early seventeenth centuries, sacred painting was considered noble because its subject matter was noble.[46] Within this conceptual framework, a painting that was of mediocre quality but of a "good" subject was better than a stylistically excellent painting that communicated little of worth.[47] The image types that populated the upper echelons of the implicit hierarchy of artistic categories in the early modern period were those that clearly announced their connection with religion.[48]

What happened when a viewer confronted a newly repainted portrait, now decorated with a halo? According to numerous accounts, ranging from hagiographies to political treatises, images had the power to fundamentally transform their viewers, potentially even against their wills, and to catalyze correct modes of response to them. Simply seeing an image, without having recourse to other teachings and texts, could occasion a dramatic spiritual conversion.[49] According to one account, Guido Reni's altarpiece of Saint Philip Neri's vision of the Virgin and Child from Santa Maria in Vallicella produced "an internal impulse contrary to the usual one" in a recalcitrant Muslim youth, converting him to Catholicism. That episode of conversion by image was subsequently depicted in another painting.[50] To Massimo Leone, this exemplifies how "images *of* conversion," that is to say representations of people being converted, became "images *for* conversion" (emphasis original), akin to Victor Stoichita's argument that images were essential catalysts in the production of visions, which could, in turn, be represented in pictorial form.[51] Stoichita connects the increasing illusionism of early modern painting with a greater capacity of such images for causing visions, suggesting that the deceit of naturalism could trigger certain forms of spiritual autoresponse.[52] Following this interpretation, repainted portraits, which maintain their naturalistic individualization, would be more efficacious in spiritually affecting those who saw them than representations of saints that bore no features of portraiture.

In practice, however, recalling the discussion of royal portraits in chapter 4, many early modern Catholics expressed skepticism that a religious image could spontaneously generate devotion in those who saw it; in a recent study, Grace Harpster has challenged the notion that for early modern viewers an image's increased naturalism was correlated with greater spiritual efficacy.[53] To wit, Saint John of the Cross noted that some people focused more on the skill with which an image was made than on what it represented, calling this vanity: "There are many people who take more joy from the painting and ornament of [images and portraits of saints] than from that which they represent."[54] In this unvarnished reading, the religious image could affect only those viewers who were primed to view it correctly, namely for its content rather than for its form. Others could remain entirely immune to its spiritual benefits. Nevertheless, religious images were believed to be valuable, not only as didactic tools, not only for their role in serving as a conduit between those who prayed to them and the divine recipients of those prayers, but for their role in continuously bolstering and reinforcing the Church's fabric of believers. Therefore, repainted portraits became new images not only in their appearance but in the new form of influence that they could exert over the people who came into contact with them.

That images changed states is indisputable. Occasionally, however, they moved in the other direction from what we have examined thus far, that is to say, from sacred to nonsacred images. Leonardo da Vinci famously recounted having been asked to strip away the sacred accouterments from a religious painting so that the patron might lust after the represented woman, free of guilt.[55] A painting by Velázquez appears to have been subjected to a similar process of desanctification but with a differing result (fig. 52). When discovered, the painting appeared to be a portrait of a girl with an idiosyncratic likeness and arresting gaze, with her hands brought together in a gesture of prayer. Although she wears garments in red and blue, the colors traditionally associated with the Virgin, the painting had no other markers of sanctity. However, a recent cleaning revealed that at an earlier stage of the painting's life history, the figure was represented with a crown of stars around her head, akin to depictions of the Immaculate Conception (fig. 53). At an unspecified later date and for reasons unknown, the crown was covered up, removing the painting's sole explicit indication of its sacred status.[56] We can only speculate about the reasons for this intervention, but if the crown of stars was indeed original to the work, the painting

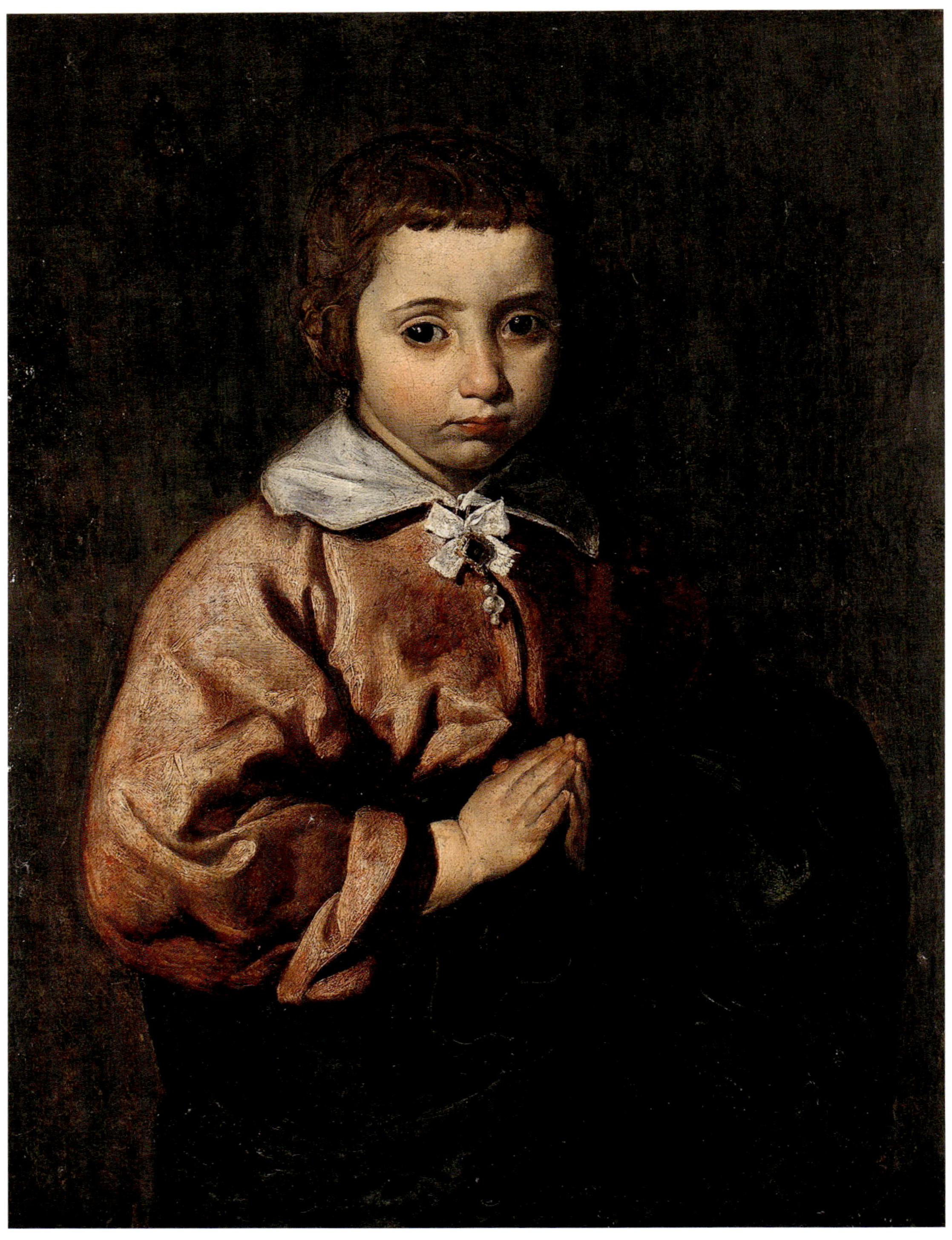

FIG. 52 Diego Velázquez, *Virgin of the Immaculate Conception*, before cleaning, before 1660. Oil on canvas, 22.625 × 17.37 in. (57.5 × 44 cm). Private collection.

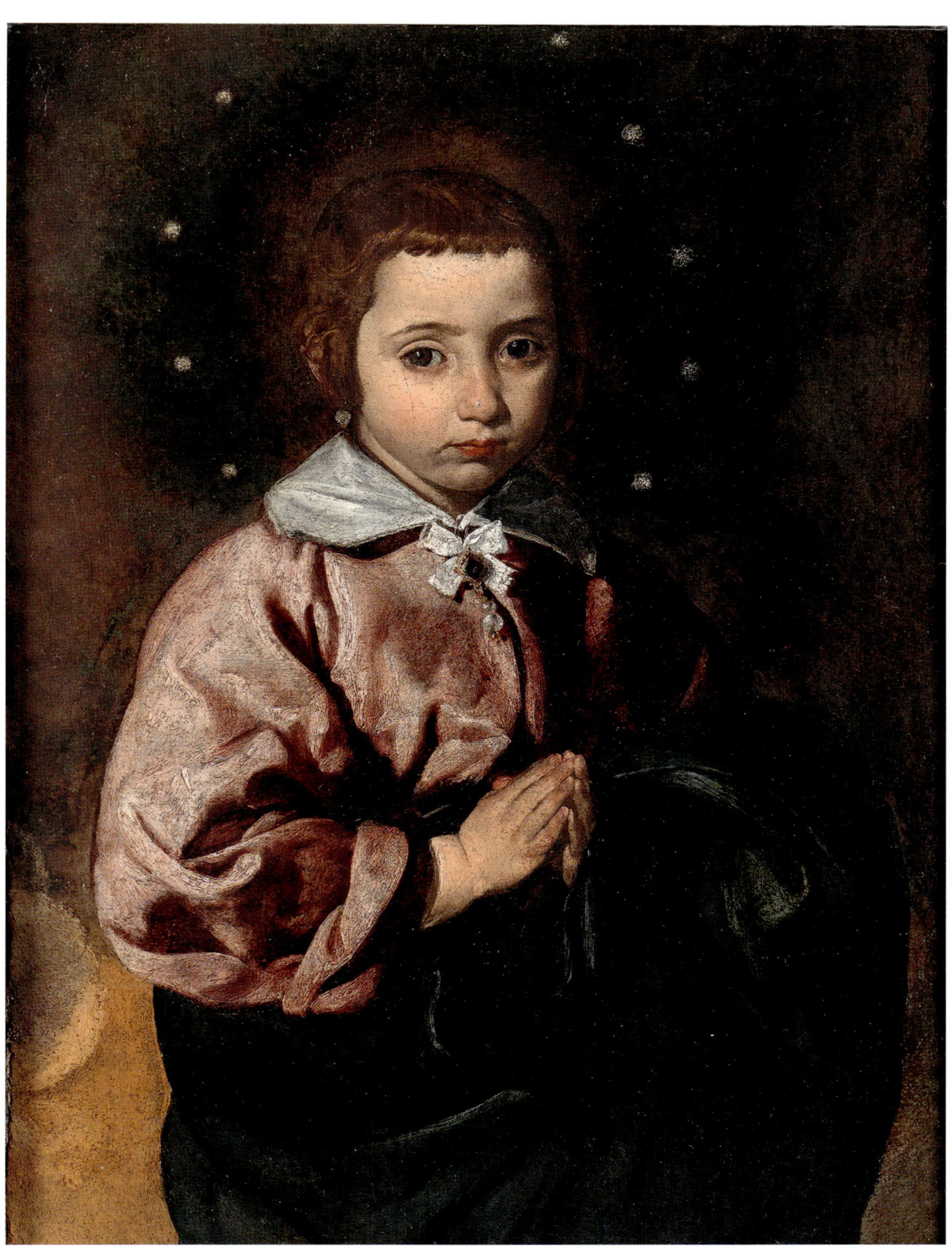

FIG. 53 Diego Velázquez, *Virgin of the Immaculate Conception*, after cleaning, before 1660. Oil on canvas, 22.625 × 17.37 in. (57.5 × 44 cm). Private collection.

may have been initially commissioned as a portrait *a lo divino* by the sitter's family and then desanctified for fear of the repercussions that such images sometimes garnered.

The Life Histories of Artworks in Early Modern Theory and Practice

The topic of an artwork's life stages commonly appeared in Renaissance treatises on painting, often building on Pliny the Elder's discussion of artists' signatures that were prefaced with different forms of the Latin verb *facere* (to make). The imperfect form *faciebat* (was making) suggested to Pliny that "art was always a thing in process and not completed, so that when faced with the vagaries of criticism the artist might have left him[self] a line of retreat to indulgence, by implying that he intended, if not interrupted, to correct any defect noted. Hence it is exceedingly modest of them to have inscribed all their works in a manner suggesting that . . . they had been snatched away from each of them by fate." Pliny added that the rare artist who used the perfect form, *fecit* (made), before his signature appeared "to have assumed a supreme confidence in his art, and consequently all these works were very unpopular."[57]

Similarly, in his *Lives*, Vasari acknowledged the benefit of oil paint in allowing for an artwork to be endlessly perfected; the labor potentially never complete. Vasari argued that in contrast to sculpture, where mistakes, either accidental or due to the sculptor's misjudgment, sometimes cause irreparable damage to the artwork, in painting, "at every slip of the brush or error of judgment that might befall them [the painters] they have time, recognizing it themselves or being told by others, to cover and patch it up with the very brush that made it; which brush, in their hands, has this advantage over the sculptor's chisels, that it not only heals, as did the iron of the spear of Achilles, but leaves its wounds without a scar."[58] Crucially, it was "the very brush that made it" that was permitted reentry onto the canvas's surface—no allowance is made in the text for posterior modifications by brushes wielded by others.[59] In his life of Jacopo da Pontormo, Vasari noted, however, that the painter would repaint his less proficient students' work to such a degree that, in the end, the perfected canvas could barely be ascribed to the student.[60] He therefore recognized the benefits of the act of repainting when it occurred in the workshop, where the master could assist, or even surpass, the pupil. Otherwise, he had little to say about its disruptive potential within the parameters of the life of a single painting, perhaps because it counteracted two of his treatise's primary objectives: a view of the history of painting as a teleological progression across time and a focus on the artistic genius of the individual.

This is not to say, however, that mutability—understood as the gradual ruination or abrupt destruction of an artwork—was not a concern for painters, patrons, and theorists of art alike.[61] For example, artists like Sebastiano del Piombo attempted to prolong the lifespan of their paintings by using durable supports such as slate and other types of stone, which speaks to an interest in conveying a painting in an unchanged state into a distant future.[62] Similarly, a painter-theorist like Pacheco took the inevitable changes of color through fading into consideration, but he also knew that little could be done to effectively counter this effect.[63] This notwithstanding, an artist's awareness of the fugitiveness of certain pigments or the sagging of canvas with time still did not allow for controlling how later viewers would engage with the finished work. Nothing in a picture's physical form could preclude the posterior imposition of new layers onto its surface.

The concerns and motivations that drove the authors of early modern art-theoretical literature do not appear to align with the wide range of artistic evidence for the practice of repainting portraits, which, as the examples under examination make clear, occurred frequently and in both elite and nonelite contexts. In practice, repainting was a standard component of the artistic process in early modern Spain, and it was associated with a battery of Spanish terms in the early modern period, including *aderezar* (dress), *retocar* (retouch), *enmendar* (amend), *renovar* (renovate), *refrescar* (refresh), and *componer* (compose).[64] Moreover, many professional painters devoted significant time to the practice as an act of conservation, given that they were entrusted with the care of paintings in vast royal, noble, and ecclesiastical collections.[65] And, of course, it was not unusual for painters to amend their own canvases, often many years later. Velázquez, in particular, appears to have reworked his paintings. For example, around 1628, he returned to one of the earliest portraits of Philip IV he had painted in Madrid and corrected the drapery of the king's cape and the position of his feet, perhaps as the result of his own artistic maturation.[66]

Even though practices of reuse in various media outside of painting have garnered scholarly interest in recent decades, there is still much research to be done on the repainting or overpainting of finished paintings in the early modern period, which, in general, has been largely ignored as a valid form of cultural production.[67] Where it is most commonly discussed is in conservation literature, which often presents repainting as a barrier to appreciating a painting's aesthetic qualities. For example, the justification of removing a sixteenth-century inscription and coat of arms that had been added to a portrait by Giovanni Battista Moroni a few years after the painter's death lay in the fact that "the historic interest of the additions was far outweighed by the aesthetic dictates of the picture."[68] Another scholar claimed that "with the removal of the halos" from portraits by Petrus Christus, "the aesthetic intentions of the artist were restored."[69] Prioritizing aesthetics in this way and focusing on repainting as merely a hindrance to perceiving a picture's original appearance, whatever that might be, is to overlook important aspects of the painting's social life, of historical practices of perception, and of the interactive and haptic forms of engaged looking that repainting represents.[70] Like the Pueblan painter Conrado, who noted matter-of-factly that other painters had likely added wings to his portraits of Palafox, the artists Moroni or Christus may have understood, and accepted, that later hands would inevitably intervene into their works, seeing the additions as part of the objects' life histories.

One Image, Many Eyes

The portrait, understood as the physiognomic likeness of a specific individual, was an elastic, manipulable image type. Furthermore, the interlocking histories of early portraiture and icon painting, the rise of ecclesiastically approved, portrait-centric religious cults in the fifteenth and sixteenth centuries, and the appealing lifelikeness achieved when images of saints drew on the conventions of portraiture all contributed to the common understanding among early modern individuals that the portrait—potentially any portrait—could be, or temporarily function as, a sacred image. But these "early modern individuals" were, of course, not a homogenous group. In the context of the transoceanic Hispanic monarchy, different individuals may have viewed the same images in entirely different ways. The American, African, Asian, or European audiences who formed part of Hispanic society in the seventeenth century brought with them differing understandings and preconceptions about representation, sanctity, and ritual. Asking the seemingly simple question about the range of responses that a single image could generate can suggest additional motivations for why images were then used in certain ways in certain places. It is also a way of working through and against the hegemonic perspectives enshrined in the archive.[71] Finally, such an approach compels us to reckon with questions of terminology. As I have suggested, the very term *portrait* in its seventeenth-century guise is nearly incompatible with its present-day usage, given how capacious a category it was in the early modern period. This capaciousness expanded even further based on where one was in the vast holdings of the Spanish Crown and on whom one asked.

With this general framework in mind and having considered a range of theories and practices relating to the physical manipulation of portraits and the manipulations of identity that they produced, we can return to Puebla de los Ángeles in 1651 and to the contentious issue of Bishop Palafox's repainted portraits. During the course of the trial, the inquisitors learned that certain portraits had been transformed through the addition of seraphic wings. More troublingly, these objects were but one manifestation of a larger set of cultic behaviors surrounding the figure of Palafox, which included the portraits' public display around the city during religious festivities. Given that the multivalent winged portraits could thus be seen by the full spectrum of the diverse colonial city's populace, the inquisitors became particularly concerned with their potentially insidious effect on its Indigenous inhabitants. This speaks to a perennial preoccupation among civil and ecclesiastical officials throughout early modern Latin America: that preconquest modes of perception, value, and belief might still linger among the region's Indigenous populations. For example, in the Guatemalan town of San Mateo Ixtatán in 1687, the parish priest lamented that the town remained "Christian in name only."[72] Such a declaration ignores the complex religiosity that developed in early modern Mexico and Central and South America. While numerous Indigenous practices and beliefs did survive into the postcontact period, those that in 1651 could trace their roots to the precontact period had inevitably been adapted and transformed in response to a century and a half of colonized reality.[73]

Two Spanish notaries, Nicolás de Valdivia and Martín de Elorriaga, declared that approximately a month prior to their deposition, while in the company of a local alderman named Juan de Llano y Losada, they visited a homestead in the primarily Indigenous neighborhood of Santiago Cholultecapan, just under a mile due west of the cathedral, where they saw that the family had displayed a portrait of Bishop Palafox in their home.[74] Llano y

Losada spoke in Nahuatl to a boy that lived there, asking him "what the name was of [the man] painted in that landscape [*paiz*] that the family had at the center of their home altar."[75] To this, "the *indisuelo* [Indian youth] promptly responded 'santo Palafox.'" This final phrase is rendered in the document, with original punctuation, as "respondio =santo Palafox=."[76] The entire party of Spaniards was "scandalized by such idolatry and discussed whether . . . in all of the other *indios*' houses they have the same portrait, with the belief and acclaim of [Palafox's] sanctity."[77]

The boy's declaration is the trial's only example of an Indigenous voice and one of the very few statements that are not mediated through reported speech. The use of direct rather than reported speech to record a response was an exceptional occurrence in inquisitorial proceedings, used typically only for declarations deemed to be particularly important.[78] However, the statement by the Indigenous child, though bracketed in marks that approximate modern quotation marks to suggest either a quotation or a fragment of particular importance, is part of the testimony of a Spanish witness and not of the Indigenous youth in question. In the multiple nested levels of highly mediated information that characterize any inquisitorial trial, even an ostensibly unmediated statement was still conveyed by the speaker to the questioner and recorded by an inquisitorial notary.[79] Faced with a dearth of information about the Indigenous speaker and his context, informed speculation can serve as a first step to reconstructing a nonhegemonic perspective onto the trial and the images on which it centered.

Why do we encounter this isolated case of direct speech in the trial, and furthermore, why is an Indigenous child privileged in this respect rather than the high-ranking Spanish clerics and officers who also testified during the proceedings? Instructions for inquisitors regularly stipulated that children could not be brought to testify in trials, given their untrustworthiness, but cases where magistrates circumvented these regulations are known.[80] Moreover, in the Puebla trial, the Indigenous child was not an actual witness but rather a source of information in another witness's declaration. Presented thusly, I argue, the boy's status as both an Indigenous person and as a child paradoxically granted his declaration the cachet of unmediated or uncorrupted authenticity. The association of Indigenous Americans with children in need of tutelage and guidance was a firmly established topos in early modern Hispanic religious and political philosophy.[81] Additionally, as a boy "who seemed to be ten years old," the *indisuelo* was also, incontrovertibly, an actual child, characterized in many sources as innocent or pure.[82] Furthermore, from the beginning of the conquest and forced evangelization of New Spain, Indigenous children were used in the identification and extirpation of idols, often employed to implicate their highborn parents' perceived misdemeanors. In 1651, the young boy tacitly reenacted such an episode from the early history of the viceroyalty by revealing his family's improper veneration.[83] His age, which by seventeenth-century standards categorized him as a child, and his ethnicity, which made him an eternal child at that, conspired to grant him an apparent lack of motive for dissimulation from the point of view both of the witnesses recounting their conversation with him and of the notary recording their testimony. The notary's inclusion of references to the speaker's youth and ethnicity enhanced, rather than subtracted from, the legitimacy of the proceedings.

Within a mile from the very center of Puebla, a self-avowed Spanish city, portraits of the controversial bishop (perhaps even some of the repainted winged portraits) would have been seen in bilingual or even monolingual Nahua households.[84] What Nahuatl terms, then, might Llano y Losada have used to question the boy? It is possible that he used a Spanish loanword, such as *pintura* (painting), which appears in the early seventeenth-century Nahuatl annals of Domingo Chimalpahin (where it is rendered as *bintura* or *bintula*).[85] In the seventeenth century, the Spanish term *imagen* (sometimes shortened to *maje*) was also common, and an image of a saint could be described synecdochally through the Spanish term *santo*.[86] However, if Llano y Losada thought of the object specifically as a *retrato* or portrait, he may also have used some form of the Nahuatl word *ixiptlatl* (such as *iixiptla* [his/her/their/its ixiptla] or *teixiptla* [somebody's ixiptla]).[87] Variants of the word that appear in colonial era metatexts are described in terms related to portraiture, widely conceived. In Alonso de Molina's lexicon of the Nahuatl language of 1571, for example, *teixiptla* is defined as "image of someone, substitute, or delegate," (*imagẽ[n] de alguno, sustituto, o delegado*) while the verbal form *ixiptlayotia* is defined as "to delegate, or to substitute for another in his/her place" (*delegar, o sostituyr a otro en su lugar*).[88] *Ixiptlayotia* is also translated as "to make something in one's/its/His image or likeness" (*hazer algo a su imagen y semejança*).[89] *Teixiptla* is implicitly connected to portraiture in this translation, which uses the same language as religious texts that describe humankind as made in the "image and likeness" of God and which often also use the term *retrato* in their explanations of this divine relationship.[90]

The focus on substitution (*sustituto, sostituyr*) in Molina's definition draws on period ideas of portraiture's substitutive capacity, as commonly used in Spanish texts. For example, in 1610, the poet Alonso de Ledesma published a set of emblems celebrating the beatification of Ignatius of Loyola.[91] The logic of the emblem titled "Concerning the miracles that [Ignatius] worked through his person, and through his portrait" hinged on the widely understood substitutive potential of portraiture—that it could stand in for distant or departed loved ones, akin to Alberti's "makes the dead seem almost alive" and "makes the absent present," or for rulers, as in the phrase *regis imago rex est*, "the image of the king is the king."[92] The pictorial portion of Ledesma's emblem does not survive, but it is described as "Blessed Ignatius was painted healing a sick person; and his portrait [was painted healing] another." In the epigram that accompanied the image, Ledesma announces that Heaven had granted Ignatius the "power of substitution [*sustitucion*]" and that he was therefore able to imbue his portrait with the same curative powers that he himself possessed.[93] In Ledesma's conceit, the portrait of Ignatius was able to do anything that Ignatius could do, including curing the sick, because his image was not a mere representation but an equivalent of the future saint.

However, the notion of *teixiptla* was far more complex than what these colonial translations, dependent on European definitions of portraiture, are able to convey. In order to fully understand its colonial usage, it is necessary to consider its precontact meanings. Generally, scholars understand *teixiptla* as the earthly manifestation or representation of a sacred entity.[94] Sometimes, *teixiptlahuan* (the plural form of *teixiptla*) were the human actors, specifically captives, who were dressed as

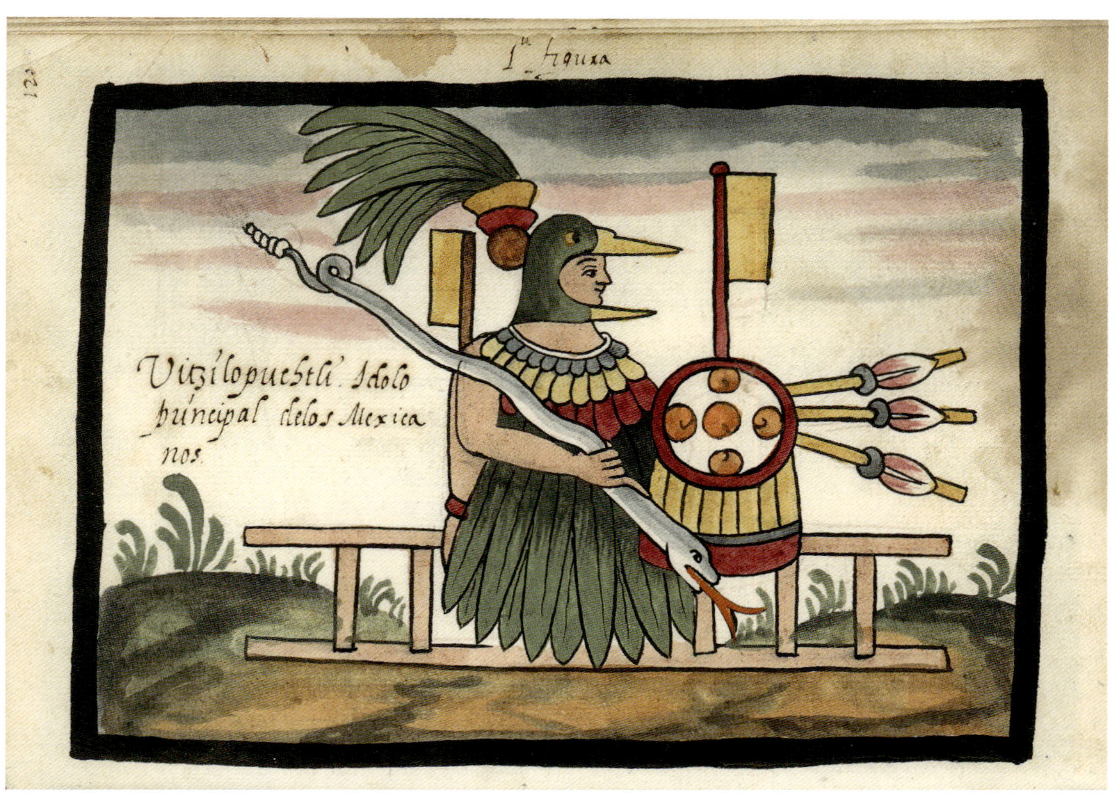

FIG. 54 Juan de Tovar, *Uitzilopuchtli, idolo principal de los Mexicanos*, fol. 120r of the *Historia de la benida de los yndios apoblar a Mexico* (Codex Tovar), ca. 1585. Ink and watercolor on European paper, 5.19 × 7.12 in. (13.2 × 18.1 cm) painting on larger page. John Carter Brown Library, Providence. Courtesy of the John Carter Brown Library.

a specific deity in order to give it form. However, humans were far from the only or most important type of *teixiptlahuan* as the term could also describe bundles, figures, wooden frames, and even painted images.[95] Even though the physical characteristics of a deity (simply put, what that deity looked like) depended on its *teixiptla*, the concept exceeds simple resemblance or masquerade. As defined by Molly Bassett, "a *teixiptla is* the being whom it embodies; it is neither an impression nor a representation of that being" (emphasis original).[96] Given its etymology, which likely derives from the flaying of a captive or the wearing of flayed skins, the term, in Bassett's understanding, can best be understood as the "concrete form of . . . someone who stands in for another by wearing the other's surface or having the other's appearance."[97] For example, an individual who wore a flayed skin became temporarily sacred given that they functioned as the *teixiptla* of a deity.[98] In form, the painting of the god Huitzilopochtli in the Codex Tovar was actually a representation of a human "deity representative" wearing Huitzilopochtli's traditional costume and regalia (fig. 54).[99] In substance, however, that previously human figure became Huitzilopochtli. What is more, the painting itself may also have been understood as a *teixiptla* or an embodiment of Huitzilopochtli. Along this line of argumentation, Diana Magaloni Kerpel has interpreted the dullness of the colored pigments used in the pages that illustrate the Nahua gods in the Florentine Codex as a way of circumscribing the very real power of those enlivened painting-deities.[100]

Molina worked with Indigenous scholars who were undoubtedly well-versed in the intricacies of both Nahuatl and the Spanish of the colonial period, and it may therefore be that the implicit reference to portraiture arose from this collaboration and from a sophisticated understanding of both the intricacies of the Nahuatl term and the semantic richness and multivalence of the Spanish word *retrato* in this period. Although the friar's lexicon preceded the Palafox case by eighty years, later dictionaries also define the term through reference to portraiture. In Juan Guerra's 1692 *Arte de la lengua Mexicana* (Art of the Mexican language), for example, *ixipta* [*sic*] is defined as "the image, or likeness" (*la imagen, ó semejanza*), while in another Nahuatl grammar, this one begun in the 1730s—eighty years *after* the Palafox case, the author Francisco Clavijero explicitly defined two entries related to the concept of *teixiptla* through the terms *retrato* (portrait) and *retratar* (to portray).[101] The terms certainly express conceptual parallels between the two cosmologies: whereas for the Aztecs *teixiptla* gave a deity physical form, in Catholicism the divine was manifested on earth in each human, all of whom were portraits of God.

The question, then, is whether in the gradual strengthening of its association with the concept of portraiture, the word *teixiptla* retained its prior precontact associations with transformation and temporary embodiment.[102] There is, I think, little doubt that it did. Bassett has established that modern-day Nahuatl speakers continue to use the term *teixiptla* to describe the making of deity bundles that, through a process of consecration, temporarily become the deities themselves. Indeed, numerous scholars have shown that drawing on the knowledge of present-day communities can shed light on preconquest histories of the foundation of those communities, suggesting the long-term survival of practices, knowledge, and beliefs.[103] What is more, regarding Catholic imagery, James Lockhart shows that while in the sixteenth century the word *ixiptlatl* was often paired in Nahuatl texts with the Spanish term *imagen*, "as if it were still necessary to explain [to Nahuatl speakers] what the Spanish word meant," in the mid-seventeenth century both terms appear to have lost much currency.[104] "It is as though," Lockhart suggests, "after experimenting with the Spanish ecclesiastical notion of emphasizing the distinction between representation and thing represented, the Nahuas had reverted to their habit (and perhaps the popular Spanish habit as well) of looking at the spiritual being and the tangible form as fully integrated. What the Nahuas had in their houses *were* the saints, in a particular manifestation, and they constantly spoke of them correspondingly."[105]

How, then, might a seventeenth-century Indigenous individual, whose understanding of the concept of divinity was tied to ideas about temporary deity-becoming, have interpreted a portrait of Bishop Palafox, such as the one that Valdivia, Elorriaga, and Llano y Losada examined in Santiago Cholultecapan?[106] Would they, to borrow from Whitney Davis, have recognized "the same, overlapping, or wholly different aspects" within the same image as did the three Spanish officials?[107] Asked about what he saw in the painting, the Indigenous child tersely described that which the painting was to him: "santo Palafox," or an image that was both a depiction of a saint and of Bishop Palafox, which to him were not exclusive identities. Although the declaration can also be translated as "holy Palafox," which would not imply the bishop's sanctity but rather his exceptional virtue, the larger parameters of the case make clear that the inquisitors' concern lay with the cultic veneration of the city's controversial bishop.[108] What the Indigenous youth performed in his response to the visiting alderman was, in part, an act of simple ekphrasis. He recognized the individual depicted in the image, and he described him by uttering his name. However, there is no mention of that particular portrait being physically amended with the attributes of sanctity in any way, unlike the portraits that are explicitly described as having added seraphic wings. Therefore, the addition of the word "santo" as a modifier to the image's identification as "Palafox" was not ekphrastic—nothing in the image itself declared the sitter's supernatural status—but was based on a conventional understanding shared by the child's family. The accepted belief in that particular Indigenous household, it seems, was that the portrait depicted a saint and not merely the local bishop. What is more, regardless of whether the object was described as an *imagen* (or *maje*), *santo* (standing in for *imagen de santo*), or some variant of *teixiptla*, the family may have deemed the image itself to be a powerful entity, an actual sacred being, endowed with quasi-magical powers. As Lockhart points out and as has been studied by scholars like William Christian and Felipe Pereda, this viewpoint represented a "popular Spanish habit," in which religious and particularly miracle-working images were deemed to be sacred in and of themselves.[109] This was also the conceit of Ledesma's emblem about the thaumaturgic powers with which Saint Ignatius's portraits were said to be imbued. Moreover, as will be examined in chapter 4, royal portraits, too, possessed a powerful capacity of standing in for their sitter in a way that far exceeded simple representation.[110] It was these varied, often unorthodox understandings that legitimized the insertion of Palafox's portrait into a grouping of other holy images (or perhaps holy beings) by its owners.

Can we use these ideas to think back on, for example, the portrait of Queen Margarita depicted as the Virgin Mary, which was the focus of chapter 1? As I have argued, for portraits *a lo divino* to function with even a minimal adherence to doctrine, the identity of their living sitters had to be subsumed entirely by that of the holy figure through a process of self-unmaking. Conversely, were Margarita's appearance to be forgotten, the painting would seem to be an entirely orthodox image for prayer and contemplation. With its portraitistic qualities suppressed, the only layer to remain in the painting would be its Catholic iconography: a representation of divine figures. In an oblique parallel, in the process of becoming *teixiptlahuan*, Nahua individuals ceded their individual personhoods, subsuming them to the needs of the impersonated deity. Once this happened, it was the sacred entity, and not they, who remained present on earth. More generally still, can we draw from the notion of *teixiptla* in its seventeenth-century guise to think about the changing states of early modern portraiture writ large? *Teixiptlahuan* served as conduits between human and divine realms, becoming deities only temporarily (even if it did often result in their sacrifice) and through community consensus. Similarly, in early modern Catholic contexts, viewers could, either consciously or misguidedly, transform portraits into images for devotion through the ways that they engaged with them. Any portrait, at any time, had within it the latent potential of being—if only to some of the persons who saw it and if only temporarily—a sacred image. Whatever correspondence there may be between portraits *a lo divino* and the concept of *teixiptla*, I do not intend to suggest that any one viewer in the early modern period, either in Mexico or in Madrid, would have made such a connection. Far from it. What this sort of contemporary free association allows us to do, however, is to take a bird's-eye view onto how certain notions—of the self, the sacred, the image, and the portrait—were being examined across the early modern Hispanic world. What emerges from such a perspective is a sense of their flexibility, a sense of their defiance toward any attempts at defining them in a straightforward, all-encompassing way.

Denying Portraithood

In 1653, the Inquisitorial Tribunal in Mexico City disseminated a decree that prohibited the making, selling, or owning of portraits of Bishop Palafox. Specifically, it indicted those people who would "paint, sell, hide, erase, or change [the portraits] into another person."[111] It appears that even actions that obscured Palafox's likeness were insufficient to undo the relic-like aura these images possessed for having once been portraits of the bishop. Even when repainted with the features of another individual entirely, the images remained threatening. Accretions could, in theory, be stripped away, explaining the inquisitors' inclusion of repainted portraits of the bishop in their decree. However, the decree's stipulation about erasure reveals that not even an iconoclastic unmaking could undo the images' potency.

It was in such cases that the boundaries of artistic categories—if not yet genres—began to ossify, heralding later conceptualizations of the portrait as an explicitly secular image type. In 1677, eighteen years after the bishop's death, a number of petitions reached the Inquisition asking permission to treat his portraits as portraits and nothing more. One individual inquired whether "without incurring any penalty he might have in his home the aforementioned portrait of the aforementioned bishop Don Juan de Palafox" because he had been a familiar of the bishop, and he wanted to "have a remembrance of him in his portrait."[112] A month later, four other citizens of Puebla stated that "for a good remembrance of [Bishop Palafox] they would want to have a portrait [of him]," adding that "because the petitioners are men of [high] station and obligations," they "would not incur any of the disadvantages for which the portraits had been prevented."[113] In their requests, the petitioners touted two things: first, that they would use the portraits as the images had ostensibly been intended, as a commemorative tool; and second, that as elite individuals, they possessed what might be summarized as the characteristic of judgment or discernment sufficient to know that the image was, and could be nothing more than, a simple portrait of a bishop.

Discernment allowed an individual to dispassionately examine an image and, in this case, prevented one from mentally imposing the category of sanctity onto a recipient who did not merit it. The quality was directly discussed in relation to class, race, and gender; its lack immediately marked one as inferior to the upper-class white Spanish male. During an earlier series of disturbances that occurred in Puebla in 1647 in support of Bishop Palafox, his followers were simply characterized as *pleve, y otras personas* (plebes, and other people), which was a class distinction rather than one ethnically or racially based. A witness in the trial following that uprising described the bishop's adherents as "lesser people: Black[s], mulattos, and boys."[114] Other witnesses added that this hostile crowd also included "mestizos and some Spaniards"[115] and that the groups that were particularly devoted to Palafox included "some Black and *chino* slaves . . . [who] expect the Lord bishop to free all of the slaves of this city."[116] *Indios*, or Indigenous individuals, were never listed among the pro-Palafox rioters, even though Palafox's supporters referred to his opponents by two, apparently derogatory, Nahuatl words: *palanca* and *palancapatli* (from *palanqui* [rotten] and *patli* [medicine]), meaning "something rotten" or "a medicine for that which is rotten."[117] In the trial of 1651, one witness declared that he "saw and heard the Lord Bishop Juan de Palafox commonly called *sancto sancto* ["saint, a saint," or "holy, holy"], especially among plebeian, foolish [*incapaz*] people who possess little judgment [*de poco discurso*]."[118] Similarly, three women who recommended that a witness pray to Palafox were characterized by their "simplicity" (*simplicidad*), while others were termed "simple people" (*gente senzilla*).[119]

By contrast, the individuals who were scandalized by the popular veneration of a number of pseudo-relics that had belonged to Bishop Palafox, including his bedclothes and the cilice he used for penance, were "knowledgeable and dispassionate people."[120] This indication of quality was similar to the petitioners of 1677, who explicitly declared their elite status and by extension their dispassionate nature, implying that they could restrict access to the paintings and that, if they were permitted to keep them, the portraits would not mutate into anything else, especially religious images. After all, various witnesses in the trial had suggested that the relative "dangers" of an image depended on its reach: the more people could see an incorrect image, the greater would be its insidious effect on the undiscerning masses, in contrast to those individuals who would ostensibly never confuse a portrait with a holy image.

In 1674, a painter from Puebla named Juan Rubí de Marimón petitioned the tribunal that he be allowed to paint a copy of a portrait of Palafox that belonged to one Francisco Lorente (or Llorente), to whom it had been sent by Palafox's biographer Rosende.[121] The portrait came with an official inquisitorial license, which permitted its owner to keep it, and Marimón, who cited the benefits that he had experienced during the bishop's tenure in the city, was granted permission to copy the portrait. Nevertheless, his license was revoked in 1680 after the tribunal received too many similar petitions.[122] It appears that, with Marimón, the tribunal had prematurely assessed that the ardor of the local devotion toward Palafox had died down. The fact that a subsequent decree prohibiting portraits of Palafox was also issued in 1691 suggests that the cult, never entirely extinguished, would flare up occasionally.[123] The decisions of 1653, 1677, and 1691 reveal that the unbridled permutations of Palafox's portraits had effectively dismantled their ability to be just portraits, at least in the eyes of the inquisitorial authority, and even nearly a half century after the events of 1651. Even when those who petitioned for the right to own a Palafox portrait advertised their ability of treating portraits qua portraits and nothing else, it was deemed that the images' lurking potential for functioning as sacred objects still posed too significant a threat.

Conclusion: The Skull in the Mirror

Palafox died in 1659, having been called back to Spain, to the provincial diocese of Osma. He had been plagued by decades of libel, excommunications, exiles, and legal attacks that resulted from his unpopular ecclesiastical and political positions, of which the 1647 and 1651 trials were but two examples. However, he had not been without friends and admirers, including the Spanish cleric Rosende, who authored Palafox's posthumous biography seven years after his death.[124] Within this text, which was instrumental in the formation of the bishop's legacy, portraits played a leading role.

Rosende's text was an ambitious attempt at vindicating Palafox and liberating him from the damage that the various legal and personal disputes had caused to his name and the ill repute that they could potentially continue to spread over his memory. Rosende likely feared that the 1651 case of the proliferation of the bishop's portraits in Puebla would be a prime target for his detractors, who could deploy the notion of the vanity of portraiture as proof of the bishop's dubious character. In anticipation of such attacks Rosende referred to a potentially apocryphal anecdote about the bishop's portraits "as testimony of how much it mortified [Palafox] to know that he was being portrayed so ubiquitously."[125] Rosende recounted that when the bishop visited a nun in Puebla:

> She mentioned to him in passing that she had a portrait of him, which gave her great consolation. He was very surprised at this, not knowing how someone might have portrayed him without his consent, and he asked to see it. The nun . . . handed it to him, as it was a small portrait, painted on tin. And when holding it in his hand he said to her: "it is clear that the painter was rushed when he painted this image, because it does not look like me. Nor are these my features. It is necessary to look at me more slowly to achieve success, [otherwise] the painter's ideas will become confused in his haste. I will have it corrected and I will return it to you." The bishop returned home, and calling upon his painter the licenciado Pedro García Ferrer . . . he ordered him to erase his face, and in its place to paint a skull, and a skeleton's hands: he did it thus . . . he returned it to the nun closed, with a note that said that this was his true portrait.[126]

That Palafox never consented to have his portrait painted is almost certainly untrue. After all, Conrado testified that Palafox himself had commissioned one of the eleven portraits that he had painted of the bishop, to send to the Philippines. Nevertheless, the conceit was as significant in the construction of his mythos—presenting Palafox as averse to the vainglories of portraiture—as it was common in the period. Ignatius of Loyola similarly refused to have his portrait taken, as examined in chapter 2, and the trope appears in countless other hagiographies and biographies of individuals, who were noteworthy for their piety, charity, or other Catholic virtues.[127]

For instance, in Pedro Salazar de Mendoza's biography of the Spanish cardinal Juan Pardo de Tavera, we read that the cardinal "showed his great modesty by objecting to sit for a portrait, even though many diligent painters and sculptors tried [to take it]."[128] In Rosende's telling, when Palafox ordered that his portrait be replaced with a skull, he effectively dismantled the roles that Alberti had attributed to portraiture, which "makes absent men present . . . and makes the dead seem almost alive."[129] The bishop's deed was a reversal of these: he made absent a familiar sitter by making his portrait likeness generic, and, more strikingly, he made a live sitter dead. In doing so, he claimed that the solace portraits were believed to provide their viewers, in this case a nun who declared that his picture provided her with "great consolation," was false.[130]

Rosende consciously highlighted the episode, which foregrounded the bishop's humility and disavowal of portraiture, because it mimicked in reverse the transformations via repainting to which people had subjected Palafox's portraits in Puebla nearly two decades prior, during his tenure as bishop of that city. In elevating Palafox's act of imposing a skeletal face onto his individualized portrait, Rosende counteracted the unsanctioned work of the "stupid or ill-intentioned individual," who had turned any number of the bishop's portraits into images of a holy figure. The erasing and repainting of Palafox's likeness with a skull pushed the image from portrait to antiportrait. Skulls, in which all viewers can see themselves and with which no one can actually identify, efface individuality, becoming identical multiples. Moreover, they appeal to the conventions of the portrait (a head with a "face," a direct "gaze") without performing any of its requisite tasks.[131] Paradoxically, when a disassociated portrait of a forgotten individual was repainted as an image of a saint, it underwent a very similar ontological transformation as Palafox's portrait-to-skull. Previously constrained by its limited relationality, the sanctified portrait now entered into a space of potentially limitless utility and universal significance—at least from the point of view of Catholic image makers and theorists.

The episode of García Ferrer's repainting is also referenced in the elaborate frontispiece for Rosende's biography, which was designed by the painter Francisco Camilo, apparently closely following Rosende's instructions, and engraved by Pedro de Villafranca y Malagón (fig. 55).[132] The engraving freely announces the multiple hands involved in its making, listing both its designer and engraver at the bottom of the page. In contrast to the practice of repainting portraits, which almost never acknowledged the identities of both painter and repainter, in prints, the notion of creation by cooperation was embedded into the very way they were made. The complex frontispiece centers on an oval portrait of the bishop, which is surrounded by a decorative frame and an array of objects, whose symbolism is carefully described in the accompanying text. Above the portrait is a mirror; its correct perspectival rendering is sacrificed so that the viewer can see its surface. In the mirror is reflected a skull, which corresponds in size and position to Palafox's head below it.[133] Adding another hand still, a later owner of the exemplar reproduced here also made his or her mark on the image, coloring it in pink and red crayon.

The inclusion of the portrait in the frontispiece and the use of the skull in the mirror to simultaneously critique it allowed Rosende to negotiate a middle ground between two seemingly incompatible goals. These were, first, the creation of a book that could compete with the most popular hagiographies of the day, which often included richly

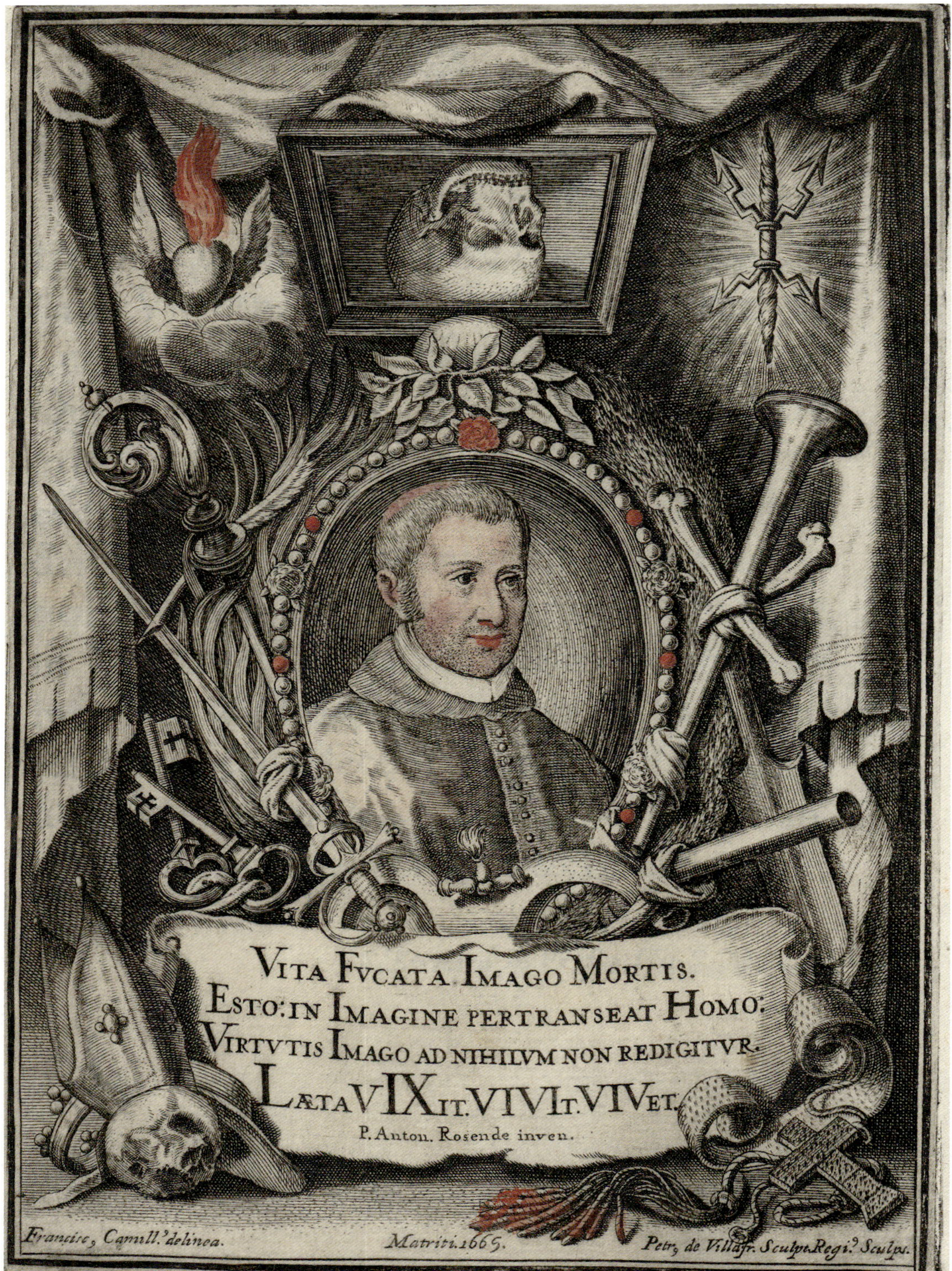
VITA FVCATA IMAGO MORTIS.
ESTO: IN IMAGINE PERTRANSEAT HOMO:
VIRTVTIS IMAGO AD NIHILVM NON REDIGITVR.
LÆTA VIXIT. VIVIT. VIVET.
P. Anton. Rosende inven.
Francisc, Camill.' delinea.
Matriti. 1665.
Petr, de Villafr. Sculpt. Regi.' Sculps.

detailed portrait frontispieces, and second, the accounting of the life of an individual purportedly driven by a singular disdain for his own portrait.[134] Rosende himself defended his decision in the following terms:

> If this man . . . had thrived in those centuries, which we did not know, nor do we discuss here, we would anxiously and curiously seek out not only his books of doctrine, but also his medals and images, in order to observe the physiognomy of a man who had so much fame. . . . For this reason, with calculated meditation, I place simultaneously before the eyes of those who would want to look upon, and consider, his books, his writings, his virtues, his face, his honor, his immortality within one sole image, all girded by the limited field that is a print, which all fits within a sheet of paper, so that he who should solicit it dispassionately, might find it all together.[135]

Although Rosende ensconced the mention of the "face," that is, Palafox's likeness, within a plethora of other symbols that stood for the bishop's achievements, characteristics, and qualities, the size and centrality of the portrait make it the most prominent and unambiguous element of the printed frontispiece. After all, in order to recognize the image in the oval as a portrait and to associate it with the subject of the biography, most readers did not need to turn to the gloss provided by Rosende, which explained the other esoteric elements that surrounded the bishop's head.

FIG. 55 Pedro de Villafranca y Malagón, after Francisco Camilo, frontispiece of Antonio González de Rosende, *Vida i virtudes del Illmo i Excmo Señor D. Juan de Palafox i Mendoza* (Madrid: Julian de Paredes, 1666). Engraving on paper, with wax crayon. Houghton Library, Harvard University, Cambridge, SC6.P1723.W666g.

In contrast to the case of Palafox's portraits, it was frequently the failure of memory or perhaps even its purposeful condemnation that resulted in a sitter's disassociation from his or her portrait and its eventual reworking. Although the recognition of a given individual may have been a portrait's primary function, a disassociated portrait still had within it a dormant potential for the conveyance of meaning, easily becoming a vehicle for other kinds of representations. Later repainters may have realized that the naturalism and the particular form of engagement with the viewer that are so typical of portraiture positively enhanced what would become depictions of saints.

It is impossible to speak of portraiture as an artistic genre in our modern, secular understanding of the term in the Hispanic world of the sixteenth and seventeenth centuries. Nevertheless, it is clear that there was, however implicit, an understanding of where one could find a physiognomic likeness, what such a likeness could do or look like, and what constituted correct or incorrect manners of interacting with it. Regardless of the multiple imbrications of portraiture and religious images in this period, there were restrictions and limitations on how those imbrications could manifest. And when those limitations were exceeded, the resulting images were often vigorously policed and effectively dismantled. It was in those instances—when inquisitors declared where a portrait was, or was not, appropriate, that we begin to observe an explicit crystallization of the notion that certain image types are distinct from others—and perhaps even distinctly secular.

But portraiture was a capacious category—and while in certain instances it was barred from religious contexts, its malleability and its incomparable ability of conveying the qualities of presence, authenticity, and likeness allowed its simultaneous existence in the sphere of the sacred. Within this early modern culture, the category of portraiture had two lives, related to each other not as a simple binary but as a constantly shifting interplay. Of these portraitures, one was constrained, closer to the modern usage of the term, and the other capacious; one was markedly self-reflective and secular, and the other still open to sacred interpretations; and, as is often the case with any form of official control, one was orthodox, while the other elicited actual lived behaviors that did not always align with official censures and could not be fully policed.[136]

PORTRAITS AS SACRED IMAGES *Chapter 4*

The Unrecognizability of the Royal Portrait

The sitter of the life-sized portrait, painted by Velázquez, wears all black, save for his white *golilla* collar and sleeve cuffs. He stands confidently, but his expression is impassive; his facial features idiosyncratic and unidealized. The background is largely undefined: a floor and wall in shades of brown and gray betray little of the sitter's location. This terse description can apply to any one of Velázquez's numerous portraits of the young king Philip IV from the mid-1620s (fig. 56), but it equally describes another portrait by the same painter thought to depict Pedro de Barberana y Aparregui, from around 1630 (fig. 57). Aside from the sitters' individualized faces, the table in the portrait of Philip, and the insignia of the Order of Santiago on Don Pedro's chest, the two portraits share much in terms of composition, monumentality, rendering of the figure, format, and even the sitters' dress. Scholars have attempted to identify certain formal solutions in royal portraits that ensured their unequivocal recognition as royal, including the sitter's emotional restraint and elegant bearing.[1] However, it would be difficult to incontrovertibly point to such qualities in the portrait of Philip IV, while denying their presence in the portrait of Barberana, who was a knight of the Order of Calatrava and a nobleman but certainly not royal. One even senses that if the sitters were to switch heads, neither image would become any more or less regal.[2] Why is the portrait of Philip not explicitly recognizable as an image of a royal individual?

Of French official portraiture, Jean-Paul Sartre writes, "We have only to note how the signs of their power are collected around Francis I or Louis XIV in their portraits. Our eyes meet royalty immediately."[3] Why are, to borrow from Sartre,

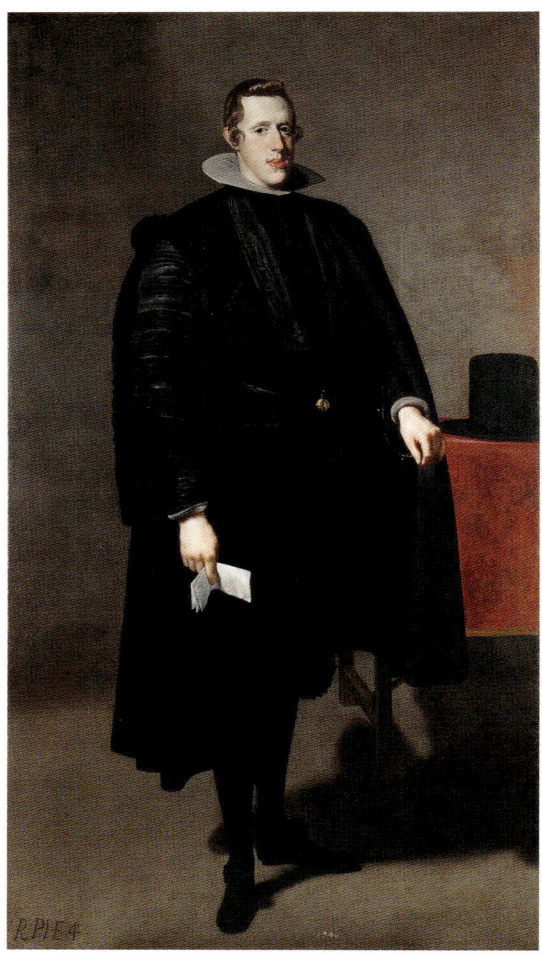

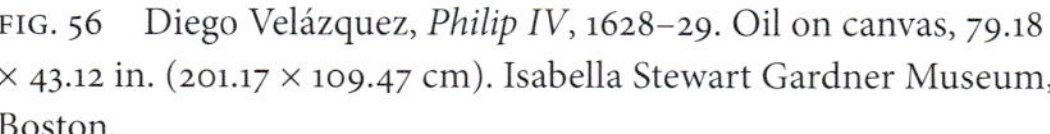

FIG. 56 Diego Velázquez, *Philip IV*, 1628–29. Oil on canvas, 79.18 × 43.12 in. (201.17 × 109.47 cm). Isabella Stewart Gardner Museum, Boston.

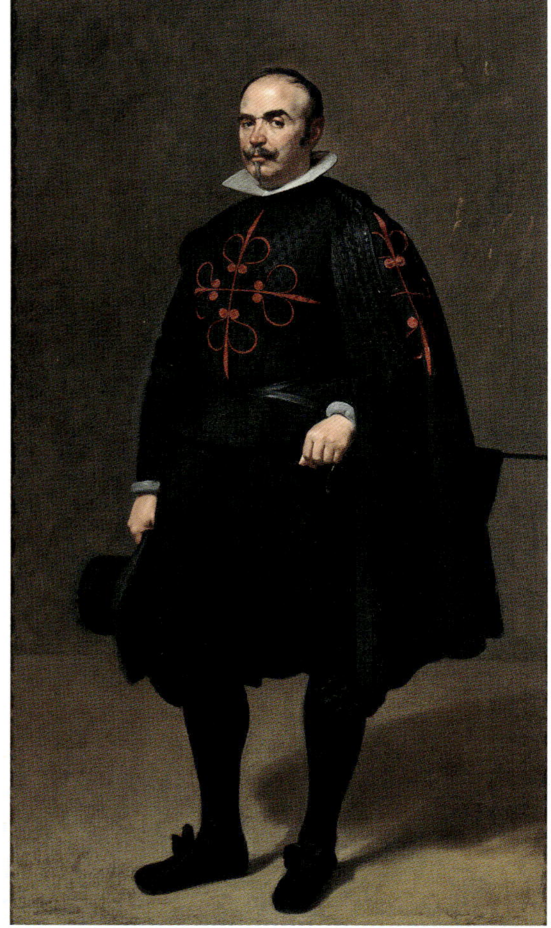

FIG. 57 Diego Velázquez, *Don Pedro de Barberana y Aparregui*, ca. 1631–33. Oil on canvas, 78 × 43 7/8 in. (198.1 × 111.4 cm). Kimbell Art Museum, Fort Worth.

Spanish royal portraits of the Habsburg period so consistently empty, entirely devoid of those "signs of power"? As discussed in chapter 1, the Habsburg kings of Spain did not claim that their rule was divinely sanctioned nor did they undertake the rituals of coronation and anointment, familiar from numerous other European contexts, which would have marked them as God's chosen representatives. By extension, they did not use symbols of royal power, such as crowns, orbs, or scepters, because those objects were inextricably tied up with the sanctifying ceremonial practices that the monarchy did not embrace. Moreover, the Spanish king was the ruler of multiple historic kingdoms, including Aragón, Portugal, and Naples, each with coronation regalia and rituals of its own, but he did not possess the overarching imperial title that, after Charles V, had passed to the Austrian Habsburgs.

By donning any one of those crowns, the argument goes, he would have excluded the other territories of which he was also king.[4] It is these qualities of early modern Spanish kingship that are at the root of what I term the unrecognizability of the royal portrait in the Hispanic world.[5]

Nevertheless, images of the king provide another avenue for understanding the overlap between portraiture and religious painting, in addition to the other forms of sacred portraiture—meditative sanctified portraits, true portraits of saints, and repainted portraits—that I have thus far examined. This may seem paradoxical given that, at casual glance, royal portraits appear to be entirely distinct from the sphere of the sacred; they are explicitly secular—and indeed, this is how they have most commonly been studied and understood. However, royal portraits were displayed with symbolically charged framing devices, such as baldachins, and they demanded specific forms of viewer response, both of which resembled the presentation and treatment of Catholic religious images.

To put it simply, to a viewer who was untrained in the specifics of the representation of privileged subjects, the royal portrait *looked* like other portraits but *functioned* akin to religious artworks. It was this dual relation—the royal portrait's formal similarity to nonroyal portraits and its functional similarity to sacred images—that forms this final conceptual conduit between the sphere of the sacred and the larger category of portraiture. As we shall see in this chapter, a nonroyal portrait—in this case once more of Bishop Palafox—could slide along this conduit, propelled by the behaviors and reactions of the audiences that saw it. Moving in one direction, it impinged upon the privileged position of the image of the king. Moving in the other, it laid claim to the seemingly unique status of religious images. The portrait's viewers created these new actualities by wanting or understanding the portrait they saw before them to be something other than what was originally intended by its artist and patrons.

Seeing Differently

That audiences affected the status of images was well understood in the sixteenth century. Paleotti notes in his *Discourse on Sacred and Profane Images* that "an image quite properly classified . . . as sacred may nonetheless be seen in another light by a viewer . . . An image may, with respect to its outer appearance, be regarded by some as religious and sacred, by others both impious and perverse as an idol, and by yet other fools as a profane picture serving merely as a diversion."[6] Paleotti acknowledges that although a picture may have been intended for religious usage, there was nothing inherent within it to ensure that it be universally recognized as such. Much the same could be said of the portrait. It was when viewers of a portrait (by analogy, Paleotti might deem them fools) did not recognize its sitter or when they attributed different qualities to the depicted figure that it became prone to accruing new layers of meaning. Echoing Paleotti, Davis discusses how various individuals apprehend identical objects in vastly differing manners, noting that each object has what he terms "forms of likeness."[7] An image can simultaneously be anything to any number of people who see it, regardless of any original intentions that may have undergirded its creation. It possesses multiple, even endless, forms of likeness.[8]

It is precisely when viewers see different things in the same images that the potential for tensions arises, as illustrated by a potentially apocryphal episode concerning a painting of María Inés Calderón (known as La Calderona), recounted by the historian Agustín González de Amezúa. Calderón, an actress and the presumed lover of King Philip IV, retired from her life at court to the Guadalajaran convent of Valfermoso de las Monjas, of which she eventually became abbess. According to the story, she may have brought with her a portrait from her days as an actress. After her death in 1646, the nuns eventually forgot that the painting, which depicted a woman in—by that time outdated—courtly dress, was a portrait. The portrait was no longer recognizable as a specific individual and appeared, instead, to simply be a painting of a figure in opulent, even fantastical, garb.[9] Eventually, the nuns of the convent came to believe that the portrait was a sacred image of the archangel Raphael and consequently moved it to a chapel in the monastic church. It is possible that this confusion was occasioned by the nuns' knowledge of any number of painterly types that existed in the gray area where portraiture and religious imagery came into conversation with each other. In the late nineteenth century, a historian visiting the convent discovered an identifying inscription on the painting and alerted the nuns to the fact that their veneration had, in fact, been misguided: it had been directed not to a depiction of an archangel but to a secular woman, whose status as the convent's abbess had apparently done little to erase her historical ill repute. The outraged nuns are said to have organized an auto-de-fé and burned the portrait, a multivalent act that may be seen both as an execution in effigy as well as an extirpation of an idol. After all, they had, for centuries, venerated an unconsecrated, inefficacious object.[10] The painting, which was originally commissioned as a portrait, did not cease being a portrait when its viewers began to treat it as a religious painting. Rather, the recognition of its status as a portrait was blocked when a certain portion of its viewers saw it only as a painting of an archangel.[11]

The nuns in Valfermoso did not transform the portrait through repainting nor did they subject it to any other permanent modification. They had not needed to since they were already convinced the image depicted a holy figure. How, then, had their principally immaterial engagements with the image affected its status, as well as the category to which it belonged? The painting's most important transformation occurred when the nuns moved the portrait into a chapel. Although donor and funerary portraits were not unusual in ecclesiastical settings, the move appears to have had the goal of bringing (what was understood to be) a sacred image into a context where performing devotions to that image would be most appropriate. Once placed within the religious frame that the entire space of the chapel provided, surrounded by flowers and candles and in the company of actual religious paintings and statues, the image could receive the nuns' prayers, serving as a link between them and the image's (perceived) holy prototype: Saint Raphael. This framing ensured that anyone who now came upon the painting was even more likely to perceive the image as sacred.

Such behaviors, because of their ephemerality and immateriality, would not have permanently affected the appearance of an image nor would they have indiscriminately communicated the image's newfound sacred status to all of its viewers. Nevertheless, this type of action, with the nuns relating with a portrait as if it were a religious picture, closely resembles the physical transformation of portraits through repainting them with halos and other attributes at some point in their afterlives, as discussed in chapter 3. It also resembles how framing elements, such as a baldachin, curtain, and dais, guaranteed that viewers would recognize that an otherwise unremarkable portrait was actually a depiction of their king, as will be discussed below. In all of these cases, the simple portraits underwent similar ontological transformations, even if only temporarily, moving from profane to sacred (or, in the case of the portrait of the king, semisacred), and from merely commemorative to powerfully efficacious. Most important, they transformed from objects that possessed relevance to only a few individuals to ones that were ostensibly universal.

To understand how the king's image linked the larger categories of sacred imagery and portraiture, this chapter will first consider period prescriptions—many of these largely implicit—for how audiences were supposed to interact with Spanish royal portraits. What I have thus far established concerning the nonsacred character of the Spanish monarchy and, relatedly, the unrecognizability of royal portraits lays the groundwork for many of these considerations. Like much of the historiography of royal portraiture, in this chapter I am interested in the power of the king's image. In contrast to prevailing scholarly notions, however, what I see in the image of the Spanish monarch is a latent, perpetually threatening powerlessness, caused, in part, by its excessive reliance on forms of display. It is these that the chapter will analyze next, considering how portraits of the king were presented to their audiences and, crucially, how those forms overlapped with religious practices. The second half of the chapter returns to the case of Bishop Palafox, partially considered in chapter 3, where the systems of royal and sacred representation, stretched thin by discontent, failed. The bishop's portraits revealed themselves to be supremely flexible, even omnivorous, easily impinging upon both of those most privileged categories: the portrait of the king and the image of the saint.

More generally, this chapter contributes to this book's larger argument that any portrait had the dormant internal potential to become a sacred image. The long, imbricated histories of religious imagery and portraiture, together with the range of sacred portraits that saturated the visual landscape of the early modern Hispanic world, meant that certain portraits, including of recently deceased saints, like Ignatius of Loyola and Teresa of Ávila, and of donors in the guise of holy figures, already functioned as religious images. It was a small conceptual leap to bring other unsanctioned portraits into that capacious category. Early modern individuals were constantly presented with opportunities for praying to portraits.

Looking at Royal Portraits

The Spanish monarchy set much stock by ceremony. Public festivities—such as *juras* or the swearing of oaths, displays of piety, processions, and proclamations—served to recapitulate its power to a broad spectrum of the populace. Within these events, the king often played a central role. However, the monarchy's colonial expansion in the sixteenth and seventeenth centuries compounded the challenges of maintaining this ceremonial character. Indeed, the Spanish Habsburg kings rarely traveled to the distant territories they controlled, and none of them ever visited the Crown's American holdings.[12] There was, however, a conceptual solution to this problem. According to the principle of *regis imago rex est* (the image of the king is the king), the royal portrait, as well as the king's coat of arms, seals, and other royal objects, could stand in for the king if he were not present.[13] Of this the playwright Juan de Zabaleta noted that through his portrait, the king "was made present continuously and simultaneously in his different states and territories,"[14] far surpassing the basic functions of the portrait as a mnemonic device or as a source of emotional comfort.[15] This capacity of the royal portrait may be considered "eucharistic," as defined by Pereda in his discussion of religious images that were believed to possess something of the divine.[16] The portrait of the king was an idiosyncratic image type in early modern Spain, based not on its appearance but on the quasi-magical characteristic of imbued presence, with which it was believed to be, or, at least, said to be, endowed. In practice, however, José Riello notes that "*every* effigy" possesses something of this substitutive power of creating presence, which in turn suggests that the royal portrait had a theoretical but not practical monopoly on this capacity.[17] This, too, contributed to its impotence.

The apparently idiosyncratic nature of royal portraits meant that they were subjected to particular strictures. In 1633, the painters Diego Velázquez and Vicente Carducho were ordered to conduct an evaluation of portraits of the king and his family that "did not resemble the royal family, [or had] indecent clothing." After collecting eighty-four portraits from shops and studios around Madrid, the two painters deemed only twelve to have been created with the decorum that the royal representation demanded. The others had the "face erased so that they might be redone and that they bear resemblance and be in conformity with the art of painting."[18] In 1679, the painters Juan Carreño de Miranda and Francisco Rizi embarked on a similar task of evaluation and censorship.[19] The erasure and repainting to which the royal portraits were subjected aimed at maintaining a uniform corpus of representations of the king. According to the logic of seriality I have explored in relation to images of saints, like Ignatius of Loyola, and which, with small exceptions, also applies to royal portraits, deviations from a corpus of hieratic images had the potential to destabilize the corpus as a whole.[20]

Considering the degree to which Madrid artists who painted royal portraits were overseen by the court, there are surprisingly few explicit instructions outlining how one was supposed to *act* in front of an image of the king. Instead, myriad texts by early modern political theorists, dramatists, and poets only obliquely suggest to their readers how to do so. How, then, was the early modern individual expected to behave before a royal portrait, particularly if it so closely resembled other portraits? According to some thinkers, the portrait of the monarch could unequivocally reveal itself as a royal image. The writer and politician Diego de Saavedra Fajardo recounted precisely such a moment of spontaneous recognition and reaction, writing that "Diego Velázquez was portraying the king Philip IV with such an exquisite movement and such an expression of the king's majestic and august face, that I was compelled to demonstrate respect [*en mí se turbó el respeto*] and I bent my knee to him and [lowered] my eyes."[21] In similar terms, Lázaro Díaz del Valle described seeing a portrait of Philip IV that was "so lifelike that, upon seeing it, it flooded me with respect [*me infundió respeto*] and provoked me toward the most appropriate veneration and reverence," which Riello analyzes in relation to the thaumaturgy of the royal image.[22] Even if unrecognized, the texts imply, the king's face could still compel a viewer to the appropriate physical reaction of reverence and servitude (even though, in practice, one could feasibly look upon a royal portrait with much greater attention than at the king himself, achieving a degree of intimacy with the simulacrum that could never occur with its original).[23] In Saavedra Fajardo's and Díaz del Valle's tellings of these episodes, the royal portraits committed a certain violence on their viewers in eliciting their respect, even though there is a certain ambiguity in both anecdotes as to whether the behavior was occasioned by Velázquez's artistry, by the power of the king's portrait qua portrait, by the sitter's qualities that were independent of that image, or, to some extent, by all three.[24]

Similarly, Pedro Jerónimo Galtero's poem "Elogio a el retrato de la magestad de Philipo IIII" (Encomium to the portrait of his majesty Philip IIII [*sic*]) of 1631 suggests that a royal portrait could provoke a spontaneous reaction of deference: "When the curtain, which contains the deity is pulled away, the body bends down [*el cuerpo inclina*]."[25] The dramatic pulling away of the curtain makes visible the royal portrait. In this instant, the revealed image appears to force the viewer's body to perform the expected choreography of bowing down or kneeling in respect and humility. That Galtero used the word "deity" is no mistake. The behaviors of reverence directed at the person and image of the king were similar to those performed in front of holy images. Some of these actions are described in the text of the twenty-fifth session of the Council of Trent, which notes that "by means of the images which we kiss and before which we uncover the head and prostrate ourselves, we adore Christ and venerate the saints whose likeness they bear."[26]

Given this similarity, the idea of kingship provides Paleotti with a convenient metaphor for clarifying particularly difficult concepts related to sacred images. For example, when describing the differences between the honorific forms of *latria*, which is adoration that is restricted to the three persons of God; *hyperdulia*, which is veneration owed only to the Virgin; and the lowest, *dulia*, which refers to the veneration directed toward the saints, Paleotti focuses on the viewer's physical movements. He acknowledges that there is no "detectable sign in us of any differentiation" between the three forms, "because we appear to kneel indifferently before the holy Sacrament, the image of the glorious Virgin, and those of the saints." Regardless of being formally the same, however, it is the "intention" that defines the type of reverence that an image's viewers perform. "We doff our cap before king and gentleman alike," Paleotti argues, "but we are saluting the king with a different intention than the gentleman."[27] Saavedra Fajardo and other theorists of royal representation could have feasibly extended this argument to counter the claim that Barberana's portrait was nearly identical in formal terms to an image of Philip IV. The two portraits were incontrovertibly different based on whom they depicted, and moreover, they were distinguished by the nature of their viewers' reactions (be they conscious or subconscious) to them.

Royal portraits were images to which even the king himself was expected to show respect.[28] The historian Baltasar Porreño wrote of Philip II that "as a consequence of his great humility, he greatly honored his progenitors, so that at their tombs and in front of their portraits he would take off his hat, and with notable care inquire as to how they were being revered and how their memory was being observed."[29] Written near the beginning of king Philip IV's reign, the statement extolling the virtuous behavior of the king's grandfather Philip II in relation to the portraits of his predecessors may

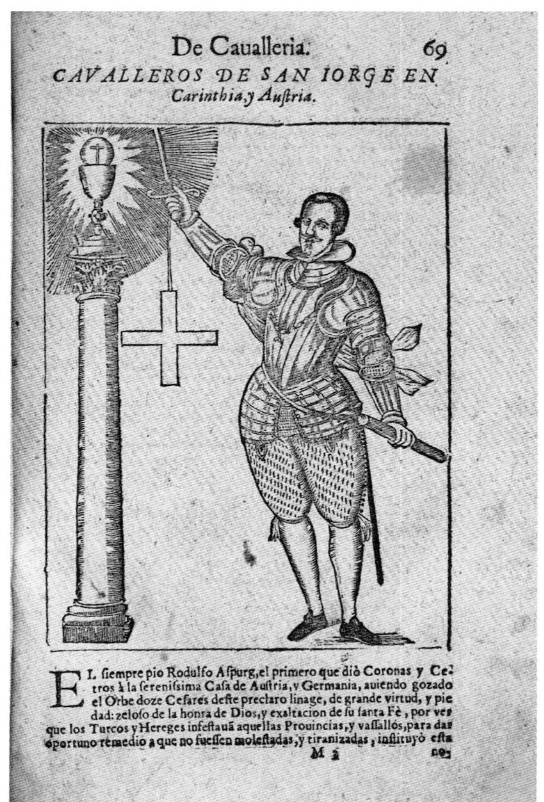

De Caualleria. 69

CAVALLEROS DE SAN IORGE EN Carinthia, y Auſtria.

EL ſiempre pio Rodulfo Aſpurg, el primero que diò Coronas y Cetros à la ſereniſsima Caſa de Auſtria, y Germania, auiendo gozado el Orbe doze Ceſares deſte preclaro linage, de grande virtud, y piedad: zeloſo de la honra de Dios, y exaltacion de ſu ſanta Fè, por ver que los Turcos y Hereges infeſtauã aquellas Prouincias, y vaſſallos, para dar oportuno remedio a que no fueſſen moleſtadas, y tiranizadas, inſtituyò eſta

M 2 no-

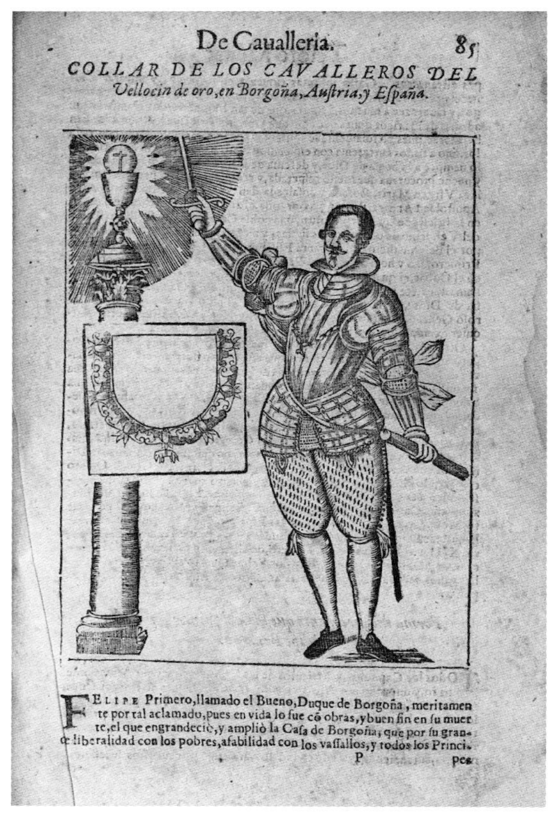

De Caualleria. 85

COLLAR DE LOS CAVALLEROS DEL Vellocin de oro, en Borgoña, Auſtria, y Eſpaña.

FELIPE Primero, llamado el Bueno, Duque de Borgoña, meritamente por tal aclamado, pues en vida lo fue cõ obras, y buen fin en ſu muerte, el que engrandeciò, y ampliò la Caſa de Borgoña, que por ſu grande liberalidad con los pobres, afabilidad con los vaſſallos, y todos los Princi-

P pes

FIG. 58 Unidentified woodcutter, after Juan de Noort, two images of King Philip IV, in José Micheli Márquez, *Tesoro militar de caualleria: Antiguo y modern modo de armas cavalleros, y professar . . .* (Madrid: Diego Díaz de la Carrera, 1642). Woodcut on paper. Bayerische Staatsbibliothek, Munich, 2 Herald. 31 h., fols. 69r and 85r.

be taken as a moralizing exhortation to the young ruler regarding proper behavior, but its message was, in effect, applicable to any inhabitant of the Spanish monarchy. When confronted with a royal portrait, even if that portrait depicted a long-deceased monarch, certain reverential gestures simply had to be performed.

However, just as there were skeptics who doubted the relationships between Christian images and their sacred prototypes, there were unquestionably early modern individuals who would have criticized the idea that royal portraits were quasi-magical substitutes for their sitters.[30] Moreover, the category of royal portraiture included not only paintings on canvas but also sculptures, portrait miniatures, manuscript illuminations in juridical documents, and printed book illustrations and broadsheets. For example, a seventeenth-century reader flipping through José Micheli Márquez's compendium of European military orders, the *Tesoro militar de cavalleria* (Military treasure of the cavalry) of 1642, would have encountered four nearly identical woodcuts that are unmistakably based on period depictions of Philip IV (fig. 58).[31] But would these simple woodcuts have been understood as *portraits* of the king? And if so, would the book's reader have performed the entire choreography of reverence that theorists and chroniclers tell us was supposed to be enacted before the royal image? This is highly doubtful. Rather, this is a case where the images' viewers would have understood them in symbolic rather than veristic terms; they represent Christian fortitude rather than the king himself and are thereby exempt from the conventional codes governing responses to royal portraiture.

Ser prudente y ser sufrido

The behaviors described by Galtero and Saavedra Fajardo stand in contrast to those explored in Juan Pérez de Montalbán's comedia *Ser prudente y ser sufrido* (To be prudent and to be uncomplaining), dateable to before 1638. The play, which has found little critical reception, is premised on the idea that one's character could be deduced by the way in which one chose to behave when confronted with the royal image.[32] The portrait's viewer, in Pérez de Montalbán's conception, was not a passive blank slate that could be acted upon by the image. Nor did the portrait have the capability of instilling decorous behavior in said viewer, as Saavedra Fajardo's unthinkingly bent knee and lowered gaze might have suggested.

Pérez de Montalbán's play begins with the medieval king Alfonso of León ordering Julio, a painter at his court, to hang his portrait, inscribed with an allegorical text, under a *mirador* (elevated window).[33] Alfonso's intention, we learn, is to hide behind the window's grate and to listen to his courtiers' remarks about the portrait. Like the ancient painter Apelles, who in Pliny's account spied on those viewing his paintings in order to hear their unmediated opinions, the king's hope is to separate the "unfaithful flattery [that] fills up all of the palace, from the first antechamber to the most hidden corner" from the truth in order to identify an honest and respectful individual for the position of his *privado* (intimate advisor).[34] From among the crowd of men who examine the portrait, all but one, Don Fernando de Quiñones, mock the *pintorcillo* (small painter), the portrait, and the inscription on it.[35] Don Fernando, on the other hand, upon realizing that it is a portrait of the king, removes his hat in front of it and declares: "Your great predecessors are exceeded by none; but in you, [the Kingdom of] León expects [you to be] the greatest of your ancestors [*el mayor de tus mayores*]."[36]

In response, Mendo, the most critical of the courtiers, quips at Fernando:

> I have been listening, and seeing
> The pious declarations
> And devout obeisances
> That you have made to this portrait;
> And because it is
> (As I suspect you know)
> a particular privilege
> reserved for painted saints
> to enjoy adoration,
> I have found it extraordinary to see you
> here idolize [*idolatrar*] [the portrait].[37]

Pérez de Montalbán leaves no doubt as to Mendo's villainousness. Nevertheless, his ability to speak poorly of the king's portrait and, by extension, the king himself is contingent upon the portrait's inability to compel appropriate reactions from its viewers. It is precisely through the contrast between the crooked Mendo's criticism of the virtuous Fernando and Fernando's attitude toward the portrait that the viewer of the play can evaluate which of the two is the more appropriate. Fernando is a decorous model for the audience to follow in their own encounters with royal portraits, and he is justly rewarded by being granted the position of the king's *privado*.

Pérez de Montalbán implicitly compares Mendo to a Protestant heretic by having him remark that the deference that one was expected to demonstrate before a royal portrait closely resembled the veneration demanded by holy images and then mockingly declare it idolatrous. The performance's early modern audiences would have understood Pérez de Montalbán's reference here. The Aragonese humanist Lorenzo Palmireno's educational manual *El estudioso de la aldea* (The scholar from the hamlet) of 1571 summarizes this notion, even if he uses Islam rather than Protestantism as a stand in for aniconic non-Catholics writ large: "Paintings and images are called *Laicorū[m] lectiones Scripturae* [readings (and) scriptures for the laity].[38] And although those of Mahomet reprimand us because we seem to them idolaters, we follow the Holy Roman Church according to the verses: God is what the image represents; but God is not the image, nor should this be believed; with the eyes of the body look at his representation, and with the soul adore what you feel."[39] Palmireno's passage highlights a central theoretical (if not practical) tenet of images in Catholicism after Trent: that they are not sacred in and of themselves but are merely representations of the sacred that assist the faithful in its contemplation.[40] By creating this exchange, Pérez de Montalbán anticipates that certain individuals might be critical of the forms of address demanded by royal portraits. He also subtly suggests that the very act of criticizing the correct manner of engaging with images of the king is blasphemous or even a form of heretical sacrilege, precisely because it mirrors Protestant critiques of Catholic visual culture. Catholics believed that Protestant characterizations of their devotional practices as idolatrous were absurd. So too, Pérez de Montalbán posits, were any challenges to the privileged status of the royal portrait.

Finally, Pérez de Montalbán's declaration that the obeisance that one was expected to demonstrate before a royal portrait closely resembles the veneration demanded by holy images is essential here. This resemblance manifests both gesturally, with Fernando removing his hat, and orally, with his respectful declarations toward that which he sees; both of these behaviors would have been appropriate forms of response toward a religious image, too. By making this observation a key point in Mendo's critique of Fernando, Pérez de Montalbán reveals that the early modern viewer would have understood how close the required modes of engagement with these two image types really were.[41]

Naples, 1647

Descriptions of viewing royal portraits in situations of political unrest reveal much about both actual and ideal forms of behavior in front of them. The chronicler Paolo Antonio di Tarsia's account of the 1647 revolt in Naples, entitled *Tumultos de la ciudad y reyno de Napoles* (Tumults of the city and kingdom of Naples), is based not on the author having witnessed the events himself—Tarsia was living in Madrid at the time—but on the various accounts of the uprising that reached the royal court in the weeks and months that followed its eruption. Tarsia was associated with the powerful Neapolitan nobleman Giangirolamo II Acquaviva, the Count of Conversano, who was suspected of supporting the French in their machinations to obtain the crown of Naples.[42] One of the pro-Spanish Tarsia's main goals was to prove the city's, and Acquaviva's, lasting loyalty to the Spanish Crown.[43] Therefore, the book must be read not for what it recounts about the events of the uprising per se but for those elements that Tarsia saw as indispensable for his text to achieve these goals, all the while making a claim to objectivity and veracity. With this in mind, it is unsurprising that the Neapolitans' behaviors toward Spanish royal images were one of the elements granted prominence in Tarsia's narrative:

> Among the noble things that were seen during the sacking . . . worthy of careful examination were the reverence, honor, and respect that the populace had towards the portraits of His Majesty the King Philip IV Our Lord, and to the other heroes of the Imperial House of Austria. During those first onslaughts, lacking in reason, not only did the [people] walk, proclaiming at each step: "*Viva* the King of Spain," but they maintained the required respect towards the portraits of His Majesty, of the Lord Emperor Charles V, and of the Lady Empress Doña Isabel, that they encountered. They took them to the market, where they had set up the seat of the armed forces, and placing them under opulent canopies, and with a guard of soldiers, they would momentarily lower their banners, and whenever they passed in front of them they inclined their heads with the deepest reverence and at night they lit torches before them, and gave other signs of veneration, *as if His Royal Person were present there* (emphasis added).[44]

Much like the behaviors exhibited by Saavedra Fajardo and the viewer of the portrait described by Galtero, here, too, the aroused Neapolitan rebels' destructive impulses could be read as having been restrained by the portraits, which compelled the populace to proper behavior. But within Tarsia's agenda of demonstrating Naples's loyalty to the Crown—and in other pro-Spanish accounts that repeated this trope—the description of the city's inhabitants' respect toward the royal portraits is actually related to the type of test that King Alfonso set his courtiers in *Ser prudente y ser sufrido*.[45] Accordingly, it was not the portrait that compelled the rebels to restraint and proper veneration. Rather, it was the rebels' inherent virtue that became apparent through their actions, in spite of the otherwise seemingly uncontrollable violence of the uprising. Like the virtuous Don Fernando from Pérez de Montalbán's play, the Neapolitans consciously made the choice to venerate the portraits for what they were—images of a sovereign—and for what they metonymically represented—the Spanish monarchy writ large.

Something similar occurred when a portrait of Charles V landed, unrecognized, in a pile of other paintings that were destined to be burned by the rebels. When passersby realized that one of the paintings depicted the emperor, they cried out, "You would burn the portrait of him who did so much good for you? That is the portrait of Charles V!" Then the populace began to shout, "Long live our benefactor!" and pulled the portrait out of the pile and placed it under a baldachin.[46] Here, contrary to Saavedra Fajardo and Galtero's poetic claims, the emperor's visage was not sufficient to convey his royal qualities to the populace. Only when someone who *knew* that the painting depicted Charles V alerted the iconoclastic mob to this fact did they respond appropriately and with decorum.

Within the pro-Spanish narratives of the uprising, however, the emphatic stress on the Neapolitan populace's supposedly positive response to the Spanish royal portraits was likely an attempt to veil actual iconoclastic abuses against them. It is hard to believe that in the fervor of the revolt, the royal portraits would have been uniformly treated in such an appropriate manner, regardless of the ingrained social behaviors that these images may have instinctively activated. And indeed, the French Duke of Guise, present in Naples during the insurrection, described a portrait of the Spanish king that was attacked, dragged through the streets, and stabbed with knives in an example of execution in effigy that was conveniently elided from Tarsia's account.[47] Similarly, some period accounts were suspicious of the respect accorded to the portraits of Charles V and Philip IV in Naples, ranging from deeming it "supernatural" to "foolish and affected," to "idolatrous," in an echo of Pérez de Montalbán's nefarious Mendo.[48]

The point here is not whether the portraits were actually venerated or destroyed during that specific event. Rather, the message that a seventeenth-century writer like Tarsia wanted to convey to his publics was that royal portraits demanded respect and veneration because they were not mere representations of the ruler they depicted. Readers at the Spanish court, including the king himself, would learn that unrest in Naples was not directed at the Spanish king nor at the Spanish monarchy as a whole but at individual viceroys, corrupted by their power and greed. As such, in Tarsia's account, Naples remained steadfastly loyal to Spain. Readers in Naples, on the other hand, and in any other place where one had to engage with a Spanish royal portrait, from Milan to Manila, would read how such loyalty had to be performed in a most correct manner, given that the portraits instantiated the king's presence in all of those places.

Tehuantepec, 1660

The specific manner in which the royal portrait was understood to instantiate the king's presence across space is illustrated by the role that it played in another situation of unrest, this time within the New Spanish viceregal administration's official response to a 1660 Zapotec rebellion in the town of Tehuantepec, in the present-day state of Oaxaca in Mexico. In contrast to the numerous royal portraits that could be found all across Naples, which was a viceregal capital, there was no portrait of the king in Tehuantepec. In order to mitigate the crisis, Cristóbal Manso de Contreras, a *regidor* (council member) from the city of Antequera (Oaxaca), approximately 150 miles away, was charged with, among other things, delivering a portrait of Philip IV to Tehuantepec, which he did with "veneration and care."[49] It was believed that the king's painted face could convey his interior qualities, "manifesting in his decorous countenance his greatness, his majesty, his benignity and piety"[50] and that these were much needed in the benighted town. Spanish officials claimed that the presence of the royal image was indispensable in Tehuantepec to officiate the ceremony of pardoning the rebels, thereby marking their ceremonial return into the fold of the Spanish monarchy.

Once arrived from Oaxaca, the royal portrait was first installed in the *casas reales* and then set up under a baldachin made of crimson damask in order to preside over the festive event. As was customary on such occasions, the *oidor* (judge) took the document that granted the town royal amnesty and kissed it, before placing it on his head.[51] Such gestures symbolically affirmed that the figure of authority, in this case the *oidor*, intended to follow the orders contained in the document and that the ritual would be witnessed by a notary.[52] We do not have information about the medium, scale, or appearance of the royal portrait that Manso de Contreras brought with him to Tehuantepec. However, if it was a painting, it was likely painted in New Spain and based on another painting, print, or drawing. For comparison, the portrait of Philip IV that presided over the festivities of his proclamation in Lima in 1622 was fully life-size, measuring four and a half by six feet. However, Lima was a major city and, like Naples, a viceregal capital; in Tehuantepec the painting feasibly may have been smaller.[53] Manso's account also sheds no light on whether the portrait's viewers were at all skeptical of its substitutive agency and its efficacy. What we do know is that the acceptance of the portrait's symbolism was such that it justified the careful, and likely costly, rolling, packing, and transport of the canvas across a significant distance, as well as its subsequent unpacking, unrolling, stretching and mounting, framing, and display in a specially constructed and decorated setting that included a costly baldachin. It ultimately mattered little whether everyone uniformly believed that the portrait of the king actually was the king. The systems of royal representation that were in place throughout the early modern Hispanic world, from the court of Madrid to towns on the Pacific coast of Mexico, functioned as if they did.

Even though Manso de Contreras's account notes that the pardon was translated and that "the Father Prior, who is learned in that language, gave a speech in vernacular Zapotec, explaining everything that had been done, and the reasons for it," it cannot provide insight into what the town's Indigenous Zapotec population thought of the proceedings and the portrait that was displayed before them.[54] For example, what Zapotec word would the priest have used to describe the portrait of Philip IV that was brought to Tehuantepec? Perhaps *lòohuáaleçáca*, which was the term that corresponded with *retrato* (portrait) and *ymagen propia de algo ò perfecta verdadera* (befitting image of something, or perfect true [image]) in Juan de Córdoba's 1578 *Vocabulario en lengua çapoteca* (Vocabulary in the Zapotec language)?[55] If so, what connotations would that term have carried in Zapotec, and how would those meanings have intersected with the substitutive nature of the Spanish royal portrait, as understood, for instance, by Manso de Contreras? I suspect that the aspect that would have been most apparent to the town's Zapotec audiences was a fundamental characteristic of royal portraiture: that it looked like, behaved like, and was treated like a sacred image. Indeed, the portrait of Philip IV was (probably) painted in oil on canvas; it depicted an individual according to European standards of naturalistic representation of the human form; it listened to wordy declarations and received reverence from its viewers; and it was opulently displayed. All of these traits would have been familiar from how the town's priests acted before religious images, both in the church of Santo Domingo and throughout the town itself, during processions and festivities. Moreover, even if no one in the town had heard of the dramatic events surrounding Bishop Palafox's portraits in Puebla just a few years earlier, Tehuantepec's inhabitants, both Indigenous and not, would have also been sensitive to the role of religious and political images in *both* generating and soothing tensions in the unequal society that was colonial New Spain.

Framing Royal Portraits

The portrait of the Spanish king had no intrinsic markers of royalty, no explicit iconographic conventions that were exclusive to it, aside from the monarch's recognizable countenance. What marked the painting as falling into the separate category of royal portraiture was the type of engagement with the image that was expected of its viewers. How a royal portrait was framed was another feature that was essential to its proper functioning because it ensured its recognition as an image of the king.[56] The external elements of the royal portrait—its parerga—included not only the picture's frame but also the cloth of honor behind it, the curtain before it, the dais or platform under it, the guard of honor that watched over it, and, perhaps most important, the baldachin or canopy that hung above it.[57] The baldachin had been a marker of status and honor since ancient times.[58] In the medieval period, baldachins were principally the privilege of church authorities, only gradually being appropriated by secular rulers.[59] However, they were sufficiently generic in form as to cause confusion about their precise meaning, as well as about who was entitled to their use. For instance, although there was a distinction between the terms *dosel* or *baldaquín*, both of which may be translated as "canopy," the two nevertheless appear to frequently alternate in period sources, suggesting that few people were well informed of the particularities of each. In 1666, the bishop of Quito Alonso de la Peña Montenegro wrote to the court in Madrid to address a claim that he had inappropriately appeared under a baldachin at a bullfight. Montenegro noted that "if by the word 'dosel' was meant a baldachin [*baldoquin*] then I never used it during the bull fights, but if what was meant was taffeta or 'dosel' then everyone here puts them up in front of the balcony on such occasions."[60] By Montenegro's definition, a *dosel*, which is interchangeable with a simple piece of silk cloth and likely possessed the pragmatic function of providing shade, did not possess the honorific symbolism of a baldachin, even though they might have been superficially quite similar.

Bishop Montenegro's letter was part and parcel of a broader struggle between secular and ecclesiastical authorities to lay claim to the status bestowed by the baldachin. Given its extraordinary symbolic importance but also the ease with which it could be replicated by anyone with means, the baldachin was among the most highly contested objects in the Hispanic world. It is no surprise, then, that royal and ecclesiastical authorities should have repeatedly clashed over their claim to the baldachin and, relatedly, to that of the *palio*, a portable canopy used during processions.[61] For example, the prelates of Puebla de los Ángeles resisted surrendering the use of the *palio* to the king and viceroy and insisted on deploying it during the triumphal entrances of the city's bishops.[62] In 1658, the episcopal retinue feigned obedience to a viceregal decree that forbade them from using the baldachin, only to then surreptitiously bring it to be displayed during the procession.[63]

Although the baldachin was an imperative part of the display of the royal portrait, there are relatively few surviving images that show such objects in situ. A drawing from 1809, produced as a record of the decoration of the mayor's house in the town of San Bartolomé de Honda (today Honda, Colombia) for the *jura* (pledge of obedience) to Ferdinand VII, illustrates the kinds of codified furnishings that were used to frame the portrait of the king during ceremonial occasions (fig. 59). At the center of the elaborate staging, which includes ephemeral

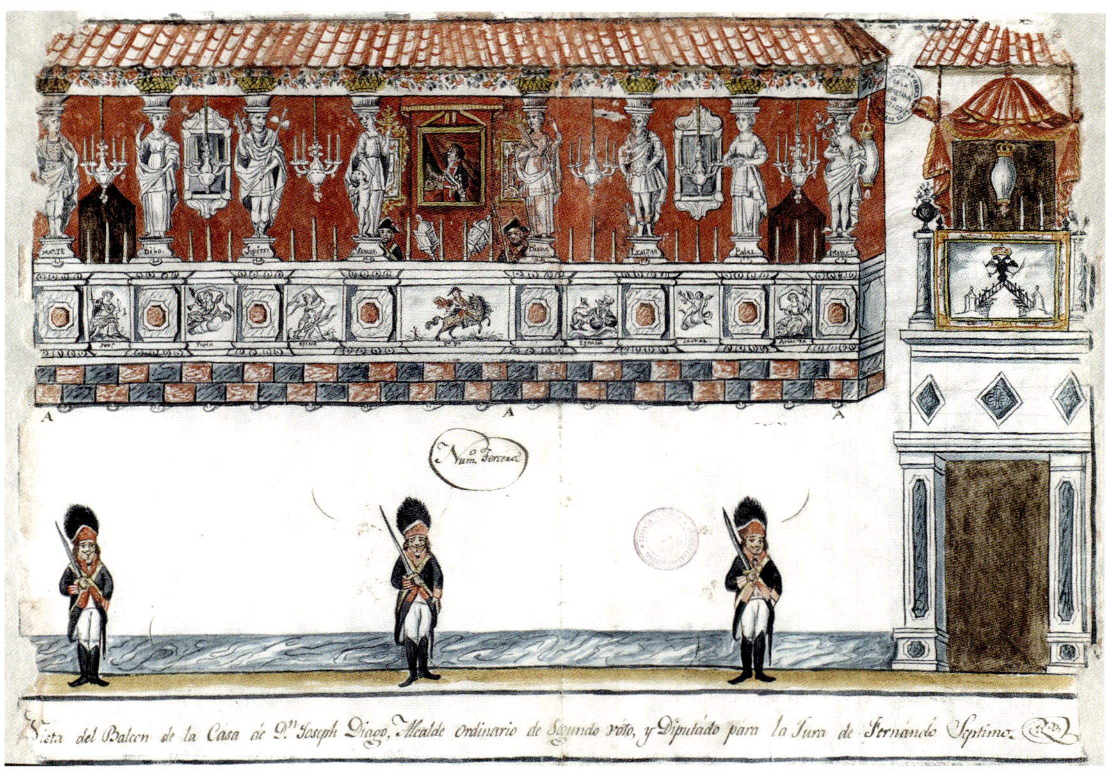

FIG. 59 Unidentified painter, *View of the House of Mayor Don Joseph Diago in San Bartolomé de Honda for the "jura" of Ferdinand VII*. Watercolor on paper, 11.4 × 16.14 in. (29 × 41 cm). Ministerio de Cultura y Deporte, Archivo Histórico Nacional, Madrid, ESTADO, MPD. 315.

decorations of Roman deities, allegories, including of Spain and of Fame, and armed guards, hangs the portrait of the new monarch under a baldachin of crimson and gold.[64] Although dating to much later than the other episodes examined in this chapter, the drawing corresponds with the innumerable early modern accounts that include descriptions of, or instructions for, the installation of royal portraits to preside over civic, royal, or religious festivities. For example, in 1660, in Tehuantepec, instructions read: "Let there be built a platform with eight steps across from the *Casas Reales* [Royal Houses], and at its head let there be placed a *dosel* [canopy] with the portrait of His Majesty, and beneath it a chair in velvet with a ceremonial *sitial* [coverlet] and a respectable table,"[65] and a 1702 text from Cuzco states that a "platform that was built next to the Casas del Cabildo . . . was [decorated] with a *sitial* and *dosel* in very rich crimson velvet, below which [hung] a portrait of Our King Lord Philip V, with three velvet-covered chairs at his feet."[66]

That these are nearly identical to how the framing devices of sacred images are described in the same period is no accident. In 1615, when the Catalan city of Mataró celebrated the beatification of Teresa of Ávila, numerous paintings of the holy nun could be found throughout the town. In

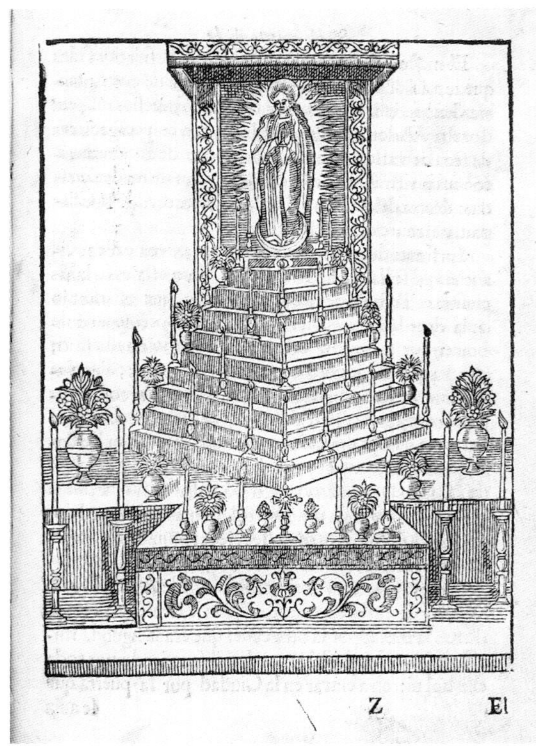

FIG. 60 Unknown artist, *Immaculate Conception Under a Canopy*, in Marco Antonio Ortí, *Siglo quarto de la conquista de Valencia* (Valencia: Juan Bautista Marçal, 1640). Woodcut on paper. Biblioteca Valenciana Nicolau Primitiu. Biblioteca Carreres, MS XII/989, between fols. 89v and 91r. Photo: Biblioteca Valenciana Digital.

the church of Saint Joseph "in the middle of the main altar there was a large painting of the saintly mother Teresa of Jesus, painted in oil by a very good hand. It was under a most beautiful *dosel*, which appeared to be of the finest brocade."[67] Similarly, in the description of an ephemeral altar set up to celebrate the four hundredth anniversary of the conquest of Valencia by King James I of Aragon, we read that a figure of the Immaculate Conception stood atop "twelve triangular steps" and "under a *dosel* of green damask." The accompanying woodcut shows the Virgin framed and mounted in this way and surrounded by dozens of lit candles and vases of flowers (fig. 60).[68] Nearby, another altar housed the Virgin of Socorro (Rescue), which was "under a rich and beautiful *dosel* of crimson velvet" and was flanked on either side by "an angel made of masonry, that illuminated the figure with two candles in its hands."[69] Walking through an early modern Hispanic city, a pedestrian would have been accustomed to seeing royal portraits and religious images displayed with the same degree of pomp and with the same general accouterments. Any differences between the image of the king and the sacred image would have been further elided by the closely related behaviors that their viewers performed before them.

The formal similarities of the painted surfaces of royal and nonroyal portraits are clear. However, given these elaborate systems of display, it was inconceivable that a portrait of Philip IV would have been confused with a portrait of a nonroyal individual, like Barberana. Barberana's portrait could have been displayed in an elegant, even ornate, frame. However—at least in theory—it would have never been granted the same symbolically charged framing and been displayed on a dais and beneath a canopy as an image of the king. According to a seventeenth-century Neapolitan account, images of the king were only placed under baldachins when they depicted the monarch as a single figure, that is to say, when they could ostensibly be confused with other nonroyal portraits.[70] When the portrait of the king was included within multifigural allegorical compositions, a baldachin was not required. Like simple repainting, which could nudge a portrait from the sphere of the secular and transform it into an efficacious religious image, here, too, the effect of a seemingly simple piece of cloth fundamentally affected the ontology of the image beneath it.

According to Alejandro Cañeque, baldachins became a quintessential marker of royalty in the early modern Hispanic world because they fulfilled the role of the absent crown as a visible symbol of royal power.[71] How, then, can we account for those portraits of Habsburg kings in which the monarch is represented with a crown?[72] In numerous childhood portraits of Charles II, for example, the young king is depicted among grandiose furnishings, with a crown, scepter, and globe. These images, produced by and after court painters, included these codified, if inaccurate, symbols of royal power in order to visually counter the young king's infirmity.[73] When crowns appear in portraits of earlier Habsburg kings, it is because the paintings were likely made outside of the purview of the court and its painter-censors, who included Velázquez, Carducho, Rizi, and Carreño. Those portraits were subjected to less stringent oversight than had they been made in Madrid, and consequently we find a greater degree of flexibility in how their makers either obeyed or ignored the codes of royal representation.[74] For example, a painting of Philip IV made in the Royal Audiencia of Santa Fé de Bogotá includes a crown, which sits on a table before the king (fig. 61).[75] The image may not derive from a Spanish painting—seemingly the most obvious source for such a representation—but from northern European engravings, which often depicted Spanish kings with scepters, ermine cloaks, or crowns, as in a print by Pieter Jode II (fig. 62).[76] Even though these were accepted accouterments of monarchical rule in the French, English, Swedish, or Polish-Lithuanian contexts that Flemish and Dutch artists were also supplying, they would have never found their way into an official portrait made in the controlled ambit of the court of Madrid.

The Bogotá painting is one of only a handful of surviving sixteenth- and seventeenth-century royal portraits from Spain's American territories.[77] In Spain, royal portraits from the period are more numerous, however, there, too, many images of the Habsburg kings are lost, as exemplified by the account of Velázquez's and Carducho's censorship of "indecent" portraits of the monarch and his family in 1633, as well as numerous iconoclastic episodes in the following centuries.[78] By extension, our understanding of what the entire corpus of royal portraits—including the orthodox and especially the unorthodox—may have looked like in the sixteenth and seventeenth centuries is fragmentary. It is possible, then, that many more royal portraits, particularly from noncourtly contexts, could have included crowns, like the Bogotá painting. Even though crowns were absent from the official repertoire of Spanish monarchical portraiture, their symbolism would have been widely understood. They appeared on coins minted across the Hispanic world, and the term "the Crown" (*la Corona*) was a common metonym for royal rule. Moreover, Christ and the Virgin were frequently depicted with crowns, including in the widespread iconography of the Coronation of the Virgin. The (admittedly infrequent) appearance of crowns in royal portraits made outside the censorious gaze of the court would have therefore likely communicated to their viewers that this was a symbol that bestowed prestige on only the most select individuals, while drawing another parallel between the categories of monarchical portraiture and sacred imagery.

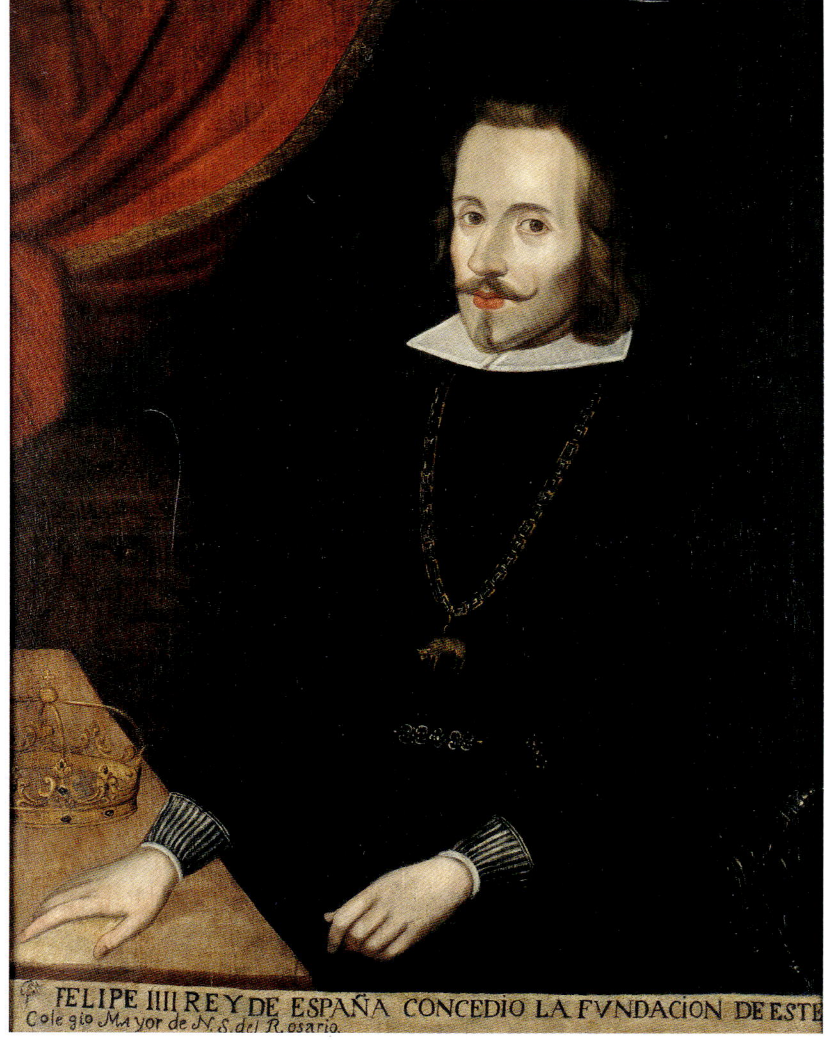

FIG. 61 Workshop of the Figueroa family, *Philip IV*, seventeenth century. Oil on canvas, 41.3 × 32 in. (105 × 81.4 cm). Museo de la Universidad del Rosario, Bogotá. Photo: Alberto Sierra.

Palafox's Omnivorous Portraits

The structural simplicity of the canopy—an apparatus of cloth and rope—was belied by its status as a deeply symbolic element of honorific display. That it signified prestige was universally accepted. However, the question of whether it was exclusive to members of the secular or the ecclesiastical hierarchies was the subject of disagreements across the early modern Hispanic world. In the realm of imagery, it was a crucial element for announcing the privileged status of paintings and sculptures of both holy figures as well as the monarch. Indeed, the agency of the baldachin could elevate an otherwise unremarkable portrait of a man posing in black to being unequivocally recognized as an image of the king. What, then, happened when a nonroyal portrait was placed beneath it?

It might seem that this is a purely theoretical question and that the fragility of the king's image that I have proposed was, at most, rhetorical. However, if we return to the trial of Palafox's portraits, we observe that the stability of the system of royal representation was challenged precisely by this inherent flexibility of both portraits and of baldachins—by the fact that they were not the exclusive domain of any one type of image nor one category of person. In the trial's proceedings, we read that a hat and collar maker named Juan de Palomares came to the tribunal in Mexico City of his own volition to report on the worrisome situation in Puebla de los Ángeles, where he had lived for five years.[79] Palomares vividly described the annual procession organized in Puebla for the celebration of Corpus Christi, which fell around five weeks prior to his deposition.[80] As the solemn retinue advanced down the Calle de la Carnicería, he narrated, it passed the portraits of Philip IV and Mariana of Austria, hanging publicly as was typical during such occasions. However, in a drastic breach of protocol and respect, the two royal images hung unadorned, "without [anyone] having put even a canopy behind them [*sin ponerles detras siquiera un dosel*]." Additionally, passersby were upset to observe that the portraits of past kings of Spain, which likely included the king's direct predecessors Philip III, Philip II, and the heavily mythologized emperor Charles V, were simply propped up (*arimados*) against a wall.[81]

Finally (and to Palomares, most shockingly), a portrait of Bishop Palafox that hung nearby—perhaps similar in appearance to the later eighteenth-century exemplar by Andrés de Islas (see fig. 44)—was displayed "with much

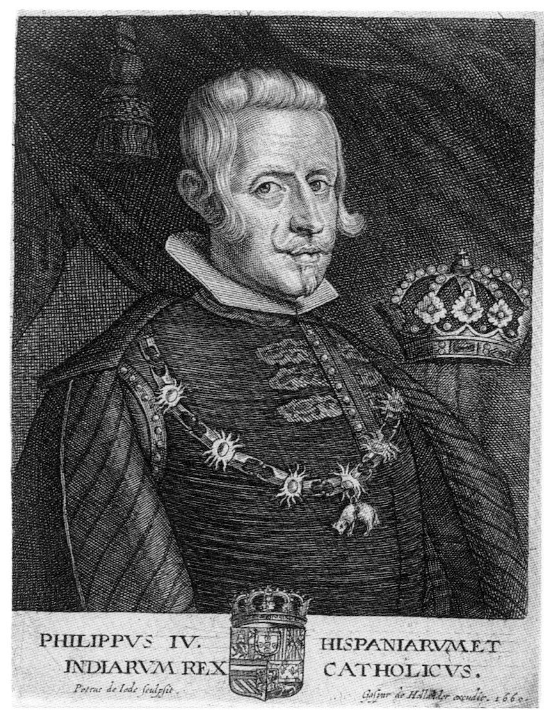

FIG. 62 Pieter de Jode II (engraver) and Gaspar de Hollander (publisher), *Philip IV*, 1660. Etching and engraving on paper, 6.8 × 5 in. (17.3 × 12.7 cm). Rijksmuseum, Amsterdam.

adornment and beneath a baldachin [*baldoquin*]." Palomares noted that some people, incensed at the impropriety asked, "Why should the portrait of the bishop have all of this majesty and adornment, and that of the king, our lord, who in fact deserves it, to have so little?"[82] Others saw no problem in this disproportion and defended the arrangement, ultimately leading the two groups to draw swords.[83] Given the deeply engrained understanding about the privileged status of the royal portrait and the often repeated claim that it was a substitute for the king, it is not surprising that an insult to the king's image would have been seen as troubling.[84]

In his testimony, Palomares suggested that while seeing a royal portrait without a

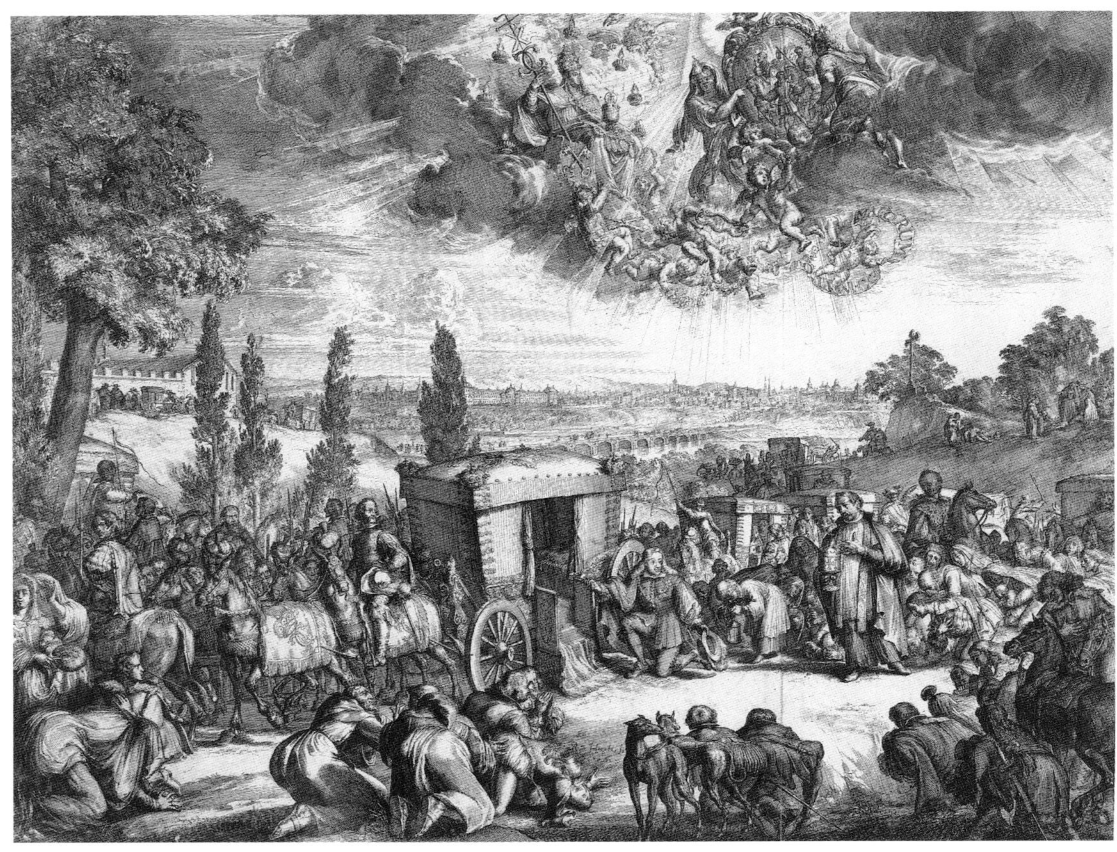

FIG. 63 Romeyn de Hooghe, *Charles II Cedes His Carriage to a Priest Carrying the Host*, 1685. Etching on paper, 12.87 × 16.45 in. (32.7 × 41.8 cm). Rijksmuseum, Amsterdam.

corresponding baldachin was surprising, the lack of even a piece of cloth behind it was disgraceful. Indeed, many members of Hispanic society would have likely never even seen a royal portrait without the framing elements of baldachin, cloth of honor, or dais, the absence of which constituted a severe breach of decorum.[85] Sixteenth- and seventeenth-century inventories attest that many people owned portraits of the king. In noble homes, paintings of the monarch were frequently exhibited as ceremoniously as in official settings, and even humble households were likely to have set store by such honorific forms of display.[86] It is important to recall here that the city's bishops used baldachins during festive occasions, in spite of royal and viceregal decrees that forbade them from doing so. By extension, such framing devices may have been accepted as appropriate for episcopal portraits, too. It is not clear from Palomares's testimony that the portrait of Palafox was displayed under a *royal* canopy—that is to say, the canopy that had been originally destined for the portraits of the royal couple. Nevertheless, the fact that the portrait of Palafox was elevated by means of a baldachin, while the royal portraits were not, gave the impression that the bishop's portrait had usurped this very particular marker of prestige.

The portrait of Palafox could comfortably inhabit the space beneath the baldachin by taking advantage of the two factors that I have outlined as defining the relation between portraiture and sacred imagery in the period. The first was the formal similarity of the portrait of the king to nonroyal portraits, caused by the lack of painted elements to mark it as idiosyncratic or privileged, and its reliance on elements of display to indicate its status as royal to its viewers. The second was the functional similarity between the royal portrait and the sacred image. Portraits of the king demanded and received the same forms of physical response—bowing, kneeling, and doffing headgear—as did religious objects. Furthermore, the baldachin's ubiquity and the similarity of how it was used in differing contexts—both royal and religious—additionally enabled the types of images displayed under it to switch their respective functions and become conflated. There was, in sum, already a widespread awareness that a portrait *could* be treated as one treats a sacred image. Furthermore, Bishop Palafox's portrait—as an image of an ecclesiastic, likely surrounded by the accouterments of his office and in spectacular robes—was more opulent than a portrait of Philip IV. The two were not interchangeable in the way that I argue the portraits of Philip and Pedro Barberana were; in fact, the portrait of Palafox registered as the visually more important one of the two.

When people placed the bishop's portrait under a baldachin, potentially displacing the portraits of the king and queen, they may have also implicitly drawn on the well-known literary and visual topos, in which Habsburg monarchs honored religious images and the Eucharist by humbling themselves in front of them, either through genuflection or by ceding them the right of way or a means of transport.[87] A print by Romeyn de Hooghe depicts the moment when King Charles II takes off his hat and gives up his carriage to a priest carrying the Eucharist through the countryside (fig. 63).[88] Such episodes can be found in the biographies and iconographies of nearly every early modern Habsburg monarch, with little to no variation, because the ceremony was hereditary.[89] After all, legitimacy was generated through uniformity, both with regularly recurring events within the lifespan of one ruler and with identical events punctuating the lives of subsequent monarchs. Because the portraits of Palafox were treated as religious images in Puebla, the displacement of the royal portrait from beneath the baldachin may have been seen as entering into the familiar and well-promoted tradition of a Habsburg monarch ceding his privileged place to a devotional object. Familiar, officially sanctioned forms of engaging with images were misinterpreted when the constitutive elements of those forms of engagement were pliable, as were both the baldachin and the royal and episcopal portraits themselves.

I argue here that the two primary characteristics of the baldachin and its related parerga were their stability in signifying power and their adaptability to whatever they shielded. Taken this way, the baldachin and other elements did not surround a stable portrait or the religious image; instead, the unstable image filled in the space under the baldachin, thereby acquiring the prestige it communicated. As the symbol of privilege par excellence, the baldachin did not rely on the royal portrait for its legitimacy: it could accommodate religious images, the Eucharist, the king, or a bishop. It could also remain unfilled and expectant, with this latency posing no threat to its future potential for bestowing status. It could, therefore, function independently of the royal portrait.

Quite the opposite was true of the image of the king, the very status of which *as royal* could be contested when stripped of the baldachin that normally elevated and enshrined it. This is precisely what occurred in Naples, where the portraits of the king went unrecognized and were threatened by destruction. That the king himself occasionally ceded his privilege to using the baldachin to objects of religious cult may have strengthened the notion of the monarch as a devotee of the Eucharist, but it paradoxically weakened his claim to the baldachin's elevating authority. In practice, the contested status of the baldachin between the royal and ecclesiastical hierarchies, its wide range of uses, and even the practical interchangeability of its nomenclature between *dosel* and *baldoquín* did not make the canopy an unequivocal marker of royal power. Therefore, as a symbol, it was too malleable and too widely applicable to unequivocally elevate and distinguish the portrait of the king.

The system of royal representation undoubtedly benefitted from the implicit association of portraits of the king with sacred images. However, as the Puebla case shows, a system where any image, when placed beneath the royal baldachin, became endowed with the otherwise restricted authority of the royal portrait, was also, to some degree, flawed. A single case, no matter how vivid, does not, of course, constitute sufficient evidence to speak of a phenomenon. It does, however, appear as a crack in the smooth face of the institution of royal representation. Evidence of additional episodes during which this system of images was destabilized will undoubtedly surface with further research in local archives in towns and parishes across what once constituted the global early modern Spanish monarchy. Royal portraits were moved, displayed, feted, removed, and stored too many times, in too many places, and for too many centuries for each event to have gone off without a hitch, for the monarch to have always been incontrovertibly recognized as himself, or for his subjects to have chosen each time to buy into the visual game they were asked to play. For an image of power, the royal portrait—which lacked the ability to advertise its own status as royal and to defend itself from misuse or misappropriation—was remarkably powerless.

Portraits for Prayer

Chapter 3 analyzed the testimony of a painter named Gaspar Conrado, who was accused of painting "a portrait of the Lord Bishop Juan de Palafox . . . with the wings of a seraph."[90] Conrado's denial of those charges and his claim that "another painter could have added the wings at the command of his masters" prompted a consideration of the practice of the sanctification of portraits in the early modern Hispanic world.[91] When the bishop's admirers added wings to his extant portraits, they declared the portraits' new status as religious images. Although these new composite images were unconsecrated and unrecognized by the Church, they could feasibly be treated by their future viewers as objects for devotion. However, the allure of portraits was such that they did not have to be subjected to any physical interventions in order to achieve this effect. A Franciscan friar named Tomás de Oviedo appeared before the Inquisitor Juan Baptista Elorriaga to describe yet another troubling way in which people engaged with the bishop's portraits. He noted that the city of Puebla was "full of [Palafox's] portraits and that even the *indios* included them in the rooms they call *santorales*, in which they kept the images of the saints to whom they are devoted."[92] As in Valfermoso, where the nuns moved a portrait they believed to be a religious image to a chapel, location would prove to be important.

One such case was described in detail by the royal administrator Enrique Dávila Pacheco, who told of his arrival at the inn in the town of Tesmeluca (today San Martín Texmelucan de Labastida), approximately twenty-five miles from the center of Puebla, on the road to Mexico City. Pacheco stated, "In a room belonging to the innkeeper and his wife my companions and I saw a portrait of Don Juan de Palafox placed in the best location, in between some pictures of saints, and corresponding to it [there were] two burning candles in two small candlesticks, placed on a board that emerged from the wall and that served as a table at the foot of said portrait." He then added, "My companions and I became scandalized, and it caused us to be amazed that such a form of cult and adoration would be given to a portrait in such a public and busy place."[93]

Dávila explained to the inquisitors that he could not, in good conscience, leave the portrait as it was, and so he took it from the inn and brought it with him in order to display before the tribunal because "he saw that the worship, and manner of adoration that those simple people performed towards the portrait greatly exceeded the reverence *that is owed to its original* on account of his episcopal dignity, his person, and the other posts that he occupies and has occupied. He was adored in a manner that is only owed to images of God our Lord, and of his mother, the holiest Virgin Mary, and of his saints, by being placed between canonized figures, by lighting candles to him, and by invoking him for one's needs" (emphasis added).[94] Although Dávila asserted that some degree of respect was owed to Palafox by virtue of his character, his prestige, and especially his position, the type of reverence that had been accorded to him in the region of Puebla far exceeded that which might be expected toward a still-living ecclesiastic.

In an earlier episode in the trial, one witness recounted that Bishop Palafox's supporters "treated [the witness] like a heretic, and spat upon him" for not owning a portrait of the bishop.[95] These behaviors represent the obverse to the lighting of candles in front of the bishop's portraits and must be considered alongside the attitudes that elevated their status to that of devotional or even miraculous images. The parallels to the iconoclastic and iconophilic conflicts of mid-sixteenth-century northern Europe are patent. Much like accusations of idolatry that were cast by both Protestants and Catholics, here, too, Palafox's supporters and detractors bandied the words "heretic" and "idolatry" against each other during the events leading up to and during the trial.[96] For instance, Palafox's later biographer, the Benedictine monk Gregorio Argaiz, cited a letter Palafox had written complaining of the persecutions he suffered on account of his conflict with the mendicant orders: "They defamed the dignity of the Episcopate . . . singing slanderous couplets against my person and my dignity, spreading satirical monikers that are so scandalous as to call me a heretic and to say that it was a formal heresy to defend the Holy Council of Trent."[97] Argaiz noted that "neither in London nor Wittenberg [was there] greater derision," framing the behavior of Palafox's Mexican detractors as a heresy so extreme that it exceeded that of the Anglicans and Lutherans associated with those two cities.[98]

The tribunal also heard another account from two notaries, Valdivia and Elorriaga. As discussed in chapter 3, they declared that approximately a month prior to their deposition, while in the company of a local alderman named Llano y Losada, they had entered an Indigenous household in Puebla and noticed that a portrait of Palafox "was placed between two sculptures; one of Christ Our Lord hanging from the Cross, and the other of Our Lady the Virgin Mary. In front of the portrait there were vases, bouquets of flowers, and two clay candlesticks with no candles in them, while the sculptures did not have before them bouquets or candlesticks."[99] Here the simple act of setting up flowers and burning candles before the bishop's portrait, while *denying them* to pictures of holy figures, effectively displaced the legitimate religious images from their privileged locus, just as had occurred with the portraits of the king and queen, which were denied baldachins. Precisely this type of behavior had been outlawed by Pope Urban VIII's decrees on saints, which address the concerning phenomenon of people setting up "lamps and other lights" in front of the "tombs, pictures, likenesses, and other things" of individuals whom "the Apostolic See had not distinguished with the honor of canonization or beatification."[100] The decrees are a reminder that the case of Palafox's portraits—where images of a living, nonholy individual began to function as sacred images—was not unique but simply emblematic of a larger problem that plagued figural image-making practices in early modern Catholic polities.

Indeed, a related case was brought before the Holy Office of Lima in 1704. An inquisitorial secretary and chaplain named Fernando Román de Aulestía declared to have seen a number of controversially arranged paintings on the doors of two grocers' shops near the city's Indigenous quarter. At one of the shops, the composition centered on an image of the Virgin, flanked by saints, on either side of whom hung images of the *Rey Inga* (Inca king) and his wife. Aulestía complained that this was scandalous in itself, but the larger problem lay in the fact that it suggested to the Indigenous passersby "that the same cult that is owed to the Holiest Virgin and to her saints can also be directed towards [the Inca] gentile kings, from which follows that they should be adored and venerated [*adorados y venerados*] as saints." If this arrangement was tolerated, Aulestía warned, it would constitute a "grave wrong against the Christian religion and a disparagement of its saints," and he therefore suggested that the owners of the shops be ordered to "erase and remove" all representations of the Inca royal couple.[101]

A few days later, after the shops were inspected, their owner appeared before the tribunal promising to take down the offending images of the Inca couple.[102] Aulestía and the other inquisitors did not describe the paintings of the Inca king and queen as portraits, and they were not images of contemporary curacas or Indigenous leaders.[103] Nevertheless, the images were recognizable as specific historical personages and as representations of an ancient and venerable royal lineage. The primary source of concern was the insertion of nonholy figures into a context where viewers—particularly Indigenous viewers—might mistake them as holy and therefore as capable of intercession or the receiving of prayers, as were recognized Catholic saints and the Virgin.[104] Implicitly underlying this worry was the Spaniards' fear that the Indigenous population might revert to their belief in the Inca's sacred status. Feasibly, had the depictions of the Inca rulers been hung separately from the holy images, they would not have garnered the inquisitors' attention. As in Puebla, here, too, placement was paramount.

Idolatries, Not Idols

From the point of view of ecclesiastical censorship, the relative danger of a sanctified portrait was proportionate to its visibility. In the Guatemalan denunciation discussed in chapter 1, for instance, it was the fact that Maldonado de Paz's family portrait in the guise of saints "was very normally displayed in churches and on altars during processions of the Holy Sacrament," which prompted an outraged declaration before the Holy Office.[105] Similarly, in Puebla in 1651, a Franciscan friar named Matías de Cifuentes declared that he counted fourteen portraits of the bishop during a single procession on the occasion of Corpus Christi a few weeks prior to his examination by the tribunal, which were "hung among images of saints approved by the holy Roman Catholic church, and some of them placed prominently on the streets through which the procession moved."[106] Visibility was believed to be particularly problematic in American contexts given that the regions' Indigenous inhabitants supposedly lacked the capacity of discerning the images' actual status and functions.

A second concern was the purported tendency of these populations to embrace idolatrous practices. This topic was neither new nor one specific to Spain's viceroyalties but rather a long-lasting issue at the core of Christian image making.[107] Early conceptions of idolatry had lambasted the maker of the idolatrous object, following from Old Testament proscriptions against the making of images. These were eventually supplanted with the belief that the roots of idolatry resided in the veneration of historical individuals, particularly rulers, who commemorated themselves or their familiars through images, which eventually garnered cultic status.[108] In such situations, the role of viewers was essential in catalyzing an object's transformation. For instance, Michael Camille notes of an image from a medieval French psalter book, in which a man kneels before a statue, that "it is not so much the object itself but this action toward it that transformed image into idol,"[109] while Joseph Koerner observes that "idolatry is an accusation, not a belief."[110] In Puebla, the trial's proceedings do not describe the portraits themselves as idols. Rather, attention is shifted away from the objects toward the viewers' actions, with witnesses declaring that "idolatries are performed"[111] toward the portraits, that "[some people] are idolizing [*ydolatrando*] [by] worshipping Palafox's portraits,"[112] and that viewers had directed an "undeserved and superstitious worship" at images of the bishop.[113] These actions implicitly cast the portraits as idols, without the images ever actually being termed as such.

Indeed, there was nothing inherently idolatrous in Palafox's portraits that were displayed at the inn in Tesmeluca until the arriving Spaniards observed the ways in which the locals behaved toward them and, evaluating these practices, reached the conclusion that they went against Catholic doctrine. This is similar to the case from Valfermoso, where it was the historian's revelation that informed the nuns that they had directed their veneration to an unsanctioned recipient: a portrait of an actress rather than a painting of an archangel. After all, the young boy examined by Alderman Llano y Losada, who termed the sitter of the portrait "Saint Palafox," did not think that the veneration that he and his family directed toward the image was unseemly.

Rather, the form of worship that they performed before the portrait—lighting candles, laying flowers, and saying prayers before it—approximated that which was performed in front of legitimate religious images. The quality of being an idol was therefore not inherent to the object that carried that designation but depended fully on its viewers' behaviors.

Given that the presence of idolatry in the Americas had been a foundational narrative of the conquest and a justification for the colonial enterprise, it is unsurprising that the Spaniards resident in New Spain expected to encounter idolatrous practices there, even over a century after the conquest.[114] However, as shown in chapter 2 on the example of the demonically possessed nuns of San Plácido, unorthodox "idolatrous" behaviors could be found as readily in Spain's colonial holdings as they could at the court in Madrid, the seat of the Spanish monarchy's power. Furthermore, the language used in the Puebla trial does not place blame on the *indios* who venerated Palafox. Instead, it speaks to the existence of a "pernicious" and "dangerous" force, which particularly threatened the Indigenous populations, those "barbarous people [*gente barbara*]." The childish *indios*' lack of discernment, the narrative went, prevented them from knowing that their actions were idolatrous. What was—however implicitly—at fault was the system of making and using images in Catholic contexts, into which these individuals had been introduced. This was a system in which artists both had the capacity for, and were accustomed to, making physiognomically accurate (or at least verisimilar) portraits and where anthropomorphic imagery was also used for cultic purposes. The simple but fundamental fact that depictions of humans were produced with both religious and nonreligious ends meant that the repeatedly shored-up boundary between the two categories was, in actuality, quite permeable.

Conclusion: Potent Images

Camille writes, regarding the making of images in medieval Europe: "Their potency was problematic. Once produced and set up in the world, they could be used in illegitimate as well as sanctioned rituals, private as well as public perceptions. . . . Also, being less controllable than the authorized text, images were dangerously divisive: they pretended to be what they were not. A deep-rooted distrust of the duplicitous in image-making runs through the Christian tradition."[115] This difficulty of controlling how people engaged with images was a factor that allowed for the manipulations examined here, with portraits being treated as if they were holy images or, worse still from the Church's point of view, as if the persons they depicted were actually holy. In these cases, images were duplicitous not merely because they were superficially imitative but because they could simultaneously inhabit multiple image categories, usurping forms of response that would not have typically belonged to them.

Audiences were intimately familiar with the codified signs of reverence that were performed in front of both royal portraits and religious images, many of which differed only in the intention behind them, to borrow from Paleotti's description of greeting a king or a gentleman. When people placed portraits of Palafox under baldachins, lit candles to them, and said prayers before them, these viewers perverted well-known codes of behavior, engaging in sanctioned forms of responding to images but directing them toward unsanctioned recipients. These cases must therefore be understood as improvisations that drew on a familiar repertoire of extant cultural forms rather than unorthodox behaviors that arose ex nihilo. At times they were undoubtedly accidental and unintended. At others, however, they may have constituted forms of creative resistance, weaponizing universal forms of orthodox imagistic practices in order to promote local agendas.

A portrait acquired meanings through the range of ways that its viewers engaged with it. When seen within the highly restricted and codified framing under a royal baldachin, the portrait of Bishop Palafox temporarily replaced the portrait of a king and, by extension, Palafox himself temporarily became king. When displayed with flowers and candles, the portrait of Palafox functioned as an image of a saint, and, by extension, Palafox himself temporarily became a saint. Depictions of Bishop Palafox—seemingly static, otherwise unremarkable portraits of an ecclesiastic—revealed themselves to be, in actuality, supremely flexible, easily inhabiting these seemingly discrete categories. What is more, under the right conditions, *any* early modern portrait could be equally omnivorous and equally labile.

CONCLUSION

The Life Histories of Sacred Portraits and the History of Sacred Portraiture

The story of sacred portraiture is not easily told in a linear manner. It weaves back and repeats itself. As it moves forward through time, it may briefly appear to align with larger narratives of the Renaissance portrait as a harbinger of post-medieval humanistic individualism and, by extension, of modernity, only to suddenly challenge them. In part, the story of sacred portraiture is the story of early modern portraiture writ large. The difficulty of recounting it, then, stems from the fact that in the early modern Hispanic world, the very concept of *retrato*, or portrait, was much more accommodating than the constrained definition of portraiture commonly used today. It encompassed cityscapes; depictions of animals, both real and imagined; images of sacred images; and, of course, representations of humans. Within this last category, the primary function of the portrait could be the recognition of a sitter's physiognomy, but portraiture could just as easily be entirely fictitious, presenting not an actuality but a potentiality or something entirely imagined. When the concepts of portraiture and likeness were used to translate already complex, multivalent ideas from Indigenous languages, such as the Nahuatl *teixiptla*, their meanings expanded even further.

However, there are a number of reasons for which the modern definition of portraiture—a secular genre tethered to physiognomy—succeeded from among its many early modern functions and understandings. Partially, this derived from how different kinds of paintings were already organized and valued in the early modern period, second, from the codification and hierarchization of artistic genres in Enlightenment-era academies, and finally, from an overloaded historiography that claimed that Renaissance portraiture reflected an entirely new modern self. Following French models, the academies of Spain and Latin America organized different pictorial types in a seemingly straightforward manner, with history painting (which often included religious narratives and stories from the lives of saints) triumphing over portraiture, both of which stood above the lesser genres of still life or *costumbrista* (genre) imagery.[1] I contend that, along with patterns of collecting and histories of museum display, these academic hierarchies contributed to the sidelining of portraiture *a lo divino* and other difficult-to-categorize image types in later historiography, regardless of their centrality to how early modern individuals lived with images.

Furthermore, in Spain portraiture-qua-physiognomic likeness developed a high status in the eighteenth and nineteenth centuries due, in large part, to the historiographic and popular veneration bestowed upon its best historical practitioners, in particular Velázquez (and later Goya). Indeed, in an occasional text published in 1781 by the Academy of Fine Arts in Madrid, *Las meninas*, described, significantly, as "a portrait of the *Infanta Doña Margarita*," was deemed "a miracle of art."[2] The text also encouraged the young painters among its readers, whom it deemed "the honor, delight, and hope of our arts," to follow in Velázquez's footsteps.[3] In such texts, the portrait was cast as an entirely discrete image type and one with a particularly sterling pedigree at that.

Twentieth-century scholarship commonly classified early modern portraiture into types, including family portraits, official portraits, group portraits, and self-portraits. Sacred portraiture, too, might seem to be simply another subcategory or branch within this larger typological tree diagram. However, such a division effaces a fundamental quality of sacred portraits and of portraits more generally: that they signify plurally. What is more, sacred portraits were ubiquitous, peppered throughout the larger spectrum of portraitistic production in the early modern period, and there almost certainly exist images that fall under the rubric of both sacred portraiture *and* each of the subtypes I have listed above. This proliferation meant that, time and again, ecclesiastical authorities confronted incursions of portraiture into the religious sphere, which occurred in spite of ever-greater numbers of decrees that sought to forbid such practices. In their general scope, the cases that focused on such commingling changed little across time. Patrons and artists repeatedly painted living individuals in the guise of holy figures; audiences repeatedly treated depictions of living individuals as if they were saints; and, in turn, ecclesiastical censors repeatedly levied the same censures against them. In Guatemala in 1615, in Madrid in 1628, in Algete in 1639, and in Puebla de los Ángeles in 1651, the functionaries of the Holy Office had to unpack the variety of ways in which individuals engaged with portraits and to decipher whether, and how, the acceptable boundaries of such engagements had been transgressed.[4] As late as in 1738, an inquisitorial trial in Mallorca investigated a number of images that depicted deceased Carthusian friars with signs of sanctity, even though the Catholic Church had not officially recognized them as saints. The friars hoped to keep the images in their monastery because the "insignia of sanctity were subtle and the paintings, in which they are [shown], are very small, and cannot be noticed, except when examined very carefully."[5] However, these paintings, too, went against the same decrees, promulgated by Pope Urban VIII in the first half of the seventeenth century, that were referenced in nearly every inquisitorial case I have examined.

Nevertheless, in Catholic contexts and in the Hispanic world in particular, the gradual untethering of the idea of the portrait from the sphere of the sacred occurred precisely when the Holy Office of the Inquisition attempted to protect the religious image from what they saw as pollution by the profane. For instance, by forbidding that people in Puebla own portraits of Bishop Palafox for fear that they might be misinterpreted and treated as sacred images, the inquisitors were making a definitive claim about portraiture's secular status. It was *against* the images that are at the core of this book—repainted portraits, portraits *a lo divino*, unsanctioned portraitistic cults, and even the ecclesiastically authorized true portraits—that the boundaries of different artistic types began to be shored up and better defined. And it was precisely the publics that commissioned, used, and viewed images—and the ecclesiastical censors who vainly tried to control them—who articulated an operative though not explicitly verbalized theory of artistic types. In turn, this led to a practical codification of what would become modern artistic genres and to an episodic, if not yet universal, understanding of the portrait as a distinctly secular, discrete, and static image type.

This development notwithstanding, the portrait was—and continues to be—an image type of unparalleled flexibility, with its meanings shifting based on its context and audience. The same images could register as sacred to certain viewers but not to others. The conclusion that can therefore be extended to any portrait is this: the sacred portrait is not only a type of portraiture but also a *potential state of every portrait*. What the cases brought together in this book demonstrate most forcefully is that any portrait possessed the capacity to, at some stage in its life history, function as a sacred image.

We recognize certain images as sacred portraits based on their characteristic amalgamation of religious and portraitistic elements. However, it is impossible, in many cases, to determine what those images were at the time of their creation. Consider, for instance, two paintings attributed to Zurbarán (figs. 64 and 65). The works share certain portraitistic features, as well as numerous compositional and stylistic similarities, including the figures' bearing, the shadowing of their faces, the nondescript backgrounds, certain elements of their dress, and the fictive stone tablets with identifying inscriptions.[6] It is this last element, the stone block in the lower left of the composition, that challenges the first work's status as a simple portrait, identifying the depicted figure as Saint Sebastian. How can we account for these similarities and for this crucial difference? Might one have been commissioned as a portrait *a lo divino*? Or repainted at a later moment? The two paintings do not readily disclose their relationship. Indeed, equally likely is that their seemingly incontrovertible similarity is merely a coincidence. Perhaps they were painted as portraits for different patrons but near the same date: if so, their painter (or painters) could have simply drawn from a bank of formal solutions in vogue at the time. Conversely, the painting of Sebastian may have always been intended as a painting as a saint, simply drawing on the formal vocabulary of portraiture for the particular effect that naturalism could bring to bear on religious imagery. Carlo Ginzburg has written with particular relevance to this image (but also to many others examined throughout this book) that "the obstacles interfering with research in the form of lacunae or misrepresentations in the sources must become part of the account."[7] Fully acknowledging the gaps in our knowledge of these objects' histories is essential, with the images under discussion being permitted to move fluidly into different categories

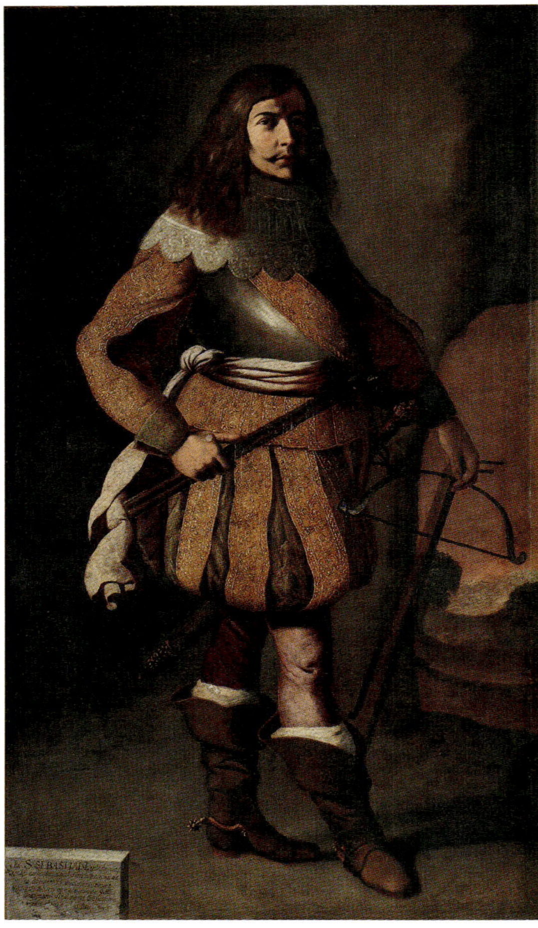

FIG. 64 Circle of Francisco de Zurbarán, *Saint Sebastian*, n.d. Oil on canvas, 75 × 44 in. (190.5 × 111.8 cm). Art Gallery of Ontario, Toronto; Goldwin Smith Collection, 1911 GS110. Photo © Art Gallery of Ontario.

or inhabiting multiple categories simultaneously should further information about their original context or history emerge.

Moreover, as I have argued in this book, early modern portraiture did not undergo a straightforward teleological development from sacred to secular (or "pure") portraiture. Indeed, the first image examined in the introduction was a mid-seventeenth-century Valencian painting of a woman depicted in the guise of the early Christian martyr Saint Barbara. Although the woman does not have a halo, a number of elements corroborate that she is meant to be understood as a depiction of the saint: her physical contact with Christ, the wreath and martyr's palm borne by the angel behind her, the inscribed sheet with the saint's name, and the red color of the garments worn by both the woman in the foreground and the one being martyred in the background vignette. The distances between saint and sitter, between past and present, and between sacred and nonsacred are entirely collapsed. By contrast, another work that was painted—also in Spain, also in the same decade—by the Madrid painter Francisco Caro, presents a radically different solution to a pair of patrons' similar challenging request that their physiognomies be included in a religious image (see fig. 11).[8] At the center of the large canvas is Saint Francis, kneeling in the midst of a miraculous vision of the Virgin and Christ at the Portiuncula, while the painting's donors, María de Amezquita and Antonio de Contreras, are portrayed in the picture's lower register. Caro's innovation resided in his subversion of the traditional format of the donor portrait wherein the commissioners shared space with a religious image's sacred protagonists. By contrast, Amezquita's and Contreras's likenesses appear as framed paintings, which are as real within the pictorial space as the tiled floor and the carpet-draped steps.

The painted frames separate the time and space of the donors from the space in which Saint Francis's vision occurs. What is more, they separate categories, distinguishing between what the artist or his patrons apparently saw as discrete artistic types. As images, the portraits of the donors are of a kind with one another but not with the sacred scene that envelops them. In everything, the two types seem binarily opposed. The portraits are iconic, with static single figures whose idiosyncratically imperfect faces are finely finished. The visionary scene, on the other hand, is narrative and teeming with idealized figures in motion, with large swaths rendered in painterly brushwork. Typologically, the portraits are cast as entirely distinct—in appearance, style, meaning, and function, from the sacred image that surrounds them. Even though the manner in which Caro's *Saint Francis* compartmentalizes its constitutive sacred and secular elements into discrete parts registers as more "modern" than the portrait of the woman as Saint Barbara, the two paintings are contemporaneous. Moreover, there exist examples of portraiture in the guise of saints and, more broadly, of sacred portraiture in the Hispanic world from at least the late fifteenth to the nineteenth centuries, far post-dating the Saint Barbara example; the disordered history of this image type from the eighteenth century until the present remains nearly entirely unexamined.

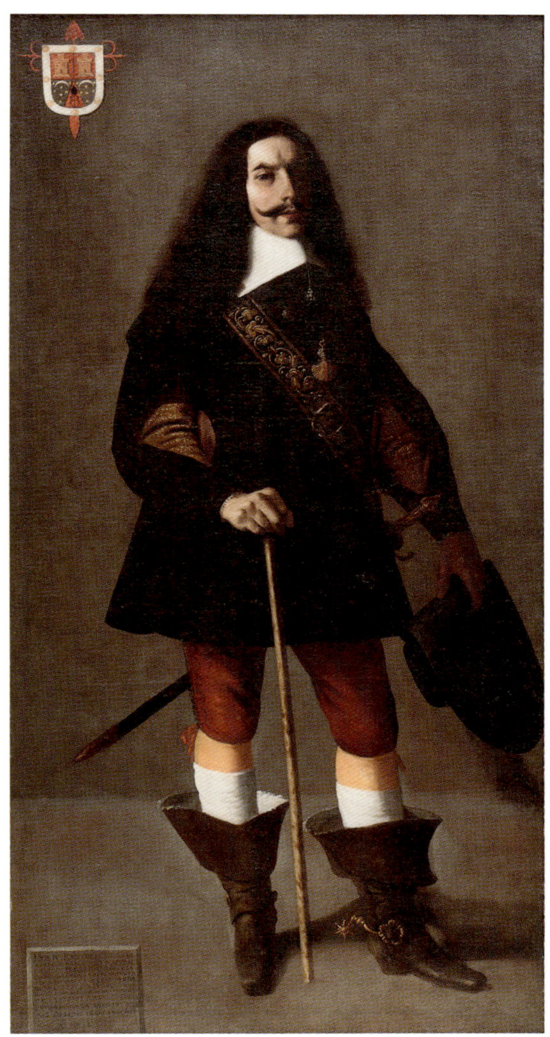

FIG. 65 Francisco de Zurbarán, *Don Juan Bazo de Moreda*, ca. 1655. Oil on canvas, 78.625 × 40.25 in. (199.7 × 102.2 cm). Detroit Institute of Arts, museum purchase, Robert H. Tannahill Foundation Fund, Jill Ford Murray Fund, and Joseph M. de Grimme Memorial Fund, 2015.13.

Nevertheless, many of this book's arguments about sacred portraiture can be extended forward in time. For example, in a 1721 portrait, in tapestry, the queen of Spain Isabel de Farnesio is represented as the *Virgen de los Desamparados* (Our Lady of the Helpless), an important advocation based in Valencia, which was widely venerated throughout the Hispanic world (fig. 66). Although she is not crowned with a halo nor with any other marker of divinity, the image is immediately recognizable both as a portrait of the queen (and perhaps also of her offspring) and as a Marian image, having been made after a print of the Valencian sculpture.[9] Even though we have little evidence for how the 1721 image was used, we can draw a direct line from this image back to the 1605 portrait of Queen Margarita of Austria and her daughter enacting the Annunciation, examined in chapter 1. The two cases are separated by over a century, and, moreover, they

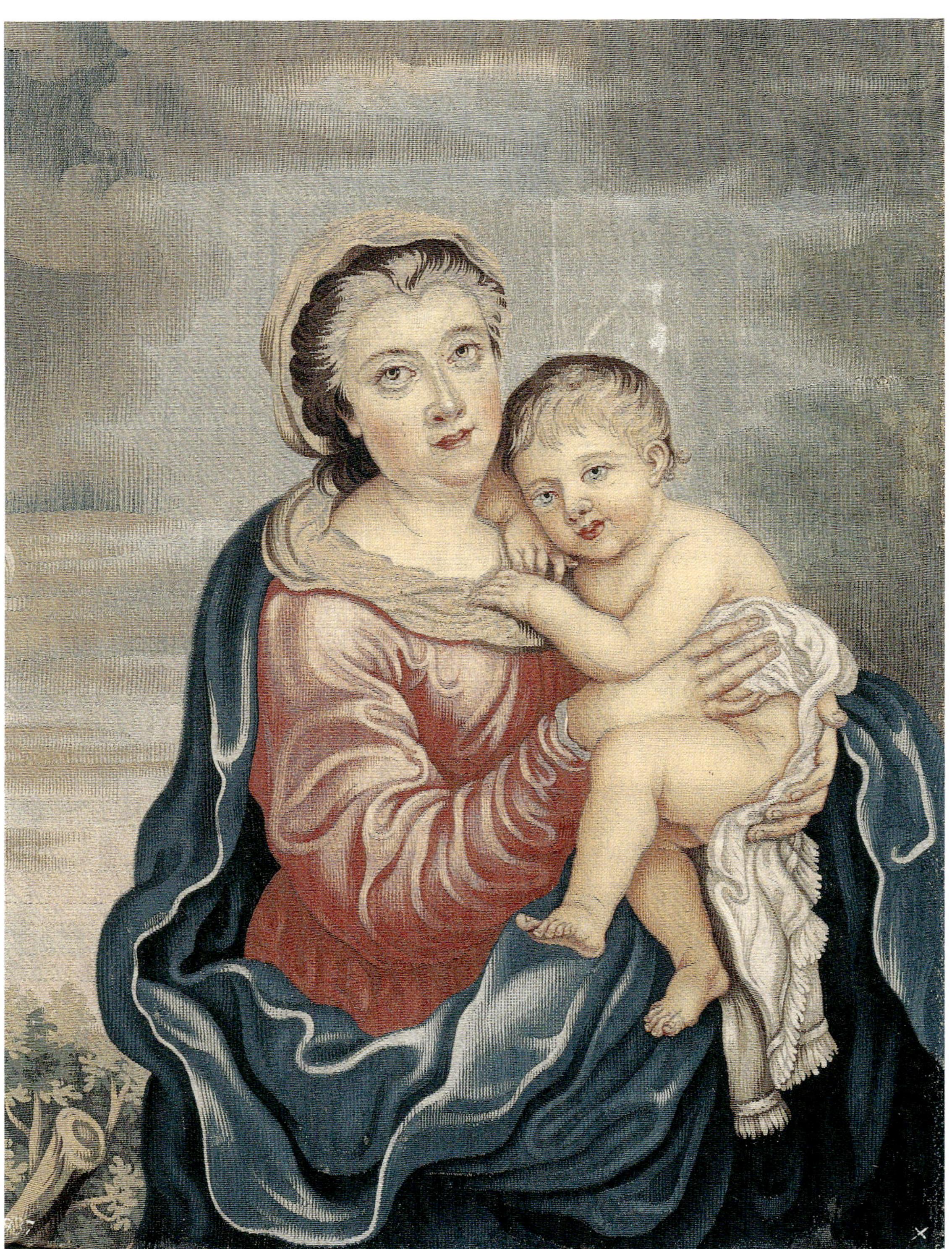

fall on either side of the historiographic chasm that is the year 1700, which is a boundary that, in separating both centuries and dynasties (the Habsburg Charles II was succeeded by the Bourbon Philip V in that year), gives the false impression that the periods are not continuous but merely contiguous. Nevertheless, the two images share crucial commonalities, even beyond the fact that they both associate a Spanish queen with the Mother of God.

Indeed, in an inventory of 1734, the textile panel is identified only by its religious aspect, with the description reading, "Our Lady with the Child in her arms, [who] rests his head on his mother's shoulder," ignoring or obscuring the fact that it is also a portrait of the queen.[10] Like Queen Isabel's woven portrait, the painting of Margarita is not, to my knowledge, inventoried as both a religious image and a portrait either. In these two cases their potentially problematic duality is entirely elided from the documentary record. The numerous painters who were tasked with creating inventories of paintings (as *tasadores*, or appraisers) often also worked as *calificadores* (assessors) for the Holy Office of the Inquisition and thereby possessed significant knowledge of ecclesiastical image regulations.[11] Placed between the royal or aristocratic patron, whose collection they were inventorying, and an ecclesiastical censor, an appraiser could simply have chosen to reduce the composite portrait *a lo divino* to only one of its constitutive elements, either the portrait or the devotional picture, thereby claiming ignorance of its heterodox character. In this way, portraits *a lo divino* may have functioned as a form of "public secret," what Michael T. Taussig characterizes as "that which is generally known, but cannot be articulated," when individuals hesitate to identify obvious facts.[12]

FIG. 66 Isabel Farnese (cartoon) and Jacobo Vandergoten the Elder (tapestry), *Queen Isabel Farnese as the Virgen de los Desamparados*, 1721. Tapestry. Palacio Real de la Granja de San Ildefonso, 10005040. Photo © Patrimonio Nacional.

Sacred portraits continued to be produced during the 1800s at various levels of society in Spain and the newly independent nation states of South and Central America, regardless of the formalization of a hierarchy of academic genres after the French model during the preceding century and a half.[13] As late as the last quarter of the nineteenth century, we encounter examples of real individuals depicted as saints, including in a now-lost painting of a woman portrayed in the guise of Saint Isabel of Hungary by the Sevillian painter Virgilio Mattoni.[14] The model of the portrait *a lo divino*, which came into popularity along with the return of the physiognomic likeness in early modern European portraiture in the fifteenth century, remained current. On the one hand, the codified language of sanctity may be read as a solution for bestowing prestige on a sitter. Indeed, the simple iconographic element of the halo was a powerful and widely understood marker of privilege. On the other hand, such was the power of the likeness, with all of its idiosyncratic imperfections, that it created sacred images that were irresistible in their currency and that actualized sacred scenes and figures in relatable terms, using portraiture to mediate between the faithful and the divine. Perhaps, from the point of view of the Catholic Church, this was an acceptable tradeoff for what was arguably a crisis in early modern sacred artistic production, expressed in the recurring inquisitorial trials of images where likeness had erupted into sacred imagery.

This crisis arose in societies that produced anthropomorphic religious images and also had the desire or need to make idiosyncratic physiognomic likenesses. The Church's attempts at censorship, remarkably similar across the early modern period, were insufficient to quell the phenomenon. Images—as well as their audiences—were mutable and fast, mimicking established forms and practices as often as they created new ones. That portraiture was part and parcel of early modern sacred imagery and that any portrait had, latent within it, the potential to function as a sacred image is clear. Therefore, regardless of the careful separation of the donors' likenesses out of the realm of the sacred image that Caro and his patrons insisted upon in their painting of Saint Francis, there was still the—very real—possibility that someone who found themselves before the image might pray not to Francis, not to Christ, and not to the Virgin but to the two painted, framed portraits.

NOTES

Unless otherwise noted, all translations in the book are my own.

Introduction

1. Villegas, *Flos sanctorum*, fol. 321r (mispaginated). The original text is only included in the endnote if it comes from a manuscript source.
2. Brown, "From Spanish to New Spanish Painting," 133.
3. *Canons and Decrees of the Council of Trent*, Twenty-Fifth Session, "On the Invocation, Veneration, and Relics of Saints, and on Sacred Images," n.p.
4. For a possible attribution of this painting to Mosén Domingo Saura, see Pérez Sánchez, *Pintura española*, 126.
5. Pierce, *Companion to Spanish Colonial Art*, 89.
6. Felipe Pereda has defined sacred images as "object(s) imbued with special virtue," which actually possessed something of the sacred (*Images of Discord*, 20). He opposes these to devotional images, which were representations of holy prototypes that were meant to be transcended in prayer. I treat the term "sacred images" more loosely, as images that derived from, represented, or mediated, the sphere of the sacred. Like Pereda, I see them as flexible, possessing the potential to function as both private, devotional images and as cultic or miraculous images, at different moments and to different audiences.
7. Vincent-Cassy, "Francisco de Zurbarán," 240.
8. Gasquoine Hartley, *Record of Spanish Painting*, 94; Lafuente Ferrari, *Breve historia*, 357; Riegl, *Historical Grammar*, 105. Similarly, museum exhibitions often include both portraits and religious paintings but corralled into separate sections; for example: Kasl, *Sacred Spain* (Indianapolis); Bray, *The Sacred Made Real* (Washington, DC); Soler de Campo, *The Art of Power* (Madrid); Katzew, *Painted in Mexico* (Los Angeles); Marías, *El Greco of Toledo* (Toledo); Haag, *Velázquez* (Vienna); and Brown, *Art and Empire* (San Diego).
9. On portrait-like paintings of saints, see Vincent-Cassy, "Francisco de Zurbarán," 240.
10. Some notable exceptions include Cherry, "Portraiture in the Divine Style?," 190–94; Vincent-Cassy, *Saintes vierges et martyres*, 335–64; Vincent-Cassy, "Retrato *a lo divino*"; Bieñko Peralta, "*Verae efigies*," 255–82; and Bassegoda, "Retratos y otros anacronismos," 93–117.
11. Guibovich Pérez, "Fortunas y adversidades," 39–60; Guibovich Pérez, *En defensa de Dios*.
12. See, for example, García-Frías Checa and Jordán de Urriés y de la Colina, *Retrato en las Colecciones Reales*.
13. See Hall, *Sacred Image*; Lingo, *Federico Barocci*; and Loh, "Early Modern Horror." See also Jasienski, "Disgust and the Sacred Image."
14. A recent study has suggested that contemporary viewers first visually "scan" the faces in those figural representations that lack represented movement, such as portraits: Massaro et al., "When Art Moves the Eyes," 12. See also Wallraven et al., "Aesthetic Appraisal of Art," 137–44.
15. Baxandall, *Painting and Experience*, 71–76.
16. The complexities of these processes are examined in Hsia and Palomo, "Religious Identities," 77–105.
17. Prodi, introduction to *Discourse on Sacred and Profane Images*, by Paleotti, 10. For overviews of the vast literature on Catholic artistic theory before and after Trent, see, among others, Freedberg, "Johannes Molanus," 229–45; Pereda, *Images of Discord*; Hall, *Sacred Image*; Lingo, *Federico Barrocci*; Locker, "Introduction: Rethinking Art," 1–18; Franco Llopis, *Pintura valenciana*; and Velandia Onofre, "Jaime Prades," 185–94.
18. Paleotti, *Discourse on Sacred and Profane Images*, 119.
19. Valadés, *Rhetorica Christiana*, 112. See also González García, *Imágenes sagradas*, 421–22; Braddock, "Mestizo Mnemonics," 123–24; Cummins, "From Lies to Truth," 158–63; Fernández Salvador, "Imágenes locales y retórica sagrada," 79–91; and Alcalá, "'Call to Action,'" 594–617.
20. See Báez Rubí, *Mnemosine novohispánica*, 253–64.

21. See, for example, Navarrete Prieto, *Murillo*, 51.
22. Quesada Valera, "El Salvador," 126–31.
23. Portús Pérez, "Jester Pablo de Valladolid," 453.
24. Lafuente Ferrari, "Ensayo preliminar," 37.
25. Portús Pérez, "Varied Fortunes," 20.
26. Covarrubias, *Tesoro*, s.v. "Retrato."
27. Pacheco, *Arte de la pintura*, 525–26. See also Pereda, "Twin Brothers," 99–112.
28. On physiognomic likeness, see Perkinson, *Likeness of the King*, 4–9. See also Zerner, "Portrait, Likeness, and Recognition," 21–24.
29. See, for example, Barthes, "Effet de réel," 84–89, and Berger, "Fictions of the Pose," 108–9.
30. Bass, *Drama of the Portrait*.
31. On this, see Portús Pérez, "Varied Fortunes," 20–21.
32. See, for instance, Bassegoda, "Retratos y otros anacronismos," 99.
33. Exceptions that prominently feature sacred portraits are the exhibition catalogs by García-Frías Checa and Jordán de Urriés y de la Colina, *Retrato en las Colecciones Reales*; and Oettinger, Jr., Bretos, and Kinder Carr, *Retratos: 2,000 Years*.
34. See, for instance, the case of Simón Pereyns's artistic practice in Toussaint, introduction to "Proceso y denuncias," xiii, and Stanfield-Mazzi, "Cult, Countenance, and Community," 431.
35. Portús, *Concepto de Pintura Española*, 61–74.
36. González García, *Imágenes sagradas*, 79.
37. Cherry, "Portraiture in the Divine Style?," 190.
38. Perkinson, *Likeness of the King*, 7.
39. Nelson, "Response to *A Questionnaire on Decolonization*," 89.
40. On another related category, that of portrait-like paintings of saints, see Vincent-Cassy, *Saintes vierges et martyres*, and Eaker, "Van Dyck," 173–91.
41. Wood, "Votive Scenario," 224–26; Falque, *Devotional Portraiture*, 4–5, 14–15, 239–70; Pope-Hennessy, *Portrait in the Renaissance*, 257, 269; Sand, *Vision, Devotion, and Self-Representation*, 88–99. On terminology, see Schleif, "Kneeling on the Threshold," 195–98. For Spain, see Yarza Luaces, "Retrato medieval," 78–93; Salvador González and De la Casa Rodríguez, "Sobre la supuesta línea," 73–98; and Raquejo Grado, "Donante en la pintura española," 76–87. For political meanings of donor portraits, see Goodman, "Conspicuous in Her Absence," 163–84. For New Spain, see Vargas Lugo, "Retrato de donantes," 13–20, and Rodríguez Moya, "Devoción y nación," 109–31. For South America, see Stanfield-Mazzi, "Cult, Countenance, and Community," 429–59.
42. My argument is in contrast to that in Raquejo Grado, "Donante en la pintura española," 86. "Retratos y otros anacronismos," 101–4. Bassegoda ("Retratos y otros anacronismos," 101–4) argues that in the second half of the seventeenth century, some of the most "flagrant anachronisms," that is interferences of contemporary portraits in religious scenes, begin to disappear in French and some Italian painting—but not in Spanish art.
43. Stratton-Pruitt, "Gaspar Miguel de Berrío," 54–55.
44. Cecchi, "Giovanni Maria Butteri," 138.
45. Pérez Sánchez, "Retrato clásico español," 247; Cherry, "Portraiture in the Divine Style?," 190–94. Additionally, see Nagel, *Controversy of Renaissance Art*, 288 n. 5; Straussman-Pflanzer, "Court Culture," 109–51; Grzęda, "Portret i figuralna interpretacja historii," 123–41; Manuth, Van Leeuwen, and Koldeweij, *Example or Alter Ego?*; Van Leeuwen, "*Portrait historié*," 109–24; Van Leeuwen, "Beeltenissen van bestuurders."
46. Jacobus, "'Propria Figura,'" 72–101.
47. See Van der Ploeg, "Likeness and Presence," 103–4; Nagel and Wood, *Anachronic Renaissance*, 118–22; and Goffen, "Icon and Vision," 487–518.
48. Pereda, "Sombras y cuadros," 80–81.
49. Velandia Onofre, "Hacia una teología," 317–29; Velandia Onofre, "Jaime Prades," 185–94; Franco Llopis, "Redescubriendo a Jaime Prades," 83–93.
50. Pereda, "Sombras y cuadros," 83–85. See also Pereda, "True Painting," 393–94.
51. Hans Belting has noted that "the interaction of official use and popular cults [. . .] cannot be neatly distinguished, no matter how much one would like to do so." Belting, *Likeness and Presence*, 45. See also Reiss, *Mirages of the Selfe*, 52.
52. On "popular culture" and "popular religion," see Eire, "Concept of Popular Religion," 1–35.
53. Examples include Pereda, *Imágenes de la discordia*; Franco Llopis and Hamann, "Curioso caso," 349–68; Franco Llopis and Rusconi, "Sobre pinturas deshonestas," 97–118; Soyer, "Inquisition, Art, and Self-Censorship," 269–92; Rodríguez Gutiérrez de Ceballos, "Repercusión en España," 153–59;

Scholz-Hänsel, "Early Modern Discipline," 127; and Riello, "El Greco y la Inquisición," 109–28. An overview of the Spanish and American Inquisitions can be found in Starr-LeBeau and Lynn, "Tribunals and Jurisdictions," 52–65, and Poska, "Disciplinary Insitutions," 266–78.

54. González García, *Imágenes sagradas*, 222.
55. Cummins, "From Lies to Truth," 157.
56. Saidiya V. Hartman's approach to analyzing the corpus of interviews conducted in the 1930s with formerly enslaved Black Americans provides a framework for approaching these inquisitorial materials from sixteenth- and seventeenth-century Hispanic territories, in spite of the historical and contextual distances between them (*Scenes of Subjection*, 11).
57. See Silverblatt, "Black Legend," 99–116, and Homza, "Victims as Actors," 193–203.

Chapter 1

1. *Proceso contra fray Francisco García Calderón*, AHN, Inquisición, legajo 3691, carpeta 2, fol. 419r. The manuscript has two competing paginations, of which I use the one listed at the top middle of each folio.
2. Pinar, *Monja enterrada*; Lea, *Chapters from the History of Spain*, esp. 309–18, 488–90; Sluhovsky, "Devil in the Convent," 1380–81, 1385–86; Puyol Buil, *Inquisición y política*, esp. 22–46. Other sources include Barbeito, *Cárceles y mujeres*, 97–265; Keitt, *Inventing the Sacred*, 46–47; and González Duro, *Demonios en el convento*. See also Áviles et al., "Archivo del Consejo de la Inquisición," 509–10, and Boyle, "Inquisition and Epistolary Negotiation," 293–309.
3. *Proceso contra fray Francisco García Calderón*, AHN, Inquisición, legajo 3691, carpeta 2, July 18, 1628, fols. 421r–422r. See also Caro Baroja, *Vidas mágicas*, 1:91.
4. Pérez Sánchez, "Pintura Genovesa en España," 177–78.
5. Moncó Rebollo, *Mujer y demonio*, 156.
6. *Proceso contra fray Francisco García Calderón*, AHN, Inquisición, legajo 3691, carpeta 2, fol. 419r: "le dixo fray Juan de Baraona a este que entendia avia de llevar el retrato del d[ic]ho Fran.[co] Prior." My thanks to Santiago López-Ríos, Goretti González, and María Lumbreras, who advised on the translation of this sentence.
7. Ibid., fol. 420v: "Preg.[do] si le dixo alguna persona por que razon se pintaron estos Angeles con esta novedad y de donde era la avian tomado para la pintura / Dixo q[ue] este testigo no hizo mas de segun la mem[a] y ni preg[o] ni le dixeron otra cosa."
8. Koldeweij et al., introduction to *Example or Alter Ego?*, 136–39.
9. Wind, "Studies in Allegorial Portraiture I," 138–62.
10. Ibid., 138–42.
11. Benito, "Retrato moralizado en España," 186.
12. Manuth, Van Leeuwen, and Koldeweij, *Example or Alter Ego?*; Van Leeuwen, "*Portrait historié*," 109–24.
13. Pope-Hennessy, *Portrait in the Renaissance*, 283.
14. Alpers, *Vexations of Art*, 53.
15. Eaker, "Van Dyck," 173–91, and Polleroß, "Between Typology and Psychology," 75.
16. Noyes, *Peter Paul Rubens*, 204.
17. Polleroß, *Sakrale Identifikationsporträt*, 1:5–6.
18. Ibid., 1:7, and Kiss, "Considérations sur le portrait historié," 114.
19. *Canons and Decrees of the Council of Trent*, Twenty-Fifth Session, "On the Invocation, Veneration, and Relics of Saints, and on Sacred Images," n.p., and Paleotti, *Discourse on Sacred and Profane Images*.
20. Orozco Díaz, "Retratos a lo divino," 32, and Orozco Díaz, "Retrato a lo divino, su influencia," 351–59.
21. Pérez Sánchez, "Retrato clásico español," 248. See, for instance, Cruz, *Neptuno Alegórico*, and Tanner, *Last Descendant of Aeneas*. For France, see Schneider, *Belle comme Vénus*.
22. Vincent-Cassy, "Retrato *a lo divino*," https://doi.org/10.4000/e-spania.33921.
23. See Sitek, "Just What Is It," 1–20.
24. See Nagel, *Controversy of Renaissance Art*, 20; Zerner, "Portrait, Likeness, and Recognition," 21–24; and Bassegoda, "Retratos y otros anacronismos," 107.
25. Vincent-Cassy, "Retrato *a lo divino*." See also Bassegoda, "Retratos y otros anacronismos," 99.
26. See Nagel, "Fashion," 37.
27. Numerous studies address the painting, including Vincent-Cassy, *Saintes vierges et martyres*, 356–57; Marías, "Juan Pantoja de la Cruz," 112–14; and Carlos Varona, *Nacer en palacio*, 214–15.

28. Polleroß, "'Majesté' contre 'Saintété,'" 47.
29. Distinct versions of this argument have been made by, among others, Vincent-Cassy, "Marguerite de Habsbourg," 215; Serrera, "Alonso Sánchez Coello," 39–40; Cherry, "Portraiture in the Divine Style?," 192; and Pascual Chenel, *Retrato de Estado*, 134.
30. Broadfoot, "*Las meninas*," 219–32.
31. Mínguez Cornelles argues that Juan Bautista Maíno's painting *Recovery of the Bahía de Todos los Santos* is a symbolic depiction of royal thamaturgy—of both injured individuals and of politically disjointed territories ("Emperadores taumaturgos," 63–65). See also Ruiz, "Unsacred Monarchy," 133; Keitt, *Inventing the Sacred*, 193–201; Cañeque, *King's Living Image*, 54–55; and Starr-LeBeau, *In the Shadow of the Virgin*, 251–57.
32. Rucquoi, "Reyes que no son taumaturgos," 63–64, 79; Kantorowicz, *King's Two Bodies*; Ruiz, "Unsacred Monarchy," 132. On the sacred/unsacred nature of Spanish kingship, see Foronda, "Apoderarse del rey," 18 n. 1.
33. Río Barredo, "Felipe II," 683–84.
34. Pellicer de Salas y Tovar, *Fenix*, fol. 133r. For an analysis of this text, see Olmo, "Providencialismo y sacralidad real," https://www.sociedadesprecapitalistas.fahce.unlp.edu.ar/article/view/SPv2n1a05.
35. This argument is made in Keitt, *Inventing the Sacred*, 183–201, and Olmo, "Providencialismo y sacralidad real."
36. An opposite claim is made in Mínguez Cornelles, "Emperadores taumaurgos," 58, and Vincent-Cassy, "Retrato *a lo divino*."
37. Velandia Onofre, "Word and Image," 332–48; Klerck, "*Portrait Historié* in Passion Scenes," 159–72.
38. Nagel, "Fashion," 37. See also Falque, *Devotional Portraiture*.
39. Marías, "Juan Pantoja de la Cruz," 112–14.
40. Carlos Varona, *Nacer en palacio*, 213–15.
41. See, for instance, Pietz, "Problem of the Fetish, I," 10.
42. Nagel, *Controversy of Renaissance Art*, 23–28, and Vincent-Cassy, "Retrato *a lo divino*."
43. See Elsner, "Place, Shrine, Miracle," 8–9. I expand here on Vincent-Cassy's consideration of these images as devotional ("Retrato *a lo divino*").
44. María Cruz de Carlos Varona hypothesizes that the painting was sent to the queen's family in Graz (*Nacer en palacio*, 214).
45. Guzmán, *Reyna catolica*, fols. 129v–130r.
46. Ibid. See also Guzmán, *Memorias*.
47. Carlos Varona, *Nacer en palacio*, 214; Kusche, *Juan Pantoja de la Cruz*, 118–20; Marías, "Juan Pantoja de la Cruz," 112.
48. Pascual Chenel, *Retrato de Estado*, 130. On the role of outward facing figures in religious historiated portraits, see Schneider, *Belle comme Vénus*, 53–56.
49. Nagel, "Fashion," 37.
50. Relatedly, see Marin, "Portrait of the King's Glorious Body," 141.
51. Vieyra, *Sermoens*, 241. On the *imitatio Christi*, see Cruz González, "Beyond the Bride of Christ," 102–32.
52. On the inimitability of the Virgin, see Warner, *Alone of All Her Sex*, 77–78, and Carlos Varona, *Nacer en palacio*, 211–12.
53. Sánchez, "Confession and Complicity," 133–34, and Marín Tovar, "Jubilosa entrada de Margarita," 147–57.
54. Guzmán, cited in Martínez Millán, "Casa de una reina católica," 348.
55. Ignacio de Loyola, *Ejercicios espirituales*, 17. See also Sluhovsky, "St. Ignatius of Loyola's 'Spiritual Exercises,'" 649–74.
56. Molina, *To Overcome Oneself*, 50–66, and Palmer, *On Giving the "Spiritual Exercises,"* 109.
57. Bouza, "Biblioteca de la reina Margarita," 50, and Sánchez, "Confession and Complicity," 136.
58. Molina, *To Overcome Oneself*, 56, and Palmer, *On Giving the "Spiritual Exercises,"* 25, 109.
59. Rhodes, "Join the Jesuits," 42–44.
60. Sluhovsky, *Becoming a New Self*, 72–73, 79.
61. Palmer, *On Giving the "Spiritual Exercises,"* 7.
62. Bouza, "Biblioteca de la reina Margarita," 50, 72. On earlier texts, see Velandia Onofre, "Word and Image," 332–34.
63. Kempis, *Contemptus mundi*, 19.
64. Ibid., 338–39. See also Falque, *Devotional Portraiture*, 122–29.
65. Bouza, "Biblioteca de la reina Margarita," 62, and Fonseca, *Tratado del amor de Dios*, 456.
66. Ignacio de Loyola, *Ejercicios espirituales*, 42. On the senses in the *Spiritual Exercises*, see Pabel, "Interior Sight," 254–88.
67. Palmer, *On Giving the "Spiritual Exercises,"* 49.
68. Ibid., 50–51.
69. Rodríguez Moya, "Reinas santas," 254.
70. Palmer, *On Giving the "Spiritual Exercises,"* 69, 307.

71. Jasienski, "Disgust and the Sacred Image."
72. See Goodman, "Royal Piety," 149–50, 167–69, and Tiffany, "Little Idols," 35–48.
73. Jesús, *Exercicios de devocion*, 172.
74. Ibid., 209.
75. Ibid., 29.
76. Pinto, *Segunda parte de los dialogos*, fols. 219v–220r.
77. Fonseca, *Tratado del amor de Dios*, 570.
78. See Pereda, *Crime and Illusion*, 107.
79. On Paleotti's evaluation of portraiture, see *Discourse on Sacred and Profane Images*, esp. 203–14.
80. Pacheco, *Arte de la pintura*, 710.
81. Joannes Molanus, cited in ibid., 710.
82. Ibid., 521–33.
83. Ignacio de Loyola, *Ejercicios espirituales*, 28.
84. Ibid., 43. See Reiss, *Mirages of the Selfe*, 392–93.
85. Chipps Smith, *Sensuous Worship*, 35. See also Blanchard, "Beyond Belief," 94–108; Falque, *Devotional Portraiture*, 240–45; and Velandia Onofre, "Word and Image," 332–48.
86. Holm Monssen, "Rex Gloriose Martyrum," 133, and González García, "Técnicas jesuíticas de predicación misional," 368–85.
87. González García, "Charles V's Death," 13–18, and González García, "Empathetic Images," 487–525.
88. See Zierholz, "'To Make Yourself Present,'" 419–60.
89. On "object-based naturalism," see Ripollés, "Allure of the Object," 132, 137. On the role of depicted objects in meditative practices, see Tiffany, "Visualizing Devotion," 448–50.
90. For Italy, see Rocco, "Maniera Devota, Mano Donnesca," 76–91; for England, see Canavan and Smith, "'Needle May Convert,'" 105–26.
91. Carlos Varona, *Nacer en palacio*, 121.
92. Sluhovsky, *Becoming a New Self*, 74.
93. See García Sanz and Triviño, *Iconografía de Santa Clara*, 150–51.
94. Rojas, *Anales*, 1:164. See also García Sanz and Triviño, *Iconografía de Santa Clara*, 47–49.
95. Pérez Sánchez and Navarrete Prieto, *Luis Tristán*, 212.
96. Braider, *Experimental Selves*, 158.
97. Tiffany, "Little Idols," 45–47; Jiménez Sanz, "Casa Museo," 330.
98. Covarrubias, *Tesoro*, s.v. "Aojar."
99. Ibid.
100. *Diccionario de la lengua castellana*, s.v. "Higa." See also Stoichita, *Goya*, 249–55.
101. On amulets, see Marías, "Juan Pantoja de la Cruz," 110; Horcajo Palomero, "Amuletos y talismanes," 524; Ragazzi, "Entrecruzamentos Culturais," 34–41; and Hernando Garrido, "Antídotos contra el diablo," 225–60.
102. Covarrubias, *Tesoro*, s.v. "Aojar."
103. García Sanz and Ruiz, "Linaje regio y monacal," 146.
104. Polleroß, "Between Typology and Psychology," 83–84. See also Polleroß, *Sakrale Identifikationsporträt*, esp. 1:52–77, and Polleroß, "Anfänge des Identifikationsporträts," 17–36.
105. See Mateo Gómez, *Juan Correa de Vivar*, 33–34, and Tanner, *Last Descendant of Aeneas*, 167–69.
106. Marín Cruzado, "Retrato real," 125.
107. Ibid., 122. See also Perkinson, "Rethinking the Origins of Portraiture," 146.
108. On these objects, see Checa Cremades, *Velázquez, Bernini, Luca Giordano*, 138; Pascual Chenel, *Retrato de Estado*, 135, 168; and Azcue, "Carlos II, portapaz de plata," 58–61. If existing portraits were transformed into religious objects in the nineteenth century, as the Museo del Prado now believes of the two paxes, this would corroborate the flexibility of the portrait as an image type, as examined in chapter 3 of this book: "Carlos II, portapaz de plata," http://www.museodelprado.es, accessed on October 21, 2021. On the cult of Saint Ferdinand, see Wunder, *Baroque Seville*, 73–96.
109. I agree with Bassegoda, who suggests that Zurbarán's paintings of female saints—largely destined for convents and never thus far convincingly associated with any actual secular sitters, are not actual portraits. Bassegoda, "Retratos y otros anacronismos," 110.
110. Orozco Díaz, "Retratos a lo divino," 33–34. See also Bergmann, *Art Inscribed*, 204–36. Another sonnet, mentioned in Portús Pérez ("Varied Fortunes," 28), is titled *Al retrato de una dama en trage de Madalena penitente*.
111. Skinner, *Clodia Metelli*, 3–7.
112. For the full text, see Orozco Díaz, "Retratos a lo divino," 34. For an analysis, see Vincent-Cassy, *Saintes vierges et martyres*, 155.
113. *Diccionario de autoridades*, s.v. "Novedad." The dictionary's source for this definition is Squarzafigo, *Opusculos*.
114. Vincent-Cassy, *Saintes vierges et martyres*, 155.
115. See Sánchez Jiménez, "'Casta Susana,'" 69–80.

116. On Lerma and Margarita, see Sánchez, *The Empress, the Queen*, 145; and Martínez Millán, "Casa de una reina católica," 348–54.
117. Urban VIII, *Decreta*, 7; *Enciclopedia Cattolica*, s.v. "Canonizzazione," columns 591–94. See also Burke, "How to Be a Counter-Reformation Saint," 50; Hills, "'Face Is a Mirror,'" 549; and Leone, *Saints and Signs*, esp. 5–20, 531–33. The most extensive recent study of this issue is Noyes, *Peter Paul Rubens*.
118. Urban VIII, *Decreta*, 7.
119. Ottonelli and Cortona, *Trattato della pittura*, 187. See also Cavazzini, "On Painted Portraiture," 229–42, and Straussman-Pflanzer, "Court Culture," 146–49.
120. Two examples are *Constituciones promulgadas por el Ilustrmo y Revermo Señor D. Fr. Francisco de Roys y Mendoza . . . Obispo de Badajoz*, 203, and *Constituciones synodales del Arzobispado de Zaragoza*, 289.
121. Rodríguez Gutiérrez de Ceballos, "Repercusión en España," 153–59.
122. *Constituciones synodales del Obispado de de Veneçuela*, 326–27.
123. *Constituciones synodales del Obispado de Osma*, 273; *Constituciones synodales de El Obispado de la ciudad de Guamanga*, 83.
124. See, more generally, Rodríguez Gutiérrez de Ceballos, "Repercusión en España," 156, and Webster, "Shameless Beauty," 249–71.
125. Covarrubias, *Tesoro*, s.v. "Divinidad." See also Wardropper, *Historia de la poesía lírica*; and Bassegoda, "Retratos y otros anacronismos," 111.
126. Camargo, *Discurso theológico*, 193–94. See also Johnson, "Feeling Certainty, Performing Sincerity," 60–61.
127. Villegas, *Esposa de Cristo*, 530. See also Sánchez López, "Cielo y el mundo," 161–233.
128. Villegas, *Esposa de Cristo*, 430–31. For an analysis of such criticisms, see González García, "Hijas de Friné," 149–73.
129. *Sumario del Concilio Provincial*, 13–14.
130. Villegas, *Esposa de Cristo*, 443.
131. *Constituciones synodales del Obispado de Malaga*, 484.
132. The case is mentioned in García Sáiz, "Portraiture in Viceregal America," 78–79.
133. Ruiz del Corral, *Carta*, AGN, Inquisición, vol. 308, expediente 107, fol. 632: "a visto este denunciante un lienzo al olio y en el pintada la ymagen de nra señora y a los pies della una de St Ju.o baptista y una de S.t estevan y otra de S.ta Lucia, y a lo q[ue] aeste t.o le parese la ymagen de St. Juo baptista es retrato lo q[ue] es rostro y caveza del licendo. Juo Maldonado de Paz oydor desta real Audia, cuyo es el lienzo en q[ue] estan estas pinturas." This is also transcribed, with discrepancies, in Chinchilla Aguilar, *Sor Juana de Maldonado*, 15.
134. Ruiz del Corral, *Carta*, AGN, Inquisición, vol. 308, expediente 107, fol. 632: "la primera vez q[ue] este t.o vio el lienzo le paresio mal que debajo de figuras de sanctos se retratasen semejantes personas y particularmente la hija, no siendo ligitima y lo mesmo lea paresido todas las veces q[ue] avisto el d[ic]ho lienzo porq[ue] se a puesto muy de hordinario en yglesias y altares en las proseçiones del sanctissimo sacramento, y q[ue] a oydo este to a dibersas personas murmurar destos retratos . . ."
135. Bergmann, *Art Inscribed*, 205–6. See also Vallejo García-Hevia, "Inquisición del distrito," 241.
136. Villa-Flores, *Dangerous Speech*, 4–9.
137. Quevedo, *Vida del Buscón*, 82.
138. Villa-Flores, *Dangerous Speech*, 4. See also Burke, *Popular Culture*, 291; Rodríguez Gutiérrez de Ceballos, "Repercusión en España," 155; and Solomon, "Presence of Portraits," 49–52.
139. Estenssoro, "Plástica colonial," 421–24.
140. Marías, "Juan Pantoja de la Cruz," 114, and Feros, *Duque de Lerma*, 169–72.
141. Feros, *Duque de Lerma*, 170.
142. Marías, "Juan Pantoja de la Cruz," 112 n. 50. On Isabel de Borbón's oratory, see Carlos Varona, *Nacer en palacio*, 180.
143. Brown and Elliott, *Palace for a King*, 31.
144. See Feros, "King's Favorite," 119–21, 130–33, and Goodman, "Royal Piety," 16–19, 144–48, 164–70.
145. Vincent-Cassy argues that the paintings "played with the different levels of possible interpretation" ("Retrato *a lo divino*," https://doi.org/10.4000/e-spania.33921).
146. This point is also made by Marías, "Juan Pantoja de la Cruz," 116.
147. For a similar argument about the political image program of the "private" Torre de la Parada,

see Oliván Santaliestra, "'Decía que no se dejaba retratar,'" 22–23. See also Polleroß, "'Majesté' contre 'Sainteté,'" 47, and Carlos Varona, *Nacer en palacio*, 214. For the political uses of a royal woman's portrait in Spain, see Jasienski, "Savage Magnificence," 195–96.

148. León, *Perfecta casada*.
149. By contrast, a seventeenth-century inventory from Florence describes "a picture on canvas depicting the portrait of the Most Serene Grand Duchess Vittoria who portrays a Virgin in the act of teaching the Serene Young Prince Cosimo to read, who portrays Our Lord and behind them is the portrait of the Maiorduomo Giovanni Cosimo Gerardini, who portrays Saint Joseph." Straussman-Pflanzer, "Court Culture," 136.
150. Nagel, *Controversy of Renaissance Art*, esp. 13–16 and 23–29.
151. Kusche, *Juan Pantoja de la Cruz*, 140.
152. Ibid., 478–85; Aguirre, "Documentos relativos a la pintura," 18–19.
153. Santos, *Descripcion breve*, 62.
154. Goffen, *Giovanni Bellini*, 217; Solomon, "Presence of Portraits," 50.
155. Kusche, *Juan Pantoja de la Cruz*, 118.
156. Korbacher, "Fra Teodoro of Urbino," 373.
157. Pérez Sánchez, "Retrato clásico español," 230. On the purported vanity of such images, see Orozco Díaz, "Retratos a lo divino," 32–33, and García Sanz and Ruiz, "Linaje regio y monacal," 148.
158. Schryver, *Prayer Book*, 17.
159. Braider, *Experimental Selves*, 136–37; Perkinson, *Likeness of the King*, 4. Bassegoda argues that the inclusion of portraits in religious scenes "would not have been a perturbing element for the mentality of the [early modern] period" ("Retratos y otros anacronismos," 105).
160. McPherson, *Modern Portrait*, 4. For a critical evaluation of these ideas of portraiture, see Woods Marsden, *Renaissance Self-Portraiture*, 13–16, and Loh, "Renaissance Faciality," 343–63.
161. Reiss, *Mirages of the Selfe*, 385. See also Braider, *Experimental Selves*, 170. On the range of approaches to the self in early modern Spain, see Luri, *Recogimiento*.
162. Alberti, *On Painting*, 63.
163. Burke, "Sociología del retrato renacentista," 110.

Chapter 2

1. On Acuña del Adarve and the Mandylion, see Pereda, *Crime and Illusion*, 188–96. On *verae effigies*, see Quiles García, *Santidad barroca*, 59–76. On secular conceptions of true portraiture, see Hajovsky, "André Thevet's 'True' Portrait," 335–52.
2. Acuña del Adarve, *Discursos de las effigies*, fol. 141r.
3. Ibid., fol. 139v.
4. Pereda, *Crime and Illusion*, 196–99.
5. Acuña del Adarve, *Discursos de las effigies*, fol. 166v.
6. See Nicolotti, *Mandylion of Edessa*. On the impossibility of neatly corralling relics from images, see Riello, "Relíquies i imatges," 125–57.
7. Acuña del Adarve, *Discursos de las effigies*, fol. 191r.
8. Ibid., fol. 141r. On the Veronica, see Sand, *Vision, Devotion, and Self-Representation*, 27–83.
9. Acuña del Adarve, *Discursos de las effigies*, fol. 231v.
10. López, "Relación de la forma," 1:766.
11. Acuña del Adarve, *Discursos de las effigies*, fol. 143r.
12. Cicero, *De natura*, 1:28.
13. Spadaccini and Talens, "Construction of the Self," 12; Pérez-Villanueva, *Life of Catalina de Erauso*, 60; Gaylord, "True Histories," 216. See also Jasienski, "Francisco Pacheco," 413–14.
14. Cueva, *Buelos de las plumas sagradas*, 290.
15. See Braun, *Juan de Mariana*, 39.
16. Longás, *Thomae Longas . . . Enchiridion*, section 7, "Dudas contra el desagravio de la verdad ofendida," n.p.
17. On falsehood in law, see Mumford, "Forgery and *Tambos*," 24–27.
18. Camerino, *Dama beata*, 184.
19. See Pereda, *Crime and Illusion*, esp. 13–22.
20. Cummins, "From Lies to Truth," 152–74.
21. On early modern sources of authority, see Copeland and Machielsen, introduction to *Angels of Light?*, 14.
22. Ferber, *Demonic Possession and Exorcism*, 77–78, and Olmo, "Posesión diabólica," 76–84.
23. Clark, *Thinking with Demons*, 8. See also Arenal and Schlau, *Untold Sisters*, and Warner, *Alone of All Her Sex*, 76.
24. *Proceso contra fray Francisco García Calderón*, AHN, Inquisición, legajo 3691, carpeta 2, fol. 398v: "en las sandalias dixo tambien el Demonio la forma q[ue] avian de tener, y el P^{re} Prior trajo un libro donde estaban pintadas y le preg.^{do} que de qual de

aquellas maneras eran, y pareciendo mas honesta la q[ue] avia señalado el demº se hicieron asi."

25. Ibid.: "y en los platos dixo tambien el Dem.º como los usaban en tiempo de San Benito y se quitaron los que tenian en la comunidad; es verdad que siempre avian desagradado aquella manera de platos."
26. Pereda, *Crime and Illusion*, 27.
27. *Proceso contra fray Francisco García Calderón*, AHN, Inquisición, legajo 3691, carpeta 2, fol. 404r: "Ytem se acuerda q[ue] mostrando este Test.º un quadro del Glorioso Patriarca San Benito al d[ic]ho Prior con palabras obscuras u de artificio como las usa muy de ordinario dio a entender q[ue] el avia visto al propio Santo diciendo en viendo el retrato, el es . . . pero era mayor, y alla nunca acabamos de tener quien nos lo sepa retratar." See also Caro Baroja, *Vidas mágicas e Inquisición*, 1:91.
28. *Proceso contra fray Francisco García Calderón*, AHN, Inquisición, legajo 3691, carpeta 2, 399v–401v: "Y tambien fue publico que el demº de Anastasia dixo las facciones y rostro del glorioso San Benito, y de la manera que lo dixo hizo el P^{re} Prior q[ue] un pintor hiciese unos dibujos traiendolos a la d[ic]ha Anastasia la preg^{to} si alguno era conforme al rostro de S Benito; y su Demonio respondio q[ue] no." For further context, see González Duro, *Demonios en el convento*, 110.
29. *Dibujo del retrato de Fray Francisco García Calderón*, AHN, Inquisición, Mapas, planos y dibujos, 238.
30. On the cults of "para-saints," see Bailey, "Missionary Order Without Saints," 240–61. See also Hills, "'Face Is a Mirror,'" 549; Portús Pérez, "Verdadero retrato y copia fallida," 241–51; and Riello, "Mímesis de la muerte," 62.
31. Bieňko Peralta, "*Verae effigies* y los retratos simulados," 272. See also Graziano, *Wounds of Love*, 46–47.
32. Contract signed by Fernández Navarrete, cited in Zarco Cuevas, *Pintores españoles*, 40. The text is also cited in translation in Portús Pérez, "Varied Fortunes," 22.
33. Pacheco, *Arte de la pintura*, 710. On Federico Borromeo's ambitious project of collecting authoritative portraits of Christian figures, both ancient and modern, see Jones, *Federico Borromeo*, 168–206.
34. Lodovico Dolce, cited in Jones, *Federico Borromeo*, 294. Dolce is also cited in Vincent-Cassy, *Saintes vierges et martyres*, 343.
35. On tradition in Catholicism, see Poole, *Our Lady of Guadalupe*, 138. By contrast, the Jesuit Ignacio de Camargo warned that when unsanctioned practices were presented as traditional, they could become accepted in society (*Discurso theológico*, 181–85).
36. Israëls, "Absence and Resemblance," 106. On earlier uses of facial casting and the interest in exact likeness, see Jacobus, "'Propria Figura,'" 72–101, and Krass, *Nah zum Leichnam*.
37. For an overview of Ignatian iconography, see Rodríguez Gutiérrez de Ceballos, "Iconografía de San Ignacio," 39–64. On modern saints from the Jesuit and Oratorian orders, see Noyes, *Peter Paul Rubens*. See also the case studies in Niedermeier, *Ersten Bildnisse*. This book, published too late to factor substantively into my current project, advances arguments that will contribute to future research.
38. López, "Relación de la forma," 1:759. The *Relación* also appears in Ignacio de Loyola, *Cartas de San Ignacio de Loyola*. The original manuscript is at the Biblioteca Nacional de España as "Relacion de la forma que se tuuo en hazer el retrato de nuestro Sancto Padre Igna.º de Loyola y del motivo q[ue] para ello tuuo el P.^{e} P.º de Ribadeneyra. hecha por el h[e]r[man]o Xval lopez su companiero q[ue] s hallo a ello," in *Vida, obras y correspondencia del padre Pedro de Ribadeneira*, 1612, BNE Mss/6525. See also Civil, "Máscara y el retrato," 290. On early Jesuit portrait series, see Harpster, "Illustrious Jesuits," 379–97.
39. On recalcitrant sitters, see Portús Pérez, "Retrato, humildad y santidad," 169–88; Berger, "Fictions of the Pose," 98; and Oliván Santaliestra, "'Decía que no se dejaba retratar,'" 17–19.
40. López, "Relación de la forma," 1:759.
41. Santalla, *Semblantes de San Ignacio*, n.p. (177).
42. Levy, *Propaganda and the Jesuit Baroque*, 11–12, 33–35. See also Hills, "Too Much Propaganda," 446–53, and Knaap, "Meditation, Ministry, and Visual Rhetoric," 157–81. On negative attitudes toward venerating images of Saint Ignatius following the suppression of the Society of Jesus in 1767, see Rodríguez Nóbrega, *Imágenes expurgadas*, 164.
43. López, "Relación de la forma," 1:759; Hornedo, "'Vera effigies' de san Ignacio," 203–24. On the history of death masks, see López de Munain, *Máscaras mortuorias*.

44. On the challenge of taking a portrait *ad vivum* from a deceased individual and the debates over Ignatius's portrait, see Niedermeier, "Artist's Memory," 157–99.
45. López, "Relación de la forma," 1:759–60.
46. Hornedo, "'Vera effigies' de san Ignacio," 209.
47. López, "Relación de la forma," 1:760. On Ribadeneira and Ignatius, see O'Malley, "Many Lives of Ignatius," 13.
48. López, "Relación de la forma," 1:761.
49. On this portrait of Ignatius, see Zierholz, "Allegories of Light and Fire," 357–78.
50. Claudio Acquaviva, cited in Hornedo, "'Vera effigies' de san Ignacio," 215.
51. López, "Relación de la forma," 1:762.
52. *Testificacion sobre la estimacion*, fol. 8r: "lo experimento, y publicamente lo vio y oyo." This document is duplicated in AHN, Inquisición, legajo 1740, no. 3, no. 8, which is used to clarify damaged portions.
53. Spadaccini and Talens, "Construction of the Self," 10.
54. Amelang, "Tracing Lives," 33–48; Johnson, "Feeling Certainty, Performing Sincerity," 50–79.
55. Johnson, "Feeling Certainty, Performing Sincerity," 50–79. See also Pérez-Villanueva, *Life of Catalina de Erauso*, 60. On the tension between verisimilitude and truth in painting, see Riello, "Verídico no es verdadero," 347–48, 362–63.
56. López, "Relación de la forma," 1:762. See also Diego de Saavedra Fajardo's description of viewing a royal portrait, cited in Calvo Serraller, *Teoría de la pintura*, 456.
57. Acuña del Adarve, *Discursos de las effigies*, fol. 197r.
58. López, "Relación de la forma," 1:763.
59. Ibid., 1:762.
60. Ibid., 1:763.
61. Ibid., 1:760, 766.
62. Nagel and Wood, *Anachronic Renaissance*, 111.
63. Ibid., 112.
64. Hills, "'Face Is a Mirror,'" 569.
65. Tiffany, *Diego Velázquez's Early Paintings*, 61.
66. On physiognomy and virtue, see Wiens, "'Like Wax Before a Fire,'" 173–74.
67. For instance, on Carmelite images of Saint John of God, see Moreno Cuadro, "Origen andaluz de la *vera effigies*," 347–70. It bears reminding that each religious order had its own agendas, which changed based on the exigencies of time and place: see Franco Llopis, "Art of Conversion?," 179–202.
68. Nagel, "Icons and Early Modern Portraits," 421.
69. López, "Relación de la forma," 1:759–60; Hornedo, "'Vera effigies' de san Ignacio," 203–24.
70. Perkinson, *Likeness of the King*, 66–75.
71. García, *Vida, virtudes, y milagros*, 623–24.
72. Infante de Aurioles, *Magna, y canonica cirugia*, 476.
73. Covarrubias, *Tesoro*, s.v. "Cabellera."
74. Hills, "'Face Is a Mirror,'" 568.
75. On the iconography of Saint Teresa, see Roe, "Vicente Carducho, Painter and Writer," 59–77.
76. See Tiffany, *Diego Velázquez's Early Paintings*, 56. See also Salinger, "Representations of Saint Theresa," 97–108.
77. Boneta, *Gracias de la gracia*, 318.
78. Méndez Rodríguez, *Velázquez y la cultura sevillana*, 338.
79. Ribera, *Vida de la madre Teresa*, 286.
80. Gracián, *Obras*, fol. 365r.
81. María de San José, cited in Infante-Galán, "'Las moradas' de Santa Teresa," 33–34.
82. See, for instance, Murillo, *Discursos predicables*, 636.
83. Ribera, *Vida de la madre Teresa*, 287.
84. Ibid., 286.
85. See Díez Atienza, "Estudio técnico," 64. See also Díez Atienza et al., "Revisión de la obra," 6–22.
86. Interián de Ayala, *Pintor Christiano*, 2:434.
87. Winter, "What/When Is a Portrait?," 257.
88. See, for instance, Holguín Valdez, "Retrato de Santa Rosa," 46–55.
89. On this painting, see Pierce and Wilson Frick, *Glitterati*, 92.
90. Copeland, *Maria Maddalena De' Pazzi.*
91. Camerino, *Dama beata*, 183.
92. The larger case is analyzed by Keitt, *Inventing the Sacred*, 108. I also examine it in greater depth in Jasienski, "Entre el retrato y la imagen sagrada."
93. *Copia de la culpa*, AHN, Inquisición, legajo 103, no. 7, fol. 52r: "le dijo a que mirase sus pinturas p[a] ber si conoçia alguna y este las miro y reparo que estava una santa Ter.[a] y que su rostro era el de d[ic]ha eujenia y que avia ssido casso Milagrosso porque el pintor que la pinto no la conocia y la hiço Borrar dos beçes y ssiempre la saco con mas perfecçion hasta que pareçiendole casso milagrosso se determino a dejar la como oy se esta con el rostro de d[ic]ha

Eujenia." This document has two, often conflicting paginations, of which I adhere to the recto-verso pagination.

94. Ibid., fols. 203r–205r: "el d[ic]ho Joan Lopez tiene en su oratorio Retrato de la d[ic]ha Eugena [*sic*] de la torre en una Pintura que de la mitad del cuerpo arriva es dela d[ic]ha eugenia de la torre y la otra mitad es de la s^{ta} y m^{dre} teresa de Jesus."
95. See, for instance, Portús Pérez, "Verdadero retrato y copia fallida." On Valdés's painting, see Fernández López, "Pinturas de Lucas Valdés," 424–25.
96. *Copia de la culpa*, AHN, Inquisición, legajo 103, no. 7, fol. 206r: "la hiço retratar el rostro en una fingida pintura de santa Teresa siendo la cara de la d[ic]ha pintura de la d[ic]ha persona y el cuerpo y traje de la santa y con esta traça y invençion tenia en su casa el retrato de la susod[ic]ha."
97. Ibid.: "siendo la d[ic]ha persona y este reo de vida tan ronpida y costumbres relajadas quiso dar a entender que la pintura avia quedado asi por modo sobrenatural fue mendaçio y invençion."
98. Ibid., fol. 210v: "dixo que [e]ste t^{e} [tiene] un quadro de la m.^{e} teresa de jesus y por tal lo venera . . . el no lo mando retratar ni tal se provava."
99. Ibid., fol. 211r: "no juzgandolo como milagro sino como causa nat.[ural]"
100. Ibid., fols. 205v–206r: "no siendolo sino una muger de malos tratos torpe y lasçiva."
101. Jacobson Schutte, "'Questo non è il ritratto che ho fatto io,'" 424.
102. Ibid.
103. Bieñko Peralta, "*Verae efigies*," 269–77, and Crispí i Canton, "Verònica de Madona Santa Maria," 85–101.
104. See, for example, Véliz Bomford, "Velázquez Composes," 92–111. On mechanical processes involved in taking and replicating portraits, see Jacobus, "'Propria Figura,'" 72–101.
105. Yepes, *Vida, virtudes y milagros*, 135.
106. The episode is described in Pacheco, *Arte de la pintura*, 695–97. Its origins, including the text on the door in Vásquez's painting, are discussed in Reeves, *Influence of Prophecy*, 161–65.
107. On Fiore and this painting, see Fajardo de Rueda, "Milenarismo y arte," 236–58, and Fajardo de Rueda, "Presencia de Joaquín de Fiore," 101–3. See also Chicangana-Bayona and Rojas Gómez, "Príncipe del arte nacional," 216–20.
108. On how Fiore's prophecy was utilized by the Dominicans and the Franciscans, see Reeves, *Influence of Prophecy*, 71–73, 96–100, 164–65.
109. Palomino, *Museo pictórico*, 1:220.
110. Rousset, "Più antico ritratto," 317–24.
111. Schenone, *Iconografía*, 336–37. On the larger historiography surrounding the figure of Vásquez, see Rojas Cocoma, "Tradición o revolución," 54–69.

Chapter 3

1. *Informacion hecha sobre la forma*, AHN, Inquisición, legajo 1740, no. 3, no. 7, fol. 2r: "la materia tan grave, y peligrosa."
2. Ibid., fol. 5v: "Y a lo que al presente se quiere acordar el Doctor Alonso de Otamendi Gamboa racionero desta sancta iglesia Catedral le dixo a este declarante como el mismo Gaspar Conrrado Pintor avia hecho un retrato de el dicho señor obispo don Juan de Palafox pintado con alas de zerafin."
3. On Conrado, see Pérez Salazar, *Historia de la pintura en Puebla*, 77, 166, and Merlo Juárez and Morales Pérez, *Estudio, devoción y belleza*, 45–48.
4. On *obrajeros*, see Schell Hoberman, *Mexico's Merchant Elite*, 133, 321. On the trial, see Fernández Gracia, "Consideraciones sobre la riqueza," 399–428; Rubial García, "Rostro de las mil facetas," 301–24; Rubial García, "St. Palafox," 193–207; and Silva Prada, "Tribunal de la fe censurado," 148–82. On images of Palafox, see Fernández Gracia, *Iconografía de Don Juan de Palafox*, and Fernández Gracia, *Don Juan de Palafox*.
5. *Informacion hecha sobre la forma*, AHN, Inquisición, legajo 1740, no. 3, no. 7, fol. 8v: "Y hasta agora no ha hecho ningun retrato de el dicho señor obispo pintado con alas de zeraphin, y puede ser que en alguno de los muchos que ha hecho, otro pintor le aya acrescentado las alas por mandado de sus dueños, y es factible por el entrañable amor que le tienen, y porque o se le atribuian a este testigo aquellos que no ha hecho."
6. See Pointon, *Portrayal and the Search for Identity*, 9.
7. Goffen, "Icon and Vision," 487–518, and Nagel and Wood, *Anachronic Renaissance*, 118–22.
8. See Katzew, "Trastoques y elipsis," 13–32.
9. See McHam, "Oedipal Palimpsest," 37–46.
10. Tiffany, *Diego Velázquez's Early Paintings*, 49–76.

11. Cherry, "Portraiture in the Divine Style?," 192; Horcajo Palomero, "Joyas del siglo XVI," 398; Vincent-Cassy, "Marguerite de Habsbourg," 213.
12. See, for example, Amador Marrero et al., "Imagen oculta," 1465–78. See also Weddigen and Weber, "Alchemy of Colors," 55.
13. Camille, *Gothic Idol*, 19.
14. Rosende, *Vida i virtudes*, 284.
15. Ibid.
16. Urban VIII, *Decreta*.
17. See, for instance, Mujica Pinilla, "Angels and Demons," 171–210.
18. Alberti, *On Painting*, 63.
19. Perkinson, *Likeness of the King*, 15–28.
20. Roberts, *Transporting Visions*, 24.
21. Didi-Huberman, "The Portrait, the Individual, and the Singular," 166; Pointon, *Portrayal and the Search for Identity*, 14–15.
22. Ringbom, *Icon to Narrative*; Stoichita, *Visionary Experience*, 61–62.
23. Bassegoda, *El Escorial como museo*, 360; Benito, "Seda y la corona," 351; Checa Cremades, *Libros de entregas*, 264.
24. Zarco Cuevas, "Inventario," 84 (entry no. 1460).
25. Mateo Gómez et al., *Arte de la Orden Jerónima*, 205.
26. Checa Cremades, *"Libros de entregas,"* 266. According to Julián Zarco Cuevas, the Escorial's librarian until 1936, the annotation was added by one Fray Juan de San Jerónimo. On this figure, see Fernández Alba, *El Escorial*, 19.
27. Andrés, "Inventario de documentos," part 1, 63, and *Cuentas libradas por Juan de Paz, pagador*, RBME, VI-3, fol. 8r, which notes that Holanda is being paid for "un lienço de tiçiano y por una figura de la reyna elena q[ue] pinto."
28. *Certificación de Antonio de Villacastín del trabajo realizado por Rodrigo de Holanda*, RBME VII-10, fol. 9r; also transcribed in Andrés, "Inventario de documentos," part 2, 83.
29. See also Díez-Ordás Berciano, "Decoración pictórica de El Escorial," 167–68, 172, 310.
30. Freedberg, *Power of Images*, 89–98.
31. Perkinson, *Likeness of the King*, 19–21; Pereda, *Crime and Illusion*, 107.
32. Pacheco, *Arte de la pintura*, 659–712. For a selected English translation, see Pacheco, *Christian Iconography*, 183–225.
33. On the connection between *enargeia* and verisimilitude, see Webb, *Ekphrasis*, 103.
34. Ibid., 127 (emphasis added). For *enargeia* as applied to early modern painting, see van Eck, "Petrifying Gaze," n.p.
35. I have examined photographs of these paintings at the Arxiu Mas in Barcelona and at the Image Collections of the National Gallery of Art in Washington, DC.
36. See, for instance, Wunder, "Innovation and Tradition," 122.
37. For a comparison, see Étienne, *Restauration des peintures à Paris*, 93.
38. See Bartolomé Borregón et al., "Informe de restauración," 28.
39. The revised inscription on the painting reads, "La Magestad del Sr Rey Phelipe 4°, el Grande Patrón de este Real Conbento de Mi Señora" (His Majesty Lord King Philip IV, the Great Patron of this Royal Convent of My Lady).
40. Bartolomé Borregón et al., "Informe de restauración," 30.
41. Dillon, *Palimpsest*, 13–15.
42. Hall, *Sacred Image*, 6.
43. Vega, *Devocion a Maria*, 268. See also González García, *Imágenes sagradas*, 328.
44. I am grateful to Byron Hamann for alerting me to this image, on which see Capretti and Padovani, *Domenico Puligo*, 46, 76–77.
45. Gimilio Sanz, "Poder, humanismo y religiosidad," 34–39. See also Porres Benavides, "Influencias de tipos iconográficos," 527–50.
46. González García, *Imágenes sagradas*, 82.
47. Ibid., 79. See also González García, "Retórica del decoro," 58.
48. Additionally, this corroborated painting's status as a liberal art: see González García, "Velázquez y la invención," 17.
49. Jarric, *Akbar and the Jesuits*, 162.
50. The episode is known thanks to the lengthy description on the painting itself, the text of which is cited in Gasbarri, "Strano quadro," 73.
51. Leone, *Saints and Signs*, 309, and Stoichita, *Visionary Experience*, 60–77.
52. Ibid., 66. See also Pereda, *Images of Discord*, 22.
53. Harpster, "Figino's Efficacy," 18.
54. Cruz, *Obras*, 322.

55. Nagel, "Icons and Early Modern Portraits," 424. See also González García, *Imágenes sagradas*, 328.
56. Cherry, "Newly Discovered 'Immaculate Conception,'" 1028–37; Navarrete Prieto, "*Inmaculada Concepción*," 5–9.
57. Pliny the Elder, cited in Goffen, *Renaissance Rivals*, 114. The argument was also known in the Hispanic world: see Pellicer de Salas y Tovar, *Lecciones solemnes*, 240. On signing practices, see Hyman, "Inventing Painting," 121–22.
58. Vasari, *Lives*, xxxii.
59. See Ruiz De Lacanal Ruiz-Mateos, "Francisco Pacheco y la restauración," 320, 322.
60. Pilliod, *Pontormo, Bronzino, Allori*, 43.
61. Wunsch, "Watteau, Through the Cracks," 40.
62. Hessler, "Man on Slate," 20. See also McCrory, "Immutable Images," 40–54, and Nygren, "Titian's Ecce Homo on Slate," 36–66.
63. McKim Smith, Andersen-Bergdoll, and Newman, *Examining Velazquez*, 111.
64. Ruiz De Lacanal Ruiz-Mateos, "Francisco Pacheco y la restauración," 319–25.
65. Vizcaíno Villanueva, *Pintor en la sociedad*, 299.
66. Brown, *Velázquez*, 47. On *pentimenti* in Velázquez, see González García, "Velázquez y la invención," 32.
67. For an analysis of the related notion of *Nachleben*, see Didi-Huberman, "Surviving Image," 59–70. See also Brilliant and Kinney, *Reuse Value*; Aksamija, Maines, and Wagoner, *Palimpsests*; and Belting, *Likeness and Presence*. For specific cases, see, among others, Prusac, *Face to Face*; Nagel, *Controversy of Renaissance Art*, 30–40; Barahal, "Repaint, Reframe, Renew"; Hoeniger, *Renovation of Paintings in Tuscany*; Van Horn, "Dark Iconoclast," 133–67. See also Hyman, "Habsburg Re-Making of the East," 39–69; Karr Schmidt and Nichols, *Altered and Adorned*; Pullins, "State of the Fashion Plate," 136–57; and Schaffer, "Playing with Pictures," 284–91. See also Van Kessel, *Lives of Paintings*, esp. 137–52. For the Hispanic world, see Villar Movellán, "Santos travestidos," 183–94; Engel, "Changing Faces," 149–69; and Katzew, "Trastoques y elipsis," 13–32. For the renovation of architecture, see Wunder, *Baroque Seville*, 45–72.
68. Hale, "Restoring *Bartolommeo Bonghi*," 25. See also Von der Goltz and Hill Stoner, "Considerations," 498–99.
69. Ainsworth, "Intentional Alterations," 51–65.
70. See Esch, "Reuse of Antiquity," 19, 27. On "polytemporal" thinking, see Shalem, "Histories of Belonging," 1–14.
71. Hartman, *Scenes of Subjection*, 10.
72. Testimony of Alonso de León, AGI, Seville, Audiencia de Guatemala 159, cited in Lovell, "Real Country," 185.
73. See Karttunen, "After the Conquest," 239–56; Olko, "Body Language," 149–79; Solari, *Idolizing Mary*, 105–30; and Lockhart, "Some Nahua Concepts," 465–82. See also the extensive catalogue of writings by Jansen and Pérez Jiménez, including *Mixtec Pictorial Manuscripts*.
74. On this neighborhood, see Gutiérrez, "Satellite Community," 31–42.
75. *Informacion hecha sobre la forma*, AHN, Inquisición, legajo 1740, no. 3, no. 7, fol. 12r: "que como se llamaba el que estaba pintado en aquel paiz."
76. Ibid.: "y el dicho regidor en lengua Mexicana pregunto a un indisuelo pequeño al pareser de edad de diez años que estaba guardando el dicho altar, que como se llamaba el que estaba pintado en aquel paiz, y con presteza respondio el indisuelo = santo Palafox =."
77. *Informacion hecha sobre la forma*, AHN, Inquisición, legajo 1740, no. 3, no. 7, fol. 12v: "todos se escandalizaron de semejante idolatria, y discurrieron podria ser que en todas las demas cassas de los Indios tengan el mismo retrato con la propria fee, y aclamacion de santo."
78. Soyer, *Ambiguous Gender*, 14.
79. On such "ambiguous countersigns," which "are often camouflaged in the ignorance, prejudices and ethnocentric perceptual processes of European observers," see Douglas, "Indigenous Countersigns," 175. See also Zemon Davis, *Fiction in the Archives*, 24–25. On the devaluation of orality and nontextual modes of communication in Western epistemology, see Kovach, *Indigenous Methodologies*, 40–44, 82, 174–78.
80. Pereda, *Crime and Illusion*, 149–50.
81. Mendieta, "Memorial de algunas cosas," 2:8–10. See also Cañeque, *King's Living Image*, 188–89, 342 n. 8, and Pagden, *Fall of Natural Man*, 104–6.
82. Garver, "Influence of Monastic Ideals," 72; Kagan, *Students and Society*, 6–9; Mejía, *Silva de varia*

lecion, fol. 99v; Isidore of Seville, *Etymologies of Isidore of Seville*, 241.

83. Mundy, "Extirpation of Idolatry," 524, 527. See also Cuadriello, "Winged and Imagined Indians," 217–20.
84. On Puebla's "Spanishness," see Fee, "Biographical Essay," 27.
85. *Codex Chimalpahin*, 2:78–85.
86. Lockhart, *Nahuas After the Conquest*, 237–38, 546 n. 138.
87. The *locus classicus* is Hvidtfeldt, *Teotl and Ixiptlatli*. I am grateful to Allison Caplan and Emily Floyd for discussing this concept with me. I also used the Online Nahuatl Dictionary, https://nahuatl.uoregon.edu, edited by Stephanie Wood, ©2000–2020.
88. Molina, *Vocabulario*, s.v. "Teixiptla"; "Ixiptlayotia."
89. Bassett, *Fate of Earthly Things*, 54.
90. See, for instance, Vega, *Empleo y exercicio sancto*, 33.
91. On Ledesma's larger project, see Rodríguez de la Flor, "'Picta poesis,'" 119–33.
92. Ledesma, "Hieroglifico XXX," fol. 83r; Alberti, *On Painting*, 63. On the concept of *regis imago*, see Bouza, *Imagen y propaganda*, 65–66.
93. Ledesma, "Hieroglifico XXX," fol. 83r.: "Heaven granted you the power of substitution [*sustitucion*] in your activities; you bestowed upon your portrait your own capabilities." For a similar episode, see Seijas, *Asian Slaves*, 21–23.
94. Boone, "Incarnations of the Aztec Supernatural," 4; Bassett, *Fate of Earthly Things*, 3. See also Carrasco, *City of Sacrifice*, 115–39, and Hajovsky, *On the Lips of Others*, 65–76.
95. Hill Boone, "Incarnations," 4; Magaloni Kerpel, *Colores del nuevo mundo*, 12–13, 46–47.
96. Basset, *Fate of Earthly Things*, 133.
97. Ibid., 134. *Teixiptla* was not always a set of easily identifiable iconographic attributes of a specific deity but could shift depending on context: ibid., 78–87.
98. Hill Boone, "Incarnations," 10–13.
99. On costume and *teixiptla*, see Mundy, *Death of Aztec Tenochtitlan*, 66.
100. Magaloni Kerpel, *Colores del nuevo mundo*, 46–47.
101. Guerra, *Arte de la lengua Mexicana*, 57; Bassett, *Fate of Earthly Things*, 55.
102. See, for example, Murillo Gallegos, "*Ixiptla* o imagen," 39–40. While a consideration of portraiture as *teixiptla* may hold for Nahuatl-speaking territories, it may not be applicable, for instance, to Ñuu Savi (Mixtec) regions: Aguilar Sánchez, "Tiempo y espacio," 303–4.
103. Noteworthy interventions include Posselt Santoyo and Jiménez Osorio, "Líneas narrativas," 259–86; Macuil Martínez, "Tradición oral," 159–62; the essays in *Tiempo sagrado, tiempo ritual*; Aguilar Sánchez, "Re-interpreting Ñuu Savi Pictorial Manuscripts," 313–40; and Flores-Marcial, "History of Guelaguetza."
104. Lockhart, *Nahuas After the Conquest*, 237–38.
105. Ibid., 238.
106. A model for such a project, in this case among the Maya, is Solari, *Idolizing Mary*.
107. Davis, *General Theory of Visual Culture*, 36.
108. On the two meanings of *santo*, see Vincent-Cassy, "Retrato *a lo divino*."
109. Lockhart, *Nahuas After the Conquest*, 237–38; Christian, *Local Religion*; Pereda, *Crime and Illusion*.
110. This point is referenced by McDonough, "Plotting Indigenous Stories," 13, 26 n. 35. Additionally, examining, for example, Yorùbá beliefs about how the faithful can temporarily serve as embodiments for Òrìṣà deities may also provide fruitful avenues for future interpretation. See, for instance, Taiwo, "Òrìṣà," esp. 96–99. On enslaved Asian and African individuals in colonial Mexico, see Seijas, *Asian Slaves*; Bennett, *Africans in Colonial Mexico*; and Sierra Silva, *Urban Slavery*. On Christianity among early modern Black populations, see Rowe, *Black Saints*; Fromont, *Art of Conversion*; Bristol, "Black Catholicism"; and Bristol, *Christians, Blasphemers, and Witches*.
111. Ramírez Leyva, "Censura inquisitorial novohispana," 219–21.
112. *Informacion hecha sobre la forma*, AHN, Inquisición, legajo 1740, no. 3, no. 7, fol. 15r: "dice que fue criado de Don Ju.[n] de Palafox, y Mendoza obpo que fue de aquella ciudad, y murio en el de Hosma, por cuya razon, y la de tener su memoria presente con su retrato . . . para que sin incurrir en pena alguna pueda tener en su casa el d[ic]ho retrato de el d[ic]ho Don Ju.[n] de Palafox."
113. Ibid., fol. 16r: "disen que para buena memoria del s.[or] obispo Don Juan de Palafox i Mendoza . . .

quisieran tener su Retrato . . . por ser los suplicantes personas de puestos i obligaciones que no pueden incurrir ninguno de los inconvenientes por quien los Retratos se an cautelado."

114. *Autos del Tribunal de México sobre lo ocurrido en la Puebla*, AHN, Inquisición, legajo 1740, no. 1, no. 2, fol. 1r: "gente menuda: negros, y mulatos, y muchachos."
115. Ibid., fol. 3r: "mestizos, y algunos Españoles."
116. Ibid., fol. 71v: "q[ue] algunos negros, y chinos esclabos de particulares desta ciudad , han dicho aguardan al dicho señor obispo, q[ue] ha de dar libertad a todos los esclabos desta ciudad, todo lo qual pide remedio."
117. Robelo, *Diccionario de aztequismos*, 298.
118. *Testificacion sobre la estimacion*, AHN, Inquisición, legajo 1740, no. 3, no. 2, fols. 3v–4r: "vio, y oyo, llamando comunmente sancto sancto al dicho Obispo Don Juan de Palafox especialmente entre la gente pleveya, incapaz, y de poco discurso."
119. Ibid., fol. 2r.
120. *Lo actuado por el comiss° deste s^{to} oficio*, AHN, Inquisición, legajo 1740, no. 1 no. 2, fols. 11v–12r: "gente entendida, y desapassionada."
121. Quintana, "III Centenario."
122. Donahue Wallace, "Prints and Printmakers," 285. The document announcing the ban of 1680 is located at *El señor fiscal del Santo Oficio sobre los retratos del señor obispo Don Juan de Palafox*, AGN, Inquisición, volume 640, expediente 3, fol. 7r.
123. Fernández Gracia, "Consideraciones sobre la riqueza," 409.
124. See also Myers, "Testimony for Canonization," 376 n. 35.
125. González de Rosende, *Vida i virtudes*, 286.
126. Ibid.
127. See Granada, *Libro de la oracion y meditacion*, 62. See also Brilliant, *Portraiture*, 16; Córdova, "Images Beyond the Veil," 256–72; and Donahue Wallace, "Saintly Beauty," 1–16.
128. Pedro Salazar de Mendoza, cited from Riello, "Bodily Disease," 101.
129. Alberti, *On Painting*, 63.
130. González de Rosende, *Vida i virtudes*, 286; Brilliant, *Portraiture*, 20.
131. See Koerner, *Moment of Self-Portraiture*, 268; Belting, *Face and Mask*, 106–18; and Beamud, "Invisible Icon," 72–73.
132. Fernández Gracia, "Alegoría y emblemática," 170; Andrés González, "Empresas y jeroglíficos," 419–39.
133. Between them is an "indistinct mass" in the shape of a head (González de Rosende, *Vida i virtudes*, n.p. [front matter]).
134. Hills, "'Face Is a Mirror,'" 548–49.
135. González de Rosende, *Vida i virtudes*, n.p. (front matter).
136. See Eire, "Concept of Popular Religion," esp. 13–21.

Chapter 4

1. Pérez Sánchez, "Retrato clásico español," 222–23; Morán Turina, *Velázquez*, 11.
2. For a similar comparison, see Ambler, "Court Portraits," 48–51, 55. See also Schreffler, *Art of Allegiance*, 61–79.
3. Sartre, "Faces, Preceded by Official Portraits," 157.
4. This argument is made by Rodríguez Gutiérrez de Ceballos ("Retrato de Estado," 104), and expanded by Ambler ("Portrait Workshop," 81–87).
5. Ruiz, "Unsacred Monarchy," 132.
6. Paleotti, *Discourse on Sacred and Profane Images*, 83–84.
7. Davis, *General Theory of Visual Culture*, 6, 36.
8. Ibid., 40–41.
9. González de Amezúa, "Notas sobre la Calderona," 36.
10. Ibid., 37.
11. On "blocked mimesis," see Morrison, *Mimetic Tradition of Reform*, xii.
12. Río Barredo, "Felipe II y la configuración del sistema," 1:2, 680–81 and 690–95.
13. Bouza, *Imagen y propaganda*, 65–66. See also Lisón Tolosana, *Imagen del rey*.
14. Juan de Zabaleta, cited in Pascual Chenel, "Teoría y práctica del retrato," 243.
15. See Woodall, "Introduction: Facing the Subject," 8.
16. Pereda, *Images of Discord*, 51–58.
17. Riello, "Siete vidas," 1079 (emphasis added).
18. Herrero-García, "Dictamen pericial de Velázquez," 67. I examine this episode in greater detail in Jasienski, "Velázquez and the Fragile Portrait."
19. Bodart, *Pouvoirs du portrait*, 295. See also Lafuente Ferrari, "Inspección de los retratos reales," 55–58.
20. On differences between Philip III's early and late portraits, see Ambler, "Court Portraits," 34–64.

21. Diego de Saavedra Fajardo, cited in Calvo Serraller, *Teoría de la pintura*, 456.
22. Riello, "Siete vidas," 1079, and Riello, "Mucha alma," 255.
23. Osorio, *Inventing Lima*, 96–97.
24. Riello, "Siete vidas," 1079.
25. Galtero, *Elogio a el retrato*, 1. The dedicatory is dated February 4, 1631, in Seville. See also Cornejo, *Pintura y teatro*, 175.
26. *Canons and Decrees of the Council of Trent*, Twenty-Fifth Session, "On the Invocation, Veneration, and Relics of Saints, and on Sacred Images," n.p.
27. Paleotti, *Discourse on Sacred and Profane Images*, 132–33. See also Melion, "Introduction," 9–14.
28. See Bodart, *Pouvoirs du portrait*, 263–68 and 305–6.
29. Porreño, *Dichos y hechos*, fol. 34v.
30. On religious skepticism in early modern Spain, see Pereda, "Sombras y cuadros," 69–86.
31. Pascual Chenel, "Fiesta sacra y poder político," 57–86, and Vega Loeches, "Fuente más sobre el Panteón Real," 67–101, esp. 91–94 (dealing with the print by Noort and its debts to earlier images).
32. See, for example, Portús Pérez, "Entre el divino artista," 203–4, and Pascual Chenel, "Teoría y práctica del retrato," 246. My reading of Peréz de Montalbán takes its cue from the analyses of *comedias* in Bass, *Drama of the Portrait*.
33. On this trope, see Cornejo, *Pintura y teatro*, 262–63, 288–89.
34. Pérez de Montalbán, *Ser prudente y ser sufrido*, 2, and Pliny the Elder, *Elder Pliny's Chapters*, 123.
35. Pérez de Montalbán, *Ser prudente y ser sufrido*, 10–11.
36. Ibid., 11.
37. Ibid.
38. Palmireno derived this notion from the thirteenth-century canonist William Durandus: Tatarkiewicz, *History of Aesthetics*, 146.
39. Palmireno, *Estudioso de la aldea*, 91. See also Franco Llopis, *Pintura valenciana*, 39.
40. Palmireno, *Estudioso de la aldea*, 91.
41. For a parallel case, see Bodart, *Pouvoirs du portrait*, 382.
42. Mastronardi, "Paolo Antonio Tarsia," 374, and Spagnoletti, "Giangirolamo Acquaviva," 1–24. See also Mastronardi, "Modelli classici," 3:1458.
43. Ibid., 3:1459; Tarsia, *Tumultos de la ciudad*, 82, 143–48 (mispaginated).
44. Tarsia, *Tumultos de la ciudad*, 63.
45. See Mauro, *Spazio urbano*, 247–49.
46. Camillo Tutini, cited in Bodart, *Pouvoirs du portrait*, 374. On the episode, see ibid., 377.
47. Henri de Lorraine, cited in ibid., 389. See also Osorio, "Copy as Original," 711–12.
48. Bodart, *Pouvoirs du portrait*, 381.
49. Manso de Contreras, "Relación cierta y verdadera," 10:186.
50. Ibid.
51. Ibid., 10:226.
52. Rappaport and Cummins, *Beyond the Lettered City*, 196.
53. Osorio, "King in Lima," 447.
54. Manso de Contreras, *Relacion cierta*, fol. 36v.
55. Córdoba, *Vocabulario en lengua çapoteca*, s.v. "Ymagen"; "Retrato."
56. On the term *parerga*, see Kant, *Critique of Aesthetic Judgment*, 68. See also Marin, "Frame of Representation," 82–83.
57. The symbolism of some of these devices is discussed in Cornejo, *Pintura y teatro*, 175; González García, "Spanish Religious Imagery," 450–51; Cuño, "Ritos y fiestas," 672; and Bridikhina, *Theatrum mundi*.
58. *Oxford Dictionary of Byzantium*, s.v. "Audience"; "Ciborium." On the etymology and significance of the canopy, see Bogdanović, *Framing of Sacred Space*, esp. 10–45.
59. Cañeque, "Sillas y almohadones," 621. See also Bodart, *Pouvoirs du portrait*, 299.
60. *Cartas y expedientes del obispo de Quito*, AGI, Quito, 77, no. 86, fol. 1r: "Y si por Docel se entiene baldoquin, nunca le he puesto en fiestas de toros; y si tafetan, o docel, todos le ponen delante el balcon en esta Prov.[a] en semejantes fiestas." This episode is also cited in Cuño, "Ritos y fiestas," 669.
61. Another conflict between secular and ecclesiastical authorities over the use of the baldachin is described in *Cartas y expedientes del virrey*, AGI, Mexico, 38, no. 46, fol. 1r.
62. Cañeque, "De sillas y almohadones," 622.
63. Ramos, *Identity, Ritual, and Power*, 49.
64. Rey-Márquez, "Jura de Fernando VII," 220–30. See also Rodríguez Moya and Mínguez Cornelles, "Cultura simbólica y fiestas borbónicas," 115–43.
65. Manso de Contreras, "Relación cierta y verdadera," 10:203.

66. Palma, *Anales del Cuzco*, 209.
67. Dalmau, *Relacion de la solemnidad*, fol. 123v. See also Bodart, *Pouvoirs du portrait*, 298.
68. Ortí, *Siglo quarto de la conquista*, fol. 89v.
69. Ibid., fol. 91r.
70. Mauro, *Spazio urbano*, 249.
71. Cañeque, "Sillas y almohadones," 617–18.
72. On the crown in a portrait of Philip II, see Miller, "Tale of Two Portraits," 103–16, and Ambler, "Portrait Workshop," 87–90.
73. See Schreffler, *Art of Allegiance*, 78–79; Pascual Chenel, "Juegos de imagen y apariencia," 175–204; and Pascual Chenel, "Construcción visual," 297–331.
74. Engel, *Pictured Politics*, 9, 37–43.
75. The painting is mentioned in Ibáñez, *Crónicas de Bogotá*, 178.
76. See, for example, Pascual Chenel, "Discurso político, identidad religiosa," 85–118.
77. See Rodríguez Moya, "Retratos de los monarcas españoles," 287–301. On the destruction of Spanish royal portraits, see Rodríguez Nóbrega, "Rey en la hoguera," 92–94.
78. See Schrader, "Royal Image," 293–310. On the low survival rates for paintings from duecento Italy and the early modern Netherlands, see, respectively, Garrison, "Note on the Survival," 140, and Van der Woude, "Volume and Value," 284–329.
79. On the president of the tribunal, Francisco de Estrada y Escobedo, see Nesvig, *Ideology and Inquisition*, 196–97.
80. García Figueroa, *Documentos para la historia de Méjico*, 1:179.
81. On the cult of Charles V during the reigns of his successors, see Bodart, *Pouvoirs du portrait*, 263–68, 305–6.
82. *Testificacion sobre la estimacion*, fols. 4r–4v: Un dia del corpus que en la calle de la carniceria que estava colgada para la procession, estavan colgados los retratos del Rey n[uest]ro señor, de la Reyna n[uest]ra señora, y demas Reyes de españa arimados a la mesma pared sin ponerles detras siquiera un dosel. Y poco mas adelante un retrato del dicho Obispo con mucho adorno debajo de un baldoquin puesto a lo que oyo decir por un Antonio García que tiene tienda de cacao y açucar y otras cossas; Y tan bien oyo decir que sintiendo mal algunas perssonas que que por que el retrato del obispo havia de estar con aquella Magestad y adorno, y el del Rey n[uest]ro s.[or] a quien era tan devido tenerla apoco mas o menos y de la manera que estava, y sobre defender otros que el retrato del obispo estava como avia de estar, avian llegado a sacar las espadas algunas perssonas aquel mesmo dia, y aunque se las nombraron a este declarante ya no se acuerda de los nombres.
83. For a related episode, see Slater, "Tampering with Signs of Power," 113–31, and Fee, "Rey versus reino(s)," 57–103.
84. Pascual Chenel, "Teoría y práctica del retrato," 244.
85. On the display of royal portraits in private homes, see Curiel, "Ajuares domésticos," 2:92–93.
86. Ibid; Rodríguez Nóbrega, "Rey en la hoguera," 89.
87. Mínguez, *Reyes solares*, 297–317. See also González de Zárate, *Emblemas regio-políticos*, 48–50.
88. Mínguez, *Reyes solares*, 313–17.
89. Ibid., 304. See also Bodart, *Pouvoirs du portrait*, 296.
90. *Informacion hecha sobre la forma*, AHN, Inquisición, legajo 1740, no. 3, no. 7, fol. 5v: "el mismo Gaspar Conrrado Pintor avia hecho un retrato de el dicho señor obispo don Juan de Palafox pintado con alas de zerafin."
91. Ibid., fol. 8v: "y hasta agora no ha hecho ningun retrato de el dicho señor obispo pintado con alas de zeraphin, y puede ser que en alguno de los muchos que ha hecho, otro pintor le aya acrescentado las alas por mandado de sus dueños, y es factible por el entrañable amor que le tienen, y porque o se le atribuian a este testigo aquellos que no ha hecho."
92. Ibid., fol. 5v: "asta los indios los tienen en paizes de tablas en los aposentos que llaman santorales diputados para tener los santos de su devocion."
93. *Testimonio de una peticion*, AHN, Inquisición, 1740. no. 3. no. 3, fol. 2r: Vi assimismo con todos los que me acompañaban en una sala de la vivienda del ventero y de su muger colocado en mejor lugar el retrato del señor Don Juan de Palafox, por estar en medio de algunas ymagenes de santos, y en correspondencia del dos velas encendidas en dos candeleritos puestos en una tabla que salia de la pared, y servia como de messa al pie de dicho retrato con que crecio el escandalo en mi y en las demas Personas, que me acompañaban, caussandonos admiracion, que en lugares tan publicos, y pasageros, se hiciesse aquel modo de adoracion y culto a un retrato.

94. Ibid., 2v: "biendo que el dicho culto, y modo de adoracion, que por aquella gente senzilla se hacia al dicho retrato excedia grandemente a la reverencia, que se debe al original por su Dignidad episcopal, persona, y demas puestos, que ocupa y a ocupado, y que se le daba aquella adoracion, que solo se debe a las Ymagenes de Dios nro señor, y de su madre ss.[ma] la virgen Maria, y de sus santos como es el de colocarle entre los canonizados, el de enzenderle luzes, y el de invocarle para las necesidades."
95. *Testificacion sobre la estimacion*, fol. 8r: "y le trataban de herege, y le escupian."
96. On the flexibility of the term *idolator*, see Sheehan, "Introduction," 564.
97. Argaiz, *Vida de Don Juan de Palafox*, 139.
98. Ibid.
99. *Informacion hecha sobre la forma*, AHN, Inquisición, legajo 1740, no. 3, no. 7, fol. 12r:
    Y aviendo entrado en la sala de la casa de un indio . . . reparo el dicho Regidor Don Juan de llano, que ensima de un altar que [en] la dicha sala estaba con diferentes imagenes de bulto de santos estaba puesto un paiz quadrado de tabla, y en el retratado [e]l señor obispo de este obispado, Don Juan de Palafox y Mendoza y todos tres se llegaron al dicho altar, y vieron como el paiz, en que assi estaba retratado el dicho señor obispo, estaba puesto entre dos hechuras de bulto la una de Xpto señor nuestro pendiente en la cruz, y la otra de la Virgen Maria nuestra señora, y delante de el dicho retrato estaban puestos dos jarros, ramilletes de flores, y dos candeleros de barro sin belas, y las dichas imagenes no tenian delante ramilletes, ni candeleros, y el dicho Regidor don Juan de llanos tomo en la mano el dicho retrato, y el, y estos declarantes dixeron ser mui semejante al original.
100. Urban VIII, *Decreta*, 2.
101. Mexicano Ramos, "Nota sobre la pintura," 78.
102. Ibid.
103. On portraits of Indigenous leaders, see Cummins, "We Are the Other," 203–70.
104. Mujica Pinilla, "Arte e identidad," 52–53.
105. Ruiz del Corral, *Carta de Ruiz del Corral*, AGN, Inquisición, vol. 308, expediente 107, fol. 632.
106. *Informacion hecha sobre la forma*, AHN, Inquisición, legajo 1740, no. 3, no. 7, fols. 6r–6v: "colgados entre imagenes de santos aprobados por la santa iglesia catolica Romana, y algunos puestos con prominente lugar."
107. Camille, *Gothic Idol*, xxvii.
108. Ibid., 27–28, 55.
109. Ibid., 2.
110. Koerner, *Reformation of the Image*, 98. Here Koerner is reading Latour, *Pandora's Hope*, 270.
111. *Informacion hecha sobre la forma*, AHN, Inquisición, legajo 1740, no. 3, no. 7, fol. 6v: "se hazen idolatrias."
112. *Peticion del Gen.[l] D. enrrique Davila*, AHN, Inquisición, legajo 1740, no. 3, no. 6 (bis), fol. 6r: "los mas estan ydolatrando prestando adoracion a los retratos del d[ic]ho obpo. D. Juan de Palafox."
113. *Informacion hecha sobre la forma*, AHN, Inquisición, legajo 1740, no. 3, no. 7, fol. 13v: "culto indevido y supersticiosso." On conceptual linkages between idolatry and disease, see Solari, *Idolizing Mary*, 84–104.
114. Cummins, "Golden Calf in America," 82–83, and Rappaport and Cummins, *Beyond the Lettered City*, 68.
115. Camille, *Gothic Idol*, xxvi.

Conclusion

1. The classification of art in nineteenth-century Spain is examined in Vázquez, *Inventing the Art Collection*, 83–84 and 118–20.
2. *Distribucion de los premios*, 79.
3. Ibid., 71.
4. Given the Holy Office's international character and the fact that inquisitors often produced manuals, it is possible that, in each of these cases, the tribunals may have read of their colleagues' earlier tribulations with sacred portraits: Lynn, "Judges and Shepherds," 125.
5. *Recogida de imágenes*, AHN, Inquisición, legajo 4462, no. 20, microfilm: "por ser d[ic]has insignias de santos sutiles, y las pinturas, en que están, muy pequeñas, no se puede notar, sino mirandolas con mucho cuidado."
6. Gutiérrez Pastor, "Don Juan Bazo de Moreda," 205.
7. Ginzburg, "Microhistory," 28.
8. Portús Pérez, "San Francisco de Asís en la Porciúncula," 124. See also Lamas Delgado,

"Peintures de Carducho, Rizi et Carreño," 224–26, and Vera, *Piedras de Segovia*, 286–93.

9. Herrero Carretero, "Jacobo Vandergoten el Viejo," 407. On the global reach of this cult, see Hajovsky, "Shifting Panoramas," 34–61.
10. Herrero Carretero, "Jacobo Vandergoten el Viejo," 409.
11. See Piedra Adarves, "Vida secreta del pintor," 399 and 411.
12. Taussig, *Defacement*, 5–6.
13. Pérez Viejo, "Géneros, mercado, artistas y críticos," 27–47.
14. Lafita, "Otras obras inéditas," 182–85.

BIBLIOGRAPHY

Manuscript Primary Sources

Autos del Tribunal de México sobre lo ocurrido en la Puebla de los Ángeles por el falso nombramiento del obispo de dicha ciudad, Juan de Palafox y Mendoza, como virrey y visitador. AHN, Inquisición, legajo 1740, no. 1, no. 2.

Bautista de Elorriaga, Juan. *Carta de Juan Bautista de Elorriaga, en la que da noticia de una pintura en hoja de lata del obispo Juan de Palafox, y agradece que se le ha puesto al tanto gracias al edicto de esta ofensa a Dios*. AGN, Inquisición, vol. 1579 B, expediente 207, año 1654, n.p.

Cartas y expedientes del obispo de Quito. AGI, Quito, 77, no. 86.

Cartas y expedientes del virrey. AGI, Mexico, 38, no. 46.

Certificación de Antonio de Villacastín del trabajo realizado por Rodrigo de Holanda. RBME VII-10, 1579.

Copia de la culpa que resulta contra Juan Lop[e]z Maria Presv[iter]o V[e]z[in]o de la villa de Arjete, sacada del proçesso de Eujenia de la Torre. AHN, Inquisición, legajo 103, no. 7.

Cuentas libradas por Juan de Paz, pagador. RBME VI-3, 1577.

Dibujo del retrato de Fray Francisco García Calderón. AHN, Inquisición, Mapas, Planos, Dibujos 238.

Guzmán, Diego de. *Memorias*. RAH, colección Salazar, MS 9-3-5-G-30 9-476.

Informacion hecha sobre la forma con que en la Ciu.d de la Puebla se hacen los Retratos del obispo della, Don Juan de Palafox y Mendoza. AHN, Inquisición, legajo 1740, no. 3, no. 7.

Lo actuado por el comisso deste sto oficio cerca de lo acaecido en la ciud de la Puebla de los Angeles a los 23 y 24 de septie de 1647. AHN, Inquisición, legajo 1740, no. 1, no. 2.

López, Cristóbal. "Relacion de la forma que se tuuo en hazer el retrato de nuestro Sancto Padre Igna.o de Loyola y del motivo q[ue] para ello tuuo el P.e P.o de Ribadeneyra. hecha por el h[e]r[man]o Xval lopez su companiero q[ue] s hallo a ello." In *Vida, obras y correspondencia del padre Pedro de Ribadeneira*, 1612, BNE Mss/6525.

Peticion del Gen.l D. enrrique Davila y Pacheco; Auto a ella proveido; e informacion que en virtud de lo mandado se ba haciendo. AHN, Inquisición, legajo 1740, no. 3, no. 6 (bis).

Proceso contra fray Francisco García Calderón. AHN, Inquisición, legajo 3691, carpeta 2.

Recogida de imágenes de personas no canonizadas, en algunas cartujas de Mallorca, 1739. AHN, Inquisición, legajo 4462, no. 20, microfilm.

Ruiz del Corral, Felipe. *Carta de Ruiz del Corral denunciando que en una pintura esta un s. Juan bautista, un san Esteban y una sta. Lucia los cuales son retratos del licenciado Juan Maldonado de Paz, de Pedro Pardo y de una hija del licenciado Maldonado*. AGN, Inquisición, vol. 308, expediente 107, fol. 632.

El señor fiscal del Santo Oficio sobre los retratos del señor obispo Don Juan de Palafox. AGN, Inquisición, vol. 640, expediente 3.

Testificacion sobre la estimacion y beneracion y debocion que se tiene a los retratos del s.or D. Juan de Palafox Obispo de la Puebla. AHN, Inquisición, legajo 1740, no. 3, no. 2.

Testimonio de una peticion que en este tribunal presento el General Don enrique Davila y Pacheco cavallero del orden de Santiago. AHN, Inquisición, 1740, no. 3, no. 3.

Printed Primary Sources

Acuña del Adarve, Juan de. *Discursos de las effigies y verdaderos retratos . . .* Villanueva de Andujar: Iuan Furgolla de la Cuesta, 1637.

Aguirre, Ricardo de. "Documentos relativos a la pintura en España: Juan Pantoja de la Cruz, pintor de cámara." *Boletín de la Sociedad Española de Excursiones* 30, no. 1 (1922): 17–22.

Alberti, Leon Battista. *On Painting*. Translated by John R. Spencer. New Haven: Yale University Press, 1966.

Andrés, Gregorio de. "Inventario de documentos sobre la construcción y ornato del Monasterio del Escorial existentes en el archivo de su Real Biblioteca. (Continuación)." Part 1. Annex to *Archivo Español de Arte* 46, no. 181 (1973): 33–64 (separate pagination from main body of issue).

———. "Inventario de documentos sobre la construcción y ornato del Monasterio del Escorial existentes en el archivo de su Real Biblioteca. (Continuación)." Part 2. Annex to *Archivo Español de Arte* 46, no. 183 (1973): 65–96 (separate pagination from main body of issue).

Boneta, José. *Gracias de la gracia, saladas agudezas de los santos* . . . Barcelona: Juan Piferrer, 1719.

Camargo, Ignacio de. *Discurso theológico sobre los theatros y comedias de este siglo* . . . Lisbon: Miguel Manescal, 1690.

Camerino, José. *La dama beata*. Madrid: Pablo de Val, 1655.

The Canons and Decrees of the Council of Trent. Edited and translated by H. J. Schroeder. Charlotte: Tan, 2005.

Checa Cremades, Fernando, ed. *Los "Libros de entregas" de Felipe II a El Escorial*. Madrid: Patrimonio Nacional, 2013.

Codex Chimalpahin: Society and Politics in Mexico Tenochtitlan, Tlatelolco, Culhuacan, and Other Nahuatl Altepetl in Central Mexico (continued): The Nahuatl and Spanish Annals and Accounts Collected and Recorded by don Domingo de San Antón Muñón Chimalpahin Quauhtlehuanitzin. Vol. 2. Translated and edited by Arthur J. O. Anderson and Susan Schroeder. Norman: University of Oklahoma Press, 1997.

Constituciones promulgadas por el Ilustrmo y Revermo Señor D. Fr. Francisco de Roys y Mendoza . . . Obispo de Badajoz. Madrid: Por Ioseph Fernandez de Buendia, 1673.

Constituciones synodales de El Obispado de la ciudad de Guamanga. Lima: Geronimo de Contreras, 1677.

Constituciones synodales del Arzobispado de Zaragoza . . . Zaragoza: Por Pascual Bueno, 1698.

Constituciones synodales del Obispado de Malaga . . . Seville: Viuda de Nicolás Rodriguez, 1674.

Constituciones synodales del Obispado de Osma . . . Villa del Burgo: Diego Fernandez de Cordova, 1586.

Constituciones synodales del Obispado de Veneçuela y Santiago de Leon de Caracas. Madrid: Imprenta del Reyno, de don Lucas Antonio de Bedmar y Narvaez, 1698.

Córdoba. Juan de. *Vocabulario en lengua çapoteca* . . . Mexico: Pedro Charte and Antonio Ricardo, 1578.

Covarrubias, Sebastián de. *Tesoro de la lengua castellana, o española* . . . Madrid: Luis Sanchez, 1611.

Cruz, Juana Inés de la. *Neptuno Alegórico*. Edited by Vincent Martin and Electa Arenal. Madrid: Cátedra, 2009.

Cruz, Juan de la. *Obras del venerable i mistico dotor F. Joan de la Cruz, primer descalço, i padre de la reforma de N. S. del Carmen* . . . Madrid: Viuda de Pedro de Madrigal, 1630.

Cueva, Bernardino de la. *Buelos de las plumas sagradas defendidos de una moderna calumnia*. Barcelona: Joseph López, 1695.

Dalmau, Joseph. *Relacion de la solemnidad con que se han celebrado en la ciudad de Barcelona, las fiestas a la Beatificacion de la Madre S. Teresa de Iesus*. Barcelona: Sebastian Matevad, 1615.

Diccionario de autoridades. Vol. 4 of *Nuevo diccionario histórico del Español*, 1734. https://apps2.rae.es/DA.html.

Diccionario de la lengua castellana, en que se explica el verdadero sentido de las voces, su naturaleza y calidad . . . Madrid: En la imprenta de la Real Academia Espanola, por los Herederos de Francisco del Hierro, 1734.

Distribucion de los premios concedidos por el rey nuestro señor á los discípulos de las nobles artes . . . Madrid: Don Joachin Ibarra, 1781.

Fonseca, Cristóbal de. *Tratado del amor de Dios*. Salamanca: Guillermo Foquel, 1592.

Galtero, Pedro Gerónimo. *Elogio a el retrato de la magestad de Philipo IIII* . . . N.p., n.d.

García, Francisco. *Vida, virtudes, y milagros de S. Ignacio de Loyola* . . . Madrid: Juan Garcia Infanzon, 1685.

García Figueroa, Francisco, ed. *Documentos para la historia de Méjico*. 7 vols. Mexico City: Imprenta de Juan R. Navarro, 1853.

González de Rosende, Antonio. *Vida i virtudes del Illmo i Excmo Señor D. Juan de Palafox i Mendoza*. Madrid: Julian de Paredes, 1666.

Gracián, Jerónimo. *Obras del P. Maestro F. Geronymo Gracian* . . . Madrid: La viuda de Alonso Martin, 1616.

Granada, Luis de. *Libro de la oracion y meditacion* . . . Barcelona: Emprenta de Iayme Cendrat, 1594.

Guerra, Juan. *Arte de la lengua Mexicana*. 2nd ed. by Alberto Santoscoy. Guadalajara: Ancira y Hno., A. Ochoa Imp., 1900.

Guzmán, Diego de. *Reyna catolica: Vida y muerte de D. Margarita de Austria reyna de Espanna*. Madrid: Luis Sánchez, 1617.

Hernández, Francisco. *The Mexican Treasury: The Writings of Dr. Francisco Hernández*. Edited by Simon Varey. Translated by Rafael Chabrán, Cynthia L. Chamberin, and Simon Varey. Stanford: Stanford University Press, 2000.

Ignacio de Loyola. *Cartas de San Ignacio de Loyola Fundador de la Compañía de Jesús*. Vol. 1. Madrid: Aguado, 1874.

———. *Ejercicios espirituales*. Edited by Santiago Arzubialde. Santander: Sal Terrae, 2017.

Infante de Aurioles, Fernando. *La magna, y canonica cirugia de Guido de Cavliaco, principe della* . . . Madrid: Maria de Quiñones, 1658.

Interián de Ayala, Juan. *El pintor christiano, y erudito, ò tratado de los errores que suelen cometerse freqüentemente en pintar, y esculpir las Imágenes Sagradas*. Vol. 2. Madrid: Joachín Ibarra, 1782.

Isidore of Seville. *The Etymologies of Isidore of Seville*. Edited and translated by Stephen A. Barney, W. J. Lewis, J. A. Beach, and Oliver Berghof. Cambridge: Cambridge University Press, 2006.

Jarric, Pierre du. *Akbar and the Jesuits: An Account of the Jesuit Missions to the Court of Akbar by Pierre du Jarric, SJ*. Translated by C. H. Payne. Edited by Sir E. Denison Ross and Eileen Power. New York: Harper Brothers, 1926.

Jesús, Francisco de. *Exercicios de devocion, y oracion, para todo el discurso del año*. Antwerp: Plantin, 1622.

Kempis, Thomas de. *Contemptus mundi, nuevamente romançado y corregido*. Translated by Luis de Granada. Antwerp: Plantin, 1572.

Ledesma, Alonso de. "Hieroglifico XXX." In Alonso de Salazar, *Fiestas, que hizo el insigne collegio de la Compañia de Iesus de Salamanca: A la Beatificacion del glorioso Patriarcha S. Ignacio de Loyola*, 83r. Salamanca: Viuda de Artus Taberniel, 1610.

León, Luis de. *La perfecta casada*. Salamanca: Antonia Ramirez viuda, 1604.

Longás, Tomás. *Thomae Longas* . . . *Enchiridion novae & antiquae medicinae dogmaticae* . . . Caesar-Augustae [Zaragoza]: Paschasium Bueno, 1689.

López, Cristóbal. "Relación de la forma que se tuvo en hazer el retrato de N.S.P. Ignacio de Loyola y del motivo que para ello tuuo el P. Pedro de Ribadeneira . . ." In *Monumenta Ignatiana ex autographis vel ex antiquioribus exemplis collecta, series quarta, scripta de Sancto Ignatio de Loyola*. 2 vols. Madrid: Typis Gabrielis López del Horno, 1904.

Macareñas, Gerónimo. "Censura del illustrissimo y reverendissimo señor don Geronimo Macareñas." In Antonio González de Rosende, *Vida i virtudes del Illmo i Excmo Señor D. Juan de Palafox i Mendoza*, unpaginated front matter. Madrid: Julian de Paredes, 1666.

Manso de Contreras, Cristóbal. *Relacion cierta, y verdadera de lo que sucediô, y a sucedido en esta villa de Guadalcaçar Provincia de Tehuantepeque desde los 22. de março de 1660: Hasta los 4 de Iulio de 1661* . . . Mexico City: Juan Ruyz, 1661.

———. "Relación cierta y verdadera de lo que sucedió y ha sucedido en esta villa de Guadalcázar, Provincia de Tehuantepec, desde los 22 de marzo de 1660 hasta los 4 de julio de 1661." In *Documentos inéditos o muy raros para la historia de México: Tumultos y rebeliones acaecidos en México*, edited by Genaro García, 10:109–229. Mexico City: Viuda de Ch. Bouret, 1907.

Mejía, Pedro de. *Silva de varia lecion*. Antwerp: Viuda de Martin Nucio, 1564.

Mendieta, Gerónimo de. "Memorial de algunas cosas que conviene representar al rey D. Felipe, Nuestro Señor, para descargo de su real conciencia." In *Códice Mendieta: Documentos Franciscanos, siglos XVI y XVII*, edited by Joaquín García Icazbalceta, 2:7–28. Mexico City: Imprenta de Francisco Díaz de León, 1892.

Molina, Alonso de. *Vocabulario en lengua castellana y mexicana*. Mexico: Antonio de Spinosa, 1571.

Murillo, Diego. *Discursos predicables sobre todos los evangelios que canta la Iglesia* . . . Zaragoza: Angelo Tavanno, 1605.

Ortí, Marco Antonio. *Siglo quarto de la conquista de Valencia*. Valencia: Juan Bautista Marçal, 1640.

Ottonelli, Giandomenico, and Pietro da Cortona. *Trattato della pittura e scultura, uso, et abuso loro*. Florence: Giovanni Antonio Bonardi, 1652.

Pacheco, Francisco. *El arte de la pintura*. Edited by Bonaventura Bassegoda i Hugas. Madrid: Cátedra, 2001.

———. *On Christian Iconography: Selections from "The Art of Painting" (1649)*. Edited and translated by Jeremy Roe and Carles Gutiérrez Sanfeliu. Philadelphia: Saint Joseph's University Press, 2017.

Paleotti, Gabriele. *Discourse on Sacred and Profane Images*. Translated by William McCuaig. Los Angeles: Getty Research Institute, 2012.

Palma, Ricardo, ed. *Anales del Cuzco: 1600 á 1750*. Lima: Imprenta de "El Estado," 1901.

Palmireno, Lorenzo. *El estudioso de la aldea*. Valencia: Pedro de Huete, 1571.

Palomino de Castro y Velasco, Antonio. *El museo pictórico y escala óptica* . . . Vol. 1. Madrid: Imprenta de Sancha, 1795.

Pellicer de Salas y Tovar, Joseph. *El Fenix y su historia natural* . . . Madrid: Imprenta del Reino, 1630.

———. *Lecciones solemnes a las obras de don Luis de Gongora y Argote, Pindaro andaluz* . . . Madrid: Imprenta del Reino, 1630.

Pérez de Montalbán, Juan. *Ser prudente y ser sufrido*. Seville: Francisco de Leefdael, n.d.

Pinar, Garci-Sánchez del. *La monja enterrada en vida ó el convento de San Plácido: Novela histórica original*. Madrid: Imprenta de Manini Hermanos, 1858.

Pinto, Hector. *Segunda parte de los dialogos de la imagen de la vida christiana*. Translated by Gonçalo de Illescas. Salamanca: En casa de Gaspar de Portonarijs, 1576.

Pliny the Elder. *The Elder Pliny's Chapters on the History of Art*. Edited by E. Sellers. Translated by K. Jex-Blake. London: Macmillan, 1896.

Porreño, Baltasar. *Dichos y hechos del Señor Rey D. Felipe II* . . . Seville: Pedro Gomez de Pastrana, 1639.

Quevedo, Francisco de. *La vida del Buscón*. In *Tres novelas del Siglo de Oro*, 53–166. Barcelona: Planeta, 1983.

Ribera, Francisco de. *La vida de la madre Teresa de Iesus fundadora de las Descalças, y Descalços Carmelitas* . . . Madrid: Imprenta Real, 1602.

Rojas, Francisco de. *Anales de la orden de los menores* . . . Valencia: Herederos de Juan Chrisostomo Garriz, por Bernardo Nogues, 1652.

Santalla, Francisco. *Semblantes de San Ignacio de Loyola* . . . N.p., 1680.

Santos, Francisco de los. *Descripcion breve del monasterio de S. Lorenzo el Real del Escorial* . . . Madrid: Imprenta Real, 1657.

Squarzafigo, Gaspar. *Opusculos*. Valencia: Geronimo de Vilagrasa, 1669.

Sumario del Concilio Provincial, que se celebro en la Ciudad de los Reyes, el año de mil y quinientos y sesenta y siete. Seville: Matias Clavijo, 1614.

Tarsia, Paolo Antonio. *Tumultos de la ciudad y reyno de Napoles en el año de 1647*. Lyon: Claudio Burgea, 1670.

Urban VIII. *Decreta servanda in canonizatione et beatificatione sanctorum* . . . Rome: Ex Typographia Rev. Cam. Apost., 1642.

Valadés, Diego. *Rhetorica Christiana*. Edited by Esteban J. Palomero et al. Translated by Tarsicio Herrera Zapién. Mexico City: Fondo de Cultura Económica, 1989.

Vasari, Giorgio. *The Lives of the Most Excellent Painters, Sculptors, and Architects*. Edited by Philip Jacks. Translated by Gaston du C. de Vere. New York: Random House, Modern Library, 2006.

Vega, Christoval de la. *Devocion a Maria: Passaporte y salvo conducto que da paso franco para una buena muerte*. Valencia: Ierono. Vilagrasa, 1666.

Vega, Diego de la. *Empleo y exercicio sancto, sobre los evangelios de las Dominicas despues de Pentecostes*. Vol. 2. Valladolid: Juan de Bostillo, 1608.

Vieyra, Antonio. *Sermoens do P. Antonio Vieyra Da Companhia de Jesu, prègador de sua magestade* . . . Lisbon: Miguel Deslandes, 1699.

Villegas, Alonso de. *Flos sanctorum, y historia general de la vida y hechos de Iesu Christo* . . . Barcelona: Sebastian de Cormellas, 1615.

Villegas, Bernardino de. *La esposa de Cristo instruida con la vida de santa Lutgarda virgen, monja de S. Bernardo*. Madrid: Imprenta Real, 1625.

Yepes, Diego de. *Vida, virtudes y milagros de la bienaventurada virgen Teresa de Jesús . . .* Lisbon: Pedro de Crasbeeck, 1616.

Zarco Cuevas, Julián. "Inventario de las alhajas, relicarios, estatuas, pinturas, tapices y otros objetos de valor y curiosidad donados por el rey don Felipe II al Monasterio de El Escorial: Años de 1571 a 1598 (Conclusión)." *Boletín de la Real Academia de la Historia* 97, no. 1 (1930): 34–144.

Secondary Sources

Aguilar Sánchez, Omar. "Re-interpreting Ñuu Savi Pictorial Manuscripts from a Mixtec Perspective: Linking Past and Present." In *Mesoamerican Manuscripts: New Scientific Approaches and Interpretations*, edited by Maarten E. R. G. N. Jansen, Virginia Lladó-Buisán, and Ludo Snijders, 313–40. Leiden: Brill, 2019.

———. "Tiempo y espacio en el Lienzo de Santo Tomás Ocotepeque." In *Tiempo y comunidad: Herencias e interacciones socioculturales en Mesoamérica y Occidente*, edited by Maarten E. R. G. N. Jansen and Valentina Raffa, 129–42, 303–4. Leiden: Leiden University Press, 2015.

Ainsworth, Maryan W. "Intentional Alterations of Early Netherlandish Painting." *Metropolitan Museum Journal* 40 (2005): 51–65.

Aksamija, Nadja, Clark Maines, and Philip Wagoner, eds. *Palimpsests: Buildings, Sites, Time*. Turnhout: Brepols, 2018.

Alcalá, Luisa Elena. "'A Call to Action': Visual Persuasion in a Spanish American Painting." *Art Bulletin* 94, no. 4 (2012): 594–617.

Alpers, Svetlana. *The Vexations of Art: Velázquez and Others*. New Haven: Yale University Press, 2005.

Alvarez de Toledo, Cayetana. *Politics and Reform in Spain and Viceregal Mexico: The Life and Thought of Juan de Palafox, 1600–1659*. Oxford: Oxford University Press, 2004.

Amador Marrero, Pablo F., Tatiana Falcón, Sandra Zetrina, Eumelia Hernández, and Elsa Royo. "La imagen oculta: Un retrato mexicano censurado del obispo canario Domingo Pantaleón Álvarez de Abreu a través de su análisis científico." In *XVII Coloquio de Historia Canario-Americana*, edited by Francisco Morales Padrón, 1465–78. Las Palmas de Gran Canaria: Cabildo Insular de Gran Canaria, 2008.

Ambler, William. "Court Portraits During the Reign of Philip III of Spain." In *Spanish Royal Patronage, 1412–1804: Portraits as Propaganda*, edited by Ilenia Colón Mendoza and Margaret Ann Zaho, 34–64. Newcastle: Cambridge Scholars, 2018.

———. "The Portrait Workshop at the Court of Philip III of Spain." PhD diss., New York University, 2014.

Amelang, James S. "Tracing Lives: The Spanish Inquisition and the Act of Autobiography." In *Controlling Time and Shaping the Self: Developments in Autobiographical Writing Since the Sixteenth Century*, edited by Arianne Baggerman, Rudolf M. Dekker, and Michael James Mascuch, 33–48. Leiden: Brill, 2011.

Andrés González, Patricia. "Empresas y jeroglíficos en un retrato de Palafox." *Boletín del Seminario de Estudios de Arte y Arqueología (BSAA)* 64 (1998): 419–39.

Arenal, Electa, and Stacey Schlau, eds. *Untold Sisters: Hispanic Nuns in Their Own Works*. Albuquerque: University of New Mexico Press, 1989.

Argaiz, Gregorio. *Vida de Don Juan de Palafox*. Edited by Ricardo Fernández Gracia. Pamplona: Edita, Asociación de Amigos del Monasterio de Fitero, 2000.

Áviles, Miguel, José Martínez Millán, and Virgilio Pinto. "El Archivo del Consejo de la Inquisición: Aportaciones para una historia de los archivos inquisitoriales." *Revista de Archivos, Bibliotecas y Museos* 81, no. 3 (1978): 459–517.

Azcue, Leticia. "Carlos II, portapaz de plata; Mariana de Neoburgo, portapaz de plata." In *Museo Nacional del Prado: Memoria de actividades 2016*, 58–61. Madrid: Ministerio de Educación, Cultura y Deporte, 2017.

Báez Rubí, Linda. *Mnemosine novohispánica: Retórica e imágenes en el siglo XVI*. Mexico City: Universidad Nacional Autónoma de México, Instituto de Investigaciones Estéticas, 2005.

Bailey, Gauvin Alexander. "A Missionary Order Without Saints: Iconography of Unbeatified and Uncanonized Jesuits in Italy and Peru, 1560–1614." In Locker, *Art and Reform*, 240–61.

Barahal, Susan. "Repaint, Reframe, Renew: Updating Sacred Images During the Early Italian Renaissance." PhD diss., Boston University, 2016.

Barbeito, Isabel, ed. *Cárceles y mujeres en el siglo XVII: Razón y forma de la galera; Proceso inquisitorial de San Plácido*. Madrid: Editorial Castalia, 1991.

Barthes, Roland. "Effet de réel." *Communications* 11, no. 1 (1968): 84–89.

Bartolomé Borregón, Rosario, Paula de la Serna Inciarte, Paloma Ruano Fernández-Hontoria, and Jorge Gómez-Acebo Garrote. "Informe de restauración." In *El retablo de Santa Ana y San Miguel, de Francisco de Comontes del Museo de Santa Cruz, Toledo*, edited by Isabel Mateo Gómez, 23–31. Toledo: Real Fundación de Toledo, 1997.

Bass, Laura. *The Drama of the Portrait: Theater and Visual Culture in Early Modern Spain*. University Park: Penn State University Press, 2008.

Bassegoda, Bonaventura. *El Escorial como museo: La decoración pictórica mueble en el monasterio de El Escorial desde Diego Velázquez hasta Frédéric Quilliet (1809)*. Barcelona: Edicions Universitat Barcelona, 2002.

———. "Retratos y otros anacronismos en la pintura religiosa española del siglo XVII." In *Los pintores de lo real*, 93–117. Madrid: Fundación Amigos del Museo del Prado, 2008.

Bassett, Molly. *The Fate of Earthly Things: Aztec Gods and God Bodies*. Austin: University of Texas Press, 2015.

Baxandall, Michael. *Painting and Experience in Fifteenth-Century Italy: A Primer in the Social History of Pictorial Style*. 2nd edition. Oxford: Oxford University Press, 1988.

Beamud, Ana Maria. "The Invisible Icon: Poetry About Portraiture in the Spanish Golden Age." PhD diss., Duke University, 1980.

Belting, Hans. *Face and Mask: A Double History*. Translated by Thomas S. Hansen and Abby J. Hansen. Princeton: Princeton University Press, 2017.

———. *Likeness and Presence: A History of the Image Before the Era of Art*. Translated by Edmund Jephcott. Chicago: University of Chicago Press, 1994.

Benito, Fernando. "El retrato moralizado en España: Contrarreforma e influencia del retrato como género." In Portús Pérez, *El retrato en el Museo del Prado*, 182–91.

Benito, Pilar. "La seda y la corona." In *España y Portugal en las rutas de seda: Diez siglos de producción y comercio entre Oriente y Occidente*, edited by Comisión Española de la Ruta de la Seda, 345–61. Barcelona: Publicacions Universitat de Barcelona, 1996.

Bennett, Herman L. *Africans in Colonial Mexico: Absolutism, Christianity, and Afro-Creole Consciousness, 570–1640*. Bloomington: Indiana University Press, 2003.

Berger, Harry, Jr. "Fictions of the Pose: Facing the Gaze of Early Modern Portraiture." *Representations* 46 (1994): 87–120.

Bergmann, Emilie L. *Art Inscribed: Essays on Ekphrasis in Spanish Golden Age Poetry*. Cambridge: Harvard University Press, 1979.

Bieñko Peralta, Doris. "Las *verae efigies* y los retratos simulados: Representaciones de los venerables angelopolitanos, siglos XVII y XVIII." In *La función de las imágenes en el catolicismo novohispano*, edited by Gisela von Wobeser, Carolina Aguilar García, and Jorge Luis Merlo Solorio, 255–82. Mexico City: Universidad Nacional Autónoma de México, Instituto de Investigaciones Históricas, 2018.

Blanchard, Jean-Vincent. "Beyond Belief: Sovereignty and the Spectacle of Martyrdom in Early Modern France." *Seventeenth-Century French Studies* 36, no. 2 (2014): 94–108.

Bodart, Diane. *Pouvoirs du portrait sous les Habsbourg d'Espagne*. Paris: CTHS-INHA, 2011.

Boer, Wietse de, Karl A. E. Enenkel, and Walter S. Melion, eds. *Jesuit Image Theory*. Leiden: Brill, 2016.

Bogdanović, Jelena. *The Framing of Sacred Space: The Canopy and the Byzantine Church*. Oxford: Oxford University Press, 2017.

Boone, Elizabeth Hill. "Incarnations of the Aztec Supernatural: The Image of Huitzilopochtli in Mexico and Europe." *Transactions of the American Philosophical Society* 79, no. 2 (1989): 1–107.

Bouza, Fernando. "La biblioteca de la reina Margarita de Austria." *Estudis* 37 (2011): 43–72.

———. *Imagen y propaganda: Capítulos de historia cultural del reinado de Felipe II*. Madrid: Akal, 1998.

Boyle, Margaret E. "Inquisition and Epistolary Negotiation: Examining the Correspondence of Teresa de la Valle y Cerda." *Letras Femeninas* 35, no. 1 (2009): 293–309.

Braddock, Alan C. "Mestizo Mnemonics: Diego de Valadés, *Rhetorica Christiana*, and the Earthly Art of Memory." In *Picture Ecology: Art and Ecocriticism in Planetary Perspective*, edited by Karl Kusserow, 114–31. Princeton: Princeton University Press, 2021.

Braider, Christopher. *Experimental Selves: Person and Experience in Early Modern Europe*. Toronto: University of Toronto Press, 2018.

Braun, Harald E. *Juan de Mariana and Early Modern Spanish Political Thought*. Aldershot: Ashgate, 2007.

Bray, Xavier, ed. *The Sacred Made Real: Spanish Painting and Sculpture, 1600–1700*. London: National Gallery, 2009.

Bridikhina, Eugenia. *Theatrum mundi: Entramados del poder en Charcas colonial*. Lima: Instituto Francés de Estudios Andinos, 2007.

Brilliant, Richard. *Portraiture*. London: Reaktion Books, 1991.

Brilliant, Richard, and Dale Kinney, eds. *Reuse Value: Spolia and Appropriation in Art and Architecture from Constantine to Sherrie Levine*. London: Routledge, 2011.

Bristol, Joan C. "Black Catholicism in Mexico." *Journal of Africana Religions* 2, no. 2 (2014): 255–63.

———. *Christians, Blasphemers, and Witches: Afro-Mexican Ritual Practice in the Seventeenth Century*. Albuquerque: University of New Mexico Press, 2007.

Broadfoot, Keith. "*Las meninas* and the King's Two Bodies." *Word and Image* 17, no. 3 (2001): 219–32.

Brown, Jonathan. "From Spanish to New Spanish Painting, 1550–1700." In *Painting in Latin America, 1550–1820*, edited by Luisa Elena Alcalá and Jonathan Brown, 103–47. New Haven: Yale University Press, 2014.

———. "La monarquía española y el retrato de aparato de 1500 a 1800 (con algunas observaciones sobre su historia subsiguiente)." In Portús Pérez, *El retrato en el Museo del Prado*, 134–59.

———. *Velázquez: Painter and Courtier*. New Haven: Yale University Press, 1986.

Brown, Jonathan, and J. H. Elliott. *A Palace for a King: The Buen Retiro and the Court of Philip IV*. New Haven: Yale University Press, 1986.

Brown, Michael A., ed. *Art and Empire: The Golden Age of Spain*. San Diego: San Diego Museum of Art, 2019.

Burke, Peter. "How to Be a Counter-Reformation Saint." In *The Historical Anthropology of Early Modern Italy: Essays on Perception and Communication*, 48–62. Cambridge: Cambridge University Press, 1987.

———. *Popular Culture in Early Modern Europe*. Aldershot: Ashgate, 2009.

———. "La sociología del retrato renacentista." In Portús Pérez, *El retrato en el Museo del Prado*, 98–115.

Calvo Serraller, Francisco. *Teoría de la pintura del Siglo de Oro*. Madrid: Cátedra, 1981.

Camille, Michael. *The Gothic Idol: Ideology and Image-Making in Medieval Art*. Cambridge: Cambridge University Press, 1989.

Canavan, Claire, and Helen Smith. "'The Needle May Convert More Than the Pen': Women and the Work of Conversion in Early Modern England." In *Conversions: Gender and Religious Change in Early Modern Europe*, edited by Simon Ditchfield and Helen Smith, 105–26. Manchester: Manchester University Press, 2017.

Cañeque, Alejandro. "De sillas y almohadones o de la naturaleza ritual del poder en la Nueva España de los siglos XVI y XVII." *Revista de Indias* 64, no. 232 (2004): 609–34.

———. *The King's Living Image: The Culture and Politics of Viceregal Power in Colonial Mexico*. New York: Routledge, 2004.

Capretti, Elena, and Serena Padovani. *Domenico Puligo, 1492–1527: Un protagonista dimenticato della pittura fiorentina*. Livorno: Sillabe, 2002.

Carlos Varona, María Cruz de. *Nacer en palacio: El ritual del nacimiento en la corte de los Austrias*. Madrid: Centro de Estudios Europa Hispánica, 2018.

Caro Baroja, Julio. *Vidas mágicas e Inquisición*. 2 vols. Madrid: Taurus, 1967.

Carrasco, Davíd. *City of Sacrifice: The Aztec Empire and the Role of Violence in Civilization*. Boston: Beacon, 1999.

Cavazzini, Patrizia. "On Painted Portraiture in Seventeenth-Century Rome: Theory, Practice and Appreciation." *Römisches Jahrbuch der Bibliotheca Hertziana* 42 (2015–16): 229–42.

Cecchi, Alessandro. "Giovanni Maria Butteri: Virgin and Child with Saint Anne and Members of the Medici Family as Saints." In *Masters of Florence: Glory and Genius at the Court of the Medici*, edited by Annamaria Giusti, 138. Memphis: Wonders, 2004.

Checa Cremades, Fernando, ed. *Velázquez, Bernini, Luca Giordano: Le corti del barocco*. Milan: Skira, 2004.

Cherry, Peter. "A Newly Discovered 'Immaculate Conception' by Diego Velázquez." *Burlington Magazine* 162 (2020): 1028–37.

———. "Portraiture in the Divine Style? Reflections on Zurbarán's Female Saints." In *Santas de Zurbarán: Devoción y Persuasión*, edited by Benito Navarrete Prieto, 190–94. Seville: Instituto de la Cultura y las Artes de Sevilla, 2013.

Chicangana-Bayona, Yobenj Aucardo, and Juan Camilo Rojas Gómez. "El príncipe del arte nacional: Gregorio Vásquez de Arce y Ceballos interpretado por el siglo XIX." *Historia Crítica* 52 (2014): 205–30.

Chinchilla Aguilar, Ernesto. *Sor Juana de Maldonado y Paz: Pruebas documentales de su existencia*. Mexico City: Hispanoamerica, 1949.

Chipps Smith, Jeffrey. *Sensuous Worship: Jesuits and the Art of the Early Catholic Reformation in Germany*. Princeton: Princeton University Press, 2002.

Christian, William A., Jr. *Local Religion in Sixteenth-Century Spain*. Princeton: Princeton University Press, 1981.

Cicero. *De natura deorum libri tres*. Edited by Joseph B. Mayor. 3 vols. Cambridge: Cambridge University Press, 1880.

Civil, Pierre. "La máscara y el retrato: Enfoques moralizadores en textos e imágenes del Siglo de Oro español." In *La maschera e l'altro*, edited by Maria Grazia Profeti, 281–97. Florence: Alinea editrice, 2005.

Clark, Stuart. *Thinking with Demons: The Idea of Witchcraft in Early Modern Europe*. Oxford: Oxford University Press, 1999.

Collingwood, R. G. *The Principles of Art*. Oxford: Oxford University Press, 1958.

Copeland, Clare. *Maria Maddalena De' Pazzi: The Making of a Counter-Reformation Saint*. Oxford: Oxford University Press, 2016.

Copeland, Clare, and Jan Machielsen. Introduction to *Angels of Light? Sanctity and the Discernment of Spirits in the Early Modern Period*, edited by Clare Copeland and Jan Machielsen, 1–16. Leiden: Brill, 2013.

Córdova, James. "Images Beyond the Veil: Funeral Portraits and Sacred Materialities in New Spain's Nunneries." *RES: Anthropology and Aesthetics* 67/68 (2016/2017): 256–72.

Cornejo, Francisco J. *Pintura y teatro en la Sevilla del Siglo de Oro: La "sacra monarquía."* Seville: Fundación el Monte, 2005.

Crispí i Canton, Marta. "La verònica de Madona Santa Maria i la processó de la Puríssima organitzada per Martí l'Humà." *Locus Amoenus* 2 (1996): 85–101.

Cruz González, Cristina. "Beyond the Bride of Christ: The Crucified Abbess in Mexico and Spain." *Art Bulletin* 99, no. 4 (2018): 102–32.

Cuadriello, Jaime. "Winged and Imagined Indians." Translated by Fernando Cervantes. In *Angels, Demons and the New World*, edited by Fernando Cervantes and Andrew Redden, 211–48. Cambridge: Cambridge University Press, 2013.

Cummins, Thomas. "From Lies to Truth: Colonial Ekphrasis and the Act of Crosscultural Translation." In *Reframing the Renaissance: Visual Culture in Europe and Latin America, 1450–1650*, edited by Claire Farago, 152–74. New Haven: Yale University Press, 1995.

———. "The Golden Calf in America." In *The Idol in the Age of Art: Objects, Devotions, and the Early Modern World*, edited by Michael W. Cole and Rebecca Zorach, 77–104. Burlington: Ashgate, 2009.

———. "We Are the Other: Peruvian Portraits of Colonial Kurakakuna." In *Transatlantic Encounters: Europeans and Andeans in the Sixteenth* Century, edited by Kenneth J.

Andrien and Rolena Adorno, 203–70. Berkeley: University of California Press, 1991.

Cuño, Justo. "Ritos y fiestas en la conformación del orden social en Quito en las épocas colonial y republicana (1573–1875)." *Revista de Indias* 73, no. 259 (2013): 663–92.

Curiel, Gustavo. "Ajuares domésticos: Los rituales de lo cotidiano." In *La ciudad barroca*, edited by Antonio Rubial García, vol. 2 of *Historia de la vida cotidiana en México*, edited by Pilar Gonzalbo Aizpuru, 81–108. Mexico City: Fondo de Cultura Económica, 2005.

Davis, Whitney. *A General Theory of Visual Culture*. Princeton: Princeton University Press, 2011.

Didi-Huberman, Georges. "The Portrait, the Individual, and the Singular: Remarks on the Legacy of Aby Warburg." Translated by Carol Plazzotta. In *The Image of the Individual: Portraits in the Renaissance*, edited by Nicholas Mann and Luke Syson, 165–88, 231–35. London: British Museum, 1998.

———. "The Surviving Image: Aby Warburg and Tylorian Anthropology." *Oxford Art Journal* 25, no. 1 (2002): 59–70.

Díez Atienza, Belén. "Estudio técnico de la producción pictórica de Antonio Bisquert en Teruel." PhD diss., Universitat Politècnica de València, 2017.

Díez Atienza, Belén, José Antonio Madrid García, and Dolores Julia Yusá Marco. "Revisión de la obra de Antonio Bisquert en la ciudad de Teruel a través de su análisis radiográfico y caracterización de materiales mediante SEM/EDX." *Ge-conservación* 16 (2019): 6–22.

Díez-Ordás Berciano, Maria Belén. "La decoración pictórica de El Escorial: Historia evolutiva de la decoración pictórica mueble de las principales estancias del monasterio de El Escorial hasta Felipe IV." PhD diss., Universidad de León, 2015.

Dillon, Sarah. *The Palimpsest: Literature, Criticism, Theory*. London: Continuum, 2007.

Donahue Wallace, Kelly. "Prints and Printmakers in Viceregal Mexico City, 1600–1800." PhD diss., University of New Mexico, 2000.

———. "Saintly Beauty and the Printed Portrait." *Aurora: The Journal of the History of Art* 8 (2007): 1–16.

Douglas, Bronwen. "Indigenous Countersigns and the Ethnohistory of Voyaging." In *Oceanic Encounters: Exchange, Desire, Violence*, edited by Margaret Jolly, Serge Tcherkézoff, and Darrell Tryon, 175–98. Canberra: Australian National University, 2009.

Eaker, Adam. "Van Dyck Between Master and Model." *Art Bulletin* 97, no. 2 (2015): 173–91.

Eck, Caroline van. "The Petrifying Gaze of Medusa: Ambivalence, *Ekplexis*, and the Sublime." *Journal of Historians of Netherlandish Art* 8, no. 2 (2016), n.p.

Eire, Carlos M. N. "The Concept of Popular Religion." In *Local Religion in Colonial Mexico*, edited by Martin Austin Nesvig, 1–35. Albuquerque: University of New Mexico Press, 2006.

Eliade, Mircea. *The Sacred and the Profane: The Nature of Religion*. Translated by Willard R. Trask. New York: Harcourt, Brace & World, 1959.

Elsner, Jaś. "Place, Shrine, Miracle." In *Agents of Faith: Votive Objects in Time and Place*, edited by Ittai Weinryb, 2–25. New Haven: Yale University Press, 2018.

Enciclopedia Cattolica. Vatican City: Ente per l'Enciclopedia Cattolica e per il libro Cattolico, 1949.

Engel, Emily A. "Changing Faces: Royal Portraiture and the Manipulation of Colonial Bodies in the Viceroyalty of Peru." In *Spanish Royal Patronage, 1412–1804: Portraits as Propaganda*, edited by Ilenia Colón Mendoza and Margaret Ann Zaho, 149–69. Newcastle upon Tyne: Cambridge Scholars, 2018.

———. *Pictured Politics: Visualizing Colonial History in South American Portrait Collections*. Austin: University of Texas Press, 2020.

Esch, Arnold. "On the Reuse of Antiquity: The Perspectives of the Archaeologist and of the Historian." Translated by Benjamin Anderson. In *Reuse Value: "Spolia" and Appropriation in Art and Architecture from Constantine to Sherrie Levine*, edited by Richard Brilliant and Dale Kinney, 13–31. London: Routledge, 2011.

Estenssoro, Juan Carlos. "La plástica colonial y sus relaciones con la gran rebelión." *Revista Andina* 9, no. 2 (1992): 415–39.

Étienne, Noémie. *La restauration des peintures à Paris (1750–1815): Practiques et discours sur la matérialité des œuvres d'art*. Rennes: Presses Universitaires de Rennes, 2012.

Fajardo de Rueda, Marta. "Milenarismo y arte: La presencia del pensamiento de Joaquín de Fiore en la Nueva Granada." *Revista Palimpsesto* 4 (2004): 236–58.

———. "La presencia de Joaquín de Fiore en la obra de Gregorio Vásquez." In *El oficio del pintor: Nuevas miradas a la obra de Gregorio Vásquez*, edited by Constanza Toquica, 95–103. Bogotá: Ministerio de Cultura, 2008.

Falque, Ingrid. *Devotional Portraiture and Spiritual Experience in Early Netherlandish Painting.* Leiden: Brill, 2019.

Fee, Nancy H. "Biographical Essay." In Juan de Palafox y Mendoza, *Virtues of the Indian / Virtudes del Indio: An Annotated Translation*, edited and translated by Nancy H. Fee (Lanham: Rowman & Littlefield, 2009).

———. "Rey versus reino(s): Palafox y los escudos de la Catedral de Puebla." In *La pluma y el báculo: Juan de Palafox y el mundo hispano del seiscientos*, edited by Montserrat Galí Boadella, 57–103. Puebla: Instituto de Ciencias Sociales y Humanidades, Benémerita Universidad Autónoma de Puebla, 2004.

Ferber, Sarah. *Demonic Possession and Exorcism in Early Modern France.* New York: Routledge, 2004.

Fernández Alba, Antonio. *El Escorial: Metáfora en piedra.* Madrid: Consejo Superior de Investigaciones Científicas, 2004.

Fernández Gracia, Ricardo. "Alegoría y emblemática en torno al retrato del virrey don Juan de Palafox." In *Emblemata aurea: La emblemática en el arte y la literatura del Siglo de Oro*, edited by Rafael Zafra and José Javier Azanza, 163–88. Madrid: Akal, 2000.

———. "Consideraciones sobre la riqueza iconográfica de Don Juan de Palafox." In *Palafox: Iglesia, cultura y estado en el siglo XVII. Congreso Internacional. IV Centenario del Nacimiento de Don Juan de Palafox y Mendoza,* edited by Ricardo Fernández Gracia, 399–427. Pamplona: Universidad de Navarra, 2001.

———. *Don Juan de Palafox: Teoría y promoción de las artes.* Pamplona: Edita, Asociación de Amigos del Monasterio de Fitero, 2000.

———. *Iconografía de Don Juan de Palafox: Imágenes para un hombre de estado y de iglesia.* Pamplona: Gobierno de Navarra, Departamento de Presidencia, Justicia e Interior, 2002.

Fernández López, José. "Pinturas de Lucas Valdés." *Boletín del Seminario de Estudios de Arte y Arqueología* 53 (1987): 413–25.

Fernández Salvador, Carmen. "Imágenes locales y retórica sagrada: Una visión edificante de Quito en el siglo XVII." *Procesos: Revisa Ecuatoriana de Historia* 25 (2007): 79–91.

Feros, Antonio. *El Duque de Lerma: Realeza y privanza en la España de Felipe III.* Madrid: Marcial Pons, 2002.

———. "The King's Favorite, the Duke of Lerma: Power, Wealth and Court Culture in the Reign of Philip III of Spain, 1598–1621." PhD diss., Johns Hopkins University, 1994.

Flores-Marcial, Xóchitl Marina. "A History of Guelaguetza in Zapotec Communities of the Central Valleys of Oaxaca, 16th Century to the Present." PhD diss., University of California, Los Angeles, 2015.

Foronda, François. "Apoderarse del rey: Un ritual de integración política en la Castilla trastámara." In *El espanto y el miedo: Golpismo, emociones políticas y constitucionalismo en la Edad Media*, 15–74. Madrid: Dykinson, 2013.

Franco Llopis, Borja. "Art of Conversion? The Visual Policies of the Jesuits, Dominicans, and Mercedarians in Valencia." In *Polemical Encounters: Christians, Jews, and Muslims in Iberia and Beyond*, edited by Mercedes García-Arenal and Gerard Wiegers, 179–202. University Park: Penn State University Press, 2019.

———. *La pintura valenciana entre 1550 y 1609: Cristología y adoctrinamiento morisco.* Lleida: Universitat de Lleida, 2008.

———. "Redescubriendo a Jaime Prades, el gran tratadista olvidado de la Reforma Católica." *Ars Longa* 19 (2010): 83–93.

Franco Llopis, Borja, and Byron Ellsworth Hamann. "Un curioso caso de destrucción de estampas en Valencia: Diego de Sevilla y las insignias de la Pasión." In *En el primer siglo de la Inquisición española: Fuentes documentales, procedimientos de análisis, experiencias de investigación*, edited by José María Cruselles Gómez, 349–68. Valencia: Universitat de València, 2013.

Franco Llopis, Borja, and Stefania Rusconi. "Sobre pinturas deshonestas, lienzos y naipes protestantes: Tres documentos inquisitoriales vinculados a la censura y tráfico de imágenes heréticas en el mundo hispánico del siglo XVI." *Manuscrits: Revista d'Història Moderna* 33 (2015): 97–118.

Freedberg, David. "Johannes Molanus on Provocative Paintings: *De Historia Sanctarum Imaginum et Picturarum*, Book II, Chapter 42." *Journal of the Warburg and Courtauld Institutes* 34 (1971): 229–45.

———. *The Power of Images: Studies in the History and Theory of Response*. Chicago: University of Chicago Press, 1989.

Fromont, Cécile. *The Art of Conversion: Christian Visual Culture in the Kingdom of Kongo*. Chapel Hill: University of North Carolina Press, 2014.

García-Frías Checa, Carmen, and Javier Jordán de Urriés y de la Colina, eds. *El retrato en las Colecciones Reales de Patrimonio Nacional: De Juan de Flandes a Antonio López*. Madrid: Patrimonio Nacional, 2014.

García Sáiz, María Concepción. "Portraiture in Viceregal America." In *Retratos: 2,000 Years of Latin American Portraits*, edited by Marion Oettinger, Jr., Miguel A. Bretos, and Carolyn Kinder Carr, 74–85. New Haven: Yale University Press, 2005.

García Sanz, Ana, and Leticia Ruiz. "Linaje regio y monacal: La galería de retratos de las Descalzas Reales." In *El linaje del emperador*, edited by Javier Portús, 134–57. Madrid: Sociedad Estatal para la Conmemoración de los Centenarios de Felipe II y Carlos V, 2000.

García Sanz, Ana, and María Victoria Triviño. *Iconografía de Santa Clara en el Monasterio de las Descalzas Reales*. Madrid: Patrimonio Nacional, Caja de Madrid, 1993.

Garrison, Edward B. "Note on the Survival of Thirteenth-Century Panel Paintings in Italy." *Art Bulletin* 54, no. 2 (1972): 140.

Garver, Valerie A. "The Influence of Monastic Ideals upon Carolingian Conceptions of Childhood." In *Childhood in the Middle Ages and the Renaissance: The Results of a Paradigm Shift in the History of Mentality*, edited by Albrecht Classen, 67–86. Berlin: De Gruyter, 2005.

Gasbarri, Carlo. "Uno strano quadro e un episodio inedito riguardante San Filippo Neri." *Strenna dei Romanisti* 22 (1961): 73–75.

Gasquoine Hartley, Catherine. *A Record of Spanish Painting*. London: Walter Scott, 1904.

Gaylord, Mary M. "The True Histories of Early Modern Writing in Spanish: Some American Reflections." *Modern Language Quarterly* 57, no. 2 (1996): 213–25.

Gimilio Sanz, David. "Poder, humanismo y religiosidad en tiempos del Patriarca Juan de Ribera en Valencia: Su colección de escultura clásica." *Espacio, Tiempo y Forma*, ser. 7, 2 (2014): 13–39.

Ginzburg, Carlo. "Microhistory: Two or Three Things That I Know About It." Translated by John Tedeschi and Anne C. Tedeschi. *Critical Inquiry* 20, no. 1 (1993): 10–35.

Goffen, Rona. *Giovanni Bellini*. New Haven: Yale University Press, 1989.

———. "Icon and Vision: Giovanni Bellini's Half-Length Madonnas." *Art Bulletin* 57, no. 4 (1975): 487–518.

———. *Renaissance Rivals: Michelangelo, Leonardo, Raphael, Titian*. New Haven: Yale University Press, 2004.

Goltz, Michael von der, and Joyce Hill Stoner. "Considerations on Removing or Retaining Overpainted Additions and Alterations." In *Conservation of Easel Paintings*, edited by Joyce Hill Stoner and Rebecca Rushfield, 497–99. New York: Routledge, 2012.

González de Amezúa, Agustín. "Unas notas sobre la Calderona." In *Estudios Hispánicos: Homenaje a Archer M. Huntington*, edited by Ramón Menéndez Pidal, 14–37. Wellesley: Spanish Department, Wellesley College, 1952.

González de Zárate, Jesús María. *Emblemas regio-políticos de Juan de Solórzano*. Madrid: Ediciones Tuero, 1987.

González Duro, Enrique. *Demonios en el convento: El conde-duque de Olivares frente a la Inquisición*. Madrid: Oberon, 2004.

González García, Juan Luis. "Charles V's Death: Crafting Words and Images for the Second Caesar." *Figura: Studies on the Classical Tradition* 4 (2016): 5–41.

———. "Empathetic Images and Painted Dialogues: The Visual and Verbal Rhetoric of Royal Private Piety in Renaissance Spain." In *Push*

Me, Pull You: Imaginative, Emotional, Physical, and Spatial Interaction in Late Medieval and Renaissance Art, edited by Sarah Blick and Laura Gelfand, 487–525. Leiden: Brill, 2011.

———. "Hijas de Friné: La cortesana como (contra) ejemplo y público de la predicación áurea." In *"Cortesanas enamoradas": La prostitución en el Siglo de Oro*, edited by Adrián J. Sáez, 149–73. Madrid: Sial Pigmalión, 2019.

———. *Imágenes sagradas y predicación visual en el Siglo de Oro*. Madrid: Akal, S.A., 2015.

———. "Retórica del decoro y censura de las imágenes en el Barroco temprano español." *Rhetorica* 32, no. 1 (2014): 47–61.

———. "Spanish Religious Imagery and Post-Tridentine Theory." *Hispanic Research Journal* 16, no. 5 (2015): 441–55.

———. "Técnicas jesuíticas de predicación misional, del Viejo al Nuevo Mundo (c. 1550–1650)." In *Barroco vivo, Barroco continúo: Otras miradas sobre la creación ibero-americana*, edited by Fernando Quiles and María del Pilar López, 368–85. Seville: Enredars, 2019.

———. "Velázquez y la invención: Mimesis y anagnórisis entre Italia y España (c. 1618–1630)." H-*ART: Revista de Historia, Teoría y Crítica de Arte* 2 (2018): 15–38.

Goodman, Eleanor. "Conspicuous in Her Absence: Mariana of Austria, Juan José de Austria, and the Representation of Her Power." In *Queenship and Political Power in Medieval and Early Modern Spain*, edited by Theresa Earenfight, 163–84. Aldershot: Ashgate, 2005.

———. "Royal Piety: Faith, Religious Politics, and the Experience of Art at the Convent of the Descalzas Reales in Madrid." PhD diss., New York University, 2001.

Graziano, Frank. *Wounds of Love: The Mystical Marriage of Saint Rose of Lima*. Oxford: Oxford University Press, 2004.

Grzęda, Mateusz. "Portret i figuralna interpretacja historii: Portret identyfikacyjny w reprezentacji władzy Jagiellonów." *Gdańskie Studia Muzealne* 1, no. 11 (2019): 123–41.

Guibovich Pérez, Pedro. *En defensa de Dios: Estudios y documentos sobre la Inquisición en el Perú*. Lima: Ediciones del Congreso del Perú, 1998.

———. "Fortunas y adversidades del Archivo de la Inquisición de Lima." In *From the Ashes of History: Loss and Recovery of Archives and Libraries in Modern Latin America*, edited by Carlos Aguirre and Javier Villa-Flores, 39–60. Raleigh: University of North Carolina Press, 2015.

Gutiérrez, Verónica A. "A Satellite Community in a Spanish City: The Barrio of Santiago Cholultecapan in Colonial Puebla de los Ángeles." *UCLA Historical Journal* 23, no. 1 (2012): 31–42.

Gutiérrez Pastor, Ismail. "Don Juan Bazo de Moreda (1614–1654), sargento mayor de los tercios de Flandes y regidor perpetuo de Logroño, pintado por Francisco de Zurbarán." *Berceo* 156 (2009): 191–212.

Haag, Sabine, ed. *Velázquez*. Munich: Hirmer, 2014.

Hajovsky, Patrick Thomas. "André Thevet's 'True' Portrait of Moctezuma and Its European Legacy." *Word and Image* 25, no. 4 (2009): 335–52.

———. *On the Lips of Others: Moteuczoma's Fame in Aztec Monuments and Rituals*. Austin: University of Texas Press, 2015.

———. "Shifting Panoramas: Contested Visions of Cuzco's 1650 Earthquake." *Art Bulletin* 100, no. 4 (2018): 34–61.

Hale, Charlotte. "Restoring *Bartolommeo Bonghi*." *Metropolitan Museum of Art Bulletin*, n.s., 51, no. 3 (1993–94): 20–25.

Hall, Marcia. *The Sacred Image in the Age of Art: Titian, Tintoretto, Barocci, El Greco, Caravaggio*. New Haven: Yale University Press, 2011.

Harpster, Grace. "Figino's Efficacy: Portraits, Votives, and Their Makers After Trent." *Oxford Art Journal* 44, no. 2 (2021): 226–45.

———. "Illustrious Jesuits: The Martyrological Portrait Series *circa* 1600." *Journal of Jesuit Studies* 9 (2022): 379–97.

Hartman, Saidiya V. *Scenes of Subjection: Terror, Slavery, and Self-Making in Nineteenth-Century America*. Oxford: Oxford University Press, 1997.

Hernando Garrido, José Luis. "Antídotos contra el diablo: Amuletos, talismanes y otros artefactos para ahuyentar espíritus malignos." In *A propósito de Satán: El submundo diabólico en tiempos del románico*, edited by Pedro Luis Huerta Huerta,

225–60. Aguilar de Campoo: Fundación Santa María la Real, 2019.

Herrero Carretero, Concha. "Jacobo Vandergoten el Viejo: Isabel de Farnesio como Virgen de los Desamparados." In *El real sitio de La Granja de San Ildefonso: Retrato y escena del rey*, edited by Delfín Rodríguez Ruiz, 406–9. Madrid: Patrimonio Nacional, 2000.

Herrero-García, Miguel. "Un dictamen pericial de Velázquez y una escena de Lope de Vega." *Revista Española de Arte* 25, no. 13.2 (1936): 66–68.

Hessler, Christiane J. "The Man on Slate: Sebastiano del Piombo's Portrait of Baccio Valori and Valori the Younger's Speech in Borghini's 'Il Riposo.'" *Source: Notes in the History of Art* 25, no. 2 (2006): 18–22.

Hills, Helen. "'The Face Is a Mirror of the Soul': Frontispieces and the Production of Sanctity in Post-Tridentine Naples." *Art History* 31, no. 4 (2008): 547–73.

———. "Too Much Propaganda." *Oxford Art Journal* 29, no. 3 (2006): 446–53.

Hoeniger, Cathleen. *The Renovation of Paintings in Tuscany, 1250–1500*. Cambridge: Cambridge University Press, 1995.

Holguín Valdez, Anthony. "Un retrato de Santa Rosa de Lima firmado por el pintor Pedro Díaz." *ILLAPA Mana Tukukq: Revista del Instituto de Investigaciones Museológicas y Artísticas de la Universidad Ricardo Palma* 16 (2019): 46–55.

Holm Monssen, Leif. "Rex Gloriose Martyrum: A Contribution to Jesuit Iconography." *Art Bulletin* 63, no. 1 (1981): 130–37.

Homza, Lu Ann. "Victims as Actors: Inquisitions." In Parker and Starr-LeBeau, *Judging Faith, Punishing Sin*, 193–203.

Hope, Charles. "Historical Portraits in the 'Lives' and in the Frescoes of Giorgio Vasari." In *Giorgio Vasari, tra decorazione ambientale e storiografia artistica: Convegno di studi (Arezzo, 8–10 ottobre, 1981)*, edited by Gian Carlo Garfagnini, 321–38. Florence: Olschki, 1985.

Horcajo Palomero, Natalia. "Amuletos y talismanes en el retrato del príncipe Felipe Próspero de Velázquez." *Archivo Español de Arte* 72, no. 288 (1999): 521–30.

———. "Joyas del siglo XVI en seis retratos infantiles de las Descalzas Reales de Madrid." *Archivo Español de Arte* 77, no. 308 (2004): 397–410.

Hornedo, Rafael María de. "La 'vera effigies' de san Ignacio." *Razón y Fe: Revista Mensual Hispanoamericana Publicada por los Padres de la Compañía de Jesús* 704/5, no. 154.3/4 (1956): 203–24.

Hsia, Ronnie Po-chia, and Federico Palomo. "Religious Identities in the Iberian Worlds (1500–1700)." In *The Iberian World, 1450–1820*, edited by Fernando Bouza, Pedro Cardim, and Antonio Feros, 77–105. New York: Routledge, 2019.

Hvidtfeldt, Arild. *Teotl and Ixiptlatli: Some Central Conceptions in Ancient Mexican Religion*. Copenhagen: Munksgaard, 1958.

Hyman, Aaron M. "The Habsburg Re-Making of the East at Schloss Schönbrunn, or 'Things Equally Absurd'." *Art Bulletin* 101, no. 4 (2019): 39–69.

———. "Inventing Painting: Cristóbal de Villalpando, Juan Correa, and New Spain's Transatlantic Canon." *Art Bulletin* 99, no. 2 (2017): 102–35.

Ibáñez, Pedro M. *Crónicas de Bogotá*. Vol. 1. 2nd ed. Bogotá: Imprenta Nacional, 1913.

Infante-Galán, Juan. "'Las moradas' de Santa Teresa y la Real Academia de Buenas Letras." *Boletín de la Real Academia Sevillana de Buenas Letras: Minervae Baeticae* 10 (1982): 33–51.

Israëls, Machtelt. "Absence and Resemblance: Early Images of Bernardino da Siena and the Issue of Portraiture." *I Tatti Studies in the Italian Renaissance* 11 (2007): 77–114.

Jacobson Schutte, Anne. "'Questo non è il ritratto che ho fatto io': Painters, the Inquisition and the Shape of Sanctity in Seventeenth-Century Venice." In *Florence and Italy: Renaissance Studies in Honour of Nicolai Rubinstein*, edited by Peter Denley and Caroline Elam, 419–31. London: Committee for Medieval Studies, Westfield College, 1988.

Jacobus, Laura. "'Propria Figura': The Advent of Facsimile Portraiture in Italian Art." *Art Bulletin* 99, no. 2 (2017): 72–101.

Jansen, Maarten E. R. G. N., and Gabina Aurora Pérez Jiménez. *Mixtec Pictorial Manuscripts: Time, Agency and Memory in Ancient Mexico*. Leiden: Brill, 2011.

Jasienski, Adam. "Converting Portraits: Repainting as Art Making in the Early Modern Hispanic World." *Art Bulletin* 102, no. 1 (2020): 7–30.

———. "Disgust and the Sacred Image in Early Modernity." In *Sacrifice and Conversion in the Early Modern Atlantic World*, edited by Maria Berbara, 243–70. Milan: Officina Libraria, 2022.

———. "Entre el retrato y la imagen sagrada: El caso de Eugenia de la Torre." In *En las sombras del barroco: Una mirada introspectiva*, edited by Adrián Contreras-Guerrero, Ángel Justo-Estebaranz, and Fernando Quiles García. Seville: EnredArs/Universo Barroco Iberoamericano, 2022 (forthcoming).

———. "Francisco Pacheco y una anunciada intervención de Fernando III el santo: Un testimonio sobre el *Libro de retratos*." *Archivo Español de Arte* 93, no. 372 (2020): 411–18.

———. "A Savage Magnificence: Ottomanizing Fashion and the Politics of Display in Early Modern East-Central Europe." *Muqarnas* 31 (2014): 173–205.

———. "Velázquez and the Fragile Portrait of the King." *Art History* 44, no. 5 (2021): 922–47.

Jenkins, Marianna. *The State Portrait: Its Origin and Evolution*. New York: College Art Association of America; Art Bulletin, 1947.

Jiménez Sanz, Carmen. "La Casa Museo Lope de Vega, nueva etapa." In *Casas museo: Museología y gestión*, edited by Asunción Cardona Suanzes, 325–38. Madrid: Ministerio de Educación, Cultura y Deporte, 2013.

Johnson, Paul Michael. "Feeling Certainty, Performing Sincerity: The Emotional Hermeneutics of Truth in Inquisitorial and Theatrical Practice." In *The Quest for Certainty in Early Modern Europe: From Inquisition to Inquiry, 1550–1700*, edited by Barbara Fuchs and Mercedes García-Arenal, 50–79. Toronto: University of Toronto Press, 2020.

Jonckheere, Koenraad. *Antwerp Art After Iconoclasm, 1566–1585*. New Haven: Yale University Press, 2012.

Jones, Pamela M. *Federico Borromeo and the Ambrosiana: Art Patronage and Reform in Seventeenth-Century Milan*. Cambridge: Cambridge University Press, 1993.

Kagan, Richard. *Students and Society in Early Modern Spain*. Baltimore: Johns Hopkins University Press, 1974.

Kant, Immanuel. *Critique of Aesthetic Judgment*. Edited and translated by James Creed Meredith. Oxford: Clarendon, 1911.

Kantorowicz, Ernst Hartwig. *The King's Two Bodies: A Study in Medieval Political Theology*. Princeton: Princeton University Press, 1997.

Karr Schmidt, Suzanne, and Kimberley Nichols, eds. *Altered and Adorned: Using Renaissance Prints in Daily Life*. Chicago: Art Institute of Chicago, 2011.

Karttunen, Frances. "After the Conquest: The Survival of Indigenous Patterns of Life and Belief." *Journal of World History* 3, no. 2 (1992): 239–56.

Kasl, Ronda, ed. *Sacred Spain: Art and Belief in the Spanish World*. New Haven: Yale University Press, 2009.

Katzew, Ilona, ed. *Painted in Mexico, 1700–1790*. Los Angeles: Los Angeles County Museum of Art, 2017.

———. "Trastoques y elipsis en un retrato de tornaviaje: La ductilidad de los mensajes." In *Tornaviaje: Tránsito artístico entre los virreinatos americanos y la metrópolis*, edited by Fernando Quiles, Pablo F. Amador, and Martha Fernández, 13–32. Santiago de Compostela: Andavira Editora, Universidad Pablo de Olavide, 2020.

Keitt, Andrew W. *Inventing the Sacred: Imposture, Inquisition, and the Boundaries of the Supernatural in Golden Age Spain*. Leiden: Brill, 2005.

Kessel, Elsje van. *The Lives of Paintings: Presence, Agency and Likeness in Venetian Art of the Sixteenth Century*. Berlin: De Gruyter, 2017.

Kiss, Imola. "Considérations sur le portrait historié." In *Les genres picturaux: Genèse, métamorphoses et transpositions*, edited by Frédéric Elsing, Laurent Darbellay, and Imola Kiss, 103–23. Geneva: Mētis, 2010.

Klerck, Bram de. "The *Portrait Historié* in Passion Scenes in Renaissance Italy." In Manuth, Van Leeuwen, and Koldeweij, *Example or Alter Ego?*, 159–72.

Knaap, Anna C. "Meditation, Ministry, and Visual Rhetoric in Peter Paul Rubens's Program for the Jesuit Church in Antwerp." In *The Jesuits II:*

Cultures, Sciences, and the Arts, 1540–1773, edited by John W. O'Malley, Gauvin Alexander Bailey, Steven J. Harris, and T. Frank Kennedy, 157–81. Toronto: University of Toronto Press, 2006.

Koerner, Joseph Leo. *The Moment of Self-Portraiture in German Renaissance Art*. Chicago: University of Chicago Press, 1993.

———. *The Reformation of the Image*. London: Reaktion Books, 2004.

Koldeweij, Jos, Rudie van Leeuwen, and Volker Manuth. Introduction to *Example or Alter Ego?* edited by Manuth, Van Leeuwen, and Koldeweij, 5–15.

Korbacher, Dagmar. "Fra Teodoro of Urbino as Saint Dominic." In *The Renaissance Portrait: From Donatello to Bellini*, edited by Keith Christiansen and Stefan Weppelmann, 371–73. New Haven: Yale University Press, 2011.

Kovach, Margaret. *Indigenous Methodologies: Characteristics, Conversations, and Contexts*. Toronto: University of Toronto Press, 2010.

Krass, Urte. *Nah zum Leichnam: Bilder neuer Heiliger im Quattrocento*. Berlin: Deutscher Kunstverlag, 2012.

Kusche, Maria. *Juan Pantoja de la Cruz y sus seguidores: B. González, R. de Villandrando y A. López Polanco*. Madrid: Fundación Arte Hispánico, 2007.

Lafita, Teresa. "Otras obras inéditas del pintor Virgilio Mattoni de la Fuente: 'San Emigdio,' 'Retrato de Adolfo López,' 'Cuaderno de apuntes,' y 'Santa Isabel de Hungría.'" *Atrio* 8/9 (1996): 173–85.

Lafuente Ferrari, Enrique. *Breve historia de la pintura española II*. Madrid: Akal, 1987.

———. "Ensayo preliminar: La interpretación del Barroco y sus valores españoles." In Werner Weisbach, *El barroco: Arte de la Contrarreforma*, translated by Enrique Lafuente Ferrari, 7–47. Madrid: Espasa-Calpe, 1942.

———. "La inspección de los retratos reales en el siglo XVII (con un autógrafo de Velázquez)." *Correo Erudito* 2 (1941): 55–58.

Lamas Delgado, Eduardo. "Les peintures de Carducho, Rizi et Carreño pour le couvent des capucins de Ségovie: Nouvelles contributions sur un mécénat méconnu, un tableau d'autel oublié et un cycle pictural disparu." *Zeitschrift für Kunstgeschichte* 75 (2012): 223–38.

Latour, Bruno. *Pandora's Hope: Essays on the Reality of Science Studies*. Cambridge: Harvard University Press, 1999.

Lea, Henry Charles. *Chapters from the History of Spain Connected with the Inquisition*. Philadelphia: Lea Brothers, 1890.

Leeuwen, Rudie van. "Beeltenissen van bestuurders en burgers als bijbelfiguren: Het bijbelse *portrait historié* in de Noordelijke en Zuidelijke Nederlanden van de zestiende en zeventiende eeuw." PhD diss., Radboud Universiteit, Nijmegen, 2018.

———. "The *portrait historié* in Religious Context and Its Condemnation." In *Pokerfaced: Flemish and Dutch Baroque Faces Unveiled*, edited by Katlijne van der Stighelen, Hannelore Magnus, and Bert Watteeuw, 109–24. Turnhout: Brepols, 2010.

Leone, Massimo. *Saints and Signs: A Semiotic Reading of Conversion in Early Modern Catholicism*. Berlin: De Gruyter, 2010.

Levy, Evonne. *Propaganda and the Jesuit Baroque*. Berkeley: University of California Press, 2004.

Lingo, Stuart. *Federico Barocci: Allure and Devotion in Late Renaissance Painting*. New Haven: Yale University Press, 2008.

Lisón Tolosana, Carmelo. *La imagen del rey: Monarquía, realeza y poder ritual en la Casa de los Austrias*. Madrid: Espasa-Calpe, 1992.

Locker, Jesse M., ed. *Art and Reform in the Late Renaissance: After Trent*. New York: Routledge, 2019.

———. "Introduction: Rethinking Art After the Council of Trent." In Locker, *Art and Reform*, 1–18.

Lockhart, James. *The Nahuas After the Conquest: A Social and Cultural History of the Indians of Central Mexico, Sixteenth Through Eighteenth Centuries*. Stanford: Stanford University Press, 1992.

———. "Some Nahua Concepts in Postconquest Guise." *History of European Ideas* 6, no. 4 (1985): 465–82.

Loh, Maria H., ed. "Early Modern Horror." Special issue, *Oxford Art Journal* 34, no. 3 (2011).

———. "Renaissance Faciality." *Oxford Art Journal* 32, no. 3 (2009): 341–63.

López de Munain, Gorka. *Máscaras mortuorias: Historia del rostro ante la muerte*. Vitoria-Gasteiz: Sans Soleil Ediciones, 2018.

Lovell, George. "The Real Country and the Legal Country: Spanish Ideals and Mayan Realities in Colonial Guatemala." *GeoJournal* 26, no. 2 (1992): 181–85.

Luri, Gregorio. *El recogimiento: La aventura del yo*. Madrid: Compañía Nacional de Teatro Clásico, 2021.

Lynn, Kimberly. "Judges and Shepherds: Inquisitions." In Parker and Starr-LeBeau, *Judging Faith, Punishing Sin*, 116–27.

Macuil Martínez, Raul. "Tradición oral nahua contemporánea y mapas coloniales." *Indiana* 36, no. 2 (2019): 159–62.

Magaloni Kerpel, Diana. *Los colores del nuevo mundo: Artistas, materiales y la creación del "Códice Florentino."* Mexico City: Universidad Nacional Autónoma de México, 2014.

Manuth, Volker, Rudie van Leeuwen, and Jos Koldeweij, eds. *Example or Alter Ego? Aspects of the* Portrait Historié *in Western Art from Antiquity to the Present*. Turnhout: Brepols, 2016.

Marías, Fernando, ed. *El Greco of Toledo: Painter of the Visible and the Invisible*. Toledo: Fundación El Greco, 2014.

———. "Juan Pantoja de la Cruz: El arte cortesano de la imagen y las devociones femeninas." In *La mujer en el arte español: VIII Jornadas de Arte*, 103–16. Madrid: Editorial Alpuerto, 1997.

Marin, Louis. "The Frame of Representation and Some of Its Figures." Translated by Wendy Waring. In *The Rhetoric of the Frame: Essays on the Boundaries of the Artwork*, edited by Paul Duro, 79–95. Cambridge: Cambridge University Press, 1996.

———. "The Portrait of the King's Glorious Body." In *Food for Thought*, translated by Mette Hjort, 189–217. Baltimore: Johns Hopkins University Press, 1989.

Marín Cruzado, Olga. "El retrato real en composiciones religiosas de la pintura de siglo XVI: Carlos V y Felipe II." In *El arte en las cortes de Carlos V y Felipe II: IX Jornadas de Arte*, 113–26. Madrid: Centro de Estudios Históricos, CSIC, 1999.

Marín Tovar, Cristóbal. "La jubilosa entrada de Margarita de Austria en Madrid." *Anales de Historia del Arte* 9 (1999): 147–57.

Martínez Millán, José. "La casa de una reina católica: Margarita de Austria (1598–1611)." In *Mujeres en la corte de los Austrias: Una red social, cultural, religiosa y política*, edited by María Leticia Sánchez Hernández, 315–60. Madrid: Ediciones Polifemo, 2019.

Massaro, Davide, Federica Savazzi, Cinzia Di Dio, David Freedberg, Vittorio Gallese et al. "When Art Moves the Eyes: A Behavioral and Eye-Tracking Study." *PLoS ONE* 7, no. 5 (2012). https://doi.org/10.1371/journal.pone.0037285.

Mastronardi, Maria Aurelia. "Modelli classici e modelli umanistici nella storiografia di Paolo Antonio di Tarsia." In *Humanismo y perviviencia del mundo clásico: Homenaje al profesor Antonio Fontán*, edited by José María Maestre Maestre, Joaquín Pascual Barea, and Luis Charlo Brea, 3:1451–62. Madrid: Alcañiz, 2002.

———. "Paolo Antonio Tarsia." In *Puglia Neo-Latina: Un itinerario fra autori e testi*, edited by Francesco Tateo, Mauro de Nichilo, and Pietro Sisto, 369–405. Bari: Cacucci Editore, 1994.

Mateo Gómez, Isabel. *Juan Correa de Vivar*. Madrid: Instituto Diego Velázquez, 1983.

Mateo Gómez, Isabel, Amelia López-Yarto Elizalde, and José María Prados García, eds. *El arte de la Orden Jerónima: Historia y mecenazgo*. Bilbao: Ediciones Encuentro Iberdrola, 1999.

Mauro, Ida. *Spazio urbano e rappresentazione del potere: Le cerimonie della città di Napoli dopo la rivolta di Masaniello (1648–1672)*. Naples: Federico II University Press, 2020.

McCrory, Martha. "Immutable Images: Glyptic Portraits at the Medici Court in Sixteenth-Century Florence." In *The Image of the Individual: Portraits in the Renaissance*, edited by Nicholas Mann and Luke Syson, 40–54. London: British Museum Press, 1998.

McDonough, Kelly S. "Plotting Indigenous Stories, Land, and People: Primordial Titles and Narrative Mapping in Colonial Mexico." *Journal for Early Modern Cultural Studies* 17, no. 1 (2017): 1–30.

McHam, Sarah Blake. "Oedipal Palimpsest." *Source: Notes in the History of Art* 27, no. 4 (2008): 37–46.

McKim Smith, Gridley, Greta Andersen-Bergdoll, and Richard Newman. *Examining Velazquez*. New Haven: Yale University Press, 1988.

McPherson, Heather. *The Modern Portrait in Nineteenth-Century France*. Cambridge: Cambridge University Press, 2001.

Melion, Walter S. "Introduction: The Jesuit Engagement with the Status and Functions of the Visual Image." In Boer, Enenkel, and Melion, *Jesuit Image Theory*, 1–49.

Méndez Rodríguez, Luis. *Velázquez y la cultura sevillana*. Seville: Universidad de Sevilla, Fundación Focus-Abengoa, 2005.

Merlo Juárez, Eduardo, and Velia Morales Pérez. *Estudio, devoción y belleza: Obras selectas de la Pinacoteca Universitaria, siglos XVII–XX*. Puebla: Benemérita Universidad Autónoma de Puebla, 2002.

Mexicano Ramos, César. "Nota sobre la pintura de los incas en dos pulperías limeñas (1704)." *Uku Pacha: Revista de Investigaciones Históricas* 1, no. 2 (2000): 77–78.

Miller, Stephanie R. "A Tale of Two Portraits: Titian's Seated Portraits of Philip II." *Visual Resources* 28, no. 1 (2012): 103–16.

Mínguez, Víctor. *Los reyes solares: Iconografía astral de la monarquía hispánica*. Castelló de la Plana: Universitat Jaume I, 2001.

Mínguez Cornelles, Victor. "Los emperadores taumaturgos: Curaciones prodigiosas desde Trajano a Napoleón." *Potestas* 5 (2012): 43–81.

Molina, J. Michelle. *To Overcome Oneself: The Jesuit Ethic and Spirit of Global Expansion, 1520–1767*. Berkeley: University of California Press, 2013.

Moncó Rebollo, Beatriz. *Mujer y demonio: Una pareja barroca (Treinta monjas endemoniadas en un convento)*. Madrid: Instituto de Sociología Aplicada, 1989.

Morán Turina, Miguel. *Velázquez*. Madrid: Akal, 2012.

Moreno Cuadro, Fernando. "Origen Andaluz de la *vera effigies* de San Juan de la Cruz y su repercusión en Flandes y en México." *Laboratorio de Arte* 25 (2013): 347–70.

Morrison, Karl F. *The Mimetic Tradition of Reform in the West*. Princeton: Princeton University Press, 1982.

Mujica Pinilla, Ramón. "Angels and Demons in the Conquest of Peru." Translated by Fernando Cervantes. In *Angels, Demons and the New World*, edited by Fernando Cervantes and Andrew Redden, 171–210. Cambridge: Cambridge University Press, 2013.

———. "Arte e identidad: Las raíces culturales del barroco peruano." In *El barroco peruano*, edited by Ramón Mujica Pinilla, 1–57. Lima: Banco de Crédito del Perú, 2002.

Mumford, Jeremy Ravi. "Forgery and *Tambos*: False Documents, Imagined Incas, and the Making of Andean Space." In *Corruption in the Iberian Empires: Greed, Custom, and Colonial Networks*, edited by Christopher Rosenmüller, 13–32. Albuquerque: University of New Mexico Press, 2017.

Mundy, Barbara E. *The Death of Aztec Tenochtitlan, the Life of Mexico City*. Austin: University of Texas Press, 2015.

———. "Extirpation of Idolatry and Sensory Experience in Sixteenth-Century Mexico." In *Sensational Religion: Sensory Cultures in Material Practice*, edited by Sally M. Promey, 515–35. New Haven: Yale University Press, 2014.

Murillo Gallegos, Verónica. "*Ixiptla* o imagen: Un problema lingüistico y culural en la evangelización novohispana." *Revista Escritos BUAP* 2, no. 2 (2017): 25–42.

Myers, Kathleen. "Testimony for Canonization or Proof of Blasphemy: The New Spanish Inquisition and the Hagiographic Biography of Catarina de San Juan." In *Women in the Inquisition: Spain and the New World*, edited by Mary E. Giles, 270–95. Baltimore: Johns Hopkins University Press, 1999.

Nagel, Alexander. *The Controversy of Renaissance Art*. Chicago: University of Chicago Press, 2011.

———. "Fashion and the Now-Time of Renaissance Art." *RES: Anthropology and Aesthetics* 46 (2004): 32–52.

———. "Icons and Early Modern Portraits." In *El retrato del Renacimiento*, edited by Miguel Falomir, 421–25. Madrid: Museo del Prado, 2008.

Nagel, Alexander, and Christopher S. Wood. *Anachronic Renaissance*. New York: Zone, 2010.

Navarrete Prieto, Benito. "La *Inmaculada Concepción* y los avances en el conocimiento del joven Velázquez." In *La "Inmaculada Concepción" o "Virgen niña" de Diego Velázquez: Creatividad y metodología de un joven genio*, edited by Rafael Romero Asenjo and Adelina Illán Gutiérrez, 5–9. Ciencia & Esencia: Cuadernos de Conservación y Tecnología del Arte 3. Madrid: Turner, 2021.

———. *Murillo: Persuasion and Aura*. Turnhout: Brepols, 2021.

Nelson, Steven. "Response to *A Questionnaire on Decolonization*." *October* 174 (2020): 89.

Nesvig, Martin. *Ideology and Inquisition: The World of the Censors in Early Mexico*. New Haven: Yale University Press, 2009.

Nicolotti, Andrea. *From the Mandylion of Edessa to the Shroud of Turin: The Metamorphosis and Manipulation of a Legend*. Leiden: Brill, 2014.

Niedermeier, Nina. "The Artist's Memory: How to Make the Image of the Dead Saint Similar to the Living; The *vera effigies* of Ignatius of Loyola." Special issue, "Le immagini vive." Edited by Carmelo Occhipinti, *Horti Hesperidum: Studi di storia del collezionismo e della storiografia artistica* 2, no. 1 (2015): 157–99.

———. *Die ersten Bildnisse von Heiligen der Frühen Neuzeit: Porträtähnlichkeit in nachtridentinischer Zeit*. Regensburg: Schnell und Steiner, 2020.

Noyes, Ruth S. *Peter Paul Rubens and the Counter-Reformation Crisis of the "Beati moderni": Sanctity in Global Perspective*. New York: Routledge, 2017.

Nygren, Christopher J. "Titian's Ecce Homo on Slate: Stone, Oil, and the Transubstantiation of Painting." *Art Bulletin* 99, no. 1 (2017): 36–66.

———. *Titian's Icons: Tradition, Charisma, and Devotion in Renaissance Italy*. University Park: Penn State University Press, 2020.

Oettinger, Marion, Jr., Miguel A. Bretos, and Carolyn Kinder Carr, eds. *Retratos: 2,000 Years of Latin American Portraits*. New Haven: Yale University Press, 2005.

Oliván Santaliestra, Isabel. "'Decía que no se dejaba retratar de buena gana': Modestia e invisibilidad de la reina Isabel de Borbón (1635–1644)." *Goya* 338 (2012): 16–35.

Olko, Justyna. "Body Language in the Preconquest and Colonial Nahua Worlds." *Ethnohistory* 61, no. 1 (2014): 149–79.

Olmo, Ismael del. "La posesión diabólica en el *Examen de ingenios para las sciencias* (1575) de Juan Huarte de San Juan: Una paradoja." *Tiempos Modernos* 33, no. 2 (2016): 70–101.

———. "Providencialismo y sacralidad real: Francisco de Blasco Lanuza y la construcción del monarca exorcista." *Sociedades Precapitalistas* 2, no. 1 (2012). https://www.sociedadesprecapitalistas.fahce.unlp.edu.ar/article/view/SPv2n1a05.

O'Malley, John W. "The Many Lives of Ignatius of Loyola, Future Saint." In *Constructing a Saint Through Images: The 1609 Illustrated Biography of Ignatius of Loyola*, 1–34. Philadelphia: Saint Joseph's University Press, 2008.

Orozco Díaz, Emilio. "El retrato a lo divino, su influencia, y unas obras desconocidas de Risueño." *Goya* 120 (1974): 351–59.

———. "Retratos a lo divino." In *Temas del Barroco: De poesía y pintura*, 29–36. Granada: Universidad de Granada, 1947.

Osorio, Alejandra B. "The Copy as Original: The Presence of the Absent Spanish Habsburg King and Colonial Hybridity." *Renaissance Studies* 34, no. 4 (2020): 704–21.

———. *Inventing Lima: Baroque Modernity in Peru's South Sea Metropolis*. New York: Palgrave Macmillan, 2008.

———. "The King in Lima: Simulacra, Ritual, and Rule in Seventeenth-Century Peru." *Hispanic American Historical Review* 84, no. 3 (2004): 447–74.

The Oxford Dictionary of Byzantium. Oxford: Oxford University Press, 1991.

Pabel, Hilmar M. "Interior Sight in Peter Canisius' Meditations on Advent." In Boer, Enenkel, and Melion, *Jesuit Image Theory*, 254–88.

Pagden, Anthony. *The Fall of Natural Man: The American Indian and the Origins of Comparative Ethnology*. Cambridge: Cambridge University Press, 1982.

Palmer, Martin E., trans. and ed. *On Giving the "Spiritual Exercises": The Early Jesuit Manuscript Directories and the Official Directory of 1599*. St. Louis: Institute of Jesuit Sources, 1996.

Parker, Charles H., and Gretchen Starr-LeBeau, eds. *Judging Faith, Punishing Sin: Inquisitions and Consistories in the Early Modern World*. Cambridge: Cambridge University Press, 2017.

Pascual Chenel, Álvaro. "La construcción visual de la imagen regia durante el reinado de Carlos II: Simulacros de magestad y propaganda política." In *Vísperas de sucesión: Europa y la Monarquía de Carlos II*, edited by Bernardo J. García García and Antonio Álvarez-Ossorio Alvariño, 297–331. Madrid: Fundación Carlos de Amberes, 2015.

———. "Discurso político, identidad religiosa y cambio dinástico: La imagen regia y la Inmaculada

Concepción entre Austrias y Borbones." In *El siglo de la Inmaculada,* edited by María Martínez Alcalde, Sergio Yago Soriano, and José Javier Ruiz Ibáñez. 85–118. Murcia: Universidad de Murcia, 2018.

———. "Fiesta sacra y poder político: La iconografía de los Austrias como defensores de la Eucaristía y la Inmaculada en Hispanoamérica." *Hipogrifo* 1, no. 1 (2013): 57–86.

———. "Juegos de imagen y apariencia: Simulación, disimulación y propaganda política durante el reinado de Carlos II." In *El universo simbólico del poder en el Siglo de Oro*, edited by Álvaro Baraibar and Mariela Insúa, 175–204. Pamplona: Universidad de Navarra, 2012.

———. *El retrato de Estado durante el reinado de Carlos II: Imagen y propaganda*. Madrid: Fundación Universitaria Española, 2010.

———. "Teoría y práctica del retrato regio en Lope de Vega." *Teatro de Palabras: Revista sobre Teatro Áureo* 7 (2013): 237–62.

Pereda, Felipe. *Crime and Illusion: The Art of Truth in the Spanish Golden Age*. Translated by Consuelo López-Morillas. London: Harvey Miller, 2018.

———. *Las imágenes de la discordia: Política y poética de la imagen sagrada en la España del cuatrocientos*. Madrid: Marcial Pons, 2007.

———. *Images of Discord: Poetics and Politics of the Sacred Image in Fifteenth-Century Spain*. Translated by Consuelo López-Morillas. London: Harvey Miller, 2018.

———. "Sombras y cuadros: Teorías y culturas de la representación en la Europa de la reforma Católica." In *'Sacar de la sombra lumbre': La teoría de la pintura en el Siglo de Oro (1560–1724)*, edited by José Riello, 69–86. Madrid: Abada Editores, Museo Nacional del Prado, 2012.

———. "True Painting and the Challenge of Hypocrisy." In *After Conversion: Iberia and the Emergence of Modernity*, edited by Mercedes García-Arenal, 358–94. Leiden: Brill, 2016.

———. "Twin Brothers: Originality and Copy in the Americas." *RES: Anthropology and Aesthetics* 71–72 (2019): 99–112.

Pérez Salazar, Francisco. *Historia de la pintura en Puebla*. Edited by Elisa Vargas Lugo de Bosch and Carlos de Ovando. 3rd ed. Mexico City: Imprenta Universitaria, 1963.

Pérez Sánchez, Alfonso E. *Pintura española de los siglos XVII y XVIII en la Fundación Lázaro Galdiano*. Madrid: Fundación Lázaro Galdiano and Fundación Pedro Barrié de la Maza, 2005.

———. "Pintura Genovesa en España en el *Seicento*." In *España y Genova: Obras, artistas y coleccionistas*, edited by Piero Boccardo, José Luis Colomer, and Clario di Fabio, 177–88. Madrid: Fernando Villaverde Ediciones, 2004.

———. "El retrato clásico español." In Portús Pérez, *El retrato en el Museo del Prado*, 213–49.

Pérez Sánchez, Alfonso E., and Benito Navarrete Prieto. *Luis Tristán*. Madrid: Fundación BBVA and Real Fundación de Toledo, 2001.

Pérez Viejo, Tomás. "Géneros, mercado, artistas y críticos en la pintura española del siglo XIX." *Espacio, Tiempo y Forma*, ser. 5 of *Historia Contemporánea* 24 (2012): 27–48.

Pérez-Villanueva, Sonia. *The Life of Catalina de Erauso, the Lieutenant Nun: An Early Modern Autobiography*. Madison: Fairleigh Dickinson University Press, 2014.

Perkinson, Stephen. *The Likeness of the King: A Prehistory of Portraiture in Late Medieval France*. Chicago: University of Chicago Press, 2009.

———. "Rethinking the Origins of Portraiture." *Gesta* 46, no. 2 (2007): 135–57.

Piedra Adarves, Álvaro. "Vida secreta del pintor José García Hidalgo." *Cuadernos de Arte e Iconografía* 8, no. 36 (2009): 395–448.

Pierce, Donna. *Companion to Spanish Colonial Art at the Denver Art Museum*. Denver: Denver Art Museum, 2011.

Pierce, Donna, and Julie Wilson Frick. *Glitterati: Portraits and Jewelry from Colonial Latin America*. Denver: Denver Art Museum, 2015.

Pietz, William. "The Problem of the Fetish, I." *RES: Anthropology and Aesthetics* 9 (1985): 5–17.

Pilliod, Elizabeth. *Pontormo, Bronzino, Allori: A Genealogy of Florentine Art*. New Haven: Yale University Press, 2001.

Ploeg, Kees van der. "Likeness and Presence in the Age Before the *Portrait Historié*." In Manuth, Van Leeuwen, and Koldeweij, *Example or Alter Ego?*, 93–108.

Pointon, Marcia. *Portrayal and the Search for Identity*. London: Reaktion Books, 2013.

Polleroß, Friedrich. "Die Anfänge des Identifikationsporträts im höfische und städtische Bereicht." *Frühneuzeit-Info* 4, no. 1 (1993): 17–36.

———. "Between Typology and Psychology: The Role of the Identification Portrait in Updating Old Testament Representations." *Artibus et Historiae* 12, no. 24 (1991): 75–117.

———. "'Majesté' contre 'Sainteté' dans les portraits des Habsbourg au début du XVIIe siècle." In *L'image du roi de François Ier à Louis XIV*, edited by Thomas W. Gaehtgens and Nicole Hochner, 33–55. Paris: Éditions de la Maison des sciences de l'homme, 2006.

———. *Das sakrale Identifikationsporträt: Ein höfischer Bildtypus vom 13. bis zum 20. Jahrhundert*. 2 vols. Worms: Wernersche Verlagsgeschellschaft, 1988.

Poole, Stafford. *Our Lady of Guadalupe: The Origins and Sources of a Mexican National Symbol, 1531–1797*. Tucson: University of Arizona Press, 1995.

Pope-Hennessy, John. *The Portrait in the Renaissance*. New York: Bollingen Foundation, 1966.

Porres Benavides, Jesús. "Influencias de tipos iconográficos paganos en obras plásticas andaluzas de la Edad Moderna." *Eikón Imago* 15 (2020): 527–50.

Portús Pérez, Javier. *El concepto de Pintura Española: Historia de un problema*. Madrid: Editorial Verbum, 2012.

———. "Entre el divino artista y el retratista alcahuete: El pintor en la escena barroca española." *Espacio, Tiempo y Forma*, ser. 7 of *Historia del Arte* 5 (1992): 185–210.

———. "The Jester Pablo de Valladolid." In *Manet/Velázquez: The French Taste for Spanish Painting*, edited by Gary Tinterow and Genèvieve Lacambre, 452–53. New Haven: Yale University Press, 2003.

———, ed. *El retrato en el Museo del Prado*. Madrid: Anaya, 1994.

———. "Retrato, humildad y santidad en el Siglo de Oro." *Revista de Dialectología y Tradiciones Populares* 54, no. 1 (1999): 169–88.

———. "San Francisco de Asís en la Porciúncula con los donantes don Antonio de Contreras y doña María Amezquita (1659): Francisco Caro." In *El retrato español en el Prado: Del Greco a Goya*, edited by Leticia Ruiz Gómez, 124. Madrid: Museo Nacional del Prado, 2006.

———. "The Varied Fortunes of the Portrait in Spain." In *The Spanish Portrait from El Greco to Picasso*, edited by Javier Portús Pérez, 17–67. Madrid: Museo Nacional del Prado, 2004.

———. "Verdadero retrato y copia fallida: Leyendas en torno a la reproducción de imágenes sagradas." In *La imagen religiosa en la Monarquía hispánica: Usos y espacios*, edited by María Cruz de Carlos, Pierre Civil, Felipe Pereda, and Cécile Vincent-Cassy, 241–51. Madrid: Casa de Velázquez, 2008.

Poska, Allyson M. "Disciplinary Institutions in the Atlantic World: Inquisitions." In Parker and Starr-LeBeau, *Judging Faith, Punishing Sin*, 266–78.

Posselt Santoyo, Emmanuel, and L. Ivette Jiménez Osorio. "Líneas narrativas en el paisaje: Un lugar de fundación compartido por tres comunidades de Ñuu Savi." In *Señoríos mixtecos: Su dimensión histórica, geográfica y territorial*, edited by Manuel A. Hermann Lejarazu, 259–86. Zinacantepec: El Colegio Mexiquense, A.C., 2021.

Prodi, Paolo. Introduction to *Discourse on Sacred and Profane Images*, by Gabriele Paleotti, 1–42. Translated by William McCuaig. Los Angeles: Getty Research Institute, 2012.

Prusac, Marina. *From Face to Face: Recarving of Roman Portraits and the Late Antique Portrait Arts*. 2nd ed. Leiden: Brill, 2016.

Pullins, David. "The State of the Fashion Plate, c. 1727: Historicizing Fashion Between 'Dressed Prints' and Dezallier's *Recueils*." In *Prints in Translation, 1450–1750: Image, Materiality, Space*, edited by Suzanne Karr Schmidt and Edward H. Wouk, 136–57. London: Routledge, 2017.

Puyol Buil, Carlos. *Inquisición y política en el reinado de Felipe IV: Los procesos de Jerónimo de Villanueva y las monjas de San Plácido, 1628–1660*. Madrid: Consejo Superior de Investigaciones Científicas, 1993.

Quesada Valera, José María. "El Salvador." In *Clausuras: Tesoros artísticos en los conventos y monasterios madrileños*, edited by Áurea de la Morena

Bartolomé, 126–31. Madrid: Real Academia de Bellas Artes de San Fernando, 2007.

Quiles García, Fernando. *Santidad barroca: Roma, Sevilla y América hispana*. Seville: Universidad Pablo de Olavide, 2018.

Quintana, José Miguel. "III Centenario de la muerte de Don Juan de Palafox y Mendoza." *Novedades* 550 (1959): n.p.

Ragazzi, Alexandre. "Entrecruzamentos Culturais: Superstição, Mito e Fé nos Amuletos de Coral." In *Arte em Ação: Anais do XXXVI Colóquio do Comitê Brasileiro de História da Arte*, 34–41. Rio de Janeiro: Comitê Brasileiro de História da Arte, 2017.

Ramírez Leyva, Edelmira. "La censura inquisitorial novohispana en algunos procesos sobre imágenes y objetos de arte." In *La abolición del arte: XXI Coloquio Internacional de Historia del Arte*, edited by Alberto Dallal, 219–39. Mexico City: Universidad Nacional Autónoma de México, Instituto de Investigaciones Estéticas, 1998.

Ramos, Frances. *Identity, Ritual, and Power in Colonial Puebla*. Tucson: University of Arizona Press, 2012.

Rappaport, Joanne, and Tom Cummins. *Beyond the Lettered City: Indigenous Literacies in the Andes*. Durham: Duke University Press, 2012.

Raquejo Grado, María Antonia. "El donante en la pintura española del siglo XVI: Su ubicación en el espacio ficticio." *Goya* 164/65 (1981): 76–87.

Reeves, Marjorie. *The Influence of Prophecy in the Later Middle Ages: A Study in Joachimism*. Oxford: Oxford University Press, 2000 (1969).

Reiss, Timothy J. *Mirages of the Selfe: Patterns of Personhood in Ancient and Early Modern Europe*. Stanford: Stanford University Press, 2003.

Rey-Márquez, Juan Ricardo. "La jura de Fernando VII en 1808, en la Villa de San Bartolomé de Honda: La *recordatio* efímera en el Antiguo Régimen neogranadino." In *Arte público y espacios políticos: Interacciones y fracturas en las ciudades latinoamericanas*, edited by José Cirillo, Teresa Espantoso Rodríguez, and Carolina Vanegas Carrasco, 220–30. Belo Horizonte: C/Arte, 2011.

Rhodes, Elizabeth. "Join the Jesuits, See the World: Early Modern Women in Spain and the Society of Jesus." In *The Jesuits II: Cultures, Sciences, and the Arts, 1540–1773*, edited by John W. O'Malley, Gauvin Alexander Bailey, Steven J. Harris, and T. Frank Kennedy, 33–49. Toronto: University of Toronto Press, 2006.

Riegl, Alois. *Historical Grammar of the Visual Arts*. Translated by Jacqueline E. Jung. New York: Zone, 2004.

Riello, José. "El Greco y la Inquisición." In *Spanische Kunst von El Greco bis Dalí: Ambiguitäten statt Stereotype*, edited by Michael Scholz-Hänsel and David Sánchez Cano, 109–28. Berlin: Frank & Timme, 2015.

———. "From the Bodily Disease to the Resurrection of the Flesh: El Greco at the Hospital Tavera." In *Creative and Imaginative Powers in the Pictorial Art of El Greco*, edited by Livia Stoenescu, 83–108. Turnhout: Brepols, 2016.

———. "Mímesis de la muerte: Alonso Berruguete, El Greco y los retratos del Cardenal Tavera." *Archivo Español de Arte* 95, no. 377 (2022): 47–66.

———. "*Mucha alma en carne viva*, que diría Díaz del Valle." *Anales de Historia del Arte* (2008): 245–56.

———. "Relíquies i imatges, i viceversa, després del Concili de Trento." In *Creure a través dels ulls*, edited by Pablo González Tornel, 125–57, 263–69. Gijón: Ediciones Trea, 2021.

———. "Las siete vidas de Velázquez (y la penúltima interpretación de *Las meninas*)." In *Scripta artium in honorem Prof. José Manuel Cruz Valdovinos*, edited by Alejandro Cañestro Donoso, 1069–90. Alicante: Universidad de Alicante, 2018.

———. "Verídico no es verdadero: Sobre *La Rendición de Breda* de Velázquez." In *La mirada extravagante: Arte, ciencia y religión en la Edad Moderna; Homenaje a Fernando Marías*, edited by María Cruz de Carlos, Felipe Pereda, and José Riello, 339–74. Madrid: Marcial Pons Historia, 2020.

Ringbom, Sixten. *Icon to Narrative: The Rise of the Dramatic Close-Up in Fifteenth-Century Devotional Painting*. Åbo: Åbo Akademi, 1965.

Río Barredo, María José del. "Felipe II y la configuración del sistema ceremonial de la monarquía católica." In *Felipe II (1527–1598): Europa y la monarquía católica*, edited by José Martínez Millán, 2:677–704. Madrid: Editorial Parteluz, 1998.

Ripollés, Carmen. "The Allure of the Object in Early Modern Spanish Religious Painting." In Locker, *Art and Reform*, 130–53.

Robelo, Cecilio A. *Diccionario de aztequismos o sea catalogo de las palabras del idioma nahuatl, azteca, o mexicano introducidas al idioma castellano bajo diversas formas*. Cuernavaca: Imprenta del autor, 1904.

Roberts, Jennifer L. *Transporting Visions: The Movement of Images in Early America*. Berkeley: University of California Press, 2014.

Rocco, Patricia. "Maniera Devota, Mano Donnesca: Women's Work and Stitching for Virtue in the Visual Culture of the Conservatori in Early Modern Bologna." *Italian Studies* 70, no. 1 (2015): 76–91.

Rodríguez de la Flor, Fernando. "'Picta poesis': Un sermón en jeroglíficos, dedicado por Alonso de Ledesma a las fiestas de beatificación de San Ignacio, en 1610." *Anales de Literatura Española* 1 (1982): 119–33.

Rodríguez Gutiérrez de Ceballos, Alfonso. "La iconografía de San Ignacio de Loyola y los ciclos pintados de su vida en España e Hispanoamérica." *Cuadernos Ignacianos* 5 (2004): 39–64.

———. "La repercusión en España del decreto del Concilio de Trento acerca de las imágenes sagradas y las censuras al Greco." In *Studies in the History of Art* 13, edited by Jonathan Brown and José Manuel Pita Andrade, 153–59. Washington, DC: National Gallery of Art, 1984.

———. "Retrato de Estado y propaganda política: Carlos II (en el tercer centenario de su muerte)." *Anuario del Departamento de Historia y Teoría del Arte* 12 (2000): 93–109.

Rodríguez Moya, Inmaculada. "Devoción y nación: El retrato de donante en los virreinatos americanos." *Norba* 38 (2018): 109–31.

———. "Las reinas santas y el retrato de la 'divina' Isabel Clara Eugenia." In *La piedad de la casa de Austria: Arte, dinastía, devoción*, edited by Víctor Mínguez and Inmaculada Rodríguez, 247–70. Gijón: Ediciones Trea, 2018.

———. "Los retratos de los monarcas españoles en la Nueva España: Siglos XVI–XIX." *Anales del Museo de América* 9 (2001): 287–301.

Rodríguez Moya, Inmaculada, and Víctor Mínguez Cornelles. "Cultura simbólica y fiestas borbónicas en Nueva Granada. De las exequias de Luis I (1724) a la proclamación de Fernando VII (1808)." *CS* 9 (2012): 115–43.

Rodríguez Nóbrega, Janeth. *Las imágenes expurgadas: Censura del arte religioso en el período colonial*. León: Universidad de León, 2008.

———. "El rey en la hoguera: La destrucción de los retratos de la monarquía en Venezuela." In *Imagen del poder: VI Encuentro Internacional sobre Barroco*, edited by Norma Campos Vera, 89–95. La Paz: Editorial Visión Cultural, 2012.

Roe, Jeremy. "Vicente Carducho, Painter and Writer: His Contributions to the *iconografía teresiana* and Reflections on St Teresa and the Perfection of Religious Paintings." In *St Teresa of Avila: Her Writings and Life*, edited by Terence O'Reilly, Colin Thompson, and Lesley Twomey, 59–77. Cambridge: Legenda, 2018.

Rojas Cocoma, Carlos. "Tradición o revolución: La invención del arte colonial en la historiografía colombiana, en la década de 1960." *Memoria y Sociedad* 16, no. 32 (2012): 54–69.

Rousset, Jean. "Il più antico ritratto di Gioacchino da Fiore." *Archivio Storico per la Calabria e la Lucania* 3 (1933): 317–24.

Rowe, Erin. *Black Saints in Early Modern Global Catholicism*. Cambridge: Cambridge University Press, 2019.

Rubial García, Antonio. "El rostro de las mil facetas: La iconografía palafoxiana en la Nueva España." In *Juan de Palafox y Mendoza: Imagen y discurso de la cultura novohispana*, ed. José Pascual Buxó, 301–24. Mexico City: Universidad Nacional Autónoma de México, Instituto de Investigaciones Bibliográficas, 2002.

———. "St. Palafox: Metaphorical Images of Disputed Sainthood." In *Colonial Saints: Discovering the Holy in the Americas, 1500–1800*, edited by Allan Greer and Jodi Billinkoff, 193–207. New York: Routledge, 2003.

Rucquoi, Adeline. "De los reyes que no son taumaturgos: Los fundamentos de la realeza en España."

Relaciones: Estudios de Historia y Sociedad 13, no. 51 (1992): 55–100.

Ruiz, Teofilo F. "Unsacred Monarchy: The Kings of Castile in the Late Middle Ages." In *Rites of Power: Symbolism, Ritual, and Politics Since the Middle Ages*, edited by Sean Wilentz, 109–44. Philadelphia: University of Pennsylvania Press, 1985.

Ruiz de Lacanal Ruiz-Mateos, María Dolores. "Francisco Pacheco y la restauración." *Laboratorio de Arte* 7 (1994): 319–25.

Salinger, Margaretta. "Representations of Saint Theresa." *Metropolitan Museum of Art Bulletin* 8, no. 3 (1949): 97–108.

Salvador González, José María, and Cristina de la Casa Rodríguez. "Sobre la supuesta línea de desarrollo de la retratística medieval: Del donante al retrato individual." *Mirabilia Ars* 3, no. 2 (2015): 73–98.

Sánchez, Magdalena. "Confession and Complicity: Margarita de Austria, Richard Haller, S.J., and the Court of Philip III." *Cuadernos de Historia Moderna* 14 (1993): 133–49.

———. *The Empress, the Queen, and the Nun: Women and Power at the Court of Philip III of Spain*. Baltimore: Johns Hopkins University Press, 1998.

Sánchez Jiménez, Antonio. "'Casta Susana': El baño de Susana, voyeurismo y écfrasis en un soneto de Lope de Vega." *Neophilologus* 93, no. 1 (2009): 69–80.

Sánchez López, Juan Antonio. "El cielo y el mundo: Mujer vestida de santa, santa vestida de mujer." In *Iconografía y creación artística: Estudios sobre la identidad femenina desde las relaciones de poder*, edited by Rosario Camacho Martínez and Aurora Miró Domínguez, 161–233. Málaga: Centro de Ediciones de la Diputación de Málaga, 2001.

Sand, Alexa. *Vision, Devotion, and Self-Representation in Late Medieval Art*. Cambridge: Cambridge University Press, 2014.

Sartre, Jean-Paul. "Faces, Preceded by Official Portraits." Translated by Anne P. Jones. In *Essays in Phenomenology*, edited by Maurice Natanson, 157–63. The Hague: Martinus Nijhoff, 1966.

Schaffer, Talia. "Playing with Pictures: The Art of Victorian Photocollage." *Victorian Literature and Culture* 39, no. 1 (2011): 284–91.

Schell Hoberman, Louisa. *Mexico's Merchant Elite, 1590–1660: Silver, State, and Society*. Durham: Duke University Press, 1991.

Schenone, Héctor H. *Iconografía del arte colonial*. Vol. 1, *Los santos*. Buenos Aires: Ediciones Tarea, 1992.

Schleif, Corine. "Kneeling on the Threshold: Donors Negotiating Realms Betwixt and Between." In *Thresholds of Medieval Visual Culture: Liminal Spaces*, edited by Elina Gertsman and Jill Stevenson, 195–216. Woodbridge: Boydell, 2012.

Schneider, Marlen. *Belle comme Vénus: Le portrait historié entre Grand Siècle et Lumières*. Zurich: Diaphanes, 2021.

Scholz-Hänsel, Michael. "Early Modern Discipline and the Visual Arts." In *Social Control in Europe*, vol. 1, *1500–1800*, edited by Herman Roodenburg and Pieter Spierenburg, 113–31. Columbus: Ohio State University Press, 2004.

Schrader, Jeffrey. "The Royal Image and Modern Spanish Iconoclasm." In *Los estatutos de la imagen: Creación, manifestación, percepción; XXXVI Coloquio Internacional de Historia del Arte*, edited by Linda Báez Rubí and Emilie Carreón Blaine, 293–310. Mexico City: Universidad Nacional Autónoma de México, Instituto de Investigaciones Estéticas, 2014.

Schreffler, Michael. *The Art of Allegiance: Visual Culture and Imperial Power in Baroque New Spain*. University Park: Penn State University Press, 2007.

Schryver, Antoine de. *The Prayer Book of Charles the Bold: A Study of a Flemish Masterpiece from the Burgundian Court*. Translated by Jessica Berenbeim. Los Angeles: J. Paul Getty Museum, 2008.

Seijas, Tatiana. *Asian Slaves in Colonial Mexico: From Chinos to Indians*. Cambridge: Cambridge University Press, 2014.

Serrera, Juan Miguel. "Alonso Sánchez Coello y la mecánica del retrato de corte." In *Alonso Sánchez Coello y el retrato en la corte de Felipe II*, edited by Juan Miguel Serrera, 38–63. Madrid: Museo del Prado, 1990.

Shalem, Avinoam. "Histories of Belonging and George Kubler's Prime Object." *Getty Research Journal* 3 (2011): 1–14.

Sheehan, Jonathan. "Introduction: Thinking About Idols in Early Modern Europe." *Journal of the History of Ideas* 67, no. 4 (2006): 561–70.

Sierra Silva, Pablo Miguel. *Urban Slavery in Colonial Mexico: Puebla de los Ángeles, 1531–1706*. Cambridge: Cambridge University Press, 2018.

Silva Prada, Natalia. "El Tribunal de la fe censurado: Prácticas rituales, pasquines y rumores contra la Inquisición novohispana (1602–1734)." *Fronteras de la Historia* 21, no. 1 (2016): 148–82.

Silverblatt, Irene. "The Black Legend and Global Conspiracies: Spain, the Inquisition, and the Emerging Modern World." In *Rereading the Black Legend: The Discourse of Religious and Racial Difference in the Renaissance Empires*, edited by Margaret R. Greer, Walter D. Mignolo, and Maureen Quilligan, 99–116. Chicago: University of Chicago Press, 2008.

Sitek, Masza. "Just What Is It That Makes Identification-Portrait Hypotheses So Appealing? On Why Hans Süss von Kulmbach 'Must' Have Portrayed John Boner." *Journal of Art Historiography* 17 (2017): 1–20.

Skinner, Marilyn B. *Clodia Metelli: The Tribune's Sister*. Oxford: Oxford University Press, 2011.

Slater, John. "Tampering with Signs of Power: Juan de Palafox, Historiography, and the Limits of Heraldry." In *Signs of Power in Habsburg Spain and the New World*, edited by Jason McCloskey and Ignacio López Alemany, 113–31. Lewisburg: Bucknell University Press, 2013.

Sluhovsky, Moshe. *Becoming a New Self: Practices of Belief in Early Modern Catholicism*. Chicago: University of Chicago Press, 2017.

———. "The Devil in the Convent." *American Historical Review* (2002): 1379–411.

———. "St. Ignatius of Loyola's 'Spiritual Exercises' and Their Contribution to Modern Introspective Subjectivity." *Catholic Historical Review* 99, no. 4 (2013): 649–74.

Solari, Amara. *Idolizing Mary: Maya-Catholic Icons in Yucatán, Mexico*. University Park: Penn State University Press, 2019.

Soler de Campo, Álvaro, ed. *The Art of Power: Royal Armor and Portraits from Imperial Spain*. Madrid: Sociedad Estatal para la Acción Cultural Exterior, 2009.

Solomon, Xavier F. "The Presence of Portraits in Paolo Veronese's Narrative Paintings." *Colnaghi Studies Journal* 3 (2019): 42–59.

Soyer, François. *Ambiguous Gender in Early Modern Spain and Portugal: Inquisitors, Doctors and the Transgression of Gender Norms*. Leiden: Brill, 2012.

———. "Inquisition, Art, and Self-Censorship in the Early Modern Spanish Church, 1563–1834." In *The Art of Veiled Speech, Self-Censorship from Aristophanes to Hobbes*, edited by Han Baltussen and Peter J. Davis, 269–92. Philadelphia: University of Pennsylvania Press, 2015.

Spadaccini, Nicholas, and Jenaro Talens. "Introduction: The Construction of the Self. Notes on Autobiography in Early Modern Spain." In *Autobiography in Early Modern Spain*, edited by Nicholas Spadaccini and Jenaro Talens, 9–40. Minneapolis: Prisma Institute, 1988.

Spagnoletti, Angelantonio. "Giangirolamo Acquaviva: Un barone meridionale tra Conversano, Napoli e Madrid." In *Giangirolamo II Acquaviva: Un barone meridionale nella crisi del Seicento (dai memoriali di Paolo Antonio di Tarsia)*, edited by Angelantonio Spagnoletti and Giuseppe Patisso, 1–24. Conversano: Centro Ricerche di Storia ed Arte, Congedo Editore, 1999.

Stanfield-Mazzi, Maya. "Cult, Countenance, and Community: Donor Portraits from the Colonial Andes." *Religion and the Arts* 15 (2011): 429–59.

Starr-LeBeau, Gretchen D. *In the Shadow of the Virgin: Inquisitors, Friars, and Conversos in Guadalupe, Spain*. Princeton: Princeton University Press, 2003.

Starr-LeBeau, Gretchen, and Kimberly Lynn. "Tribunals and Jurisdictions: Inquisitions." In Parker and Starr-LeBeau, *Judging Faith, Punishing Sin*, 52–65.

Stoichita, Victor I. *Visionary Experience in the Golden Age of Spanish Art*. London: Reaktion, 1995.

Stoichita, Victor I., and Anna Maria Coderch. *Goya: The Last Carnival*. London: Reaktion, 1999.

Stratton-Pruitt, Suzanne L. "Gaspar Miguel de Berrío." In *Journeys to New Worlds: Spanish and Portuguese Colonial Art in the Roberta and Richard Huber Collection*, edited by Suzanne L. Stratton-Pruitt and Mark A. Castro, 54–55. Philadelphia: Philadelphia Museum of Art, 2013.

Straussman-Pflanzer, Eve. "Court Culture in 17th-Century Florence: The Art Patronage of Medici Grand Duchess Vittoria della Rovere (1622–1694)." PhD diss., New York University, 2010.

Taiwo, Olufemi. "Òrìṣà: A Prolegomenon to a Philosophy of Yorùbá Religion." In *Òrìṣà Devotion as World Religion: The Globalization of Yorùbá Religious Culture*, edited by Jacob K. Olupona and Terry Rey, 84–105. Madison: University of Wisconsin Press, 2008.

Tanner, Marie. *The Last Descendant of Aeneas: The Hapsburgs and the Mythic Image of the Emperor*. New Haven: Yale University Press, 1993.

Tatarkiewicz, Władysław. *History of Aesthetics II: Medieval Aesthetics*. Edited by C. Barrett. Translated by R. M. Montgomery. The Hague: Mouton, 1970.

Taussig, Michael T. *Defacement: Public Secrecy and the Labor of the Negative*. Palo Alto: Stanford University Press, 1999.

Teresi, Rebecca Quinn. "Images of the Immaculate Conception and the Rhetorics of Purity in Golden Age Spain." PhD diss., Johns Hopkins University, 2021.

Tiempo sagrado, tiempo ritual: El "xantolo" y el "micailhuitl" entre los pueblos nahuas de Hidalgo. Pachuca: Consejo Estatal para la Cultura y las Artes de Hidalgo, 2020.

Tiffany, Tanya. *Diego Velázquez's Early Paintings and the Culture of Seventeenth-Century Seville*. University Park: Penn State University Press, 2012.

———. "Little Idols: Royal Children and the Infant Jesus in the Devotional Practice of Sor Margarita de la Cruz (1567–1633)." In *The Early Modern Child in Art and History*, edited by Matthew Knox Averett, 35–48. London: Pickering & Chatto, 2015.

———. "Visualizing Devotion in Early Modern Seville: Velázquez's 'Christ in the House of Martha and Mary.'" *Sixteenth Century Journal* 36, no. 2 (2005): 433–53.

Toussaint, Manuel. Introduction to "Proceso y denuncias contra Simón Pereyns en la Inquisición de México." *Anales del Instituto de Investigaciones Estéticas* 2, supplement (1938): xvii–xxi.

Vallejo García-Hevia, José María. "La inquisición del distrito de la Audiencia de Guatemala (1569–1609)." *Anuario de Historia del Derecho Español* 71 (2001): 161–266.

Van Horn, Jennifer. "The Dark Iconoclast: African Americans' Artistic Resistance in the Civil War South." *Art Bulletin* 99, no. 4 (2018): 133–67.

Vargas Lugo, Elisa. "El retrato de donantes y el autorretrato en la pintura novohispana." *Anales del Instituto de Investigaciones Estéticas* 13, no. 51 (1983): 13–20.

Vázquez, Oscar E. *Inventing the Art Collection: Patrons, Markets, and the State in Nineteenth-Century Spain*. University Park: Penn State University Press, 2001.

Vega Loeches, José Luis. "Una fuente más sobre el Panteón Real de El Escorial: Fray Martín de la Vera y su *Instrucción de eclesiásticos* (1630)." *Imafronte* 23 (2014): 67–101.

Velandia Onofre, Darío. "Hacia una teología de la imagen: Mística, oratoria y pintura en la España del Siglo de Oro." PhD diss., University of Barcelona, 2014.

———. "Jaime Prades y las imágenes sagradas: La defensa de su adoración y uso." *Hispania Sacra* 69, no. 139 (2017): 185–94.

———. "Word and Image in Saint Ignatius of Loyola: The Shaping of Visual Culture in Spain After the Council of Trent." *Word and Image* 34, no. 4 (2018): 332–48.

Véliz Bomford, Zahira. "Velázquez Composes: Prototypes, Replicas, and Transformations." *Colnaghi Studies Journal* 3 (2018): 92–111.

Vera, Juan de. *Piedras de Segovia: Apuntes para un itinerario heráldico y epigráfico de la ciudad*. Segovia: Instituto Diego de Colmenares, 1950.

Villa-Flores, Javier. *Dangerous Speech: A Social History of Blasphemy in Colonial Mexico*. Tucson: University of Arizona Press, 2006.

Villar Movellán, Alberto. "Santos travestidos: Imágenes condenadas." *Cuadernos de Arte e Iconografía* 2, no. 4 (1989): 183–91.

Vincent-Cassy, Cécile. "Francisco de Zurbarán y el retrato sacro: Las santas vírgenes y mártires del maestro y su taller." *Tiempos Modernos* 33, no. 2 (2016): 236–54.

———. "Marguerite de Habsbourg (1584–1611), épouse de Philippe III d'Espagne, et la sanctification des membres féminins de la maison d'Autriche." In

Donne, potere, religione: Studi per Sara Cabibbo, edited by Marina Caffiero, Maria Pia Donato, and Giovanna Fiume, 207–22. Milan: Franco Angeli, 2017.

———. "El retrato *a lo divino*: Intención y realces de una forma híbrida." *e-Spania: Revue Interdisciplinaire d'Études Hispaniques Médiévales et Modernes* 35 (2020). https://doi.org/10.4000/e-spania.33921.

———. *Les saintes vierges et martyres dans l'Espagne du XVIIe siècle: Culte et image*. Madrid: Casa de Velázquez, 2011.

Vizcaíno Villanueva, María A. *El pintor en la sociedad madrileña durante el reinado de Felipe IV*. Madrid: Fundación Universitaria Española, 2005.

Wallraven, Christian, Douglas William Cunningham, J. Rigau, Miguel Feixas, and Mateu Sbert. "Aesthetic Appraisal of Art: From Eye Movements to Computers." In *Computational Aesthetics in Graphics, Visualization, and Imaging*, edited by Oliver Deussen and Peter Hall, 137–44. Geneva: Eurographics Association, 2009.

Warburg, Aby. "The Art of Portraiture and the Florentine Bourgeoisie: Domenico Ghirlandaio in Santa Trinita; The Portraits of Lorenzo de' Medici and His Household (1902)." In *Aby Warburg: The Renewal of Pagan Antiquity; Contributions to the Cultural History of the Renaissance*, edited by Kurt W. Forster, translated by David Britt, 185–222. Los Angeles: Getty Research Institute for the History of Art and the Humanities, 1999.

Wardropper, Bruce W. *Historia de la poesía lírica a lo divino en la cristianidad occidental*. Madrid: Revista de Occidente, 1958.

Warner, Marina. *Alone of All Her Sex: The Myth and the Cult of the Virgin Mary*. New York: Vintage, 1983.

Webb, Ruth. *Ekphrasis, Imagination and Persuasion in Ancient Rhetorical Theory and Practice*. London: Routledge, 2016.

Webster, Susan Verdi. "Shameless Beauty and Worldly Splendor: On the Spanish Practice of Adorning the Virgin." In *The Miraculous Image in the Late Middle Ages and Renaissance*, edited by Erik Thunø and Gerhard Wolf, 249–71. Rome: L'Erma di Bretschneider, 2004.

Weddigen, Tristan, and Gregor J. M. Weber. "The Alchemy of Colors: Titian Portrays His Pigment Merchant Alvise 'dai Colori' dalla Scala." In *Titian: Lady in White*, edited by Stephan Koja and Andreas Henning, 50–63. Dresden: Sandstein, 2018.

Wiens, Gavin. "'Like Wax Before a Fire: Sainthood and Image Theory in Some Early Portraits of Bernardino of Siena." *RES: Anthropology and Aesthetics* 75/76 (2021): 168–82.

Wind, Edgar. "Studies in Allegorial Portraiture I." *Journal of the Warburg Institute* 1, no. 2 (1937): 138–62.

Winter, Irene J. "What/When Is a Portrait? Royal Images of the Ancient Near East." *Proceedings of the American Philosophical Society* 153, no. 3 (2009): 254–70.

Wood, Christopher S. "The Votive Scenario." *RES: Anthropology and Aesthetics* 59/60 (2011): 206–27.

Wood, Stephanie, ed. *Online Nahuatl Dictionary*. 2000–2020. https://nahuatl.uoregon.edu.

Woodall, Joanna. "Introduction: Facing the Subject." In *Portraiture: Facing the Subject*, edited by Joanna Woodall, 1–25. Manchester: Manchester University Press, 1997.

Woods Marsden, Joanna. *Renaissance Self-Portraiture: The Visual Construction of Identity and the Social Status of the Artist*. New Haven: Yale University Press, 1998.

Woude, Ad van der. "The Volume and Value of Paintings in Holland at the Time of the Dutch Republic." In *Art in History, History in Art: Studies in Seventeenth-Century Dutch Culture*, edited by David Freedberg and Jan de Vries, 284–329. Los Angeles: Getty Center for the History of Art and the Humanities, 1991.

Wunder, Amanda. *Baroque Seville: Sacred Art in a Century of Crisis*. University Park: Penn State University Press, 2017.

———. "Innovation and Tradition at the Court of Philip IV of Spain (1621–1665): The Invention of the *Golilla* and the *Guardainfante*." In *Fashioning the Early Modern: Dress, Textiles, and Innovation in Europe, 1500–1800*, edited by Evelyn Welch, 111–33. Oxford: Oxford University Press, 2017.

Wunsch, Oliver. "Watteau, Through the Cracks." *Art Bulletin* 100, no. 2 (2018): 37–60.

Yarza Luaces, Joaquín. "El retrato medieval: La presencia del donante." In Portús Pérez, *El retrato en el Museo del Prado*, 66–97.

Zarco Cuevas, Julián. *Pintores españoles en San Lorenzo el Real de El Escorial (1566–1613)*. Madrid: Instituto de Valencia de Don Juan, 1931.

Zemon Davis, Natalie. *Fiction in the Archives: Pardon Tales and Their Tellers in Sixteenth-Century France*. Stanford: Stanford University Press, 1987.

Zerner, Henri. "The Portrait, Likeness, and Recognition." *Seminar* 415 (March 1994): 21–24.

Zierholz, Steffen. "Allegories of Light and Fire: Ignatian Effigies Painted on Copper." *Journal of Jesuit Studies* 9 (2022): 357–78.

———. "'To Make Yourself Present': Jesuit Sacred Space as Enargetic Space." In Boer, Enenkel, and Melion, *Jesuit Image Theory*, 419–60.

INDEX

Italicized page references indicate illustrations. Endnotes are referenced with "n" followed by the endnote number.